THE
BARE ESSENTIALS
PLUS

THE
BARE ESSENTIALS
PLUS

THIRD EDITION

SARAH NORTON

BRIAN GREEN

NELL WALDMAN

THOMSON

NELSON

Australia   Canada   Mexico   Singapore   Spain   United Kingdom   United States

THOMSON
NELSON

**The Bare Essentials Plus,
Third Edition**

by Sarah Norton, Brian Green,
and Nell Waldman

**Associate Vice President,
Editorial Director:**
Evelyn Veitch

Editor-in-Chief:
Anne Williams

Marketing Manager:
Sandra Green

Director, Development:
Lenore Spence

Permissions Coordinator:
Nicola Winstanley

Senior Production Editor:
Natalia Denesiuk

Copy Editor:
June Trusty

Proofreader:
Sarah Robertson

Indexer:
Edwin Durbin

Production Coordinator:
Ferial Suleman

Design Director:
Ken Phipps

Interior Design:
Sonya V. Thursby, Opus House
Incorporated

Cover Design:
Rocket Design

Cover Image:
Photodisc Blue/Getty Images

Illustrations:
Kathryn Adams

Compositor:
Carol Magee

Printer:
Transcontinental

**Library and Archives Canada
Cataloguing in Publication**

Norton, Sarah, date–

The bare essentials plus /
Sarah Norton, Brian Green,
Nell Waldman.—3rd ed.

Includes index.
ISBN 0-17-640700-6

1. English language—
Composition and exercises.
2. English language—Textbooks
for second language learners.
I. Green, Brian II. Waldman,
Nell Kozak, 1949– III. Title.

PE1128.N67 2006   808'.042
C2006-901458-2

Preface

To the Instructor

The Bare Essentials Plus, Third Edition, is a new addition to the *Essentials* series, the comprehensive set of texts that has helped more than half a million Canadian students learn to write for college and the workplace. *The Bare Essentials Plus* incorporates the practical, accessible features that distinguish the *Essentials* series: straightforward explanation of each point, copious examples, and plenty of exercises—both in the text and on the comprehensive Web site at www.essentialsplus3e.nelson.com—to ensure mastery. The *Plus* in the title refers to Unit 6, which focusses on the needs of second-language writers, a growing segment of the college population in many parts of Canada. Unit 6 is a specialized add-on that can be integrated into class work or assigned as homework for students who need it.

Teachers familiar with the first two editions of *The Bare Essentials Plus* will notice that instruction in this book is organized and presented differently. A major difference between student writing today and student writing 25 years ago is that spelling mistakes are no longer the most obvious errors in student assignments. Thanks to word processors, most spelling errors can be caught and corrected by conscientious writers before papers are submitted. Homonyms, of course, are the exception to the rule, so we've highlighted the problems they present in Chapter 2. The three spelling rules, still useful, but no longer deserving the prominence they previously enjoyed, have been moved to Appendix A, "Spelling Matters."

Here is an overview of major changes to content and organization that are new to this edition:

- Chapter 1 focusses on audience-appropriate language. Today, with the ubiquity of colloquialisms in advertising and short forms in text messaging, the formerly fine line between prose and speech has become all but invisible. To help students find and use an appropriate register in their writing, *The Bare Essentials Plus* now begins with an overview of what levels and kinds of language are (and are not) appropriate in written messages designed for specific audiences and purposes.

- Units 1, 2, 3, 4, and 6 conclude with a Rapid Review—a comprehensive exercise that complements the introductory Quick Quiz. By comparing their scores on the preliminary quiz and the final review, students can see for themselves how far they've progressed.

- Unit 5, on paragraphs and essays, has been expanded to include a more flexible definition of thesis statements and a more comprehensive treatment of outlines, ranging from the informal scratch outline to the detailed formal outline. We have added exercises to each stage of the revision process (Chapter 26) to give students practice in working through the three steps of a thorough revision.

- Unit 7 contains ten essays, seven of them new to this edition, that exemplify and support the instruction in Units 1 through 5. The last three essays are examples of short, documented papers. New questions for discussion and suggestions for writing follow each essay.

- In response to reviewers' requests, we have included more information on format and documentation and posted an introduction to MLA and APA styles on our Web site. We have added to Chapter 20 more examples of how to punctuate titles, including those from electronic sources, and have deleted the use of punctuation marks in direct speech.

- A new Appendix B, "A Review of the Basics," defines and illustrates the kinds and parts of sentences and the parts of speech.

- The List of Grammatical Terms (Appendix C) simply and clearly explains terms that appear in bold print in the text, together with definitions and examples of other grammatical terms with which students should be familiar.

- On the page facing the inside back cover, we have reproduced a list of commonly used editing and proofreading symbols, their interpretation, and extra space in which students can record their instructor's preferred editing/proofreading symbols.

The Bare Essentials Plus provides students with all they need to progress from basic sentence correctness through paragraph development to the organization and presentation of short college papers. We have tried to present these critical concepts clearly, in a friendly tone, with encouragement, motivation, and humour.

The "essentials" are presented in the traditional way, from words (Unit 1) to syntax (Unit 2) to grammar (Unit 3) to punctuation (Unit 4) to paragraphs and essays (Unit 5). Unit 6 contains instruction designed to support advanced second-language learners, but everyone can benefit from reviewing the information in Chapters 27 and 28. Readings that provide examples and inspiration are presented in Unit 7. The units are independent of each other, so instructors can choose to present them in whatever order suits them and their curriculum. The chapters within each unit, however, should be introduced in the order in which they appear. The exercises within each unit are cumulative: those in later chapters often include questions that assume mastery of skills covered in earlier chapters.

Almost all of the exercises can be completed in the text, and the answers, in Appendix D, are easy to find. The first exercise in each chapter refers students to the page on which the answers for that chapter begin, and all exercises are numbered by chapter as well as by exercise (e.g., Exercise 5.4 refers to the fourth exercise in Chapter 5). We instruct students to check their answers as soon as they have completed an exercise in order to get immediate feedback, learn from their mistakes, and avoid reinforcing their errors. **We urge instructors to emphasize the importance of this procedure.** Students who need more practice than the exercises in the text provide will find supplementary, self-scoring exercises on the Web site. Web icons in Chapters 2 through 31 identify when and where to find these additional exercises.

Answers to the chapter Mastery Tests are not included in the textbook. They are posted on the Instructor Resources page of the Web site and printed in the *Instructor's Manual*. Both resources also offer an alternative set of Mastery Tests, equivalent to those in the book in number and difficulty.

On the inside front cover is a Quick Revision Guide that students can use as a checklist to guide them as they edit their work. Instructors can duplicate the guide, attach a copy to each student's paper, and mark ✔ or ✘ beside each point in the guide to identify the paper's strengths and weaknesses. This strategy provides students with comprehensive and consistent feedback and saves hours of marking time.

Instructor Resources

Web Site: www.essentialsplus3e.nelson.com

On page viii there is an outline of the contents of our new Web site. In the Instructor Resources, The Creative Classroom is new, and consists of interactive exercises designed especially for this edition of the book. The Student Resources page is divided into three major sections: More Exercises (linked to the Web icons in Chapters 2 to 31), More Information, and More Practice. The Supplementary Readings, which are linked to both the Instructor and the Student pages, are designed for students who need elementary, unambiguous examples of the five-paragraph essay. These essays are less sophisticated in language and structure than those in Unit 7.

Instructor Resources	Student Resources

The Creative Classroom
Answers to Chapter Mastery Tests
Alternative Chapter Mastery Tests &
    Answers
Answers to Discussion Questions (Unit 7)
Supplementary Readings
PowerPoint Slides and Transparencies
The Essentials Test Manual
Authors' Forum
	More Exercises (Chapters 2–31)
	More Information
	    Additional Examples for Chapters 2–31
	    Research Papers: Format and
	      Documentation
	      • MLA Style
	      • APA Style
	    Student Survival Skills
	More Practice
	    Practice Tests
	    Supplementary Readings
	Ask the Authors

THE ESSENTIALS TEST MANUAL

The Essentials Test Manual is a comprehensive test bank that includes pre-course diagnostic tests as well as pre- and post-tests for each unit and chapter. The manual concludes with Answer Keys.

INSTRUCTOR'S MANUAL

This print resource includes teaching tips, classroom activities, answers to the Mastery Tests for each chapter, an alternative set of Mastery Tests and answers, additional readings for analysis, and transparency masters that summarize chapter contents. The last 20 slides define and illustrate parts of speech and sentences and provide a quick review of major syntax, grammar, and punctuation errors.

Like its predecessors, *The Bare Essentials Plus,* Third Edition, has been designed not only for college students but also for their teachers who are dedicated to providing students with correct and effective writing skills as efficiently and painlessly as possible. While *The Bare Essentials Plus* can successfully be used to support self-instruction and independent study, it works best for students lucky enough to have a teacher to guide them enthusiastically through its contents, adjusting the pace and level of instruction to the needs of each class, and providing regular feedback and encouragement. These heroic individuals are the people to whom the *Essentials* series owes its 25 years of success. We hope this latest edition will fulfil their expectations and merit their endorsement.

Please let us know what you think of the new *Bare Essentials Plus*. You can reach us directly via the Authors' Forum at www.essentialsplus3e.nelson.com.

Acknowledgments

We are indebted to our reviewers, whose comments, criticisms, and suggestions helped to make this a more useful book:

Rick Erlendson, Grande Prairie Regional College
Paul Hedlin, Vanier College
Tanya Lewis, Langara College
Linda Laporte Power, Dawson College
Rose To, University of Calgary

We owe special thanks to Valerie Grabove, consultant at the Centre for Professional Development at Niagara College, who developed the teaching strategies and classroom activities that support and enhance this new edition.

Sarah Norton
Brian Green
Nell Waldman

Introduction

To the Student: Why You Need This Book

College and university composition courses have always had a public-relations problem. Writing skills is not a "core" course, and students often wonder why they are required to take it. The fact is that writing skills are as valuable to your career success as any other subject you will take. That's why English composition is part of your curriculum: program advisory boards and curriculum committees know that graduates who can communicate well will get hired more quickly, advance more quickly, and climb higher in their professions than graduates with poor communication skills. Companies from Gulf Oil to IBM, from CBC to Ford, from the Royal Bank to Bell Canada, not to mention all levels of government, hospitals, police forces, and the Canadian military, have gone on record as demanding superior communication skills as an essential hiring criterion.

To any employer, an employee is more valuable if he or she can write well. Fairly or unfairly, no matter what field you're in, employers, peers, and subordinates will judge your ability largely on the basis of your communication skills. In most careers, your ability to write well will be tested every day.

The good news is that writing skills can be learned. There is no reason you can't write clear and correct reports, memoranda, and even e-mails. This book is intended to help you do exactly that, just as it has helped thousands of Canadian students in the 12 years since it was first published. All you need is the desire to improve. If you have the will, you'll invest the time, effort, and care needed to make the concepts in this book work for you.

What's in This Book

There is more to this text than meets the eye. In addition to the book you're holding in your hand, you have access to a vast Web site that provides more exercises, information, and practice. Together, the book and the Web site give you the tools and resources you need to improve your writing.

If you turn to the Table of Contents (page xv), you'll see that the book is divided into seven units. Units 1 through 4 will help you identify and eliminate errors in your writing.

> A writing error is a failure of communication. Miscommunication occurs when a message fails to meet the reader's expectations, or the writer's purpose, or both.

Unit 5 explains and illustrates how to organize and develop your ideas in effective paragraphs, essays, and reports. Unit 6 reviews those aspects of English that second-language students find troublesome. Unit 7 consists of 10 readings on a variety of topics we hope you will find interesting. These essays illustrate a number of common organizational patterns as well as the range of language, from formal to informal, writers can choose from to suit their subject, audience, and purpose.

Four appendixes follow Unit 7: Appendix A is devoted to the essentials of spelling; B covers basic grammatical points—the kinds and parts of sentences and the parts of speech; and C lists the grammatical terms used in the book. Whenever you find a **technical term** in bold type, you can turn to Appendix C to discover its definition and examples of its correct use. Appendix D contains answers to most of the exercises in the first six units, and a comprehensive index concludes the book.

On the Web site, under "More Information," you'll find additional examples for every point explained and illustrated in the book. In most chapters, a computer icon tells you when and where exercises are available on the Web site for extra practice. The Web exercises are electronically scored, which means you can get immediate feedback about your progress. Also on the Web site are practice tests that check your knowledge of each rule or principle. (We suggest you do these practice tests before you try the chapter Mastery Tests.)

GO TO WEB

EXERCISE

For students who are required to write research papers as part of their composition course, the Web site offers explanations and examples of both MLA and APA format and documentation styles. Since few of us have the courage (or common sense) to begin work on a major assignment as soon as it is assigned, the Web site provides a chapter on Student Survival Skills, which covers topics that range from understanding course outlines to overcoming procrastination and writer's block.

A special feature of our Web site is the **Ask the Authors** button. Click this button to send us questions that you don't want to raise in class: you may be afraid they'll sound "dumb"; your instructor is pressed for time and lets you know it; or you're too shy to ask questions in class. **Ask the Authors** questions are e-mailed to us, and one of us will get back to you and answer your question. As far as we know, there are few "dumb" questions about writing, so feel free to ask us about whatever is puzzling you. We also encourage you to tell us what you like and don't like about our book.

How to Use This Book

In each chapter, we do three things: explain a point, illustrate the point with examples, and provide exercises to help you master it. The exercises are arranged in sets that get more challenging as you go along. After some of the exercises, you'll find a symbol directing you to the *Bare Essentials* Web site (www.essentialsplus3e.nelson.com), where we have provided additional exercises for those who need extra practice. By the time you finish a chapter, you should have a good grasp of the skill. Then it's up to you to apply that skill *every* time you write. Competence in writing is no different from any other competence: it results from combining knowledge with practice.

Here's how to proceed:

1. Read the explanation. Do this even if you think you understand the point. Make sure you understand the concept, and get help from your teacher if it's not completely clear.
2. Study the highlighted rules and the examples that follow them.
3. If you find an explanation easy and think you have no problem with the skill, try the last set of exercises that follow the explanation. Then check your answers. If you've made no errors, go on to the next point.

   If you're less confident, don't skip anything. Start with the first set and work through all the exercises, including those on the Web site, until you are sure you understand the point. (As a general rule, getting three exercises in a row entirely correct demonstrates understanding and competence.)
4. **Always check your answers to one set of exercises before you go on to the next.** This step is crucial. Only by checking your results after each set can you identify errors and correct them right away, instead of repeating and possibly reinforcing them.

5. When you find a mistake, go back to the explanation and examples. Study them again; then look up the additional examples for that point on the Web site. If you are truly stuck, check with your instructor. Your brain cannot learn anything as complex as the structure of written language unless you clear up problems as you go. Continue with the exercises only when you are sure you understand where you went wrong and are confident that you won't repeat the error.

You can reinforce your understanding—and prepare for in-class tests— by doing the practice tests posted on the Student Resources page of the *Bare Essentials Plus* Web site.

WHAT THE SYMBOLS MEAN

GO TO WEB

EXERCISE

When this symbol appears in the text, it means that you will find on the *Bare Essentials Plus* Web site information or exercises to supplement the chapter you are working on. Once you've logged on to the Web site, click on the "More Exercises" button. The exercises are posted by chapter, so to get to the exercises for the apostrophe, for example, click on Chapter 3 in the list, then go to the numbered exercises identified for you below the icon. Web exercises are marked automatically, so you will know instantly whether or not you have understood the material.

This symbol beside an exercise means the exercise is designed for two or more students working together. Often you are instructed to begin work in a pair or group, then to work individually on a writing task, and finally to regroup and review your writing with your partner(s). (Of course, your instructor may choose to modify these exercises for students working independently.)

This symbol means "note this." We've used it to highlight writing tips, helpful hints, hard-to-remember points, and information that you should apply whenever you write, not just when you are dealing with the principle covered in the paragraph marked by the icon.

When an exercise is marked with this icon, it means the activity is a Mastery Test—an exercise designed to check your level of understanding of the principles covered in the chapter you have just completed. The answers to these exercises are not in the back of the book; your instructor will provide them.

When this symbol appears in the margin beside a paragraph or an exercise, it means that the information is specifically designed to help second-language learners master a point that many find troublesome.

TWO FINAL SUGGESTIONS

Inside the front cover, you'll find a Quick Revision Guide. Use it to help you revise your papers before handing them in. This book is meant to be a practical tool, not a theoretical reference. Apply the lessons in all the writing you do. Explanations can identify writing problems and show you how to solve them; exercises can give you practice in eliminating errors; but only writing and revising can bring real and lasting improvement.

Inside the back cover, you'll find a Time Line that summarizes verb tenses in a quick, easy-to-read chart. On the page facing the inside back cover, we've provided a list of the most common editing and proofreading symbols—the shorthand forms instructors often use when grading your papers to signal where you've made mistakes. We explain and illustrate the standard symbols and also leave space for you to write in your own instructor's preferred symbol or abbreviation for each type of error. See Chapter 26 for suggestions about using this list to maximize your improvement from one essay to another.

Contents

PREFACE . . . v

INTRODUCTION . . . x
    To the Student: Why You Need This Book . . . x
    What's in This Book . . . xi
    How to Use This Book . . . xii

UNIT 1   WORDS
    Quick Quiz . . . 2
1 Choosing the Right Words . . . 4
    The Writer's Toolkit . . . 4
    Levels of Language . . . 10
    Wordiness . . . 11
    Slang . . . 13
    Pretentious Language . . . 15
    Offensive Language . . . 17
    Abusages . . . 17
2 Hazardous Homonyms . . . 22
3 The Apostrophe . . . 38
    Contraction . . . 39
    Possession . . . 42
    Plurals . . . 47
4 Capital Letters . . . 50
    Rapid Review . . . 57

UNIT 2   SENTENCES
    Quick Quiz . . . 60
5 Cracking the Sentence Code . . . 62
    Finding Subjects and Verbs . . . 63
    More about Verbs . . . 67
    More about Subjects . . . 70
    Multiple Subjects and Verbs . . . 74

6 Solving Sentence-Fragment Problems . . . 79
"Missing Piece" Fragments . . . 79
Dependent Clause Fragments . . . 84

7 Solving Run-On Sentence Problems . . . 90
Comma Splices . . . 90
Fused Sentences . . . 90

8 Solving Modifier Problems . . . 99
Misplaced Modifiers . . . 99
Dangling Modifiers . . . 103

9 The Parallelism Principle . . . 110

10 Refining by Combining . . . 117
Sentence Combining . . . 117
Review of Conjunctions and Relative Pronouns . . . 119
    A. Using Conjunctions to Combine Clauses . . . 119
    B. Using Relative Pronouns to Combine Clauses . . . 120

Rapid Review . . . 131

UNIT 3 GRAMMAR
Quick Quiz . . . 134

11 Choosing the Correct Verb Form . . . 137
The Principal Parts of Verbs . . . 137
The Principal Parts of Irregular Verbs . . . 140
Choosing between Active and Passive Voice . . . 146

12 Mastering Subject–Verb Agreement . . . 153
Singular and Plural . . . 153
Four Special Cases . . . 158

13 Keeping Your Tenses Consistent . . . 168

14 Choosing the Correct Pronoun Form . . . 173
Subject and Object Pronouns . . . 174
Using Pronouns in Contrast Constructions . . . 177

15 Mastering Pronoun–Antecedent Agreement . . . 181
Pronoun–Antecedent Agreement . . . 181
    1. Pronouns Ending in *-one*, *-body*, *-thing* . . . 182
    2. Vague Reference . . . 186
    3. Relative Pronouns . . . 189

16 Maintaining Person Agreement . . . 194
Rapid Review . . . 201

UNIT 4   PUNCTUATION
Quick Quiz . . . 204

17 The Comma . . . 207
Five Comma Rules . . . 208

18 The Semicolon . . . 219

19 The Colon . . . 226

20 Quotation Marks . . . 232
Quoted Material . . . 232
Titles . . . 236

21 Question Marks, Exclamation Marks, and Punctuation Review . . . 240
The Question Mark . . . 240
The Exclamation Mark . . . 241
Punctuation Review . . . 244
Rapid Review . . . 248

UNIT 5   PARAGRAPHS AND ESSAYS
22 Finding Something to Write About . . . 252
Choose a Satisfactory Subject . . . 253
Discover Your Thesis and Main Points . . . 255
Testing Your Main Points . . . 261
Organizing Your Main Points . . . 263

23 The Thesis Statement . . . 269

24 The Outline . . . 281
Scratch Outline . . . 282
Informal Outline . . . 282
Formal Outline . . . 283

25 Paragraphs . . . 288
Developing Your Paragraphs . . . 289
Writing Introductions and Conclusions . . . 298
Keeping Your Reader with You . . . 300
Transitions . . . 300
Tone . . . 301

26 Revising Your Paper . . . 305
What Is Revision? . . . 305
Step 1: Revise Content and Organization . . . 306
Step 2: Revise Paragraphs and Sentences . . . 310

Step 3: Edit and Proofread . . . 313
    Tips for Effective Proofreading . . . 316

UNIT 6   FOR ESL LEARNERS: A REVIEW OF THE BASICS
Introduction . . . 319
Quick Quiz . . . 320
27 Choosing the Correct Verb Tense . . . 322
Verb Tense Formation . . . 323
The Present Tenses . . . 326
    A. The Simple Present Tense . . . 326
    B. The Present Progressive Tense . . . 326
    C. The Present Perfect Tense . . . 329
    D. The Present Perfect Progressive Tense . . . 330
The Past Tenses . . . 332
    A. The Simple Past Tense . . . 332
    B. The Past Progressive Tense . . . 332
    C. The Past Perfect Tense . . . 333
    D. The Past Perfect Progressive Tense . . . 335
The Future Tenses . . . 338
    A. The Simple Future Tense . . . 338
    B. The Future Progressive Tense . . . 339
    C. The Future Perfect Tense . . . 340
    D. The Future Perfect Progressive Tense . . . 341
Using Present Tenses to Indicate Future Time . . . 342

28 More about Verbs . . . 346
Forming Negatives . . . 346
Participial Adjectives . . . 348
Modal Auxiliaries . . . 351

29 Solving Plural Problems . . . 359
Singular vs. Plural Nouns . . . 359
Count vs. Non-Count Nouns . . . 365
Quantity Expressions . . . 371

30 Using Articles Accurately . . . 376
The Indefinite Article: *A/An* . . . 376
The Definite Article: *The* . . . 380
No Article (Zero Article) . . . 386
Using *The* or No Article in Geographical Names . . . 387

31 Practising with Prepositions . . . 394

Prepositions That Indicate Time Relationships . . . 396
Prepositions That Indicate Place or Position . . . 398
Prepositions That Indicate Direction or Movement . . . 400
Other Prepositional Relationships . . . 401
Rapid Review . . . 407

UNIT 7   READINGS
Brian Green, "Career Consciousness" . . . 412
Sun-Kyung Yi, "An Immigrant's Split Personality" . . . 414
Eva Tihanyi, "Resolving Conflict in the Workplace" . . . 416
Shandi Mitchell, "Baba and Me" . . . 418
Germaine Greer, "Ottawa vs. New York" . . . 421
Sarah Norton, "Metamorphosis" . . . 425
Jeffrey Moussaieff Masson, "Dear Dad" . . . 427
Deenu Parmar, "Labouring the Wal-Mart Way" . . . 431
Nell Waldman, "The Second-Language Struggle"
   (MLA Documentation Style) . . . 434
Aliki Tryphonopoulos, "A City for Students"
   (APA Documentation Style) . . . 438

APPENDIXES
A   Spelling Matters . . . 444
Three Basic Rules . . . 444
Rule 1: Dropping the Final *e* . . . 444
Rule 2: Doubling the Final Consonant . . . 446
Rule 3: Words Containing *ie* or *ei* . . . 447
Spelling Spoilers . . . 448

B   A Review of the Basics . . . 451
Sentences: Kinds and Parts . . . 451
   Function: Four Kinds of Sentences . . . 451
   Structure: Basic Sentence Patterns . . . 452
   The Parts of a Sentence . . . 454
Parts of Speech . . . 456
   1. Nouns . . . 456
   2. Verbs . . . 457
   3. Pronouns . . . 458
   4. Adjectives . . . 460

5. Adverbs . . . 461

6. Prepositions . . . 461

7. Conjunctions . . . 462

8. Articles . . . 463

9. Expletives . . . 463

C   List of Grammatical Terms . . . 464

D   Answers to Exercises . . . 473

INDEX . . . 537

CREDITS . . . 545

CORRECTION ABBREVIATIONS AND SYMBOLS . . . 546

Words

Quick Quiz

1 Choosing the Right Words

The Writer's Toolkit

Levels of Language

Wordiness

Slang

Pretentious Language

Offensive Language

Abusages

2 Hazardous Homonyms

3 The Apostrophe

Contraction

Possession

Plurals

4 Capital Letters

Rapid Review

QUICK QUIZ

The following quick quiz will let you see at a glance which chapters of Unit 1 you need to pay special attention to. The paragraph below contains a total of 15 errors in word choice, homonyms, apostrophes, and capital letters. When you've made your corrections, turn to page 473 and compare your version with ours. For each error you miss, the answer key directs you to the chapter you need to work on.

[1]I decided to buy a new radio for my car, so I went to a local store who's reputation I trusted to see what new products were available. [2]Their, the clerk told me they were having a sale on Voice-Activated car radio's. [3]He demonstrated by saying, "louder," which had the affect of increasing the radio's volume. [4]Then he said, "Hip Hop" and the radio changed to a Hip-Hop station. [5]I thought this radio was really cool, so, despite the fact that it cost more then ordinary radios, I bought it. [6]In actual fact, I felt that it was safer than radios that needed to be adjusted manually, by hand, while I was driving the car. [7]It was more attractive than the others, too. [8]I excepted the store's offer to install it for a small additional cost. [9]Soon I was driving

along the road calling out, "Louder" to increase the volume and "Oldie's" to get a station playing songs from the past. [10]As I was turning a corner, however, another driver suddenly cut in front of me. [11]Surprised and annoyed, I yelled, "Stupid!" and the radio suddenly and abruptly switched to a call-in show.

1

Choosing the Right Words

The purpose of this book is to help you learn to write effective, error-free English. However, there are some considerations beyond correctness that you should address if you are to be a competent communicator. These considerations include, first, choosing an appropriate level of language; and second, avoiding wordiness, slang, pretentiousness, offensive language, and non-standard expressions (the words and phrases we call "abusages").

The key to successful communication is consideration of your "receiver," the person who is going to read your words. Readers do two things at once: they look for meaning, and they form an impression (often unconsciously) of the writer. In this chapter, we give you some tips to help you ensure that your writing is easy to understand and makes a good impression on the reader.

Before you get started, you need to equip yourself with a few essential resources and some basic knowledge of what kind of language is appropriate when you write.

The Writer's Toolkit

No one expects a writer to write without assistance. In fact, our first recommendation to beginning writers is to get help! Every writer needs three basic tools and to know how to use them.

1. Buy and use a good dictionary.

A dictionary is a writer's best friend. You will need to use it every time you write, so if you don't already own a good dictionary, you need to buy one. For Canadian writers, a good dictionary is one that is Canadian, current, comprehensive (contains at least 75,000 entries), and reliable (published by an established, well-known firm).

A convenient reference is the *Gage Canadian Dictionary*, available in an inexpensive paperback edition. It is the dictionary on which we have based the examples and exercises in this chapter. Also recommended are the *Nelson Canadian Dictionary of the English Language* (Thomson Nelson, 1997) and, for those whose native language is not English, the *Oxford Advanced Learner's Dictionary*, 7th ed. (Oxford, 2004). Unfortunately, no comprehensive Canadian dictionary is available on the Internet.

A good dictionary packs a lot of information into a small space. Take a look at the *Gage Canadian Dictionary* entry for the word *graduate*, for example. The circled numbers correspond to the numbers in the list of information dictionary entries provide, which follows the entry.

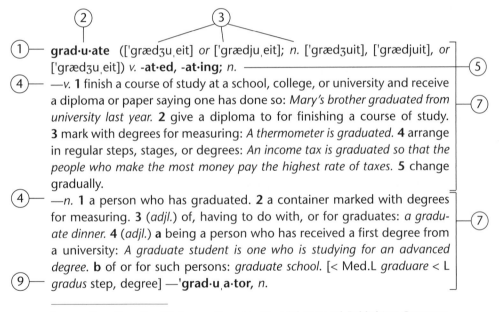

grad·u·ate (['grædʒuˌeit] *or* ['grædjuˌeit]; *n.* ['grædʒuit], ['grædjuit], *or* ['grædʒuˌeit]) *v.* **-at·ed, -at·ing;** *n.*

—*v.* **1** finish a course of study at a school, college, or university and receive a diploma or paper saying one has done so: *Mary's brother graduated from university last year.* **2** give a diploma to for finishing a course of study. **3** mark with degrees for measuring: *A thermometer is graduated.* **4** arrange in regular steps, stages, or degrees: *An income tax is graduated so that the people who make the most money pay the highest rate of taxes.* **5** change gradually.

—*n.* **1** a person who has graduated. **2** a container marked with degrees for measuring. **3** (*adjl.*) of, having to do with, or for graduates: *a graduate dinner.* **4** (*adjl.*) **a** being a person who has received a first degree from a university: *A graduate student is one who is studying for an advanced degree.* **b** of or for such persons: *graduate school.* [< Med.L *graduare* < L *gradus* step, degree] —'**grad·u**ˌa·**tor,** *n.*

Source: *Gage Canadian Dictionary.* Toronto: Gage Educational Publishing Company, 2000. 667.

In a dictionary entry, you will find some or all of the following information.

1. **Spelling:** if there are two or more acceptable spellings, the most common one is normally given first
2. **Syllables:** Small, centred dots (·) show you where hyphens can go if you need to break a word at the end of a line
3. **Pronunciation:** if there is more than one acceptable pronunciation, the most common one is listed first

4. **Grammatical form(s)**: e.g., noun *(n.)*, verb *(v.)*, adjective *(adj.)*
5. Any **irregular forms** of the word, such as the plural form of a noun, or the past tense and past participle of a verb
6. **Usage restrictions**: e.g., slang, informal, archaic, offensive
7. **Definition(s)**: the most common meanings are given first, followed by the technical or specialized meanings, together with phrases or sentences illustrating how the word is used
8. **Idioms** using the word
9. **Origins** of the word (etymology)
10. **Other helpful information**: e.g., homonyms (words that sound the same as the entry word); synonyms (words that are similar in meaning to the entry word); antonyms (words opposite in meaning); and special variations in grammar, spelling, pronunciation, and usage

Unless you have already done so (and most people haven't) begin by reading the "Guide to the Dictionary." The information in the Guide may not be very entertaining, but it is essential if you want to understand how to read your dictionary accurately. No two dictionaries are alike. Only if you are familiar with your dictionary's symbols, abbreviations, and the format of its entries, will you be able to use it efficiently.

Knowing what is in the Guide will also save you time. For example, you may not need to memorize long lists of irregular plurals. Good dictionaries include irregular plurals in their entries. They also include irregular forms of verbs, adjectives, and adverbs. And if you've forgotten how regular plurals, verbs, adjectives, and adverbs are formed, you'll find that information in the Guide as well.

Take half an hour to read the Guide in your dictionary; then do the following exercises. Be sure to check your answers to each set before you go on to the next. Starting with Exercise 1.2, answers for exercises in this chapter begin on page 473.

Exercise 1.1

1. Find two pronunciations for *lieutenant* and *schedule*. Which of the pronunciations is favoured in Canada?
2. What is another spelling of the word *humour*? Which spelling is used when an ending like *–ous* or *–ist* is added to the root word?
3. The prefix *–ir* put at the beginning of some words reverses their meaning. For example, *irregular* is the opposite of *regular*. Find six other words that have this characteristic. Note the pronunciation of *irreparable*!
4. Is *tatoo* spelled correctly? Is the word a noun or a verb? Find two different meanings of the word.

5. Find alternative spellings for the words *programme, centre, skillful, traveler,* and *judgement.* In each case, indicate the spelling favoured in Canada.

Exercise 1.2

Write the plural form of each word.

1. ratio	6. data
2. criterion	7. mother-in-law
3. analysis	8. nucleus
4. personnel	9. appendix
5. crisis	10. formula

Exercise 1.3

Combine each root word with the ending given.

1. delay + ed	6. lonely + ness
2. journey + s	7. policy + s
3. play + er	8. easy + er
4. destroy + ing	9. lazy + ness
5. repay + ment	10. necessary + ly

After you have checked your answers to this exercise, go back and look closely at the questions. What do the root words in questions 1 to 5 have in common? What do the root words in questions 6 to 10 have in common? How do these similarities affect the way they are spelled when an ending is added?

Exercise 1.4

Using hyphens, show where each word could be divided at the end of a line. (Some words can be divided in two or more places: *po-li-tics*, for example.)

1. discuss	6. create
2. management	7. solution
3. accommodate	8. technician
4. distribute	9. conscience
5. through	10. business

Exercise 1.5

The following words are not pronounced the way you might expect if you've had no previous experience with them. Working in teams of two, look them up in your dictionary and, in the space beside each word, write out its pronunciation (the information given immediately after it in parentheses). Take turns with your partner sounding out each word, one syllable at a time, using your dictionary's pronunciation key to help you. No answers are given for this exercise.

1. preferable
2. epitome
3. impotent
4. comparable
5. subtle

6. eulogy
7. indict
8. irreparable
9. corps
10. chassis

2. Use spelling and grammar checkers responsibly.

- Good spell-check programs can find typing errors and some common spelling mistakes. They have limitations, however. They can't tell if you meant to write "your" or "you're" and will not flag either word, even if it's used incorrectly. (You'll learn more about such words in Chapter 2, "Hazardous Homonyms.") Also, since we use Canadian English, our spelling is sometimes different from American spelling, on which most word-processing programs are based. If your program can be set to Canadian spelling, make that adjustment. If it cannot, be aware that words such as *colour*, *honour*, and *metre*—all correct Canadian spellings—will be flagged as errors.
- Another useful tool is a hand-held spell checker. Conveniently pocket-sized and not expensive, these devices contain a large bank of words and can provide the correct spelling if the "guess" you type in is not too far off. Some checkers even pronounce the word for you. Ask your instructor if you can use this device (sound turned off, please) when you are writing in class and during exams.

- Electronic translating dictionaries are available online and as hand-held devices. Some of them even "talk"—they pronounce the word as a native speaker would. (Of course, the accuracy of the pronunciation depends on the knowledge and skill of the programmer.) Do not use the voice feature in class! Most of the translating dictionaries are limited in their capability, so look for one that is both comprehensive and accurate. And be careful not to seize on the first definition that appears for a word you are looking for. Read through all the options given. Computers cannot grasp ambiguity, irony, or idioms the way the human mind does. Sometimes the speed and convenience of electronic dictionaries can lead to embarrassing linguistic lapses; for example, a European vacuum cleaner manufacturer translated its slogan into English as "Nothing sucks like our product." Print dictionaries are almost always more reliable than their electronic counterparts.

- The best advice we can give you about grammar checkers (they announce their presence by producing wavy green lines under words or sentences as you write on your word processor) is to use them with caution. So far, no grammar checker has been able to account for most, let alone all, of the subtleties of English grammar. A grammar program is as likely to flag a perfectly good sentence, even to suggest a "fix" that is incorrect, as it is to ignore a sentence full of errors. "I done real good on my grammar test," for example, escapes the dreaded wavy green line.

3. Buy and use a good thesaurus.

If you use the same words over and over, you will bore your reader. A thesaurus is a dictionary of synonyms—words with similar meanings. For any word you need to use repeatedly in a document, a good thesaurus will provide a list of alternatives.

Please note that synonyms are not identical in meaning. Only you (or a knowledgeable friend) can decide which of the words listed in your thesaurus may be suitable for your message. Your dictionary will help you decide which terms are acceptable and which are not. We do not recommend that you rely on the thesaurus in your word-processing program. For any given word, a WP thesaurus provides a list, in alphabetical order, of more-or-less synonyms, with no usage labels or examples. "More-or-less" is not good enough. The minimum information you need is whether the synonyms offered are nouns or verbs and whether they are in general use or are informal, technical, derogatory, or even obsolete. For this information, you need a book. Buy a good thesaurus and use it in conjunction with your dictionary.

Two thesauruses are available in inexpensive paperback editions: *The Oxford Thesaurus of English* (Oxford, 2004), and *Roget's Thesaurus* (Penguin, 2000).

Inexperienced writers sometimes assume that long, obscure words will impress their readers. In fact, the opposite is usually true. Most readers are annoyed by unnecessarily "fancy" language (see "Pretentious Language," page 15).

NEVER use a word whose meaning you do not know. When you find a possible but unfamiliar synonym, look it up in your dictionary to be sure it means what you want it to say.

Levels of Language

Communication can occur at many levels, from grunts and mumbles to inspiring speeches; from unintelligible graffiti to moving poetry. Different levels of language are appropriate for different messages and different audiences. In academic and professional writing, you will be expected to use what is called standard written English. Anything less than that will be thought inappropriate by your readers.

Levels of language are defined by vocabulary, by the length and complexity of the sentences and paragraphs, and by tone (how the writing "sounds"). Most of the communication you will encounter or be required to write will be at the **general level**, which is the level used in college and business. Outside of school and off the job, it is appropriate for you to communicate at the **informal level**, which is used in personal writing and in conversation.

The following chart outlines the characteristics of general and informal English.

	Informal	General
Vocabulary	Casual, everyday; some slang and colloquial expressions; contractions commonly used	The language of educated persons; non-technical; readily understood by most readers; few if any colloquial expressions; no slang, few contractions
Sentences and paragraphs	Short, simple sentences; some sentence fragments; dashes acceptable; short paragraphs	Complete sentences of varying lengths; paragraphs usually between 75 and 200 words
Tone	Casual, conversational; sounds like ordinary speech	Varies from light to serious to suit message and purpose of writer
Typical uses	E-mail between friends; some fiction; some newspaper columns; advertising	Most of what we read, including newspapers, magazines, most textbooks, business correspondence

Examples:

Informal: She's not going to go for the job.
General: She will not be applying for the position.

Informal: I'm dying to take these cool wheels for a spin.
General: I'd like to test-drive this sports car.

Informal: We're fed up with you people, so we're getting somebody else.
General: We are not satisfied with your service, so we have decided on another supplier.

From the chart and these examples, you can see why the general level is preferred for written communication. It's more precise, and it's clear to a wide audience of readers. Informal English is best reserved for conversation or other communication between friends.

Exercise 1.6

Write two short reports explaining how you like your program so far. One is an e-mail to a good friend; the other is a report required by the director of your program. Adapt your level of language so that it is appropriate to each situation.

Wordiness

One of the barriers to clear communication is **wordiness**. This problem is caused by using two or more words where one would do. As a matter of courtesy to your reader, you should make your writing as concise as possible.

Here's an example of what we mean. Read through the following passage. Then read it a second time and cross out the unnecessary words and phrases. Finally, compare your revision to the original to see how much shorter and clearer you have made the message.

Recycling, it seems to me, is, in fact, an idea that is so timely and current that it ought to be enforced by the laws of the land. If people in this country, no matter where or who, were required by legislation from our political leaders to recycle wherever, whenever, and whatever possible, then and only then would recycling take on the importance and significance it so rightly deserves.

By eliminating the redundant phrases, you probably came up with a sentence similar to this one: "Recycling is so important that it should be enforced by law." This sentence is concise, clear, and forceful. And it has the added advantage of not irritating readers.

Careless writers fall into the bad habit of using phrases that they think sound important but are actually redundant—that is, they say the same thing twice. The following is a list of some common examples.

Wordy	Concise
a large number of	many
absolutely nothing/everything/ complete	nothing/everything/complete
actual (*or* true) fact	fact
almost always	usually
at that point in time	then
at the present time	now
continue on	continue
could possibly (*or* may possibly, might possibly)	could (*or* may, might)
due to the fact that	because
equally as good	as good
few and far between	rare
final conclusion	conclusion
for the reason that	because
I myself (*or* you yourself, etc.)	I (*or* you, etc.)
I personally think/feel	I think/feel
in every instance	always
in my opinion, I think	I think
in the near future	soon
in today's society/in this day and age	now (*or* today)
is able to	can
personal friend	friend
real, genuine leather (*or* real antique, etc.)	leather (*or* antique, etc.)
red in colour (*or* large in size, etc.)	red (*or* large, etc.)
repeat again	repeat
really, very	These words add nothing to your meaning. Leave them out.
8:00 a.m. in the morning	8:00 a.m.
such as, for example	such as
take active steps	take steps
totally destroyed	destroyed
very (most, quite, almost, rather) unique	unique

By studying these examples, you can see how these and many other phrases add words without adding any meaning to your message. Teachers and editors call these phrases "fill" or "padding," and they urge students to eliminate them from their writing if they want to build a good relationship with their readers.

Exercise 1.7

Revise these sentences to make them shorter and clearer. Then compare your answers with our suggestions on page 474.

1. Several of my close personal friends and I myself have discussed it among ourselves and decided to go to the gym.

2. We were amazed and surprised to learn that the art painting hanging in our residence was a real, genuine work by a really famous and well-known artist.

3. Though small in size and light in weight, in actual fact she is the best forward on our team.

4. There is absolutely no way that we can ever be completely free of the violence that seems to surround us on all sides in today's society.

5. The professor at that point in time totally destroyed my concentration by announcing and saying that we had only five minutes left, no more.

Slang

Rad, wicked, chewy, dude: are these slang expressions familiar to you? **Slang** is "street talk": non-standard language used in conversation among people belonging to the same social group. Because slang words go out of date quickly and are understood by a limited group of people, you should avoid them in all but your most informal conversations and personal e-mails.

If you are in doubt about a word, check a dictionary. If the word you want is a slang term, it will have *sl.* beside it. Some words—for example, *cool*, *neat*, *bombed*—have both a standard meaning and a slang meaning. By taking the time to choose words and expressions that are appropriate to written English, you will increase your chances of communicating clearly and gaining your readers' respect.

"Yo dude! I'm here, like, for the interview. You guys want a junior executive, I need a job. We're cool!"

Exercise 1.8

Working with a partner write a list of 10 slang expressions in current use. Now "translate" these words or phrases into general-level English that would be appropriate in writing. Here are some examples to get you started:

fly	that's dope
messy	he's money
crib	bling

Pretentious Language

If slang is language that is too casual for informal writing, its opposite is **pretentious language**: words that are too formal for general writing. Never use a long, difficult, or obscure word when a simpler word will do. Your writing will be easier to read and your message clearer and more convincing if you write to inform rather than to impress.

You can recognize pretentious language easily: the words are long, unfamiliar, and sound unnatural. If the average reader needs a dictionary to "translate" your words into general English, then your writing is inflated and inappropriate. Consider these examples:

> Before we embark on our journey, we must refuel our vehicle.
>
> The refrigerator is bare of comestibles, so it is time to repair to the local emporium and purchase victuals.

With your dictionary in hand, you could translate these pompous sentences into plain English.

> Before we leave, we need to put gas in the car.
>
> The refrigerator is empty, so it's time to go to the store and buy some food.

But why would you? It's the writer's job to communicate, and a pretentious writer makes the reader do too much work. Here is a list of the most common offenders, together with their general-level equivalents.

"Madam, I am presenting myself in response to your company's request for an interpersonal conference with respect to a trainee-level position."

Pretentious	Clear
ascertain	find out
commence	begin
endeavour	try
facilitate	help
finalize	finish
manifest	show
reside	live
transmit	send
utilize	use

The cure for pretentious language is simple: be considerate of your readers. If you want your readers to understand and respect you, write in a simple, straightforward style.

Exercise 1.9

Revise the following sentences to eliminate pretentious language in favour of plain English. You may need to use your dictionary to complete this exercise. Compare your answers with our suggestions.

1. One should exercise diligence when utilizing an axe.

2. We reside at the conjunction of Maple Street and Rue Érable in the metropolis of Sherbrooke.

3. After we had finalized our survey of the task we had been assigned, we knew assistance would be necessary.

4. When we detected the presence of storm clouds in advance of our position, we knew that precipitation was imminent.

5. His gym teacher is conscious of the fact that Tom has an aversion to physical exertion.

Offensive Language

The last thing you want to do when you write is to offend your reader, even if you are writing a complaint. As we've seen above, some words occasionally used in speech are always inappropriate in writing. Swear words, for example, are unacceptable in a written message. So are obscene words, even "mild" ones. Offensive language appears much stronger in print than in speech and can provoke, shock, or even outrage a reader. Racist language and blasphemy (the use of names or objects that are sacred to any religion) are always unacceptable and are deeply offensive.

E-mail is especially dangerous. Many writers have experienced the acute embarrassment of having a message read by people for whom it was not intended. What may have seemed when you wrote it to be an innocent joke or an emphatic expression might, if it is read by someone other than the intended audience, prove hateful to readers and mortifying to the writer. THINK before you click "Send."

It is wise to avoid all questionable, let alone unacceptable, expressions in your writing. Language has power. As many linguists have observed, our language actually shapes as well as reflects our attitudes and values. Those who use racist, blasphemous, sexist, or profane terms not only reinforce the attitudes contained in those terms, but also project a profoundly negative image of themselves to their readers.

Abusages

Some words and phrases, even ones we hear in everyday speech, are *always* incorrect in written English. Technically, they are also incorrect in speech, but most people tolerate them as part of the casual standard that is common in informal conversation. If these expressions appear in your writing, your reader will assume you are uneducated, ignorant, or worse. Even in some conversations, particularly in academic and professional environments, these expressions make a poor impression on your listeners.

Carefully read through the following list and highlight any words or phrases that sound all right to you. These are the ones you need to find and fix when you revise.

Alot	There is no such word. Use *much* or *many*. ("A lot" is acceptable in informal usage.)
Anyways (anywheres)	The *s* on these words betrays the writer as uneducated.

Can't hardly (couldn't hardly)	The correct expression is *can* (or *could*) *hardly* (or *scarcely*, or *barely*, etc.).
Could of (would of, should of)	Using the preposition *of* instead of the auxiliary verb *have* in these verb phrases is a common error. Write *could have*, *would have*, and *should have*.
Didn't do nothing	All double negatives are wrong. Some familiar examples are "couldn't see nothing," "won't go nowhere," and "can't find nobody." Write *didn't do anything, couldn't see anything, won't go anywhere*, and *can't find anybody*.
***Good* used as an adverb**	"How are you?" "I'm good." This all-too-common expression is incorrect (unless you mean to state that you are moral or ethical or saintly). If you want to say that you are healthy, then say, "I'm *well*."
Irregardless	There is no such word. *Regardless* is the word you may want, but check your thesaurus for other, possibly more appropriate, choices.
***Media* used as singular**	The word *media* is plural. It is incorrect to say, "television is a mass media." It is a mass *medium*. Newspapers and magazines are print media. Radio, television, and the Internet are electronic media.
Off of	Use *off* by itself. "I fell *off* the wagon."
***Prejudice* used as an adjective**	It is incorrect to write "She is *prejudice* against blondes." Use *prejudiced*.
Prejudism	There is no such word. Use *prejudice* (a noun). "He showed prejudice in awarding the prize to his daughter."
***Real* used as an adverb**	"Real good," "real bad," and "real nice" are not acceptable. You could use *really* or *very* and be correct, but such filler words add nothing to your meaning.
The reason is because	Write *the reason is that*: "The reason is that my dog ate my essay."

Sort of speak	If you must use this expression, get the words right: "So to speak."
Suppose to	Like "use to," this phrase is incorrect. Write *supposed to* and *used to*.
Themselfs	Also "ourselfs," "yourselfs." The plural of *self* is *selves*: *ourselves, yourselves,* and *themselves.* "Theirselves" is also non-standard English and is not used by educated speakers/writers.
Youse	There is no such word. *You* is both the singular and the plural form of the pronoun. While occasionally heard in restaurants or retail stores, "Can I help youse?" labels the speaker as uneducated.

Exercise 1.10

Working with a partner, revise the following sentences to eliminate any abusages. Then compare your revisions with our suggestions on page 474.

1. Abdullah is real talented, so he could of chosen alot of different careers.

2. Irregardless of what you think, I believe the media is generally reliable.

3. We should of told Kevin there wasn't nothing he could of done to help.

4. The reason youse are failing is because you don't do no homework.

5. Between you and I, Karl didn't do real well at today's practice.

6. Sonji's father isn't prejudice; he can't hardly stand any of her boyfriends, irregardless of their backgrounds.

7. For this party, you're suppose to dress the way you use to when you were in primary school.

8. She shouldn't be driving anywheres; we should of taken the car keys off of her.

9. We were real sure of ourselves going into the race, but once we fell off of our bikes, we couldn't hardly hope to win.

10. Our instructor doesn't have no patience with people who should of been coming to class and now can't write real well.

Exercise 1.11

Eliminate the 15 abusages from the following. Ask your instructor for answers to this exercise after you complete it.

When I get up, I can barely move until I get my first cup of strong coffee. I like my coffee strong enough to peel the glaze off of the coffee cup. Over the years, I have become use to my morning caffeine jolt, and now my body depends on it to get going. Between you and I, I could cut back on my coffee consumption, I guess, but I enjoy the taste of it so much that I don't really want to do nothing that would deprive me of that pleasure

There are alot of people who are more addicted to caffeine than I am; some of my friends can't hardly get through the day without 10 or more cups. I believe the media is at least partly responsible for our addiction because it promotes caffeine-laden drinks as healthy, fun beverages. The commercials imply that these drinks are suppose to be good for us. One of my former classmates always carried high-caffeine soft drinks in her backpack when she should of been carrying fruit juice or water. Halfway through the term, she got sick and had to drop out. I am convinced the reason was because of her caffeine addiction.

I guess caffeine is like anything else: fine in moderation, but dangerous in excess. Anyways, until some study proves us wrong, my friends and I will enjoy our caffeine fixes, comforting ourselfs with the knowledge that there are far worse addictions.

2

Hazardous Homonyms

This chapter focuses on **homonyms**—words that sound alike or look alike and are easily confused: *accept* and *except*; *weather* and *whether*; *whose* and *who's*; *affect* and *effect*. Your word processor will not help you find spelling mistakes in these words because the "correct" spelling depends on the sentence in which you use the word. If you use the wrong one, you'll muddle the meaning of the sentence and throw your reader off-track. Writers must be alert to the hazards of easily confused words, just as drivers must be alert to road hazards.

For example, if you write, "Meat me hear inn halve an our," no spelling checker will find fault with your sentence. And no reader will understand what you're talking about—unless he or she takes the time to read the sentence aloud, then "translate" the sounds into meaningful spellings and thus puzzle out what you meant to say in the first place. The writer's job is to make reading as easy as possible for the audience. When you use incorrect spellings, you force the reader off the road to understanding (and sometimes around the bend).

Below you will find a list of the most common homonym hazards. Careful pronunciation can sometimes help you tell the difference between words that are often confused. For example, if you pronounce the words *accept* and *except* differently, you'll be less likely to use the wrong one when you write. It's also useful to make up memory aids to help you remember the difference in meaning between words that sound or look alike. The list that follows includes several examples that we hope you will find helpful.

Only some of the words on this list will cause you trouble. Make your own list of problem pairs and keep it where you can easily refer to it. Tape it inside the cover of your dictionary, or post it over your computer. Get into the habit of checking your document against your list every time you write.

accept
except

Accept means "take" or "receive." It is always a verb. *Except* means "excluding."

> I *accepted* the spelling award, and no one *except* my mother knew I cheated.

advice
advise

The difference in pronunciation makes the difference in meaning clear. *Advise* (rhymes with *wise*) is a verb. *Advice* (rhymes with *nice*) is a noun.

> I *advise* you not to listen to free *advice*.

affect
effect

Affect as a verb means "change." Try substituting *change* for the word you've chosen in your sentence. If it makes sense, then *affect* is the word you want. As a noun, *áffect* means "a strong feeling." *Effect* is a noun meaning "result." If you can substitute *result,* then *effect* is the word you need. Occasionally, *effect* is used as a verb meaning "to bring about."

> Learning about the *effects* (results) of caffeine *affected* (changed) my coffee-drinking habits.
> Depressed people often display inappropriate *affect* (feelings).
> Antidepressant medications can *effect* (bring about) profound changes in mood.

a lot
allot

A lot (often misspelled *alot*) should be avoided in formal writing. Use *many* or *much* instead. *Allót* means "distribute" or "assign."

>   *many*   *much*
> He still has a~~ lot of~~ problems, but he is coping a~~ lot~~ better.
> The teacher will *allot* the marks according to the difficulty of the questions.

allusion
illusion

An *allusion* is an implied or indirect reference. An *illusion* is something that appears to be real or true but is not what it seems. It can be a false impression, idea, or belief.

> Many literary *allusions* can be traced to the Bible or to Shakespeare.
> A good movie creates an *illusion* of reality.

are
our

Are is a verb. *Our* shows ownership. Confusion of these two words often results from careless pronunciation.

> Where *are our* leaders?

beside
besides

Beside is a preposition meaning "by the side of" or "next to." *Besides* means "also" or "in addition to."

> One evening with Mario was more than enough. *Besides* expecting me to buy the tickets, the popcorn, and the drinks, he insisted on sitting *beside* Lisa rather than me.

choose
chose

Pronunciation gives the clue here. *Choose* rhymes with *booze*, is a present tense verb, and means "select." *Chose* rhymes with *rose*, is a past tense verb, and means "selected."

> Please *choose* a topic.
> I *chose* to write about fuel cell technology.

cite
sight
site

To *cite* means "to quote from" or "to refer to."

> A lawyer *cites* precedents; writers *cite* their sources in articles or research papers; and my friends *cite* my e-mails as examples of comic writing.

Sight means "vision," the ability to see. It can also mean something that is visible or worth seeing.

> She lost her *sight* as the result of an accident.
> With his tattoos and piercings, Izzy was a *sight* to behold.

A *site* is the location of something: a building, a town, or an historic event.

> The *site* of the battle was the Plains of Abraham, west of Quebec City.

coarse
course

Coarse means "rough, unrefined." (The slang word **arse** is co**arse**.) For all other meanings, use *course*.

> That sandpaper is too *coarse* to use on a lacquer finish.
> *Coarse* language only weakens your argument.
> Of *course* you'll do well in a *course* on the history of pop music.

complement **compliment**	A *complement* completes something. A *compliment* is a gift of praise.

A glass of wine would be the perfect *complement* to the meal.
Some people are embarrassed by *compliments*.

conscience **conscious**	Your *conscience* is your sense of right and wrong. *Conscious* means "aware" or "awake"—able to feel and think.

After Ann cheated on the test, her *conscience* bothered her.
Ann was *conscious* of having done wrong.
The injured man was *unconscious*.

consul **council** **counsel**	A *consul* is a government official stationed in another country. A *council* is an assembly or official group. Members of a *council* are *councillors*. *Counsel* can be used to mean both "advice" and "to advise."

The Canadian *consul* in Venice was very helpful.
The Women's Advisory *Council* meets next month.
Maria gave me good *counsel*.
She *counselled* me to hire a lawyer.

desert **dessert**	A *désert* is a dry, barren place. As a verb, *desért* means "to abandon" or "to leave behind." *Dessért* is the part of a meal you'd probably like an extra helping of, so give it an extra *s*.

The tundra is Canada's only *desert* region.
If you *desert* me, I'll be all alone.
I can't resist any *dessert* made with chocolate.

dining **dinning**	You'll spell *dining* correctly if you remember the phrase "wining and dining." You'll probably never use *dinning*. It means "making a loud noise."

The dog is not supposed to be in the *dining* room.
We are *dining* out tonight.
The sounds from the karaoke bar were *dinning* in my ears.

does **dose**	Pronunciation provides the clue. *Does* rhymes with *buzz* and is a verb. *Dose* rhymes with *gross* and refers to a quantity of medicine.

> Josef *does* drive fast, *doesn't* he?
> My grandmother used to give me a *dose* of cod liver oil every spring.

forth **fourth**	*Forth* means "forward." *Fourth* contains the number **four**, which gives it its meaning.

> Please stop pacing back and *forth*.
> The Raptors lost their *fourth* game in a row.

hear **here**	*Hear* is what you do with your **ear**s. *Here* is used for all other meanings.

> Now *hear* this!
> Ranjan isn't *here*.
> *Here* is your assignment.

it's **its**	*It's* is a shortened form of *it is*. The apostrophe takes the place of the *i* in *is*. If you can substitute *it is*, then *it's* is the form you need. If you can't substitute *it is*, then *its* is the correct word.

> *It's* really not difficult. (*It is* really not difficult.)
> The book has lost *its* cover. ("The book has lost *it is* cover" makes no sense, so you need *its*.)

It's is also commonly used as the shortened form of *it has*. In this case, the apostrophe takes the place of the *h* and the *a*.

> *It's* been a bad month for software sales.

knew
new

Knew is the past tense of *know*. *New* is an adjective meaning "having recently come into being," "fresh," or "original."

> We *knew* our *new* pool would attract friends just as surely as fruit attracts flies.
> Who would have thought that cropped pants, a style from the 1950s, would be considered a *new* fashion 50 years later?

know
no

Know is a verb meaning "to understand" or "recognize." *No* can be used as an adverb to express refusal or denial, or as an adjective to express a negative state or condition.

> *No*, we do not *know* the results of the test yet.
> Why are there *no* cookies left in the jar?

later
latter

Lāter refers to time and has the word **lāte** in it. *Lătter* means "the second of two" and has two *t*'s. It is the opposite of *former*.

> It is *later* than you think.
> You take the former, and I'll take the *latter*.

lead
led

Lead is pronounced to rhyme with *speed* and is the present tense of the verb *to lead*. (*Led* is the past tense of the same verb.) The only time you pronounce *lead* as "led" is when you are referring to the writing substance in a pencil or the soft, heavy, grey metal used to make bullets or leaded windows.

> You *lead*, and I'll decide whether to follow.
> Your suitcase is so heavy it must be filled with either gold or *lead*.

loose
lose

Pronunciation is the key to these words. *Loose* rhymes with *moose* and means "not tight" or "unrestricted." *Lose* rhymes with *ooze* and means "misplace" or "be defeated."

There's a screw *loose* somewhere.
When Moosehead beer is served, people say, "The moose is *loose*!"
Some are born to win, some to *lose*.
You can't *lose* on this deal.

miner
minor

A *miner* works in a **mine**. *Minor* means "lesser" or "not important," or a person who is legally not an adult.

Liquor can be served to *miners*, but not if they are *minors*.
For some people, spelling is a *minor* problem.

moral
morale

Again, pronunciation provides the clue you need. *Móral* refers to the understanding of what is right and wrong. *Morále* refers to the spirit or mental condition of a person or group.

Most religions are based on a *moral* code of behaviour.
Despite his shortcomings, he is basically a *moral* man.
Low *morale* is the reason for our employees' absenteeism.

passed
past

Passed is the past tense of the verb *pass*, which has several meanings, most of which have to do with movement on land or water, but some of which have to do with sports or games. *Past* describes something that happened or existed in an earlier time. *Passed* is always a verb; *past* can be a noun, adjective, adverb, or preposition, but it is never a verb.

George *passed* the puck to Henry, who slammed it *past* the goalie to win the game.

peace
piece

Peace is what we want on **Earth**. *Piece* means a part or portion of something, as in "a **pie**ce of **pie**."

Everyone hopes for *peace* on Earth.
A *piece* of the puzzle is missing.

personal
personnel

Pérsonal means "private." *Personnél* refers to the group of people working for a particular employer or to the office responsible for maintaining employees' records.

The letter was marked "*Personal* and Confidential."
We are fortunate in having highly qualified *personnel*.
Yasmin works in the *Personnel* Office.

principal **principle**	*Principal* means "main." A *principle* is a rule. A *principal* is the main administrator of a school. The federal government is the *principal* employer in Summerside, Prince Edward Island. The *principal* and the interest totalled more than I could pay. (In this case, the *principal* is the main amount of money.) One of our instructor's *principles* is to refuse to accept late assignments.
quiet **quite**	If you pronounce these words carefully, you won't confuse them. *Quiet* has two syllables (pronunced *kwý-et); quite* has only one. The chairperson asked us to be *quiet*. We had not *quite* finished our assignment.
stationary **stationery**	*Stationary* means "fixed in place." *Stationery* is writing paper. A *stationary* bicycle will give you a good cardio workout without stressing your knees. Please order a new supply of *stationery*.
than **then**	*Than* is used in comparisons: bigger than, better than, slower than, etc. Pronounce it to rhyme with *can. Then* refers to time and rhymes with *when*. Kim is a better speller *than* I. I'd rather be here *than* there. Pay me first, *then* you can have my notes.
their **there** **they're**	*Their* indicates ownership. **There** points out something or indicates place. It includes the word **here**, which also indicates place. *They're* is a shortened form of *they are.* (The apostrophe replaces the *a* in *are.*) It was *their* fault. *There* are two weeks left in the term. Let's walk over *there*. *They're* late, as usual.

threw
through

Threw is the past tense of the verb *throw*. *Through* can be used as a preposition, adjective, or adverb, but never as a verb.

> James *threw* the ball *through* the kitchen window. When he climbed *through* to fetch it, his mother angrily told him that his days of playing catch in the yard were *through*.

too
two
to

The *too* with an extra *o* in it means "more than enough" or "also." *Two* is the number after one. For all other meanings, use *to*.

> It's *too* hot, and I'm *too* tired *to* go for another hike.
> There are *two* sides *to* every argument.
> The *two* women knew *too* much about each other *to* be friends.

wear
were
where
we're

If you pronounce these words carefully, you won't confuse them. *Wear* rhymes with *tear* and is a noun. *Were* rhymes with *fur* and is a verb. **Where** is pronounced "hwear," includes the word **here**, and indicates place. *We're* is a shortened form of *we are* and is pronounced "weer."

> After 360,000 km, you shouldn't be surprised that your car is showing signs of *wear* and tear.
> You *were* joking, *weren't* you?
> *Where* did you want to meet?
> *We're* on our way.

weather
whether

Weather refers to climatic conditions: temperature and humidity, for example. *Whether* means "if" and is used in indirect questions or to introduce two alternatives.

> We're determined to go camping this weekend, no matter what the *weather* is like. We'll pack enough gear to be prepared *whether* it rains or shines.

who's
whose

Who's is a shortened form of *who is* or *who has*. If you can substitute *who is* or *who has* for the *who's* in your sentence, then you have the right spelling. Otherwise, use *whose*.

> *Who's* coming to dinner? (*Who is* coming to dinner?)
> *Who's* been sleeping in my bed? (*Who has* been sleeping in my bed?)

Whose paper is this? (*"Who is* paper" makes no sense, so you need *whose*.)

woman **women**	Confusing these two is guaranteed to irritate your women readers. *Woman* is the singular form; compare **man**. *Women* is the plural form; compare **men**.

One *woman* responded to our ad.
Our company sponsors both a *women*'s team and a men's team.

you're **your**	*You're* is a shortened form of *you are*. If you can substitute *you are* for the *you're* in your sentence, then you're using the correct form. If you can't substitute *you are,* use *your.*

You're welcome. (*You are* welcome.)
Unfortunately, *your* hamburger got burned. (*"You are* hamburger" makes no sense, so *your* is the word you want.)

In the exercises that follow, choose the correct word. If you don't know an answer, go back and re-read the explanation. Check your answers after each set. Answers for exercises in this chapter begin on page 475.

Exercise 2.1

1. This is a (coarse/course) that I should be able to pass easily.
2. My sister is a (woman/women) who (heres/hears) everything and forgets nothing.
3. (Who's/Whose) radio is disturbing the (piece/peace) and quiet?
4. (They're/Their) still in bed because they stayed up (to/too) late.
5. This college values (its/it's/its') students.
6. I'd like to (lose/loose) four kilograms by Christmas, but I can't resist (deserts/desserts).

Exercise 2.2

1. (Its/It's) the perfect (site/sight) for a small house.
2. I won't (accept/except) assignments submitted (later/latter) than Thursday.
3. Our (moral/morale) was given a lift by the (compliments/complements) we received.

4. (They're/Their) eating habits are having an (effect/affect) on their health.
5. It was the (fourth/forth) quarter of the game, and we (lead/led) by 20 points.

Exercise 2.3

1. Is there anyone (who's/whose) (advice/advise) you will listen to?
2. (Your/You're) confidence in statistics is an (allusion/illusion).
3. Sometimes my (conscious/conscience) bothers me when I send (personnel/personal) e-mails on the office computer.
4. (Whose/Who's) turn is it to go to the storeroom for more (stationary/stationery)?
5. I believe in the (principle/principal) of fairness more (than/then) the deterrent of punishment.

Exercise 2.4

1. After lunch, we (lead/led) them to the (sight/site) of the old mine.
2. She (cited/sited) my essay in her paper on the (effects/affects) of poor grammar.
3. If we (except/accept) your (council/counsel), will you guarantee success?
4. He was still (conscience/conscious) after falling from his (stationery/stationary) bike.
5. My overindulgence at the (dining/dinning) table (lead/led) to a night of discomfort.

GO TO WEB

EXERCISES 2.1, 2.2

Exercise 2.5

1. (Choose/Chose) carefully, because the candidate (who's/whose) hired will (effect/affect) all of us.
2. This company makes a better product (then/than) any of (it's/its) competitors.

3. In a situation (were/where/wear) a company has several owners, the (principle/principal) owner is the one who has the most shares.
4. (Its/It's) the law that, as a (minor/miner), she is not allowed to have ice wine with her (desert/dessert).

Exercise 2.6

Find and correct the 15 errors in the following sentences.

1. Its clear that my ability to learn is effected by my personnel well-being more then by my intellectual ability.

2. All employees, without acception, will be fined $10.00 a day until moral on the job cite improves!

3. The advise given to us by the personnel firm we hired was to chose a women who's principle qualifications were a huge ego and shoes that complimented her every outfit.

4. Emily is the supervisor whose responsible for monitoring the affects of automation on assembly-line personnel.

Exercise 2.7

Find and correct the 10 errors in this paragraph.

I had a hard time chosing between two colleges, both of which offered the coarses I wanted. Both had good placement records, and I just couldn't make up my mind. I asked my friends for advise, but they were no help.

Several were surprised that any college would even except me! Their negative view of my academic ability did nothing to improve my moral; in fact, it lead me to re-evaluate my selection of friends. My school counsellor, a women who's opinion I respect, didn't think one college was better then the other, so she suggested that I choose the school that was located were I preferred to live. I followed her advice, and I haven't regretted it.

Find and correct the 15 errors in this paragraph.

Many people today are chosing a quieter way of life. They hope to live longer and more happily by following the "slower is better" principal. Some, on the advise of they're doctors, have been forced to slow down. One heart surgeon, for example, tells his patients to drive only in the slow lane rather then use the passing lane. They may arrive a few minutes later, but their blood pressure will not be effected. Others don't need to be prompted by their doctors. They except that living at a slower pace doesn't mean loosing out in any way. In fact, the opposite is true: chosing a healthy lifestyle benefits everyone. Piece and quite in your personnel life leads to increased productivity, higher moral, and greater job satisfaction. Sometimes the improvements are miner, but as anyone who has consciencely tried to slow the pace of life can tell you, the slow lane is the fast lane to longevity.

GO TO WEB

EXERCISES 2.3, 2.4

Exercise 2.9

Below is a list of word pairs that are often confused. Use each one in a sentence that clearly differentiates the word from the word or words that have the same sound. Use your dictionary to help you. When you are finished, exchange papers with another student and check each other's work.

1. altar, alter
2. breath, breathe
3. capital, capitol
4. stake, steak
5. waist, waste

6. cite, site
7. cloths, clothes
8. emigrate, immigrate
9. hoard, horde
10. precede, proceed

Exercise 2.10

All of the words in the following paragraphs are correctly spelled; however, 15 of them are the wrong words—they don't mean what the writer intended. Can you solve the puzzle by finding the errors and supplying the correct words?

When their buying a new car, do Canadians put styling or fuel economy first? According to a recent survey, the former factor is more important to most of us than the later. In fact, fuel economy ranked 8th in the list of criteria Canadians consider when choosing a new vehicle. (It ranked 24th in the United States.) Perhaps we are willing to except high gas prices as a miner irritant, under the allusion that prices will soon go down. In fact, high gas prices are not going to go down: there hear to stay.

Here are four ways drivers can reduce there fuel consumption, no matter what vehicle they drive. First, by making the conscience decision to reduce speed on highways by 10 kph, its possible to save about $10 on a 500-km trip. Second, aggressive speeding up and breaking uses 40 percent more fuel then smooth and steady driving. On that same 500-km trip, you can save enough to pay for an evening's dinning out. Third, using "low fuel con-sumption" tires and inflating them properly will significantly extend the time between fill-ups. Forth, take off that roof rack. Removing it will not only reduce the amount of fuel you use by more than 10 percent, it will also significantly reduce noise when your driving on the highway.

3

The Apostrophe

Can you spot how this job applicant's letter revealed his poor writing skills? Here's a sentence from his application:

I would like to be an active participant in you're companies success as it enters it's second decade of outstanding service to customer's.

Misused apostrophes display a writer's ignorance or carelessness. They can also confuse, amuse, and sometimes annoy readers. The example above contains four apostrophe errors, which irritated the reader so much that the applicant didn't even make it to the interview stage.

- Sometimes you need an apostrophe so that your reader can understand what you mean. For example, there's a world of difference between these two sentences:

  The instructor began class by calling the students' names.
  The instructor began class by calling the students names.

- In most cases, however, misused apostrophes just amuse or irritate an alert reader:

  The movie had it's moments.
  He does a days work every week.
  The Lion's thank you for your contribution.

It isn't difficult to avoid such mistakes. Correctly used, the apostrophe indicates either **contraction** or **possession**. It never makes a singular word plural. Learn the simple rules that govern these uses and you'll have no further trouble with apostrophes.

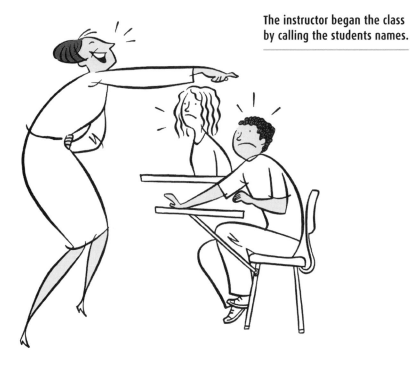

The instructor began the class by calling the students names.

Contraction

Contraction is the combining of two words into one, as in *they're* or *can't*. Contractions are common in conversational, informal English. Unless you are quoting someone else's words, however, you should avoid them in the writing you do for college or work.

The rule about where to put an apostrophe in a contraction is one of the few rules to which there are no exceptions.

When two words are combined into one, and one or more letters are left out, the apostrophe goes in the place of the missing letter(s).

Here are some examples.

I am	→ I'm		they are	→ they're
we will	→ we'll		it is	→ it's
she is	→ she's		it has	→ it's
do not	→ don't		who has	→ who's

Exercise 3.1

Place apostrophes correctly in these words, which are intended to be contractions. Notice that when the apostrophe is missing, the word often has a different meaning. Answers for exercises in this chapter begin on page 476.

1. cant
2. shed
3. hell
4. wed
5. lets

6. hasnt
7. youre
8. wont
9. shell
10. well

Exercise 3.2

Make these sets of words into contractions.

1. they are
2. I will
3. it has
4. can not
5. everyone is

6. could not
7. who has
8. you are
9. we would
10. will not

GO TO WEB

EXERCISES 3.1, 3.2

Exercise 3.3

Correct these sentences by placing apostrophes where they are needed.

1. Wed be glad to help if theyd ask us.
2. There wont be a problem if youre on time.
3. Im sure that contractions shouldnt be used in formal writing.
4. Theyre acceptable in conversation and for informal writing.

5. Dont worry about your heart; itll last as long as you do.

6. Your sisters very nice, but your brothers weird.

7. Its certain that hell be late.

8. Well help you with your essay, but youll have to get started right away.

9. In my culture, a birthdays the most important day of the year, and any-one whos celebrating is the centre of attention.

10. Its a shame that theyre arriving for a three-week visit on the same day that youre leaving to go home.

Exercise 3.4

In some formal kinds of writing—academic, legal, and technical, for example—contractions are not acceptable. A good writer is able not only to contract two words into one, but also to expand any contraction into its original two-word phrase. In the following paragraph, find and expand each contraction into its original form.

I'm writing to apply for the position of Webmaster for BrilloVision.com that you've advertised in the *Daily News*. I've got the talent and background you're looking for. Currently, I work as a Web designer for an online publication, Vexed.com, where they're very pleased with my work. If you click on their Web site, I think you'll like what you see. There's little in the way of Web design and application that I haven't been involved in during the past two years. But it's time for me to move on to a new challenge, and BrilloVision.com promises the kind of opportunity I'm looking for. I guarantee you won't be disappointed if I join your team!

Possession

The apostrophe is also used to show ownership or possession. Here's the rule that applies in most cases.

> Add *'s* to the word that indicates the *owner*.
> If the resulting word ends in a double or triple *s*, delete the last *s*, leaving the apostrophe in place.[1]

Here are some examples that illustrate the rule.

singer + 's = singer's voice	women + 's = women's voices
band + 's = band's instruments	student + 's = student's report card
players + 's = players's uniforms	students + 's = students's report cards
ships + 's = ships's crews	colleges + 's = colleges's teams

To form a possessive correctly, you must first identify the word in the sentence that indicates possession and determine whether it is singular or plural. For example, "the managers duties" can have two meanings, depending on where you put the apostrophe:

the manager's duties (the duties belong to one *manager*)
the managers' duties (the duties belong to two or more *managers*)

> To solve an apostrophe problem, follow this two-step process:
> 1. Find the owner word.
> 2. Apply the possession rule.

Problem: Gretas hair is a mess.
Solution: 1. The word that indicates possession is *Greta* (singular).
            2. Add *'s* to *Greta*.

Greta's hair is a mess.

---

[1] Many writers today prefer to keep the final *s* when it represents a sound that is pronounced, as it is in one-syllable words such as *boss* (*boss's*) and *class* (*class's*), and in some names such as *Harris* (*Harris's*) and *Brutus* (*Brutus's*).

Problem: The technicians strike halted the production.
Solution: 1. The word that indicates possession is *technicians* (plural).
2. Add *'s* to *technicians*, then delete the second *s*, leaving the apostrophe.

The *technicians'* strike halted the production.

Sometimes the meaning of your sentence is determined by where you put the apostrophe.

Problem: The writer was delighted by the critics response to her book.

Now you have two possibilities to choose from, depending on your meaning.

Solution A: 1. The owner word is *critic* (singular).
2. Add *'s* to *critic*.

The writer was delighted by the *critic's* response to her book.

Solution B: 1. The owner word is *critics* (plural).
2. Add *'s* to *critics*, then drop the second *s*, leaving the apostrophe.

The writer was delighted by the *critics'* response to her book.

Both solutions are correct, depending on whether the book was reviewed by one critic (A) or by more than one critic (B).

Possession does not have to be literal. It can be used to express the notion of "belonging to" or "associated with." That is, the owner word need not refer to a person or group of people. Ideas or concepts (abstract nouns) can be "owners" too.

today's new = the news of today
a month's vacation = a vacation of one month
a year's salary = the salary of one year

Exercise 3.5

In each of the following phrases, make the owner word possessive.

1. woman beauty
2. heaven gate
3. families budgets
4. children school

5. the soldiers uniforms

6. the books title

7. the Thousand Islands climate

8. the Simpsons daughters

9. the oldest child responsibility

10. our country flag

GO TO WEB

EXERCISES 3.3, 3.4

Note that a few words, called **possessive pronouns**, are already possessive in form, so they don't have apostrophes.[2]

yours

hers/his/its

ours

theirs

whose

His business provides excellent service to *its* customers.
Whose cellphone is ringing, *yours* or mine?
This classroom is *theirs*. *Ours* is across the hall.

Four possessive words are often confused with the contractions that sound like them. When you are trying to decide which spelling to use, expand the contraction into its original two words and try those words in your sentence. If the sentence still makes sense, use the contraction. If it doesn't, use the possessive.

Possessive	Contraction
its = *It* owns something	it's = it is/it has
their = *They* own something	they're = they are
whose = *Who* owns something	who's = who is/who has
your = *You* own something	you're = you are

---

[2] If you add an apostrophe to any of these words, you create an error. There are no such words as *your's*, *her's*, *their's*, or *our's*.

Error: They're (they are) going to sing they're (~~they are~~) latest song.
Revision: They're going to sing *their* latest song.

Error: It's (it is) you're (~~you are~~) favourite song.
Revision: It's *your* favourite song.

Error: Who's (~~who is~~) CD are you listening to?
Revision: *Whose* CD are you listening to?

Error: That car has a hole in it's (~~it is~~) muffler.
Revision: That car has a hole in *its* muffler.

Exercise 3.6

Make the words in parentheses possessive. This exercise will help you discover how well you understand the difference between possessive pronouns and their sound-alike contractions.

1. (Juri) greatest fear is his (mother) disapproval.

2. (Students) supplies can be expensive, so I buy mine at (Danny) Dollar Store.

3. My parents would like to know (who) yogurt was left in (they) fridge for three months.

4. After only a (month) wear, my (sons) new jacket fell apart.

5. Unfortunately, the (book) cover was much more interesting than (it) contents.

6. Our (team) biggest win came at the same time as our (league) other teams all lost.

7. (Texas) record of executing people is one of the (United States) most notorious statistics.

8. This year, our (family) Thanksgiving celebration will be a quiet one, as we think of other (families) poverty.

9. This weeks *Fashion* magazine devotes four pages to (men) clothing and twelve pages to women's.

10. One way of overcoming writer's block is to disconnect (you) computer from (it) monitor, so you can't see (you) work as you type.

In the two exercises that follow, correct the sentences by placing apostrophes where they are needed in contractions and possessive constructions. Delete any misused apostrophes. Work with a partner in Exercise 3.7, but do Exercise 3.8 on your own. There are 10 errors in each exercise.

Exercise 3.7

1. Theres a rumour that youre going to quit smoking.

2. Its true. My family doctors concerns about my health finally convinced me to quit.

3. Whos perfect? I am, in my mothers opinion, at least.

4. Its a fact that most mothers opinions about their children are unrealistically positive.

5. Most fathers opinions are highly negative when they first meet their daughters boyfriends.

Exercise 3.8

1. The candidates debate was deadly boring until the fans started fighting in their seats.

2. Todays styles and tomorrows trends will be featured in our display window.

3. Hockeys playoff schedule puts the final's into the middle of June.

4. My in-laws home is about four hours drive north of Red Lake.

5. Todays paper features a short article entitled "Its Clear the Apostrophes Days Are Numbered."

GO TO WEB

EXERCISE 3.5

Plurals

The third apostrophe rule is very simple. Memorize it, apply it, and you will instantly correct many of your apostrophe errors.

Never use an apostrophe to make a word plural.

The plural of most English words is formed by adding *s* to the root word, not *'s*. The *s* alone tells the reader that the word is plural: e.g., *memos, letters, files, broadcasts, newspapers, journalists*. If you add an apostrophe + *s*, you are telling your reader that the word is either a contraction or a possessive.

Incorrect: Never use apostrophe's to make word's plural.
Correct: Never use apostrophes to make words plural.

Exercise 3.9

Correct the misused and missing apostrophes in the following sentences. There are 10 errors in this exercise.

1. When you feel like a snack, you can choose between apples or Timbit's.

2. Annas career took off when she discovered its easy to sell childrens toys.

3 The Olympic Game's are held every two years.

4. Pokers an easy game to play if you are dealt ace's more often than your opponent's are.

5. Nobodies perfect, but if you consistently make mistakes, you demonstrate that you don't understand apostrophe's.

GO TO WEB

EXERCISES 3.6, 3.7

Correct the misused and missing apostrophes in the two exercises that follow. There are 10 errors in each exercise.

Exercise 3.10

1. Ive posted a sign on my front lawn: "Salespersons' welcome. Dog foods expensive."

2. The leader's of the European Union country's are meeting in Brussels.

3. Do you really think your employee's will be disappointed when they hear that you've cancelled the companies annual picnic?

4. In Canada, when it's warm enough to expose you're skin to the sun, the insects feeding season is at it's height.

Exercise 3.11

1. Candy is dandy, but liquors quicker. (Ogden Nash)

2. The storm devastated the two small town's in it's path.

3. Thank you for the flower's you sent us on the occasion of the twins graduation.

4. Somebodys going to be very disappointed when the panel releases its decision.

5. Four months work was wasted by a few minutes carelessness.

6. Don't forget your three o'clock appointment at the Finger's and Toe's salon.

Before you do the final exercise in this chapter, you may want to review what you've learned about using apostrophes correctly. See the Summary box on the next page.

Summary

- When contracting two words into one, put an apostrophe in the place of the missing letters.
- Watch for owner words: they need apostrophes.
- To indicate possession, add *'s* to the owner word. (If the owner word already ends in *s*, just add the apostrophe.)
- Possessive pronouns (e.g., *their, its, ours*) do not take apostrophes.
- Never use an apostrophe to form the plural of a word.

Exercise 3.12

This exercise will test your mastery of the apostrophe. There are 20 errors in the following sentences. Find and correct them.

1. In just a weeks time, womens' fashion's will go on sale in our downtown store.

2. Our year-end sale is you're opportunity to stock up on some of the seasons most exciting suit's, coat's, and casual wear.

3. While you browse through our impressive womens wear collections, the man in you're life will be happy to head to the fifth floors year-end sale of tools for his home workshop.

4. Its the perfect opportunity for woodworker's and auto enthusiast's to update their tool collection's.

5. We also offer a childrens' program that let's you drop off your kid's in a professional daycare for only $5.00 an hour.

6. If your husband is the problem, you can drop him off at the Mens' Lounge on the fifth floor, where he can while away the time playing dart's and pinball, thus allowing you to get in a whole days guilt-free shopping.

4

Capital Letters

Capital letters belong in a few specific places and nowhere else. Some writers suffer from "capitalitis." They put capital letters on words without thinking about their position or function in a sentence.

Not many people have this problem. If you are in the majority who generally use capitals correctly, skip this chapter and go on to something else. If you are puzzled about capital letters, though, or have readers who are puzzled by your use of them, read on.

Capitalize the first letter of a word that fits into one of the six categories listed below:

> 1. The first word of a sentence, a direct quotation, or a sentence from a quoted source.

Are you illiterate? Write to us today for free help.
The novel began, "It was a dark and stormy night."
Lister Sinclair claims that the only thing Canadians have in common is that "We all hate Toronto."

Exercise 4.1

Add the eight missing capital letters to the following sentences. Answers for exercises in this chapter begin on page 478.

1. the pen is mightier than the sword.

2. Pietro hurried back inside and said, "it's too cold to go to school today."

3. my parents have a bumper sticker that reads, "money isn't everything, but it sure keeps the kids in touch."

4 taped to the door, there was a sign that read "not to be used as an exit or entrance."

5. in conclusion, I want you to think about the words of Wendell Johnson: "*always* and *never* are two words you should always remember never to use."

---

2. The names of specific people, places, and things.

Names of people (and their titles):

> Shania Twain, Governor General Michaëlle Jean, the Rev. Henry Jones, Professor Sandra Chin, Senator Anne Cools, Sergeant Preston, Ms. Akila Hashemi

Names of places, regions, and astronomical bodies (but not general geographic directions):

> Stanley Park, Lake Superior, Cape Breton Island; Nunavut, the Prairie Provinces, the Badlands; Saturn, Earth, the Moon, the Asteroid Belt; south, north

Names of buildings, institutions, organizations, companies, departments, products, etc.:

> the Empress Hotel; McGill University, Red Deer College; the Liberal Party, the Kiwanis Club; Petro-Canada, Giant Tiger; the Department of English, the Human Resources Department; Kleenex, Volvo, Labatt's

Exercise 4.2

Add capital letters where necessary in the following sentences. There are 20 errors in this exercise.

1. After a brief stay in the maritimes, captain Tallman and his crew sailed west up the st. lawrence.

2. The broadcast Department of niagara College has ordered six sony cameras for its studios in welland, Ontario.

3. Do you find that visa is more popular than American express when you travel to faraway places such as Mexico, France, or Jupiter?

4. Our stay at the Seaview Hotel, overlooking the pacific ocean, certainly beat our last vacation at the bates motel, where we faced west, overlooking the city dump.

5. As a member of the alumni association I am trying to raise funds from companies like Disney, toyota, microsoft, and the cbc, where our graduates have positions.

---

3. Names of major historical events, historical periods, religions, holy texts, and holy days.

World War II, the Depression, the Renaissance; Islam, Judaism, Christianity, Buddhism, Hinduism; the Torah, the Koran, the Bible, the Upanishads; Ramadan, Yom Kippur, Easter

Exercise 4.3

Add the 20 capital letters that are missing from the following sentences.

1. The crusades, which were religious wars between muslims and christians, raged through the middle ages.

2. The hindu religion recognizes and honours many gods; islam recognizes one god, allah; buddhism recognizes none.

3. The koran, the bible, and the torah agree on many principles.

4. The jewish festival of hanukkah often occurs near the same time that christians are celebrating christmas.

5. After world war I, many jews began to emigrate to Palestine, where they and the muslim population soon came into conflict.

GO TO WEB

EXERCISE 4.1

4. The days of the week, months of the year, and specific holidays (but not the seasons).

Wednesday; January; Remembrance Day, Canada Day; spring, autumn

Exercise 4.4

The following sentences contain both missing and unnecessary capitals. Find and correct the 15 errors.

1. My favourite months are january and february because I love all Winter sports.

2. This monday is valentine's day, when messages of love are exchanged.

3. In the summer, big meals seem to be too much trouble; however, after thanksgiving, we need lots of food to survive the winter cold.

4. A National Holiday named flag day was once proposed, but it was never officially approved.

5. Thursday is canada day and also the official beginning of my Summer Vacation.

5. The major words in titles of published works (books, magazines, films; essays, poems, songs; works of art; etc.). Do not capitalize minor words (articles, prepositions, conjunctions) in titles unless the word is the first word in the title.

The Empire Strikes Back   *The Thinker*
Of Mice and Men   "An Immigrant's Split Personality"
Maclean's   "In Flanders Fields"
Harry Potter and the Half-Blood Prince   "O Canada"

Exercise 4.5

Add the 30 capital letters that are missing from the following sentences.

1. The review of my book, *the life and times of a chocoholic*, published in *the globe and mail*, was not favourable.

2. Clint Eastwood fans will be delighted that the two early movies that made him internationally famous, *a fistful of dollars* and *for a few dollars more*, are now available on dvd.

3. Joseph Conrad's short novel *heart of darkness* became the blockbuster movie *apocalypse now*.

4. My poem, "a bright and silent place," was published in the april issue of *landscapes* magazine.

5. Botticelli's famous painting, "birth of venus," inspired my poem "woman on the half shell."

Pay special attention to this next category. It is one that causes everybody trouble.

6. The names of specific school courses

Marketing 101, Psychology 100, Mathematics 220, English 110,

but   a) NOT the names of general school subjects

marketing, sociology, mathematics

b) *unless* the subjects are languages or pertain to specific geographical areas whose names are capitalized.

English, Greek, the study of Chinese history, modern Caribbean literature, Latin American poetry

(Names of languages, countries, and geographical regions are always capitalized.)

Exercise 4.6

Add capital letters where necessary in the following sentences. There are 15 errors in this exercise.

1. I want to take introductory french this term, but it is not offered until Winter.

2. Although my favourite subject is Math, I'm not doing very well in Professor Truman's course, business finance 101.

3. We began our study of sociology with the concept of relationships.

4. Laurie is studying to be a chef and is taking courses called food preparation, restaurant management, and english.

5. The prerequisite for Theology 210 is introduction to world religions, taught by professor Singh.

GO TO WEB

EXERCISE 4.2

Exercise 4.7

In the two exercises that follow, correct the spelling by adding or deleting capital letters as necessary. There are 20 errors in each exercise.

1. Our youth group meets in the ottawa mosque every second thursday.

2. You must take some Science courses, or you'll never get into the program you want at college in the Fall.

3. Gore Vidal, author of *the best man*, once said, "it is not enough to succeed; others must fail."

4. After the game, we went to the burger palace for a late snack and then went home to watch *this Hour Has 22 minutes* on television.

5. In our english course at caribou college, we studied *the englishman's boy*, a novel about life among the settlers of the american and canadian west.

Exercise 4.8

1. I own a ford and wear levi's jeans but hope someday to drive a porsche and wear armani.

2. Two of Vancouver's religious leaders, rabbi David Mivasair and imam Fode Drome, held a joint service last month to bring their two Communities together.

3. In an award ceremony that president george w. bush did not attend, he was given the prize for stupidest political statement of 2005 for his remark, "they are always thinking of ways to harm america, and so are we."

4. I plan to travel on air canada to asia next summer to visit sri lanka, india, and pakistan, where I have many relatives.

Exercise 4.9

The following exercise is the Mastery Test and contains 25 errors. Before you begin, it would be a good idea to review the six capitalization rules, which are highlighted on pages 50–54.

1. In cambridge, england, there is a small Café where students like to gather. On the wall is a sign that reads, "in case of fire, pay bill promptly."

2. We enjoyed our english course because professor alzhari made the subject interesting and our text, *the bare essentials plus*, was both enlightening and fun.

3. We travelled North to nunavut, where we boarded a de haviland beaver float plane for the journey up to rankin inlet.

4. One of Canada's most famous painters was tom thomson, whose painting called "the jack pine" is widely known. He died under mysterious circumstances when his canoe overturned in algonquin park in 1917.

RAPID REVIEW

As a final check of your mastery of the information in Unit 1, correct the 15 errors in the following paragraphs. Then check your answers on pages 479–80 to see if you need to review any of the material you've covered.

[1]Recently I read a book, published in 1908, in which the author, travelling in the Nova Scotia wilderness, reports being thrilled out of his mind when he cited a beaver dam. [2]Beavers were almost extinct at that time; he'd never seen one before, and he might never get a chance to see another. [3]The author's excitement interested me because, far from being extinct, the beaver is now so common and so prolific that its being hunted and trapped as a nuisance across Canada. [4]Did you know that Canadian trapper's are issued a quota for the number of beavers they are aloud to trap in their regions, and they must reach that quota or loose their trapping licences?

[5]Were not alone in our struggle to control these humongous, pesky rodents, either. [6]A *Canadian Geographic* film called *The super beaver* documents the creatures introduction to Tierra del Fuego, at the tip of South America, which has led to the complete and total devastation of the

ecosystem there. [7]The film tells us that only coral and humans have had a greater impact on Earth's environment than beavers. [8]They have now migrated to the mainland of South America and, without radical government intervention, they threaten to destroy millions of hectares of Argentinas land as they expand their territory northward. [9]It's difficult to except the fact that only 100 years ago, travellers in Canadas wilderness longed for a glimpse of what was then a rare and exotic animal.

UNIT 2

Sentences

Quick Quiz

5 Cracking the Sentence Code
Finding Subjects and Verbs
More about Verbs
More about Subjects
Multiple Subjects and Verbs

6 Solving Sentence-Fragment Problems
"Missing Piece" Fragments
Dependent Clause Fragments

7 Solving Run-On Sentence Problems
Comma Splices
Fused Sentences

8 Solving Modifier Problems
Misplaced Modifiers
Dangling Modifiers

9 The Parallelism Principle

10 Refining by Combining
Sentence Combining
Review of Conjunctions and Relative Pronouns

Rapid Review

QUICK QUIZ

This quick quiz will show you which chapters of Unit 2 you need to focus on. The passage below contains 15 errors: fragments, run-ons, misplaced and dangling modifiers, and lack of parallelism. When you've made your corrections, turn to pages 480–81 and compare your version with ours. For each error you miss, the answer key directs you to the chapter you need to work on.

[1]You know that the heart pumps blood through our bodies, but did you also know that the word "heart" appears in the English language in other interesting ways? [2]Let's look at some of the idioms using the word "heart." [3]An idiom being a phrase whose meaning is difficult to figure out from the meaning of its individual words. [4]For example, "heart of gold" and "heart of stone." [5]Some "heart" idioms have positive connotations, negative connotations cling to others, and some are neutral. [6]Some have to do with love and loss, others have nothing at all to do with romance.

[7]After "losing your heart," the romance begins. [8]As the relationship develops, you have many "heart-to-heart" talks, you love each other "from the bottom of your hearts." [9]However, your "heart sinks" confronting the end of the relationship. [10]You might "cry your heart out." [11]Because you are "heartbroken" and your lover is "heartless."

[12]Turning away from romance, many other heart idioms that apply to all aspects of life. [13]For example, learning something "by heart" (memorizing it) and having your "heart set" on something (wanting it very much). [14]Scared nearly out of your wits, the "heart-stopping" movie you are watching is truly frightening. [15]The "heartland" the most important part of a country. [16]Asking someone to "have a heart" meaning to ask for sympathy. [17]To describe people as "young at heart" means they are youthful in spirit, though not in years.

[18]English idioms using the word "heart" have a bewildering number of meanings that we only learn through experience. [19]Experience teaches us not to say that spicy food gave us "heartache." [20]Or that an ex-lover caused us to have "heartburn." [21]My "heart goes out" to the many language learners who are confused by the difference!

5

Cracking the Sentence Code

A baby's first word is a big step, one that all parents mark as a significant stage of development. Not all parents recognize that an even more significant step in a baby's progress is the first time she puts together the two elements of a complete sentence: a subject and a verb. *Words* enable us to communicate images; *sentences* are the tools with which we communicate ideas.

There is nothing mysterious or difficult about sentences. You've been speaking them successfully since you were two. The difficulty arises when you try to write—not sentences, oddly enough, but paragraphs. Most college students, if asked to write 10 sentences on 10 different topics, could do so without error. But when those same students write paragraphs, then fragments, run-ons, and other sentence faults appear.

The solution to sentence-structure problems has two parts.

Be sure every sentence you write
1. has both a subject and a verb and
2. expresses a complete thought

If English is your first language, your ear may be the best instrument with which to test your sentences. If you read a sentence aloud, you may be able to tell by the sound whether it is complete and clear. Sometimes, however, your ear may mislead you, so this chapter will show you, step by step, how to decode your sentences to find their subjects and verbs. When you know how to decode sentences, you can make sure that every sentence you write is complete.

Read these sentences aloud.

Kiteboarding is one of the world's newest sports.
Although kiteboarding is still a young sport.

The second "sentence" doesn't sound right, does it? It does not make sense on its own and is in fact a sentence fragment.

Testing your sentences by reading them aloud won't work if you read your paragraphs straight through from beginning to end. The trick is to read from end to beginning. That is, read your last sentence aloud and *listen* to it. If it sounds all right, then read aloud the next-to-last sentence, and so on, until you have worked your way back to the first sentence you wrote.

Now, what do you do with the ones that don't sound correct? Before you can fix them, you need to decode each sentence to find out if it has both a subject and a verb. The subject and the verb are the bare essentials of a sentence. Every sentence you write must contain both. There is one exception:

In a **command**, the subject is suggested rather than stated.

Consider these examples.

Sign here. = [You] sign here. (The subject you is implied or understood.)
Charge it. = [You] charge it.
Play ball! = [You] play ball!

Finding Subjects and Verbs[1]

A sentence is about *someone* or *something*. That someone or something is the **subject**. The word (or words) that tells what the subject *is* or *does* is the **verb**. In the following sentences, the subject is underlined once and the verb twice.

Snow falls.
Meiling dislikes winter.
We love snowboarding.
Mt. Whistler offers excellent opportunities for winter sports.
In Canada, winter is six months long.
Some people feel the cold severely.

The subject of a sentence is always a **noun** (the name of a person, place, thing, or concept) or a **pronoun** (a word such as *I, you, he, she, it, we,* or *they*

---

[1] If you have forgotten (or have never learned) the parts of speech and the basic sentence patterns, you will find this information in Appendix B (page 451).

used in place of a noun). In the examples above, the subjects include persons (*Meiling, we, people*); a place (*Mt. Whistler*); a thing (*snow*); and a concept (*winter*). In one sentence, a pronoun (*we*) is the subject.

> Find the verb first.

One way to find the **verb** in a sentence is to ask what the sentence says about the subject. There are two kinds of verbs:

- **Action verbs** tell you what the subject is doing.
  In the examples above, *falls, dislikes, love,* and *offers* are action verbs.
- **Linking verbs** link or connect a subject to a noun or adjective describing that subject. In the examples above, *is* and *feel* are linking verbs.
  Linking verbs tell you the subject's condition or state of being. (For example, "Tadpoles *become* frogs," "Frogs *feel* slimy.") The most common linking verbs are forms of *to be* (*am, is, are, was, were, have been,* etc.) and verbs such as *look, taste, feel, sound, appear, remain, seem,* and *become*.

Another way to find the verb in a sentence is to put a pronoun (*I, you, he, she, it,* or *they*) in front of the word you think is the verb. If the result makes sense, it is a verb. For example, you could put *it* in front of *falls* in the first sentence listed above: "It falls" makes sense, so you know *falls* is the verb in this sentence. Try this test with the other five example sentences.

Keep this guideline in mind as you work through the exercises below.

> To find the subject, ask <u>who</u> or <u>what</u> the sentence is about.
> To find the verb, ask what the subject <u>is</u> or <u>is doing</u>.

In each of the following sentences, underline the <u>subject</u> with one line and the <u>verb</u> with two. Answers for exercises in this chapter begin on page 481. If you make even one mistake, go to the Web site and do the exercises listed under the Web icon that follows this exercise. Be sure you understand this material thoroughly before you go on.

Exercise 5.1

1. Canadians love doughnuts.

2. They eat more doughnuts than any other nation.

3. Most malls contain a doughnut shop.

4. Doughnuts taste sweet.

5. Glazed doughnuts are my favourite.

6. Hot chocolate is good with doughnuts.

7. Try a bran doughnut for breakfast.

8. It is good for your health.

9. Doughnut jokes are common on television.

10. Dentists like doughnuts too, but for different reasons.

GO TO WEB

EXERCISES 5.1, 5.2

Exercise 5.2

Underline the subject with one line and the verb with two.

1. My computer is usually reliable.

2. Today, however, it keeps crashing.

3. Turn it off.

4. Maybe the processor is tired.

5. Perhaps the operator needs a vacation.

6. Computing is a necessary part of my life.

7. My work depends on it.

8. Without a functioning computer, I feel frustrated and angry.

9. Eventually, I decided to hit it with my fist.

10. The computer booted right up!

GO TO WEB

EXERCISE 5.3

Usually, but not always, the subject comes before the verb in a sentence.

Occasionally, we find the subject after the verb:

- In sentences beginning with *Here* + some form of *to be* or with *There* + some form of *to be*

  Here and *there* are never the subject of a sentence.

  Here <u>are</u> your test <u>results</u>. (Who or what <u>are</u>? <u>Results</u>.)
  There <u>is</u> a <u>fly</u> in my soup. (Who or what <u>is</u>? A <u>fly</u>.)

- In sentences that are deliberately inverted for emphasis

  Finally, at the end of the long, boring joke <u>came</u> the pathetic <u>punch line</u>.
  Out of the stadium and into the pouring rain <u>marched</u> the <u>demonstrators</u>.

- In questions

  <u>Are</u> <u>we</u> there yet?
  <u>Is</u> <u>she</u> the one?

  But notice that in questions beginning with *who, whose, what,* or *which,* the subject and verb are in "normal" order: subject followed by verb.

  <u>Who</u> <u>ate</u> my sandwich?   Whose <u>horse</u> <u>came</u> first?
  <u>What</u> <u>caused</u> the accident?   Which <u>car</u> <u>uses</u> less gas?

Exercise 5.3

Underline the subject with one line and the verb with two. Watch out for inverted-order sentences. If you made even one mistake, do the Web exercises that follow this exercise.

1. Is Tomas still on the team?

2. Consider it done.

3. Here are the answers to yesterday's quiz.

4. Is it your birthday today?

5. Into the pool leaped the terrified cat.

6. Where are the children?

7. There were only two students in class today.

8. Which elective is easier?

9. Are you happy with your choice?

10. Who let the dogs out?

GO TO WEB

EXERCISES 5.4, 5.5

More about Verbs

The verb in a sentence may be a single word, as in the exercises you've just done, or it may be a group of words. When you are considering whether or not a word group is a verb, there are two points you should remember.

1. No verb preceded by *to* is ever the verb of a sentence.[2]
2. **Helping verbs**[3] are often added to main verbs.

The list below contains the most common helping verbs.

be (all forms of	can	must/must have
to *be* can act as	could/could have	ought
helping verbs: e.g.,	do/did	shall/shall have
am, are, is, was, were,	have/had	should/should have
will be, have/had	may/may have	will/will have
been, etc.)	might/might have	would/would have

The complete verb in a sentence consists of
the main verb together with any helping verbs.

[2] The form *to* + verb—e.g., *to speak, to write, to help*—is an infinitive. Infinitives can act as subjects or objects, but they are never verbs.

[3] If you are familiar with technical grammatical terms, you will know these verbs as **auxiliary verbs**. They also include modal auxiliaries (see Chapter 28).

Below are a few of the forms of the verb *to take*. Study this list carefully, and note that when the sentence is in question form, the subject comes between the helping verb and the main verb.

We <u>are taking</u> a required
   English course.
You <u>can take</u> it with you.
<u>Could</u> Ravi <u>have taken</u> it?
<u>Did</u> you <u>take</u> your turn?
The money <u>has been taken</u>.
We <u>have taken</u> too much time.
You <u>may take</u> a break now.

We <u>might have taken</u> your advice.
You <u>must take</u> the bus.
Lucy <u>ought to have taken</u> a course
   in stress management.
<u>Shall</u> we <u>take</u> his offer?
I <u>should take</u> more time.
We <u>will take</u> the championship.
We <u>should have taken</u> the gold medal.

One verb form ALWAYS requires a helping verb. Here's the rule.

> A verb ending in *-ing* MUST have a helping verb (or verbs) before it.

Here are a few of the forms a verb ending in *-ing* can take.

Ralph <u>is taking</u> the test.
<u>Am</u> I <u>taking</u> your place?
You <u>are taking</u> an awfully long time.
Samantha <u>will be taking</u> over your duties.
<u>Have</u> you <u>been taking</u> French lessons?

Exercise 5.4

Underline the complete verb with a double line.

1. Your sister is calling from Mexico.

2. Carina will arrive from Finland tomorrow.

3. Have you arranged accommodation for our guests?

4. The restaurant could have prepared a vegetarian meal.

5. They might have moved away from the city.

6. Xue should have completed her diploma by now.

7. Do you know anything about Linux?

8. They have visited Venezuela twice.

9. We must have practised enough by now.

10. I will be looking for verbs in my sleep.

GO TO WEB

EXERCISES 5.6, 5.7

Beware of certain words that are often confused with helping verbs.

Words such as *always, ever, just, never, not, often, only,* and *sometimes* are NOT part of the verb.

These words sometimes appear in the middle of a complete verb, but they are modifiers, not verbs. Do not underline them.

Sofia <u>is</u> always <u>chosen</u> first.
They <u>have</u> just <u>been</u> married.
That question <u>has</u> not often <u>been asked</u>.

<u>Do</u> you ever <u>have</u> doubts about
  your ability?
<u>Will</u> you never <u>learn</u>?
I <u>have</u> often <u>wondered</u> about that.

In the following exercises, underline the subject with one line and the verb with two. Check your answers to the first set before going on to the next.

Exercise 5.5

1. I am making a nutritious breakfast.

2. It does not include Coca-Cola.

3. You can add fresh fruit to the cereal.

4. The toast should be almost ready now.

5. My doctor has often recommended yogurt for breakfast.

6. I could never eat yogurt without fruit.

7. With breakfast, I will drink at least two cups of coffee.

8. I don't like tea.

9. I simply cannot begin my day without coffee.

10. I should probably switch to decaf.

Exercise 5.6

1. Winners are always watching for opportunities.

2. Losers are usually looking for lucky breaks.

3. I should be riding my bicycle to work.

4. My bike has been broken for nearly two years.

5. I cannot ride a broken bike.

6. My broken bike is really just an excuse.

7. Given the opportunity, I will always drive.

8. Also, I have been waiting for the bicycle fairy to fix it.

9. Wouldn't that be a lucky break?

10. Maybe I should simply start working on it myself.

GO TO WEB

EXERCISES 5.8, 5.9

More about Subjects

Often groups of words called **prepositional phrases** come before the subject in a sentence or between the subject and the verb. When you're looking for the subject in a sentence, prepositional phrases can trip you up unless you know the following rule.

The subject of a sentence is never in a prepositional phrase.

You must be able to identify prepositional phrases so that you will know where *not* to look for the subject.

A prepositional phrase is a group of words that begins with a preposition and ends with a noun or pronoun that answers the question *what* or *when.*

This noun or pronoun is called the object of the preposition, and it is this word that, if you're not careful, you might think is the subject of the sentence.

Below is a list of prepositional phrases. The italicized words are prepositions; the words in regular type are their objects.

about your message	*between* them	*near* the wall
above the door	*by* the way	*of* the memo
according to the book	*concerning* your request	*on* the desk
after the meeting	*despite* the shortfall	*onto* the floor
against the wall	*down* the corridor	*over* the page
along the hall	*except* the contract	*through* the window
among the staff	workers	*to* the staff
around the office	*for* the manager	*under* the table
before lunch	*from* the office	*until* the meeting
behind my back	*in* the filing cabinet	*up* the corridor
below the window	*inside* the office	*with* permission
beside my computer	*into* the elevator	*without* the software

Before you look for the subject in a sentence, cross out all prepositional phrases.

A bird ~~in the hand~~ <u>is</u> messy. (What <u>is</u> messy? The <u>bird</u>, not the hand.)

This deck ~~of cards~~ <u>is</u> unlucky. (What <u>is</u> unlucky? The <u>deck</u>, not the cards.)

Several houses ~~on our block~~ <u>need</u> painting. (What <u>needs</u> painting? The <u>houses</u>, not the block.)

In the following exercises, first cross out the prepositional phrase(s) in each sentence. Then underline the subject with one line and the verb with two. Check your answers on page 482, and if you make even one error in Exercise 5.7, do the Web exercises before going on to Exercise 5.8.

Exercise 5.7

1. Many people in the crowd were confused.

2. Fifty of her friends gave her a surprise party.

3. The official opening of the new city hall will be held tomorrow.

4. In the movies, the collision of two cars always results in a fire.

5. A couple of burgers should be enough for each of us.

6. Please decide on dessert before dinnertime.

7. Only a few of us have finished our homework.

8. After class, the people in my car pool meet in the cafeteria.

9. There is a show about laser surgery on television tonight.

10. In the land of the blind, the one-eyed man is king. (Erasmus)

GO TO WEB

EXERCISES 5.10, 5.11

Exercise 5.8

1. A party in our neighbours' apartment kept us awake until dawn.

2. The meeting of all students in our class solved nothing.

3. From the hallway came the sound of a loud argument.

4. According to the news, the temperature in Yellowknife fell 20°C overnight.

5. My naps in the afternoon are necessary because of my late night activities.

6. Nothing in this world travels faster than a bad cheque.

7. For many students, lack of money is probably their most serious problem.

8. The plural of "choose" should be "cheese."

9. After my acceptance to this college, I became interested in learning more about the city.

10. My guarantee of an A in this course is valid only under certain conditions.

Exercise 5.9

1. In my opinion, the fear of flying is entirely justifiable.

2. In our basement are stacks of magazines dating from the 1950s.

3. The rats in our building have written letters of complaint to the Board of Health.

4. Why did Kai insist on purple for the bathroom?

5. For reasons of privacy, I am listed in the telephone book under my dog's name.

6. Into the classroom and up to the front marched a tall woman with a determined look in her eyes.

7. Most of the students in the class instantly decided not to argue with her.

8. In future, be sure to read through your notes before the exam.

9. In your brochure, you advertise a "semi-annual after-Christmas sale" of quality items.

10. According to my dictionary, the word "semi-annual" means twice a year.

GO TO WEB

EXERCISES 5.12, 5.13

Multiple Subjects and Verbs

So far, you have been decoding sentences containing a single subject and a single verb, even though the verb may have consisted of more than one word. Sentences can, however, have more than one subject and one verb. Multiple subjects are called **compound subjects**; multiple verbs are **compound verbs**.

Here is a sentence with a multiple subject.

<u>French fries</u> and <u>onion rings</u> <u>are</u> Brian's idea of a balanced diet.

This sentence has a multiple verb.

Selena <u>walks</u> and <u>dresses</u> like a supermodel.

And this sentence contains both a multiple subject and a multiple verb.

<u>Alan</u> and <u>Vijay</u> <u>drove</u> to the mall and <u>shopped</u> for hours.

The parts of a multiple subject are usually joined by *and* (sometimes by *or*). Compound subjects and verbs may contain more than two elements. Look at the following examples.

<u>Clarity</u>, <u>brevity</u>, and <u>simplicity</u> <u>are</u> the basic qualities of good writing.

<u>Raj</u> <u>deleted</u> his work, <u>shut down</u> the computer, <u>unplugged</u> it, and <u>dropped</u> it out of the window.

Identify the subjects and verbs in the three exercises that follow. First, cross out any prepositional phrases. Then underline the subjects with one line and the verbs with two. Be sure to underline all elements of a multiple subject or verb (there may be more than two). Check your answers to each set, and if you you've made any errors, do the Web exercises before you go on to the next exercise.

Exercise 5.10

1. My mother and father support me in college.

2. I could study tonight or go to the movies.

3. My parents and the rest of my family are expecting me to do well in school.

4. Entertainment and clothing are not included in my budget.

5. Tuition, books, lab fees, and rent take all my money.

6. A student's life can be sad and lonely.

7. In my letters home, I whine and moan at every opportunity about my lack of money.

8. Unfortunately for me, my mother and father were students too and had the same experience.

9. They laugh and shake their heads and tell me about their college days.

10. According to my parents, they ate only Kraft Dinner, lived in a shack, wore hand-me-down clothes, and walked 10 kilometres to school.

GO TO WEB

EXERCISES 5.14, 5.15

Exercise 5.11

1. Verbs and subjects are sometimes hard to find.

2. Farmers, loggers, and fishers need and deserve the support of consumers.

3. Open the bottle, pour carefully, taste, and enjoy.

4. Where do you and your roommates get the energy for school, work, and fun?

5. Werner, Italo, and Pierre discussed and debated recipes all night.

6. During the following week, each one chose and prepared a meal for the other two.

7. Werner's sauerbraten and Black Forest cake amazed and delighted his friends.

8. Italo chopped, sliced, simmered, and baked a magnificent Italian meal.

9. Pierre and his sister worked in the kitchen for two days and prepared a delicious cassoulet.

10. By the end of the week, Pierre, Italo, and Werner were ready for a diet.

GO TO WEB

EXERCISE 5.16

Exercise 5.12

1. A fool and his money are soon parted.

2. I dream of success and worry about failure.

3. Nur and Aman paddled and portaged for 10 days.

4. From the back seat of the tiny car emerged a basketball player and a Newfoundland dog.

5. In the mist of early morning, a Brontosaurus and a Tyrannosaurus Rex sniffed the moist air and hunted for food.

6. Study my methods, use my research, but do not copy my work.

7. Why are goalies in hockey and kickers in football so superstitious?

8. In my dreams, the maid, butler, housekeeper, and chef wash the dishes, vacuum the floors, do the laundry, and make the meals.

9. According to the official course outline, students in this English course must take notes during every class and submit their notes to their instructor for evaluation.

10. In the opinion of many Canadians, the word *politician* is a synonym for "crook."

GO TO WEB

EXERCISE 5.17

Here's a summary of what you've learned in this chapter. Keep it in front of you as you write the Mastery Test.

Summary

- The subject is *who* or *what* the sentence is about.
- The verb tells what the subject *is* or *does*.
- The subject normally comes before the verb (exceptions are questions, sentences that begin with *here* or *there*, and sentences that begin with a series of prepositional phrases and are inverted for effect.)
- An infinitive (a phrase consisting of *to* + verb) is never the verb of a sentence.
- The complete verb consists of a main verb + any helping verbs.
- By itself, a word ending in *-ing* is not a verb.
- The subject of a sentence is never in a prepositional phrase.
- A sentence can have more than one subject and verb.

Exercise 5.13

This exercise will test your ability to identify subjects and verbs in different kinds of sentences. First, cross out any prepositional phrases. Next, underline the subject(s) with one line and the verb(s) with two. Be sure to underline all elements in a multiple subject or verb.

1. Provide a passport photo and self-addressed return envelope.

2. Maryam and Amal have often won academic honours.

3. We bought bread and tomatoes and made sandwiches for the group.

4. Many early immigrants to Canada arrived in Halifax and took the train west.

5. For most of the twentieth century, they arrived by ship, were cleared through Customs at Pier 21 in Halifax, and were welcomed by hard-working volunteers.

6. Among the hopeful signs in our city are increased overall prosperity, less violent crime, and higher levels of employment.

7. On the groom's face were a bolt through the nose, a pin through one eyebrow, two rings through the left ear, and a stud through the cheek.

8. Muslims, Buddhists, Hindus, Christians, Jews, Sikhs, Baha'is, and Zoroastrians participated in the ceremony and together prayed for peace.

9. The rain is getting heavier, the tent is beginning to flood, and I am getting soaked!

10. According to its campaign promises, the new government will provide jobs for all, eliminate the national debt, lower taxes, and offer free post-secondary education, all in its first year of office.

6

Solving Sentence-Fragment Problems

Every complete sentence has two characteristics. It contains a subject and a verb, and it expresses a complete thought. Any group of words that is punctuated as a sentence but lacks one of these characteristics is a **sentence fragment**. Fragments are appropriate in conversation and in some kinds of writing, but normally they are not acceptable in college, technical, or business writing.

There are two kinds of fragments you should watch out for: the "missing piece" fragment and the dependent clause fragment.

"Missing Piece" Fragments

Sometimes a group of words is punctuated as a sentence but is missing one or more of the essential parts of a sentence, the subject and verb. Consider these examples.

1. Found it under the pile of clothes on your floor.

(Who or what <u>found</u> it? The sentence doesn't tell you. The subject is missing.)

2. Their arguments about housework.

(The sentence doesn't tell you what the arguments <u>were</u> or <u>did</u>. The verb is missing.)

3. During my favourite TV show.

(<u>Who</u> or <u>what</u> <u>was</u> or <u>did</u> something? Both subject and verb are missing.)

4. The programmers working around the clock to trace the hacker.

(Part of the verb is missing. Remember that a verb ending in *-ing* needs a helping verb to be complete.)

Finding fragments like these in your work when you are revising is the hard part. Fixing them is easy. There are two ways to correct sentence fragments. Here's the first one.

> To change a "missing piece" fragment into a complete sentence, add whatever is missing: a subject, a verb, or both.

1. You may need to add a subject:

Your <u>sister</u> found it under the pile of clothes on your floor.

2. You may need to add a verb:

Their arguments <u>were</u> about housework. (linking verb)
Their arguments about housework eventually <u>destroyed</u> their relationship. (action verb)

3. You may need to add both a subject and a verb:

My <u>mother</u> always <u>calls</u> during my favourite TV show.

4. Or you may need to add a helping verb:

The programmers <u>have been</u> working around the clock to trace the hacker.

Don't let the length of a fragment fool you. Students sometimes think that if a string of words is long, it must be a sentence. Not so. No matter how long the string of words, if it doesn't contain both a subject and a verb, it is not a sentence. For example, here's a description of a traffic jam:

Inching, inching, each hard-won car length a minute-long test of patience, six lanes of powerful, brightly coloured machines capable of cruising 130 km in the time it takes to crawl one on this day, their drivers hermetically sealed behind steel and glass, resigned to the wait, listening to the radio in their streamlined steel capsules, developing fleeting relationships with the drivers in the adjacent lanes as they inch forward in unison.

At 71 words, this "sentence" is long, but it is a fragment. It lacks both a subject and a verb. If you add "The <u>commuters</u> <u>were</u>" at the beginning of the fragment, you would have a complete sentence.

Exercise 6.1

In the following exercise, decide whether each group of words is a complete sentence or a "missing piece" fragment. Put S before each complete sentence and F before each fragment. Make each fragment into a complete sentence by adding whatever is missing: the subject, the verb, or both. Then compare your answers with our suggestions. Answers for exercises in this chapter begin on page 484.

1. _____ One type of sentence-fragment error.

2. _____ Glad to be able to help you.

3. _____ Hoping to hear from you soon.

4. _____ Saved by the bell.

5. _____ To prevent a similar tragedy from happening again.

6. _____ Not a good idea.

7. _____ Attaching a DVD player to the television.

8. _____ Close the door quietly on your way out.

9. _____ No choice but to get up early.

10. _____ Working as a server, for example, can be exhausting.

GO TO WEB

EXERCISES 6.1, 6.2

Most of us have little difficulty identifying a fragment when it stands alone. But when we write, of course, we write in paragraphs, not in single sentences. Fragments are harder to identify when they occur in a context, as you'll see in the next exercise.

Exercise 6.2

Read the following selections carefully and decide whether each question contains only complete sentences or whether it contains one or more sentence fragments. Put S beside the questions that contain only sentences. Put F beside those that contain fragments. Then check your answers.

1. _____ This apartment suits me in every way. Except for the price. I can't afford it.

2. _____ In track and field, this college is very well respected. Our team won the championship last year. Setting three new provincial records.

3. _____ Whenever I go fishing, the fish aren't biting, but the mosquitoes are. Maybe I should give up fishing. And start collecting insects as a hobby instead.

4. _____ My son is a genius. On his last birthday, he was given a toy that was guaranteed to be unbreakable. Used it to break all his other toys.

5. _____ We weren't lost, but we were certainly confused. I realized this when we passed City Hall. For the third time.

6. _____ I've had bad luck with cars. I wrecked two in three years. Perhaps this is why my parents don't let me borrow their car.

7. _____ My husband and I often go to the hockey arena. Not to watch sports, but to hear the concerts of our favourite local bands. These concerts give new meaning to the word "cool."

8. _____ According to the weather reporter at our local radio station, a storm with high winds and heavy rains is approaching our region. Yesterday, when the temperature hit 0°C, she predicted light snow.

9. _____ I enjoy reading travel books. About faraway, exotic places that I have never visited and will probably never get to see. The fun is in the dreaming, not the doing.

10. ___ Spending my remaining days skiing and the nights dining and dancing. That's how I picture my retirement. Unfortunately, by then I'll be too old to enjoy it.

Once you have learned to identify fragments that occur within a paragraph, it's time to consider the best way to correct them. You could fix all of them the way we've identified above, by adding the missing piece or pieces to each one, and in some cases, that is your only choice. However, there is another, shorter, way that can often be used to correct fragments in context. You need to be familiar with this "fragment fixer."

> You can sometimes correct a "missing piece" fragment by attaching it to a complete sentence that comes before or after it—whichever one makes sense.

Sometimes you need to put a comma between a missing piece fragment and the complete sentence to which you attach it. (See Chapter 17, "The Comma," Rule 3, page 210, and Rule 4, page 211.)

Exercise 6.3

Now go back to the sentences in Exercise 6.2 and correct the fragments. As you go through the exercise, try to use both techniques we've identified for fixing fragments:

- add the missing piece(s)
- join the fragment to a complete sentence next to it

When you've finished, compare your answers with ours on page 484.

Exercise 6.4

Read through the following paragraph, and put S before each complete sentence and F before each fragment. Then check your answers.

(1) _____ I decided to take swimming lessons for several reasons. (2) _____ First, knowing that swimming is one of the best activities for physical fitness. (3) _____ Second, safety. (4) _____ You never know when the ability to

swim might save your life. (5) ____ Or the life of someone you're with.
(6) ____ Third, being able to enjoy water sports such as diving and
snorkelling instead of being stuck on shore watching others have fun.
(7) ____ By summer, I hope to be a confident swimmer. (8) ____ Able to
enjoy myself in and on the water. (9) ____ I can hardly wait!

Exercise 6.5

Now correct the fragments you identified in the paragraph above. Use both
fragment-fixing techniques that are highlighted on pages 80 and 83. Then
compare your answers with ours on page 485.

Dependent Clause Fragments

Any group of words containing a subject and a verb is a **clause**. There are
two kinds of clauses. An **independent clause** is one that makes complete
sense. It can stand alone, as a sentence. A **dependent clause**, as its name
suggests, cannot stand alone as a sentence. It depends on another clause to
make complete sense.

Dependent clauses (also known as **subordinate clauses**) begin with
dependent clause cues (technically known as **subordinating conjunctions**):

Dependent Clause Cues

after	that
although	though
as, as if	unless
as long as	until
as soon as	what, whatever
because	when, whenever
before	where, wherever
even if, even though	whether
if	which, whichever
since	while
so that	who, whose

Whenever a clause begins with one of these words or phrases, it is
dependent.

> A dependent clause must be attached to an independent clause. If it stands alone, it is a sentence fragment.

Here is an independent clause:

I am a poor speller.

If we put one of the dependent clause cues in front of it, it can no longer stand alone:

Because I am a poor speller

We can correct this kind of fragment by attaching it to an independent clause:

Because I am a poor speller, I have a PDA with a spell checker.

Exercise 6.6

Let's start with an easy exercise. Put an S before each clause that is independent and therefore a sentence. Put an F before each clause that is dependent and therefore a sentence fragment. Circle the dependent clause cue in each fragment. Then compare your answers with those on page 485.

1. _____ After class is over.

2. _____ When you wish upon a star.

3. _____ Since then, I have been on time.

4. _____ Once the batteries are charged.

5. _____ Who encouraged us to keep trying until we succeeded.

6. _____ Take a picture.

7. _____ Even if there is an earthquake.

Most sentence fragments are dependent clauses punctuated as sentences. Fortunately, this is the easiest kind of fragment to fix.

> To correct a dependent clause fragment, join it either to the sentence that comes before it or to the one that comes after it—whichever linkage makes the most sense.

Problem: Learning a new language is difficult. When you are an adult. It can be done, though.

The second "sentence" is incomplete; the dependent clause cue *when* is the clue you need to identify it as a sentence fragment. You could join the fragment to the sentence that follows it, but then you would get " Learning a new language is difficult. When you are an adult, it can be done, though," which doesn't make sense. The fragment should be linked to the sentence before it.

Revision: Learning a new language can be difficult when you are an adult. It can be done, though.

If, as in the example above, your revised sentence *ends* with the dependent clause, do not put a comma before it. If, however, your revised sentence *begins* with the dependent clause, put a comma between it and the independent clause that follows.

Although it is difficult to learn a new language when you're an adult, it can be done. (See Chapter 17, "The Comma," Rule 3, on page 210.)

Exercise 6.7

Correct the fragments in Exercise 6.6 by attaching each one to an independent clause that you have made up. Then compare your answers with our suggestions. Be sure to put a comma after a dependent clause that comes at the beginning of a sentence.

Check your fragment-finding skills by trying the following exercises. The items in these exercises each contain three clauses, one of which is dependent, and therefore a fragment. Highlight the dependent clause in each item.

Exercise 6.8

1. Walking is probably the best form of exercise there is. Unless you're in the water. Then swimming is preferable.

2. Rain doesn't bother me. I like to stay inside and read. When the weather is miserable.

3. Please try this curry. After you've tasted it. I am sure you'll be able to tell me what's missing.

4. The report identifies a serious problem that we need to consider. Whenever our Web site is revised or updated. It is vulnerable to hackers.

5. Sanir and Jade asked us what we thought about their recent engagement. Since they want to go to Canada's Wonderland for their honeymoon. We think they are probably too young to get married.

GO TO WEB

EXERCISE 6.3

Exercise 6.9

1. I keep the temperature in my apartment very low. In order to save money. My friends have to wear sweaters every time they visit.

2. Your idea that we should ask for directions was a good one. If we had relied on the hand-drawn map we were given. We would still be lost right now.

3. Home decoration isn't all that difficult. When you don't have enough money for furniture, carpets, or curtains. You have no choice but to be creative.

4. I believe that honesty is the best policy. If I found a million dollars in the street and discovered that it belonged to a poor, homeless person. I'd give it right back.

5. The names of many Canadian landmarks have been changed over the years. The Oldman River, for example, which runs through Lethbridge, used to be called the Belly River. Until local residents petitioned for a change to a more dignified name.

GO TO WEB

EXERCISE 6.4

Exercise 6.10

Correct the sentence fragments you highlighted in Exercises 6.8 and 6.9 above. Make each fragment into a complete sentence by attaching it to the independent clause that precedes or follows it, whichever makes better sense. Remember to punctuate correctly: if a dependent clause comes at the beginning of your sentence, put a comma after it. Check your answers after each exercise.

Exercise 6.11

In the following paragraph, you'll find a mixture of "missing piece" fragments and dependent clause fragments. Revise the six fragments any way you choose: either by adding the missing piece(s), or by joining fragments to appropriate independent clauses. Check your punctuation carefully.

Because the chances of winning are so small. Lotteries have been called a tax on people with poor math skills. Buying a lottery ticket will gain you about as much as betting that the next U.S. president will come from Moose Jaw. Or that the parrot in the pet store speaks Inuktitut. While winning a lottery is not impossible. It is so unlikely that you'd do better to use your money to light a nice warm fire. Though the winners are highly publicized. No one hears about the huge numbers of losers. Whose money has gone to pay the winners. In order for the lottery corporation to make its enormous profits. Millions of dollars must be lost whenever a lucky winner is declared.

GO TO WEB

EXERCISES 6.5, 6.6

Exercise 6.12

Find and fix the 10 fragment errors in this paragraph.

Some basic truths about the differences between men and women. While a woman marries a man expecting he will change. He won't. While a man marries a woman expecting that she will not change. She will. A woman worries about the future. Until she gets a husband. A man never worries about the future. Until he gets a wife. A woman will dress up, do her hair, and apply make-up to go shopping, get the mail, put out the garbage, water the plants, or go to the gym. While a man gets dressed up only for weddings and funerals. When it comes to her children. A woman knows all about them. Their dental appointments and secret fears, best friends and romances, favourite foods, and hopes and dreams. A man, on the other hand, is vaguely aware of some short people living in the house. And finally, arguments. A woman has the last word in any argument. If a man says anything after the woman has the last word. He starts a new argument.

7

Solving Run-On Sentence Problems

Some sentences lack essential elements and thus are fragments. Other sentences contain two or more independent clauses that are incorrectly linked together. A sentence with inadequate punctuation between clauses is a **run-on.** Run-ons tend to occur when you write in a hurry, without taking time to organize your thoughts first. If you think about what you want to say and punctuate carefully, you shouldn't have any problems with run-ons.

There are two kinds of run-on sentence to watch out for: comma splices and fused sentences.

Comma Splices

As its name suggests, the **comma splice** occurs when two complete sentences (independent clauses) are joined (or spliced) by a comma. Consider these examples:

Tea may be good for you, coffee is not.
This film is boring, it has no plot.

Fused Sentences

A **fused sentence** occurs when two complete sentences are joined together with no punctuation between them. For example:

Tea may be good for you coffee is not.
This film is boring it has no plot.

There are four ways you can fix comma splices or fused sentences.

1. Make the independent clauses into separate sentences.

Tea may be good for you. Coffee is not.
This film is boring. It has no plot.

This solution works well if you do not use it too often. Writing that consists of nothing but single-clause sentences lacks smoothness and sounds immature.

2. Separate the independent clauses with a comma and one of these words: *and, but, or, nor, for, so, or yet.*[1]

Tea may be good for you, but coffee is not.
This film is boring, for it has no plot.

3. Make one clause dependent on the other by adding one of the dependent clause cues listed on page 84.

Tea may be good for you although coffee is not.
This film is boring because it has no plot.

4. Use a semicolon, either by itself or with a transitional expression, to separate the independent clauses.[2]

Tea may be good for you; coffee is not.
This film is boring; for one thing, it has no plot.

Note: All four solutions to comma splices and fused sentences require you to use a word or punctuation mark strong enough to come between two independent clauses. A comma by itself is too weak, and so is a dash.

---

[1] These words are called coordinating conjunctions because they are used to join equal (or coordinating) clauses. See Appendix B, page 462, for an explanation and illustration of the different kinds of conjunctions and how to use them.

[2] If you are not sure when or why to use a semicolon, see Chapter 18, pages 219–20.

The sentences in the following exercises will give you practice in correcting comma splices and fused sentences. Revise the sentences where necessary (note that there is one correct sentence in each set), and then check your answers. Answers for exercises in this chapter begin on page 486. Since there are four ways to fix each incorrect sentence, your answers may differ from our suggestions. If you are unsure about when to use a semicolon and when to use a period, be sure to read Chapter 18 before going on.

Exercise 7.1

1. Press on the wound that will stop the bleeding.

2. Get going the others are waiting.

3. I can't read it the print is too small.

4. Here is my number, give me a call.

5. I'm busy right now, you'll have to wait.

6. I'm not afraid to die, I just don't want to be there when it happens.
   (Woody Allen)

7. Eat sensibly exercise regularly die anyway.

8. That was a great dive, you get a perfect 10.

9. Listen to this man play, he's a jazz–blues musician who calls himself Dr. John.

10. While you were out, you received one phone call, it was from a telemarketer.

Exercise 7.2

1. I hate computers they're always making mistakes.

2. I'm trying to stop playing computer games, they take up too much of my time.

3. My watch has stopped, I don't know what time it is.

4. I'm innocent, this is a case of mistaken identity.

5. This desk is made of pine with maple veneer the other is solid oak.

6. I'm going to stay up all night tonight I don't want to miss my 8:30 class.

7. The microwave oven is the most important appliance in my home, without it, I'd starve.

8. Money may not be everything, it is far ahead of whatever is in second place.

9. There are two kinds of people in the world: those who are at their best early in the morning, and those who are at their best late at night.

10. Teachers are finding more and more students who went from printing straight to a keyboard, they have never learned cursive script.

GO TO WEB

EXERCISE 7.1

Exercise 7.3

1. His favourite music is the blues, it complements his personality and temperament.

2. This restaurant is terribly slow, it will be dinnertime when we finally get our lunch.

3. I'm investing all my money in this week's lottery the jackpot is over 10 million dollars.

4. Smile when you speak, you can get away with saying almost anything.

5. Parking your car facing the wrong way on a city street is illegal and could cost you a fine.

6. If I never again see a fast-food breakfast, it will be too soon, the last one I ate nearly put me in the hospital.

7. The fine art of whacking an electronic device to get it to work again is called "percussive maintenance," nine times out of ten, it works.

8. The English language makes no sense, why do people recite at a play and play at a recital?

9. I write in my journal every day when I'm 90, I want to read about all the important events in my life.

10. We have not inherited the Earth from our ancestors we are borrowing it from our children.

GO TO WEB

EXERCISE 7.2

Exercise 7.4

In the paragraph that follows, correct the 10 run-on errors any way you choose. This would be a good time to review the four solutions to run-ons highlighted on page 91. Your goal is to produce a paragraph in which the sentences are both correct and effective. Then compare your revision to our suggestions on page 487.

Last year, an exchange student from the south of France came to live with us her name was Simone, she came to Canada to practise her English and learn something about our culture. Simone was amazed by ice hockey, she had never seen a game before and thought it was very exciting. In her first months here, Simone was surprised by what she perceived as Canadians' devotion to everything American, from television shows, to sports events, to music, to fast food, she confessed that she couldn't see much that was uniquely Canadian she was disappointed by our lack of a distinct culture, after she made a week's trip to Chicago, she began to understand some of the differences between the two countries, the relative cleanliness of Canada's cities, our support of multiculturalism, and our respect for law and order impressed her, the vast size of our country, with its huge expanses of untouched wilderness, intimidated her a little.

Although she was homesick, especially in the first few weeks, Simone enjoyed her year in Canada when she was packing up to return to Provence, she was already planning her next visit, she wants to go camping on Prince Edward Island.

Exercise 7.5

In the following exercise, correct the 10 run-on errors using a variety of the solutions listed on page 91. Our answers, on pages 487–88, are only suggestions.

Once upon a time, three travellers came upon a raging river, it prevented them from continuing their journey, luckily, however, they got to the river just in time to rescue a magic elf from the rushing water, she was so grateful to them for saving her life that she told them she would grant each of them one wish so the first man wished for the strength to be able to cross the river and instantly his arms and legs developed powerful muscles that enabled him to swim easily to the other side and the second man wished for a boat that would carry him across and his wish was granted in the form of a sturdy rowboat and strong oars, it allowed him to make his way safely to the other side. The third man, having observed the success of his two companions, wanted to show that he could outsmart them, he asked for the intelligence that would enable him to cross the water with the least possible effort and he was immediately transformed into a woman who realized there was a bridge a few metres downstream and walked across it to the other shore.

Exercise 7.6

The following exercise will provide you with a double challenge of your sentence-structure expertise. In this exercise, you will find both fragments and run-ons. Work through it slowly and carefully, and check your results with our suggestions on page 488.

1. The newspaper tells us that the weekend has set records. Both for high temperatures and traffic accidents the two records are probably connected.

2. Computers are not intelligent, if they were, they wouldn't allow humans to touch their keyboards.

3. The snow continues to fall, hasn't let up for three days.

4. The pen is mightier than the sword, why is it that they confiscate swords but not pens at the airport check-in?

5. I have always driven a small car, I think gas-guzzling SUVs, vans, and pickup trucks are ridiculous for city driving. Wastefulness on wheels.

6. A cup of coffee in the morning gets me started, another at midday helps keep me alert after lunch.

7. CRNC is the home of the million-dollar guarantee, you give us a million dollars we guarantee to play any song you want.

8. We often hear people complain about the cost of gasoline for their cars, the same people don't hesitate to spend $1.50 for a bottle of water. The same water they get free from the tap.

9. Television is a mass medium, there is an old saying that it is called a medium because it rarely does anything well. Never truer than in today's 300-channel world.

10. Winter is my favourite season, a blanket of white snow covers the ugliness of the city. Making the world seem fresh, clean, and pure.

GO TO WEB

EXERCISE 7.3

Exercise 7.7

The following exercise contains 10 run-on errors. We suggest you review the four ways to correct these errors (page 91) before you tackle this exercise. Your goal is to produce paragraphs in which all sentences are correct and effective.

An acquaintance of mine recently became a Canadian citizen, when she told me about her citizenship hearing, I couldn't bring myself to offer the congratulations she expected. Before her hearing, she was given a small book containing basic facts about Canada, she was told that the judge who interviewed her would question her on the information in that book, she didn't study the book, she never even opened it.

At the hearing, the judge asked her a few simple questions, such as the name of the governor general, some advantages of being a Canadian citizen, and whether health care was a federal or a provincial responsibility but since she couldn't answer any of these questions, my friend just shrugged and waited for the judge to give her the answers. She expected to be told to come back when she had learned more about her adopted country, she was astonished when the judge congratulated her for successfully completing the interview and set a date to confirm her citizenship.

I find the judge's decision appalling for several reasons first, my friend's refusal to read the book suggests she doesn't have much respect for Canadian citizenship, second, her low opinion of our country's citizenship process was confirmed when the judge approved her application. Third, I can't help but feel she was passed because she is an attractive blonde teacher who speaks with a slight English accent, if she had been a man or woman of colour, or spoken little or no English, I can't help but think her application would have been rejected, it deserved to be.

8

Solving Modifier Problems

Having been underwater for more than 150 years, Dr. Philbrick found the warship in excellent condition.

Both students were expelled as a result of cheating *by the college registrar*.

Peng visited his family, who live in China *during the summer*.

How could Dr. Philbrick stay underwater for 150 years? Was the college registrar cheating? Does Peng's family live in China during the summer, or did Peng visit them during the summer? As you can see, the meaning in these examples is not clear. The confusion comes from problems with modifiers.

A **modifier** is a word or phrase that adds information about another word in a sentence. In the examples above, the italicized words are modifiers. Used correctly, modifiers describe or explain or limit another word, making its meaning more precise. Used carelessly, modifiers cause confusion or, even worse, amusement.

You need to be able to recognize and solve two kinds of modifier problems: **misplaced modifiers** and **dangling modifiers**.

Misplaced Modifiers

Modifiers must be as close as possible to the words they apply to. Readers usually assume that a modifier modifies whatever it's next to. It's important to remember this because, as the following examples show, changing the position of a modifier can change the meaning of your sentence.

(Only) I love you. (No one else loves you.)

I (only) love you. (I have no other feelings for you.)

I love (only) you. (You are the only one I love.)

> To make sure a modifier is in the right place, ask yourself "What does it apply to?" and put it beside that word or phrase.

When a modifier is not close enough to the word it refers to, it is said to be misplaced. A **misplaced modifier** can be a single word in the wrong place:

My supervisor told me that the payroll department needs someone who can use accounting software (badly).

Is some company really hiring people to do poor work? Or does the company urgently need someone familiar with accounting software? The modifier *badly* belongs next to the word it applies to, *needs*:

My supervisor told me that the payroll department (badly) needs someone who can use accounting software.

> Be especially careful with these words: *almost, nearly, just, only, even, hardly, merely, scarcely*. Put them right before the words they modify.

Misplaced: I (nearly) passed every course I took in college.

Correct: I passed (nearly) every course I took in college.

Misplaced: Clive (almost) lost 5 kg while studying for exams.

Correct: Clive lost (almost) 5 kg while studying for exams.

Misplaced: Emilia (only) writes with her left hand.

Correct: Emilia writes (only) with her left hand .

A misplaced modifier can also be a group of words in the wrong place:

(Babbling contentedly), the new mother watched her baby.

The modifier, *babbling contentedly*, is too far away from the word it applies to: *baby*. It seems to modify *mother*, making the sentence ridiculous. We need to revise the sentence.

The new mother watched her baby (babbling contentedly).

Look at this example:

I worked for my aunt, who owns a variety store (during the summer.)

During the summer applies to *worked* and should be closer to it:

(During the summer,) I worked for my aunt, who owns a variety store.

Notice that a modifier need not always go right next to what it modifies. It should, however, be as close as possible to it.

Occasionally, as in the examples above, the modifier is obviously out of place. The writer's intention is clear, and the sentence is easy to correct. Sometimes, however, modifiers are misplaced in such a way that the meaning is not clear, as in this example:

My boss told me (on Friday) I was being let go.

Did the boss speak to the employee on Friday? Or did she tell the employee that Friday would be his last day? To avoid confusion, we must move the modifier and, depending on the meaning we want, write

(On Friday), my boss told me I was being let go.

Or

My boss told me I was being let go (on Friday).

Rewrite the following sentences, placing the modifiers correctly. Check your answers to each set before going on. Answers for this chapter begin on page 488.

Exercise 8.1

1. They just closed before five.

2. We were splashed with mud by every car that passed almost.

3. The flag was just raised at sunrise.

4. She was exhausted after merely walking 300 metres.

5. After the fire, she took her clothes to the cleaners with the most smoke damage.

6. The French nearly drink wine with every meal, including lunch.

7. The suspect scarcely gave the police any information.

8. He was nearly underwater for two minutes before surfacing.

9. We camped in a national park with lots of wildlife during August.

10. A huge tree can be cut by any idiot with a chainsaw, even one more than 300 years old.

Exercise 8.2

1. The president only fired those who had failed to meet their sales quotas.

2. I have been fired nearly every week that I have worked here.

3. I had scarcely answered 12 of the 25 questions when time was up.

4. Braying loudly, Matti couldn't force the donkey to take a single step.

5. We have computers for all office staff with little memory and constant breakdowns.

6. Canadians practically enjoy the highest standard of living in the world.

7. We bought gifts for the children with batteries included.

8. Although six of us went to the beach, Kevin only took pictures of his girlfriend.

9. This is a book for avid readers with real weight and depth.

10. Vince crouched in the long grass and watched the lion with binoculars.

GO TO WEB

EXERCISES 8.1, 8.2

Dangling Modifiers

A **dangling modifier** occurs when there is no *specific word* or *idea* to which the modifier can sensibly refer. With no appropriate word to refer to, the modifier seems to apply to whatever it's next to, often with ridiculous results:

After a good night's sleep, my teachers were impressed by my alertness.

(This sentence seems to say that the teachers had a good night's sleep.)

While paying for our purchases, a security guard watched closely.

(The security guard paid for our purchases?)

Dangling modifiers are harder to fix than misplaced ones. You can't simply move danglers to another spot in the sentence. There are two ways to correct them. One way requires that you remember the following guideline.

> When a modifier comes at the beginning of the sentence, it modifies the subject of the sentence.

This rule means that you can avoid dangling modifiers by choosing the subjects of your sentences carefully.

> 1. Make sure the subject is an appropriate one for the modifier to apply to.

Using this method, we can write our two examples by changing the subjects.

After a good night's sleep, I impressed my teachers with my alertness.

While paying for our purchases, we were closely watched by a security guard.

> 2. Another way to correct a dangling modifier is to change it into a dependent clause.

After I had had a good night's sleep, my teachers were impressed with my alertness.
While we paid for our purchases, a security guard watched us closely.

Sometimes a dangling modifier comes at the end of a sentence.

A Smart is the car for me, looking for efficiency and affordability.

Can you correct this sentence? Try it; then look at the suggestions provided at the end of this chapter.

Summary

1. Ask "What does the modifier refer to?"
2. Be sure there is a word or phrase in the sentence for the modifier to apply to.
3. Put the modifier as close as possible to the word or phrase it refers to.

The sentences in Exercises 8.3 and 8.4 contain dangling modifiers. Correct them by changing the subject of each sentence to one the modifier can appropriately apply to. There is no one right way to correct these sentences. Our answers on page 489 are only suggestions.

Exercise 8.3

1. When running competitively, a thorough warm-up is necessary.

2. As a college teacher, dangling modifiers are annoying.

3. After revising her résumé, filling out the application, and going through the interview, the position was taken by someone else.

4. Getting to the meeting room 20 minutes late, everyone had left.

5. After cooking all day long, the gourmet meal was worth the effort.

6. Having arrived so late, the meal was cold.

7. Driving recklessly, the police stopped André at a roadblock.

8. Dressed in a new miniskirt, her boyfriend thought Jessa looked terrific.

9. After waiting for 20 minutes, the server finally came to our table.

10. Having been convicted of breaking and entering, the judge sentenced Bambi to two years in prison.

Exercise 8.4

1. Travelling in Quebec, knowing even a little French is useful.

2. Her saddle firmly cinched, Marie led the mare out of the barn.

3. After being seasick for two days, the ocean became calm.

4. Standing in the water for more than an hour, the cold numbed him to the bone.

5. Being very weak in math, the job was out of my reach.

6. Looking for a job, a good résumé is vital to success.

7. After spending two weeks quarrelling non-stop, their relationship was over.

8. In less than a minute after applying the ointment, the pain began to ease.

9. Living kilometres away from anything, a car is a necessity.

10. Having had the same roommate for three years, my parents suggested

that I look for another.

Exercise 8.5

Correct the dangling modifiers in Exercise 8.3 by changing them into dependent clauses.

Exercise 8.6

Correct the dangling modifiers in Exercise 8.4 by changing them into dependent clauses.

Correct the misplaced and dangling modifiers in Exercises 8.7 and 8.8 in any way you choose. Our answers on page 490 are only suggestions.

Exercise 8.7

1. The sign said that students were only admitted to the pub.

2. Swimming in these waters, the undertow can be dangerous.

3. The lion was recaptured before anyone was mauled or bitten by the trainer.

4. Swimming isn't a good idea if polluted.

5. Suddenly slamming on the brakes, several passengers were thrown to the floor.

6. Employees who are late often are dismissed without notice.

7. After waiting for you for more than an hour, the evening was ruined.

8. Munching on chicken wings during the game, our appetites for dinner were ruined.

9. We hired the first designer who applied because of her experience.

10. The president spoke glowingly of the retiring workers who had worked long and loyally for 20 minutes.

Exercise 8.8

1. Everyone stared as she rode through town on a horse in a polka-dot bikini.

2. Though drunk daily, many residents don't trust city water.

3. Being a music lover, an MP3 player is always in my pocket.

4. Although Jan lives more than 50 km away, he nearly manages to come to every class.

5. Before beginning to write the exam, prayer is a recommended strategy.

6. After giving birth to a litter of 12, my sister had her Dachshund neutered.

7. I heard about the team's star player being hurt on a sports phone-in show.

8. Listening to the rumours, the newlyweds are already on the road to separation.

9. Before buying a used car, the police recommend checking the ownership records.

10. We were shot almost the first day we went into the forest during hunting season.

GO TO WEB

EXERCISES 8.3, 8.4

Exercise 8.9

Now test your mastery of modifiers. Correct the errors in this final exercise.

1. It is very annoying when notes are handed out to students with no holes punched in them.

2. It's so cold today that my neighbour is walking her dog wearing earmuffs.

3. Now that he's agreed to take over the cooking, my husband frequently says he will make Chicken Vindaloo.

4. While answering my e-mail, the computer crashed, and I lost all my addresses.

5. Having a college education, a large accounting firm offered Sue a management position with a generous salary.

6. When roasted, you will see how delicious beets can taste.

7. Being thoroughly prepared for the meeting, a few drinks with friends could not do any harm.

8. Dennis was informed that his application had been rejected by a secretary who kindly offered him a handkerchief.

9. Snorkelling in the clear Caribbean water, schools of colourful fish swam by in a brilliant parade.

10. Having decided which computer to buy, a salesclerk was summoned to complete the transaction.

Here are two suggestions for handling the Smart car sentence on page 104:

1. **Add an appropriate subject:** (Looking for efficiency and affordability,) I decided a Smart was the car for me.
2. **Change the dangler to a dependent clause:** A Smart is the car for me since I am looking for efficiency and affordability.

9

The Parallelism Principle

Brevity, clarity, and force: these are three characteristics of good writing style. **Parallelism** will reinforce these characteristics in everything you write.

When your sentence contains a series of two or more items, they must be grammatically parallel. That is, they must be written in the same grammatical form. Consider this example:

Shefali likes *dancing, skiing,* and *to travel.*

The three items in this series are not parallel. Two end in *-ing*, but the third, *to travel*, is the infinitive form of the verb. To correct the sentence, you must put all the items in the same grammatical form. You have two choices. You can write

Shefali likes *dancing, skiing,* and *travelling.*

Or you can write

Shefali likes *to dance, to ski,* and *to travel.*

Now look at an example with two non-parallel elements:

Most people seek happiness in *long-term relationships* and *work that provides them with satisfaction.*

Again, you could correct this sentence in two ways. You could write "Most people seek happiness *in relationships that are long-term* and *in work that provides them with satisfaction,*" but that solution produces a long and clumsy

NEL

sentence. The shorter version works better: "Most people seek happiness in *long-term relationships* and *satisfying work.*" This version is concise, clear, and forceful.

> Correct faulty parallelism by writing all items in a series in the same grammatical form; that is, all words, or all phrases, or all clauses.

One way to tell whether the items in a series are parallel is to write them out in list form, one below the other. That way, you can see at a glance if all the elements are in the same grammatical form.

Not Parallel	**Parallel**
My ex-boyfriend is *messy, rude,* and *an obnoxious person.*	My ex-boyfriend is *messy, rude,* and *obnoxious.*
(This list has two adjectives and a noun phrase.)	(This list has three adjectives.)
I support myself by *delivering pizza, poker,* and *shooting pool.*	I support myself by *delivering pizza, playing poker,* and *shooting pool.*
(This list has two phrases and one single word as objects of the preposition *by.*)	(This list has three phrases as objects of the preposition *by.*)
Jules wants a job that *will interest him, will challenge him,* and *pays well.*	Jules wants a job that *will interest him, (will) challenge him,* and *(will) pay him well.*
(This series of clauses contains two future tense verbs and one present tense verb.)	(All three subordinate clauses contain future tense verbs.)

As you can see, achieving parallelism is partly a matter of developing an ear for the sound of a correct list. A parallel sentence has a smooth, unbroken rhythm. Practice and the exercises in this chapter will help. Once you have mastered parallelism in your sentences, you will be ready to develop ideas in parallel sequence—in thesis statements, for example—and thus to write clear, well-organized prose. Far from being a frill, parallelism is a fundamental characteristic of good writing.

Correct the sentences where necessary in the following exercises. As you work through these sentences, try to spot parallelism errors from the change in rhythm that the faulty element produces. Then revise each sentence to bring the faulty element into line with the other elements in the series. Check your answers to each set of 10 before going on. Answers for this chapter begin on page 490.

Exercise 9.1

1. This is a book to read, enjoy, and keep in your memory.

2. The new brochure on career opportunities is attractive and contains lots of information.

3. Except that it was too long, too much violence, and too expensive, it was a great movie.

4. He ate his supper, did the dishes, watched television, and bedtime.

5. Barking dogs and children who never stop screaming keep me from enjoying the park.

6. In this clinic, we care for the sick, the injured, and also those who are disabled.

7. If she wasn't constantly eating chips, playing bingo, and cigarette smoking, she'd have plenty of money for groceries.

8. Our team could win the Cup because it has speed, size, youthful players, and talent.

9. So far, the countries I have enjoyed most are China for its people, France for its food, and the beaches of Brazil.

10. She was discouraged by the low pay, being forced to work long hours, and the office politics.

GO TO WEB

EXERCISES 9.1, 9.2

Exercise 9.2

1. Being unable to speak the language, I was confused, frustrated, and it's embarrassing.

2. Trying your best and success are not always the same thing.

3. I hold a baseball bat right-handed but play hockey left-handed.

4. A good student attends all classes and projects are always finished on time.

5. A good teacher motivates with enthusiasm, informs with sensitivity, and is a compassionate counsellor.

6. A good college president has the judgment of Solomon, Plato's wisdom, and the wit of Rick Mercer.

7. Licking one's fingers and to pick one's teeth in a restaurant are one way to get attention.

8. To succeed in this economy, small businesses must be creative and show flexibility.

9. Canadians must register the cars they drive, the businesses they own, the contracts they make, the houses they buy, and gun possession.

10. The test required us to read a paragraph, some questions to answer, and write a summary.

GO TO WEB

EXERCISES 9.3, 9.4

Exercise 9.3

Revise the following lists by changing the last element in each case to make it parallel with the first two.

Example: Incorrect: health   happiness   wise

         Correct: health   happiness   wisdom

1. see the sky	feel the warmth	wine could be tasted
2. read	learn	have understanding
3. tighten	adjust	make looser
4. broadcasting	nursing	being an engineer
5. insight	intelligence	being knowledgeable
6. highly motivated	fully trained	having lots of education
7. information	education	entertaining
8. evaluating carefully	waiting patiently	fully exploring

Exercise 9.4

Create a sentence for each of the parallel lists you developed in Exercise 9.3.

Example: A person who has health, happiness, and wisdom is truly rich.

Exercise 9.5

As a test of your mastery of parallel structure, correct the six errors in the following paragraph.

The dictionary is a useful and educational resource. Everyone knows that its three chief functions are to check the spelling, for finding out the meanings of words, and what the correct pronunciation is. Few people, however, use the dictionary for discovery as well as learning. There are several ways to use the dictionary as an aid to discovery. One is randomly looking at words, another is to read a page or two thoroughly, and still another is to skim the text looking for unfamiliar words. By this last method I discovered the word *steatopygous*, a term I now try to use at least once a day. You can increase your vocabulary significantly by using the dictionary, and of course a large and varied vocabulary can be used to baffle your colleagues, employers will be impressed, and your English teacher will be surprised.

Exercise 9.6

Many errors in parallelism occur in the lists of bulleted points that are commonly featured in reports and presentations. The following exercise tests your ability to correct errors in lists. Make the bulleted points in each set parallel. (Your answers may vary from our suggestions on pages 491–92, depending on which of the items in the list you choose as the model for the others to parallel.)

1. A coach has four responsibilities:
   - To encourage and motivate
   - Teaching skills and techniques
   - Developing teamwork and co-operation
   - To develop physical and mental strength

2. The college will undertake the following steps to conserve energy:
   - Building temperatures will be lowered by two degrees in winter.
   - Lights in all rooms will be put on motion sensors.
   - Raising the temperature in buildings by two degrees in summer
   - All windows will be replaced with high-efficiency glass.

3. In selecting a location for the new college residence, we must be mindful of transportation factors:
   - Convenient access to mass transit
   - Making sure there is ample parking for all residents with cars
   - Ensuring easy connections to major highways
   - Immediate access to the bicycle-path network
   - On-site availability of pedestrian walkways

4. This summer, I have five goals that I want to accomplish:
   - Learning to kiteboard
   - Read the latest Harry Potter book

- Participating in a 10-km Fun Run
- Earn enough money to pay my tuition
- Spending time with my friends at the beach

5. The duties of this position include
- Greeting customers
- Modelling the clothing we sell
- Making sales
- Stock the shelves
- Inventory
- Open and lock up the store

Exercise 9.7

As a test of your ability to correct faulty parallelism, revise the following sentences.

1. The Vancouver Canucks are a good team: hard-hitting, fast-skating, and thinking quickly.

2. The fear of losing is forgotten in the winning joyfulness.

3. Travel teaches us to be tolerant, resourceful, patience, and independence.

4. Our company hires locally, advertises nationally, and has global sales.

5. They are an odd couple: Suniti is calm and placid, while Ranjan exhibits nervousness and tension.

6. The union demands that we hire more staff, the work space should be renovated, and computer upgrades.

7. After reading the explanations and all the exercises have been completed, you'll be a better writer.

8. A good nurse is knowledgeable, kind, and has sensitivity and skill.

9. She is talkative and aggressive but also has enthusiasm and works hard.

10. In our community, two related crimes are rapidly increasing: drug abuse and stealing things.

Refining by Combining

Sentence Combining

To reinforce what you've learned about sentence structure, try your hand at **sentence combining**, a technique that enables you to avoid a choppy, monotonous, or repetitious style while at the same time producing correct sentences. Sentence combining accomplishes three things: it reinforces your understanding of sentence structure; it helps you to refine and polish your writing; and it results in a style that will keep your reader alert and interested in what you have to say.

Let's look at two short, technically correct sentences that could be combined:

My boss always arrives late.
She is cranky in the morning.

There are several ways of combining these two statements into a single sentence.

1. You can connect them with an appropriate linking word, such as *and*, *but*, *or*, *nor*, *for*, *so*, and *yet*.

My boss always arrives late *and* is cranky in the morning.
My boss is cranky in the morning, *so* she always arrives late.

2. You can change one of the sentences into a subordinate clause.

My boss, *who* is cranky in the morning, always arrives late.
Because my boss is cranky in the morning, she always arrives late.

3. You can change one of the sentences into a modifying phrase.

(*Being late*) my boss is always cranky in the morning.
My boss, (*always late*), is cranky in the morning.

4. Sometimes you can reduce one of your sentences to a single-word modifier.

My (*cranky*) boss always arrives (*late*) in the morning.

In sentence combining, you are free to move parts of the sentence around, change words, add or delete words, or make whatever other changes you find necessary. Anything goes, as long as you don't drastically alter the meaning of the base sentences. Remember that your aim in combining sentences is to create effective sentences, not long ones. Clarity is essential and brevity has force. Here's another example to consider.

Correct but choppy sentences conveying an idea:

Water is vital to life.
It is an important Canadian resource.
It must be protected.

Correct and smooth sentences conveying the same idea:

Water, which is vital to life, is an important Canadian resource that must be protected.
An important Canadian resource, water is vital to life and must be protected.
Water is an important Canadian resource that must be protected because it is vital to life.

The skills that you learn by combining sentences develop your understanding of the connections between ideas. They are useful not only in writing and speaking, but also in reading, listening, and problem-solving.

Review of Conjunctions and Relative Pronouns

Two of the most common methods of combining sentences are by using conjunctions and relative pronouns, both of which often cause problems for students whose native language is not standard English. So we will review the rule governing these two linking techniques first, before moving to the creative writing aspect of sentence combining. Those who do not need this review should turn now to Exercise 10.3.

A. USING CONJUNCTIONS TO COMBINE CLAUSES

Use only one connecting word between two clauses.

This rule holds whether you intend to create a sentence consisting of two coordinating independent clauses or one consisting of a main clause and a subordinate clause. For example, let's suppose you want to combine "I enjoy school" with "I also like my part-time job."

Incorrect: *Although* I enjoy school, *and* I also like my part-time job.
Correct: I enjoy school, *and* I also like my part-time job.
Also correct: *Although* I enjoy school, I also like my part-time job.

Now test your understanding of this important point by doing the following exercise.

Exercise 10.1

Read through the sentences below and decide whether each one is correct or incorrect. For the incorrect sentences, cross out the unnecessary conjunction. Be sure your revised sentences are correctly capitalized and punctuated. Answers to exercises in this chapter begin on page 492.

1. Although the test was difficult, so I passed it.

2. After eating our lunch, then we continued working.

3. When December is over, winter continues for two or three months.

4. Since our essay is due tomorrow, so we must stay up late tonight.

5. Even though the pictures are good, yet I hate seeing myself.

6. Before the party, she cooked food for 12 people.

7. Though having a car would be convenient, but I need the money for other things.

8. If this book will help me, so I will buy it.

9. Where a mistake has been found, so it must be corrected.

10. Although many are cold, few are frozen.

GO TO WEB

EXERCISE 10.1

B. USING RELATIVE PRONOUNS TO COMBINE CLAUSES

You can often combine two clauses by using a relative pronoun (*who, whom, whose, that, which*) to join them. (If you are not sure when to use *that/which* or *who/whom*, see Chapter 15, pages 189–90). Below are some examples of the different ways you can use a relative pronoun to join two clauses.

Separate Sentences	**Combined Sentence**
The man is waiting in the car. He is my father.	The man *who* is waiting in the car is my father. (NOT "The man who is waiting in the car he is my father.")
Yesterday Gina met Raffi. His family lives in Beirut.	Yesterday, Gina met Raffi *whose* family lives in Beirut.
I need a copy of *Frankenstein*. Ms. Lee assigned this book last week.	I need a copy of *Frankenstein, which* Ms. Lee assigned last week.
Frankenstein is a novel. It was written in 1818 by Mary Shelley.	*Frankenstein* is a novel *that* was written in 1818 by Mary Shelley.

Exercise 10.2

Combine the following sentences, using the relative pronoun given in parentheses as the link. Then check your answers on page 492.

1. I have a teacher. The teacher always wears a tie. (who)

2. Here is the car. This car is always breaking down. (that)

3. I am enrolled in an art class. The class meets Wednesday evenings. (that)

4. That singer just won a Grammy. I always forget her name. (whose)

5. The pen is broken. It is the pen you gave me. (that)

6. My plant is dead. You never watered it. (which)

7. The cellphone is ringing. You always carry it. (that)

8. Lisa baby-sits for a man. The man's wife speaks only Japanese. (whose)

9. The taxi driver took me to the airport. He drove 20 km over the speed limit all the way. (who)

10. My roommate is finally moving out. His snoring keeps me awake. (whose)

GO TO WEB

EXERCISE 10.2

In the following exercises, try your solutions aloud before you write them. You may also want to refer to Chapters 17 and 18 for advice on using the comma and the semicolon, respectively.

Exercise 10.3

1. No one wants to answer.
   The teacher asks a question. (when)

_____

_____

2. Our apartment is quite large and comfortable.
   Our apartment is very reasonably priced. (yet)

   _____

   _____

3. High marks in college are a matter of luck.
   Some college students believe this. (that)

   _____

   _____

4. Our company will sponsor a marathon runner.
   One of the employees must enter the race. (but)

   _____

   _____

5. Hybrid cars are becoming more popular.
   Hybrid cars cost more than comparable gas-powered models. (even though)

   _____

   _____

6. The VJ on Channel 12 is only 24 years old.
   The VJ on Channel 12 sounds like an experienced professional. (who)

   _____

   _____

7. They won the lottery.
   They were down to their last loonie. (just when)

   _____

   _____

8. I have a migraine headache.
   My headache prevents me from working, reading, or even watching TV. (that)

   _____

   _____

9. Your choice of outfit is not appropriate for the office.
   Your outfit would look just right in an after-hours club. (but)

   _____

   _____

10. Strong coffee keeps me awake.
    I love the taste of strong coffee.
    I like my coffee very hot. (although)

    _____

    _____

In the two exercises that follow, use all four sentence-combining techniques to combine each set of statements into longer, more interesting units.
(*Hint*: Read each set of statements through from beginning to end before you begin to combine them. Try out several variations aloud or in your head before writing your preferred solution.) There are many ways to combine these short statements to make smooth, effective sentences. Our answers on page 493 are only suggestions.

Exercise 10.4

1. The cursor is blinking.
   There is no response.

   _____

   _____

   _____

2. The village is very small.
   I grew up in the village.

   _____

   _____

   _____

3. My car is in the repair shop.
   It needs a new alternator.

   _____

   _____

   _____

4. The textbook contains information.
   The information will be on the exam.
   The exam is tomorrow.

   _____

   _____

   _____

5. I have read this book from cover to cover.
   I have completed all of the exercises in this book.
   Gradually, my writing skills are improving.

   _____

   _____

   _____

6. Banging your head against a wall uses calories.
   Doing this uses 150 calories an hour.

   _____

   _____

   _____

7. The movie was terrible.
   Our car broke down.
   We had a good time anyway.

   _____

   _____

   _____

8. Many of my friends send me pictures with their e-mails.
   My computer doesn't have much memory.
   It doesn't have enough to receive the pictures.

   _____

   _____

   _____

9. This restaurant is very expensive.
   The food is good.
   The service is excellent.
   I don't mind paying the price.

   _____

   _____

   _____

10. Some people enjoy hockey.
    Others prefer soccer.
    Soccer is the world's most popular spectator sport.

    _____

    _____

    _____

Exercise 10.5

1. A good manager must have many skills.
   The most important skill is the ability to delegate.

   _____

   _____

   _____

2. The stapler is missing.
   The stapler was clearly labelled.
   It had my name labelled on it.

   _____

   _____

   _____

3. Saskatchewan is where I was born.
I was born in Weyburn.
I have not lived there since I was a baby.

_____

_____

_____

4. A sauna provides no proven health benefits.
I find a sauna very refreshing.
A sauna is refreshing when the weather is cold.

_____

_____

_____

5. English muffins were not invented in England.
French fries were not invented in France.

_____

_____

_____

6. My satellite TV reception is very poor in the summer.
It is just fine in the winter.
Leaves on the trees block the dish.

_____

_____

_____

7. Taylor is very good at reading a road map.
She can find her way anywhere.
She cannot fold it properly.

_____

_____

_____

8. Our college has a Continuing Education Department.
   The Continuing Education Department offers courses at night.
   Some of the courses are for credit.
   Others are for interest.

   _____

   _____

   _____

9. Tisa is a Canadian citizen.
   She was born in Halifax.
   She has lived most of her life in Texas.
   She has American citizenship, too.

   _____

   _____

   _____

10. My roommate is not too bright.
    He watches *60 Minutes* on television.
    It takes him an hour and a half.

    _____

    _____

    _____

GO TO WEB

EXERCISES 10.3, 10.4

Exercise 10.6

Combine each set of statements below into a single concise, smooth, and interesting sentence.

1. The train was late.
   We missed our connection.
   We didn't arrive until 4:00 a.m.

   _____

   _____

   _____

2. Your address has changed.
   Our courier could not find your location.
   She was unable to deliver your parcel.

   _____

   _____

   _____

3. It is important to choose unfamiliar passwords.
   It is important to change passwords frequently.
   Hackers can do serious damage if they break into our system.

   _____

   _____

   _____

4. Boris plays basketball.
   Boris plays for our college team.
   Boris is 2 m, 14 cm tall.
   The team won the intermural championship last year.

   _____

   _____

   _____

5. A consultant is a jobless person.
   A consultant is given huge sums of money.
   A consultant shows executives how to work.

   _____

   _____

   _____

6. My eight-year-old sister bought a giant poster.
   The poster was of Mary-Kate and Ashley Olsen.
   She hung the poster on her bedroom wall.

   _____

   _____

   _____

7. He finished high school.
   He worked for six months.
   He worked at a telemarketing company.
   He travelled in Spain for three months.

   _____

   _____

   _____

8. Our computer system is down.
   All orders must be taken by hand.
   Orders can be transferred to the computer later.

   _____

   _____

   _____

9. There is a flight leaving in half an hour.
   It will get you to Winnipeg.
   You will have to change planes in Lethbridge.

   _____

   _____

   _____

10. Mosquitoes are annoying.
    Mosquitoes can be dangerous.
    Mosquitoes carry the West Nile virus.
    Even if one stings you, you have less than a 5 percent chance of getting
    the disease.

    _____

    _____

    _____

After you have combined a number of sentences, you can evaluate your
work. Read your sentences out loud. How they *sound* is important. Test your
work against these six characteristics of successful sentences.

Summary

1. **Meaning**: Have you said what you mean?
2. **Clarity**: Is each sentence clear? Can it be understood on the first
   reading?
3. **Coherence**: Do the parts of your sentences fit together logically and
   smoothly?
4. **Emphasis**: Are the most important ideas either at the end or at the
   beginning of each sentence?
5. **Conciseness**: Is every sentence direct and to the point? Have you cut
   out all redundant or repetitious words?
6. **Rhythm**: Do your sentences flow smoothly? Are there any interrup-
   tions in the development of the key idea(s)? If so, do the interrup-
   tions help to emphasize important points, or do they distract the
   reader?

If your sentences pass all six tests of successful sentence style, you can be
confident that they are both technically correct and pleasing to the ear. No
reader could ask for more.

As a final test of your ability to use correct sentence structure, below is a passage with 15 errors. If you can spot and correct the fragments, run-ons, faulty parallel structure, dangling and misplaced modifiers in this review, you are well equipped to move on to Unit 3. If you fail to identify an error or if you make a mistake, the Answer Key on page 494 will direct you to the chapter you should review.

[1]Imagination is the ability to visualize things that are not physically present. [2]Often thought to be important to artists, but not to anyone else. [3]Of course, artists depend on imagination, their creativity consists of picturing things that do not exist in the real world and giving form to their visions in paintings, sculptures, music, or literature. [4]Artists, however, are not only the ones who rely on imagination for a living. [5]To be able to see a new way to accomplish a familiar task or a different approach to an old problem. [6]This is a critical skill in many fields. [7]Among them, science, doctors, technology, construction, manufacturers, and lawmaking. [8]Being vital to innovation and invention, you will find leaders in all fields have highly developed imaginations. [9]The critical importance of imagination applies not to just leaders, either. [10]All humans use imagination to find ways to

improve their lives. [11]And entertaining themselves with books, films, and games of all kinds.

[12]Lack of imagination leads to rigidity and stagnation, to doing the same old things in the same old way. [13]It is true that some people only are comfortable in an environment in which there is little or no change. [14]Such people become anxious, even helpless, when jobs are assigned them requiring even a minimal amount of creativity. [15]There is a story about two men who were observed at work in a city park. [16]One was digging holes the other was filling in the holes. [17]Being curious, they were asked by a bystander what they were doing. [18]They replied that each of them had a job: Henry dug the holes, the trees were planted by Bill, and John filled the holes. [19]Being sick today, Henry and John had to do their jobs without Bill.

Grammar

Quick Quiz

11 Choosing the Correct Verb Form
The Principal Parts of Verbs
The Principal Parts of Irregular Verbs
Choosing between Active and Passive Voice

12 Mastering Subject–Verb Agreement
Singular and Plural
Four Special Cases

13 Keeping Your Tenses Consistent
Subject and Object Pronouns
Using Pronouns in Contrast Constructions

14 Choosing the Correct Pronoun Form

15 Mastering Pronoun–Antecedent Agreement
Pronoun–Antecedent Agreement
    1. Pronouns Ending in *-one, -body, -thing*
    2. Vague Reference
    3. Relative Pronouns

16 Maintaining Person Agreement
Rapid Review

The following quick quiz will let you see at a glance which chapters of Unit 3 you need to pay special attention to. The paragraphs below contain 15 errors in grammar: verb forms, subject–verb agreement, verb tense consistency, pronoun forms, pronoun–antecedent agreement, and pronoun consistency.

When you've made your corrections, turn to pages 494–95 and compare your revisions with ours. For each error you miss, the Answer Key directs you to the chapter you need to work on.

[1]"What's in a name?" Shakespeare asked. [2]The answer is, "a great deal." For instance, your name may indicate the decade in which you were born. [3]Like skirt length, tie width, and hairstyles, names will be going in and out of fashion. [4]If your grandparents were born in the 1940s or '50s, the chances are good that him and her will be called Robert, Mark, or Richard; and Linda, Barbara, or Patricia. [5]Interestingly, the name Michael first appeared on the top 10 list in the '50s and then tops the charts as the most popular male name for the next 40 years.

[6]In the 1960s, the most popular female name is Lisa. [7]Other favourites include Kimberley, Donna, and Michelle. [8]If you were born in the '70s,

one's parents may well have named you Jennifer, Amy, or Jessica; or Christopher, Matthew, or Justin. [9]In the '80s, baby boys were likely to be named Joshua, Daniel, or Jason. [10]Those little boys probably go to kindergarten with little girls called Amanda, Ashley, and Tiffany. [11]In the 1990s, the most popular names for boys were Jacob, Nicholas, and Tyler; for girls, Emily, Brittany, and Megan.

[12]What about the future? [13]A Web site called Babyzone.com offers advice for couples who will be expecting a child. [14]The "power names" for the new century includes one-syllable names such as Grace, Cole, and Claire. [15]Place names also rank high on the list: Dakota, Dallas, and Brooklyn (for boys or girls); China and India (for girls). [16]New parents that want to be on the leading edge of the naming culture often look to celebrities for guidance.

[17]Babyzone advises that Bob Geldof and his wife names his three daughters Peaches, Pixie, and Fifi Trixibelle. [18]And, of course, everyone under 30 know about Gwyneth's daughter, Apple.

[19]If you are interested in traditional English names, Babyzone posts a list of names found in Shakespeare's plays, which are full of beautiful names— at least for women: Miranda, Olivia, Ariel. [20]But if you're tempted to choose a Shakespearean name for your baby, the play should be read by you first. [21]Burdening a helpless infant with a name such as Malvolio, Goneril, or Caliban is a form of child abuse!

11

Choosing the Correct Verb Form

Errors in grammar are like flies in soup. Most of the time, they don't affect meaning any more than flies affect flavour, but they are distracting and irritating. You must eliminate grammar errors from your writing if you want your readers to pay attention to what you say rather than to how you say it.

The verb is the most complex and essential part of a sentence. In fact, a verb is to a sentence what an engine is to a car: the source of power and a frequent cause of trouble.[1]

This chapter looks at two verb problems that occur in many people's writing: incorrect use of irregular verbs and difficulties with the passive voice.

The Principal Parts of Verbs

All verb formations are based on one of the verb's **principal parts**. Technically, the principal parts are not the **tenses** (time indicators) of the verb; they are the elements that are used to construct the various tenses.

> Every verb has four forms, called its principal parts.
> 1. The **infinitive** form: the form used with *to*
> 2. The **simple past** (also called the **past** form)
> 3. The **present participle** (the *-ing*) form
> 4. The **past participle**: used with *has* or *have*

Here are some examples:

---

[1] Verb tenses are reviewed in Chapter 27. Negatives, modals, and participial adjectives (e.g., *confused* vs. *confusing*) are reviewed in Chapter 28.

Errors in grammar are like flies in soup: distracting and irritating.

Infinitive	Simple Past	Present Participle	Past Participle
A. (to) call	called	calling	(has) called
(to) dance	danced	dancing	(has) danced
(to) work	worked	working	(has) worked
B. (to) do	did	doing	(has) done
(to) eat	ate	eating	(has) eaten
(to) say	said	saying	(has) said

If you study the list above, you will notice an important feature of principal parts. In the first group of three verbs (A), the simple past and the past participle are identical: they are both formed by adding *-ed* (or simply *-d* if the verb ends in *-e*, as *dance* does). When both the simple past and the past participle of a verb are formed with *-ed*, the verb is called a **regular verb**. Fortunately, most of the many thousands of English verbs are regular.

In the second group (B), the verbs are called **irregular verbs** because the simple past and past participle are not formed by adding *-ed*. With *do* and *eat*, the simple past and the past participle are different words: *did/done, ate/eaten*. The simple past and past participle of *say* are the same, *said*, but they are not formed with the regular *-ed* ending.

Unfortunately, although there are only a few hundred irregular verbs in English, they are some of the most common verbs in the language; for example, *begin, come, do, go, see,* and *write* are all irregular. Consider the following sentences, all of which are grammatically incorrect:

I begun classes yesterday.

He come to see me last week.

I done it before.

She has went away on vacation.

He seen his girlfriend with another man.

I have wrote you an e-mail answering your questions.

Depending on your experience with English, these sentences may or may not sound wrong to you, but if you look at the irregular verbs listed on pages 140–42, you will understand *why* they are incorrect. What are the correct forms of the verbs in the sentences above? Write them in above the incorrect forms.

If you are not sure of the principal parts of a verb, check your dictionary. If the verb is irregular, you will find the principal parts listed after the entry for the infinitive form. For instance, if you look up *sing* in your dictionary, you will find *sang* (simple past), *sung* (past participle), and *singing* (present participle). If no principal parts are listed after the verb you are checking, it is regular and forms its simple past and past participle by adding *-ed*.

The verbs in the list on pages 140–42 are used so frequently you should take the time to learn their principal parts. We have not included the present participle (the *-ing* form) because it rarely causes difficulty. The good news is that not every verb on this list will cause you trouble.

Here's how to identify your problem verbs. With a blank piece of paper, cover the middle and right-hand columns of the verb list (i.e., cover up the simple past and past participle forms). Move the paper down the page until the infinitive form of the first verb, *be*, appears. Now say the past tense and past participle of *be* and move the paper to the right to check your responses. If your answers were correct, move the paper down again until the next verb, *bear*, appears in the left-hand column. Again, say the past tense and the past participle, check your responses, and move on to the next verb.

When you come to a verb whose past tense or past participle you aren't sure of or misidentify, highlight that verb across all three columns. In this way, after you've gone through the list once, you'll have a quick and easy reference to the correct forms of verbs that cause you trouble.

The Principal Parts of Irregular Verbs

Infinitive (Use with *to* and with helping/auxiliary verbs)	Simple Past	Past Participle (Use with *has*, *have*, *had*)
be (am, is)	was/were	been
bear	bore	borne
beat	beat	beaten
become	became	become
begin	began	begun
bend	bent	bent
bind	bound	bound
bite	bit	bitten
bleed	bled	bled
blow	blew	blown
break	broke	broken
bring	brought (*not* brang)	brought (*not* brung)
broadcast	broadcast	broadcast
build	built	built
burst	burst	burst
buy	bought	bought
catch	caught	caught
choose	chose	chosen
cling	clung	clung
come	came	come
cost	cost	cost
cut	cut	cut
deal	dealt	dealt
dig	dug	dug
dive	dived/dove	dived
do	did (*not* done)	done
draw	drew	drawn
dream	dreamed/dreamt	dreamed/dreamt
drink	drank (*not* drunk)	drunk
eat	ate	eaten
fall	fell	fallen
feed	fed	fed
feel	felt	felt
fight	fought	fought
find	found	found

Infinitive (Use with *to* and with helping/auxiliary verbs)	Simple Past	Past Participle (Use with *has, have, had*)
flee	fled	fled
fling	flung	flung
fly	flew	flown
forbid	forbade	forbidden
forget	forgot	forgotten/forgot
forgive	forgave	forgiven
freeze	froze	frozen
get	got	got/gotten
give	gave	given
go	went	gone (*not* went)
grow	grew	grown
have	had	had
hear	heard	heard
hide	hid	hidden
hit	hit	hit
hold	held	held
hurt	hurt	hurt
keep	kept	kept
know	knew	known
lay (to put or place)	laid	laid
lead	led	led
leave	left	left
lie (to recline)	lay	lain (*not* layed)
light	lit/lighted	lit/lighted
lose	lost	lost
make	made	made
mean	meant	meant
meet	met	met
mistake	mistook	mistaken
pay	paid	paid
raise	raised	raised
ride	rode	ridden
ring	rang	rung
rise	rose	risen
run	ran	run
say	said	said
see	saw (*not* seen)	seen
seek	sought	sought
sell	sold	sold

Infinitive (Use with *to* and with helping/auxiliary verbs)	Simple Past	Past Participle (Use with *has, have, had*)
set	set	set
shake	shook	shaken (*not* shook)
shine	shone	shone
shoot	shot	shot
show	showed	shown
shrink	shrank	shrunk
sing	sang	sung
sink	sank	sunk
sit	sat	sat
sleep	slept	slept
slide	slid	slid
speak	spoke	spoken
speed	sped	sped
spend	spent	spent
spin	spun	spun
stand	stood	stood
sting	stung	stung
strive	strove	striven
steal	stole	stolen
stick	stuck	stuck
strike (hit)	struck	struck
strike (affect)	struck	stricken
swear	swore	sworn
swim	swam	swum
swing	swung (*not* swang)	swung
take	took	taken
teach	taught	taught
tear	tore	torn
tell	told	told
think	thought	thought
throw	threw	thrown
understand	understood	understood
wear	wore	worn
weave	wove	woven
win	won	won
wind	wound	wound
withdraw	withdrew	withdrawn
write	wrote	written

The sentences in the exercises below require both the simple past and the past participle of the verb shown at the left. Write the required form in each blank. Do not add or remove helping verbs. Be sure to check your answers after each set. Answers for this chapter begin on page 495.

Exercise 11.1

1. wear   You _____ your good hiking boots only once, but after you have

_____ them several times, you won't want to take them off.

2. give   The tourists _____ Terry a tip after she had _____ them direc-

tions to the hotel.

3. begin   After the project had _____ , the members of the team soon

_____ to disagree on how to proceed.

4. eat   I _____ as though I had not _____ in a month.

5. cost   The vacation in Cuba _____ less than last year's trip to Jamaica

had _____ and was much more fun.

6. bring   If you have _____ your children with you, I hope you also _____

enough toys and movies to keep them out of trouble during

your stay.

7. grow   The noise from the party next door _____ louder by the hour,

but by midnight I had _____ used to it, and went to sleep.

8. sit   Marc _____ in front of the TV all morning; by evening he will

have _____ there for eight hours—a full working day!

9. write   After she had _____ the essay that was due last week, she _____

e-mails to all her friends.

10. pay   I _____ off my credit cards, so I have not _____ this month's

rent.

Exercise 11.2

1. ride   I had never _____ in a stretch limo until I _____ in one at Jerry's

wedding.

2. sing   She _____ a silly little song that her mother had _____ when she was a baby.

3. teach   Harold had been _____ to play poker by his father, and he _____ his daughter the same way.

4. find   He _____ the solution that hundreds of mathematicians over three centuries had not _____ .

5. fly   Suzhu had once _____ to Whitehorse, so when she _____ north to Tuktoyaktuk, she knew what to expect.

6. feel   At first, they had _____ silly in their new pink uniforms, but after winning three games in a row, they _____ much better.

7. lie   The cat _____ right where the dog had _____ all morning.

8. go   We _____ to our new home to find that the movers had _____ to the wrong address to deliver our furniture.

9. lose   The reason you _____ those customers is that you have _____ confidence in your sales technique.

10. steal   I _____ two customers away from the sales representative who earlier had _____ my best account.

GO TO WEB

EXERCISE 11.1

Exercise 11.3

1. think   I had _____ that you were right, but when I _____ more about your answer, I realized you were wrong.

2. buy   If we had _____ this stock 20 years ago, the shares we _____ would now be worth a fortune.

3. do   They _____ what was asked, but their competitors, who had _____ a better job, got the contract.

4. show   Today our agent _____ us a house that was much better suited to our needs than anything she had _____ us previously.

5. hurt   Budget cuts had _____ the project, but today's decision to lay off two of our workers _____ it even more.

6. throw   The rope had not been _____ far enough to reach those in the water, so Mia pulled it in and _____ it again.

7. lay   Elzbieta _____ her passport on the official's desk where the other tourists had _____ theirs.

8. put   I have _____ your notebook in the mail, but your pen and glasses I will _____ away until I see you again.

9. fight   My parents _____ again today, the way they have _____ almost every day for the last 20 years.

10. break   She _____ the Canadian record only six months after she had _____ her arm in training.

GO TO WEB

EXERCISE 11.2

Exercise 11.4

Correct the 20 verb errors in the following sentences.

1. I have not forgave Tran for copying the essay that had took me three weeks to write.

2. Our cans of pop had froze solid, but once they thawed, we drunk them anyway.

3. Sneaking into class late, Viktor lay his essay on the desk with the others; he had wrote it during his lunch break.

4. First we swum out to the wreck and then we doved to look for the treasure.

5. Too late, after they had ate all the salad and pasta they could hold, they seen the dessert table.

6. The last time I saw my niece was when she blowed out the four candles on her birthday cake. Now she has grew into a lovely young woman.

7. They had ran all the way to school while their boyfriends had rode in an air-conditioned car.

8 We brung a suitcase full of souvenirs when we come home from Taiwan.

9. My husband gave the contractor a bonus because he done the job on time, forgetting that I had already payed the man and that he hadn't filled the huge hole he digged in our basement.

Choosing between Active and Passive Voice

Verbs have another quality besides tense (or time). Verbs also have what is called "voice," which means the quality of being either active or passive. In sentences with **active voice verbs**, the "doer" of the action is the grammatical subject of the sentence.

> Active voice: Good <u>parents</u> <u>support</u> their children.
> A <u>car</u> <u>crushed</u> the cat.
> <u>Someone</u> <u>will show</u> a movie in class.

In sentences with **passive voice verbs**, the grammatical subject of the sentence is the "receiver" of the action (that is, the subject is "passively" acted upon), and the "doer" becomes an object of the preposition *by* or is absent from the sentence entirely, as in the third example below.

> Passive voice: <u>Children</u> <u>are supported</u> by good parents.
> The <u>cat</u> <u>was crushed</u> by a car.
> A <u>movie</u> <u>will be shown</u> in class.

Notice that active and passive verbs can be in any tense. Present, past, and future tense verbs are used in both sets of examples above. Can you tell which is which?

Passive voice verbs are formed by using a form of *be* + the past participle form of the verb. This is another situation where you need to know the past participle form of irregular verbs; for instance, in the third example above, the correct passive construction is *will be shown*, not *will be showed*. In the examples below, note the different tenses and pay special attention to the passive voice verb forms.

	Active	**Passive**
present	The boss signs the cheque.	The cheque is signed by the boss.
past	The boss signed the cheque.	The cheque was signed by the boss.
future	The boss will sign the cheque.	The cheque will be signed by the boss.
present progressive	The boss is signing the cheque.	The cheque is being signed by the boss.
past progressive	The boss was signing the cheque.	The cheque was being signed by the boss.

Exercise 11.5

Use two lines to underline the verbs in the sentences below. Then identify the verbs as either active (A) or passive (P). The first one is done for you. The answers to this exercise begin on page 496.

1. __A__ Our professor <u>checks</u> our homework every day.

2. _____ The report is being prepared by the marketing department.

3. _____ The car was being driven by a chauffeur.

4. _____ Eva will invite Kiefer to the party.

5. _____ The CN Tower is visited by hundreds of people every day.

6. _____ Sula designs bracelets, necklaces, and earrings.

7. _____ *The English Patient* was written by Canadian author Michael Ondaatje.

8. _____ Hollywood made the book into a successful movie.

9. _____ The song was performed by Eminem.

10. _____ Two metres of snow had to be shovelled off the driveway.

Exercise 11.6

Now rewrite the sentences in Exercise 11.5, changing active voice verbs to passive and passive voice verbs to active. Use two lines to underline the verbs. We've done the first sentence for you as an example.

1. Our homework <u>is checked</u> by our professor every day.

2.

3.

4.

5.

6.

7.

8.

9.

10.

Active voice verbs are more direct and emphatic than passive verbs. Good writers use the active voice unless there is a specific reason to use the passive. There are three situations in which the passive voice is preferable.

1. The person or agent that performed the action is not known.

The telephone <u>had been left</u> off the hook for two days.
Primate Road is the name that <u>has been given</u> to our street.
This work station <u>is</u> not ergonomically <u>designed</u>.

2. You want to place the emphasis on the person, place, or object that was affected by an action rather than on the subject performing the action.

The computer lab <u>was broken</u> into by a group of angry students.

This sentence focusses the reader's attention on the computer lab rather than on the students. If we reconstruct the sentence in the active voice, we produce a quite different effect.

A group of angry students <u>broke</u> into the computer lab.

3. You are writing a technical report, a scientific report, or a legal document.

Passive verbs are the appropriate choice when the focus is on the facts, methods, or procedures involved in an experiment, situation, or event rather than on the person(s) who discovered or performed them. Passive verbs establish an impersonal tone that is appropriate to these kinds of writing. Contrast the emphasis and tone of these sentence pairs:

Passive: The heat <u>was increased</u> to 150°C and <u>was maintained</u> at that temperature.
Active: My lab partner and I <u>increased</u> the heat to 150°C and <u>maintained</u> it at that temperature.

Passive: Our annual report <u>was approved</u> by the board on February 15.
Active: The board <u>approved</u> our annual report on February 15.

In general, because active verbs are more concise and forceful than passive verbs, they add focus and strength to your writing. When you find a passive verb in your writing, think about *who* is doing *what* to *whom*. Ask yourself why the *who* is not the subject of your sentence. If there is a good reason, then use the passive voice. Otherwise, change the verb.

Exercise 11.7

Rewrite the sentences below, changing the verbs from passive to active voice. You may need to add a word or phrase to identify the doer of the action expressed by the verb.

1. The gas for the trip was bought by Lisa.

2. The dishes were washed by our houseguests.

3. His business card was given to me by the sales representative.

4. An error in your bill was made by our computer.

5. The short route home was taken by my brother.

6. On our first anniversary, our portrait was taken by a professional photographer.

7. American election practices are not always understood by Canadians.

8. Very little about Canada is known by most Americans.

9. In today's class, your research papers will be worked on by all of you.

10. All the information you need to become a competent writer is contained in this book.

Exercise 11.8

Rewrite the sentences below, changing the verbs from passive to active voice. Then compare your revision to the original and, with the three reasons for choosing the passive voice in mind (pages 148–49), decide which sentence is more effective.

1. The professor was told by Bambi that she was finding the course too difficult.

2. This document was not typed by a member of our staff.

3. The burning building was carefully entered by three firefighters.

4. My ability to read was helped by my new bifocals.

5. The lights had been left on all the time we were away.

6. At 4:00 each afternoon, the linens are laid and the tables are set by the dining room servers.

7. In the parade around the stadium, the Olympic flag was carried by a biathlete.

8. The project was delayed because of poor communication among the members of the team.

9. His bookcase is used by my brother to hold his bowling trophies and empty fast-food containers.

10. A state of emergency has been declared and a special fund to aid the flood victims has been set up by the provincial government.

GO TO WEB

EXERCISES 11.3, 11.4

Exercise 11.9

Rewrite the following paragraph, changing verbs from passive voice to active voice where appropriate. You should find 10 verbs that need to be revised.

[1]The relationship between Americans and Canadians has been described by some as similar to that between an elephant and a mouse. [2]By others, it has been described as similar to the relationship between a dominant older sibling and a submissive younger one. [3]I think our relationship with our southern neighbour is best illustrated by the following story. [4]On his first visit to Texas, a Canadian was being shown around the state by a native Texan. [5]The sightseeing tour was begun in Austin, and as they drove from place to place, both host and guest began to learn about each other. [6]During their conversation, the Canadian was asked if he owned any land in Canada. [7]He replied that a few hectares were owned by his family, and then, of course, what a "hectare" was had to explained to the puzzled Texan.

[8]After that concept had been clarified, the Texan bragged that he owned so much land his pickup truck could be driven in any direction for seven hours without leaving his property! [9]This remark was considered by the Canadian for several seconds before he replied, "I had a pickup truck like that once, too."

12

Mastering Subject–Verb Agreement

Singular and Plural

One of the most common writing errors is lack of agreement between subject and verb. Both must be singular, or both must be plural. If one is singular and the other plural, you have an agreement problem. You have another kind of agreement problem if your subject and verb are not both in the same "person" (see Chapter 16).

Let's clarify some terms. First, it's important to distinguish between **singular** and **plural**.

- "Singular" means one person or thing.
- "Plural" means more than one person or thing.

Second, it's important to know what we mean when we refer to the concept of **person**:

- "First person" is the person(s) speaking or writing: *I, me; we, us*
- "Second person" is the person(s) being addressed: *you*
- "Third person" is the person(s) being spoken or written about: *he, she, it; they, them*

Here's an example of the singular and plural forms of a regular verb in the present tense:

	Singular	Plural
first person	I win	we win
second person	you win	you win
third person	she wins (*or* he, it, the horse wins)	they win (*or* the horses win)

The third-person form often causes trouble because the verb endings do not match the subject endings. Third-person singular present tense verbs end in -*s*, but their singular subjects do not. Third-person plural verbs never end in -*s*, while their subjects normally do. Look at these examples:

A <u>fire</u> <u>burns</u>.
The <u>car</u> <u>skids</u>.
The <u>teacher</u> <u>helps</u> the children learn to read.

The three singular verbs, all of which end in -*s* (*burns*, *skids*, *helps*), agree with their singular subjects (*fire*, *car*, *teacher*), none of which ends in -*s*. When the subjects become plural, the verbs change form, too.

Four <u>fires</u> <u>burn</u>.
The <u>cars</u> <u>skid</u>.
The <u>teachers</u> <u>help</u> the children learn to read.

Now all of the subjects end in -*s*, and none of the verbs do. This is **subject–verb agreement**.

Subjects and verbs must either be both singular or both plural.

This rule causes difficulty only when the writer doesn't know which word in the sentence is the subject and so makes the verb agree with the wrong word. As long as you decode the sentence correctly (see Chapter 5), you'll have no problem making every subject agree with its verb.

If you have not already done so, now is the time to memorize this next rule.

The subject of a sentence is NEVER in a prepositional phrase.

Here's an example of how errors occur:

Only <u>one</u> ~~of the 2,000 ticket buyers~~ are going to win.

What is the subject of this sentence? It's not *buyers*, but *one*. The verb must agree with *one*, which is clearly singular. The verb *are* does not agree with *one*, so the sentence is incorrect. It should read

Only <u>one</u> ~~of the 2,000 ticket buyers~~ <u>is</u> going to win.

If you are careful about identifying the subject of your sentence, even when it is separated from the verb by other words or phrases, you'll have no difficulty with subject–verb agreement. Before you try the exercises in this chapter, reinforce what you've learned by studying these examples.

Incorrect: One of my sisters speak five languages.
Correct: One ~~of my sisters~~ <u>speaks</u> five languages.

Incorrect: Xue, one of the few girls on the team, keep trying for a perfect score.
Correct: <u>Xue</u>, one ~~of the few girls on the team~~, <u>keeps</u> trying for a perfect score.

Incorrect: One of the students continually write graffiti on the walls of the staff room.
Correct: <u>One</u> ~~of the students~~ continually <u>writes</u> graffiti ~~on the walls of the staff room~~.

Exercise 12.1

Underline the subject in each sentence. Answers for exercises in this chapter begin on page 498.

1. The key to power is knowledge.
2. Here are the invoices for this shipment of software.
3. In the future, instead of live animals, people may choose intelligent machines as pets.
4. At the front of the line stood Professor Temkin, waiting to see Santa.
5. Jupiter and Saturn, the solar system's largest planets, appear close together in the western sky.

Pay special attention to words that end in *-one*, *-thing*, or *-body*. They cause problems for nearly every writer.

Words ending in *-one*, *-thing*, or *-body* are always singular.

When used as subjects, these pronouns require singular verbs.

anyone	anything	anybody
everyone	everything	everybody
no one	nothing	nobody
someone	something	somebody

The last part of the pronoun subject is the tip-off here: every*one*, any*thing*, no*body*. If you focus on this last part, you'll remember to use a singular verb with these subjects. Usually, these words cause trouble only when modifiers crop up between them and their verbs. For example, you would never write "Everyone are here." The trouble starts when you insert a group of words in between the subject and the verb. You might, if you weren't careful, write this: "Everyone involved in implementing the company's new policies and procedures are here." The meaning is plural: several people are present. But the subject (*everyone*) is singular, so the verb must be *is*.

More subject–verb agreement errors are caused by violations of this rule than any other. Be sure you understand it. Memorize it, and then test your understanding by doing the following exercise before you go any further.

Exercise 12.2

Circle the correct verb for each of the following sentences.

1. Somebody with a taste for Smarties (has/have) found my hidden stash of candy.
2. I wonder why it is that everyone in my photos (has/have) red eyes.
3. Nothing (succeed/succeeds) like success.
4. Everybody on the team (show/shows) great respect for the coach.
5. No one carrying a pager, a cellphone, or a recording device (is/ are) permitted into the theatre.

GO TO WEB

EXERCISE 12.1

Exercise 12.3

Change the subject and verb in each sentence from plural to singular. Underline the subject once and the verb twice. Then check your answers.

1. Our papers are due on Tuesday.

2. Our passport photos are hideous!

3. The technicians are away on a professional development course.

4. Under our back porch live two huge raccoons.

5. Have the lucky winners collected the lottery money?

6. The articles in this journal give you the background information you need.

7. Hotels within walking distance of the arena are a necessity for our team.

8. Only recently have our track coaches become interested in chemistry.

9. So far, only two of your answers have been incorrect.

10. The pressures of schoolwork and part-time work have caused many students to drop out.

GO TO WEB

EXERCISE 12.2

Exercise 12.4

Rewrite each sentence, switching the positions of the main elements and revising the verb accordingly. Then check your answers. For example:

Peanuts <u>are</u> my favourite snack.
My favourite <u>snack</u> <u>is</u> peanuts.

1. Hockey players are a good example.
2. A healthy type of oily fish is sardines.
3. Palm-sized computers are a necessity in my job.
4. What irritates us is noisy speedboats on our quiet lake.
5. Fresh fruits and vegetables are an important part of a balanced diet.

Exercise 12.5

This exercise will challenge your ability to use singular and plural subjects and verbs correctly. Rewrite the following paragraph, changing its nouns and verbs from plural to singular. Then check your answers. Your first sentence will be "A **dog seems** to understand the **mood** of **its owner**."

Dogs seem to understand the moods of their owners. They are tuned in to any shifts in emotion or changes in health of the humans they live with.

Doctors will often suggest adding pets to households where there are people suffering from depression or emotional problems. Dogs are sympathetic companions. The moods of elderly people in retirement homes or even hospital wards can be brightened by visits from pet owners and their dogs. Dogs never tire of hearing about the "good old days," and they are uncritical and unselfish in giving affection. Doctors will often encourage epilepsy sufferers to adopt specially trained dogs. Such dogs are so attuned to the health of their owners that they can sense when seizures are about to occur long before the owners can. The dogs then warn the owners of the coming attack, so the owners are able to take safety precautions.

So far, so good. You can find the subject, even when it's hiding on the far side of the verb or separated from the verb by one or more prepositional phrases. You can match up singular subjects with singular verbs and plural subjects with plural verbs. Now let's take a look at a few of the complications that make subject–verb agreement such a disagreeable problem.

Four Special Cases

Some subjects are tricky. They look singular but are actually plural, or they look plural when they're really singular. There are four kinds of these slippery subjects, all of them common and all of them likely to trip up the unwary writer.

> 1. Multiple subjects joined by *or; either . . . or; neither . . . nor;* or *not . . . but.*

Most multiple subjects we've dealt with so far have been joined by *and* and have required plural verbs, so agreement hasn't been a problem. But watch out when the two or more elements of a compound subject are joined by *or*; *either . . . or*; *neither . . . nor*; or *not . . . but*. In these cases, the verb agrees in number with the nearest subject. That is, if the subject closest to the verb is singular, the verb will be singular; if the subject closest to the verb is plural, the verb must be plural too.

Neither the <u>federal government</u> nor the <u>provinces</u> effectively <u>control</u> pollution.

Neither the <u>provinces</u> nor the <u>federal government</u> effectively <u>controls</u> pollution.

Exercise 12.6

Circle the correct verb for each of the following sentences. Then check your answers.

1. Either Pierre or his sisters (live/lives) at home, but not both.
2. Neither the photos nor the painting (reveal/reveals) her true beauty.
3. Not one teacher but more than a dozen students (has/have) come to help.
4. Fast cars, powerful boats, or any video about them (fascinate/fascinates) five-year-old Josh.
5. Neither the landlord nor the tenants (know/knows) who is responsible for the break-in.

GO TO WEB

EXERCISE 12.3

2. Subjects that look multiple but really aren't.

Don't be fooled by phrases beginning with words such as *with*, *like*, *as well as*, *together with*, *in addition to*, and *including*. These prepositional phrases are

NOT part of the subject of the sentence. Since they do not affect the verb, you can mentally cross them out.

> My math professor, ~~as well as my counsellor,~~ has advised me to change my major.

Two people were involved in the advising; nevertheless, the subject (math professor) is singular, so the verb must be singular (<u>has advised</u>).

> All my courses, ~~including English,~~ are easier this term.

If you mentally cross out the phrase "including English," you can easily see that the verb (<u>are</u>) must be plural to agree with the plural subject (<u>courses</u>).

Exercise 12.7

Circle the correct verb for each of the following sentences. Then check your answers.

1. Anar, like her sisters, (want/wants) to be a nurse.
2. One hot dog with ketchup, mustard, and pickles (has/have) more calories than you can imagine.
3. In addition to a tripod and three rolls of film, my camera (was/were) stolen from my van.
4. Eddie, together with his band, (is/are) featured tonight in the student pub.
5. "People" skills, such as a sense of humour, (doesn't/don't) usually appear on a résumé although they are essential in the workplace.

GO TO WEB

EXERCISE 12.4

3. Collective nouns.

A collective noun is a word naming a group. Some examples are *audience, band, class, committee, company, crowd, family, gang, group,* and *majority.*

When you are referring to the group acting all together, as a unit, use a singular verb. When you are referring to the members of the group acting individually, use a plural verb.

The <u>team</u> <u>is</u> sure to win tomorrow's game.

(Here *team* refers to the group acting as one unit.)

The <u>team</u> <u>are</u> going to shower and then talk to the reporters.

(The members of the team are acting individually.)

Exercise 12.8

Circle the correct verb in each case.

1. This club (is/are) open to people of all ages.

2. Our audience (thinks/think) we are better than the Rolling Stones!

3. The committee (recommends/recommend) stricter rules for parking.

4. The jury (wants/want) to spend the long weekend with their families.

5. The crowd (was/were) mostly dressed in jeans and T-shirts.

4. Units of money, time, mass, length, and distance.

These expressions require singular verbs.

<u>Four dollars</u> <u>is</u> too much to pay for a cup of coffee.

<u>Two hours</u> <u>seems</u> like four in our sociology class.

<u>Eighty kilograms</u> <u>is</u> the mass of an average man.

<u>Ten kilometres</u> <u>is</u> too far to walk.

Exercise 12.9

Circle the correct verb for each of the following sentences. Then check your answers.

1. Do you think $50 (is/are) too much to pay for a used set of Madonna videos?
2. A12-kg turkey (is/are) far too large for 10 people.
3. If you have good equipment and move at a steady speed, the 19 km of the ski trail (go/goes) by very quickly.
4. Five hundred grams of grapes (was/were) more than I could eat.
5. Five centimetres of ice and slush (take/takes) longer to clear than the same amount of snow.

GO TO WEB

EXERCISE 12.5

Exercise 12.10

The next three exercises review all of the troublesome aspects of subject–verb agreement. Correct the errors in each exercise, and then check your answers before going on. Answers for this section of the chapter begin on page 499.

1. Not the weekly quizzes, but the final exam are what I'm worried about.

2. Unfortunately, not one of the women agree to pose nude for a publicity photo.

3. Either the tires or the alignment are causing the steering vibration.

4. This province, along with six others, have voted in favour of the federal government's health care proposal.

5. Anything that could possibly go wrong, including wind, rain, hail, and snow, have gone wrong during this event.

6. When Kim emptied her pockets, she found that $2.00 were all she had left to buy lunch.

7. Neither the puppies nor their mother were enjoying the veterinarian's physical examination.

8. Get ready: 400 km of mountain roads lie ahead of us.

9. Everything you've told me about Katrina and her children are untrue and hurtful.

10. It seems that in every group project, there is one team member who get stuck with most of the work.

Exercise 12.11

There are 10 errors in this exercise.

1. Each day that passes bring us closer to the end of term.

2. A Quetchua Indian living in the Andes Mountains have two or three more litres of blood than people living at lower elevations.

3. The swim team has been billeted with host families during their stay in Seattle.

4. Neither fame nor riches is my goal in life.

5. The original model for the king in a standard deck of playing cards are thought to be King Charles I of England.

6. A large planet together with two small stars are visible on the eastern horizon.

7. The lack of things to write about are my problem.

8. One faculty member in addition to a group of students have volunteered to help us clean out the lab.

9. Not only cat hairs but also ragweed make me sneeze.

10. Everyone who successfully completed these exercises deserve high praise.

GO TO WEB

EXERCISES 12.6, 12.7

Exercise 12.12

Find and correct the 10 errors in the following paragraph.

The rewards of obtaining a good summer or part-time job goes well beyond the money you earn from your labour. Contacts that may be valuable in the future and experience in the working world is an important part of your employment. Even if the jobs you get while attending school has nothing to do with your future goal, they offer many benefits. For example, when considering job applicants, an employer always prefer someone who can be counted on to arrive at the work site on time, get along with co-workers, and follow directions. Neither instinct nor instruction take the place of experience in teaching the basic facts of working life. These long-term considerations, in addition to the money that is the immediate reward, is what makes part-time work so valuable. Everyone who have worked part-time while going to school are able to confirm these observations.

GO TO WEB

EXERCISE 12.8

Exercise 12.13

Complete the sentences in the exercises below using present tense verbs. After you complete each set, check the answer section to see whether your verbs should be singular or plural.

1. Neither my boss nor the receptionist

2. Everybody with two or more pets

3. Not the lead singer but the musicians

4. A flock of birds

5. Every one of his employees

6. Ten dollars

7. The whole family, including two aunts and six cousins

8. The actors, as well as the director

9. Either a Big Mac or a Whopper

10. No one among the hundreds present

Exercise 12.14

Write your own sentences, choosing your subjects as indicated and using present tense verbs.

1. Use a unit of time as your subject (e.g., your age).

2. Use a multiple subject.

3. Use *no one* as your subject.

4. Use *everything* as your subject.

5. Use *neither . . . nor*.

6. Use *either . . . or*.

7. Use a singular subject + *together with*.

8. Use a plural subject + *in addition to*.

9. Use your own height as your subject.

10. Use a multiple subject joined by *or*.

The box below contains a summary of the rules governing subject–verb agreement. Review them carefully before you try the mastery test for this chapter.

Summary

- Subjects and verbs must agree: both must be singular, or both must be plural.
- The subject of a sentence is never in a prepositional phrase.
- Pronouns ending in *-one, -thing,* or *-body* are singular and require singular verbs.
- Subjects joined by *and* are always plural.
- When subjects are joined by *or; either . . . or; neither . . . nor;* or *not . . . but,* the verb agrees with the subject that is closest to it.
- When looking for the subject in a sentence, ignore phrases beginning with *as well as, including, in addition to, like, together with,* etc. They are prepositional phrases.
- When *each, either,* and *neither* are used as subjects, they require singular verbs.
- Collective nouns are usually singular.
- Units of money, time, mass, length, and distance are always singular.

Exercise 12.15

As a final check of your mastery of subject–verb agreement, correct the 15 errors in the following exercise.

Travel Advisory

Anyone travelling abroad are advised to remember that other countries are not like home. Caution with respect to food, language, and customs are advisable. The French, for example, consumes vast quantities of butter and garlic with their beloved *escargots*; however, no amount of butter and garlic piled on snails disguise the fact that they are slugs in a shell. And although delectable croissants is available everywhere in France, no foreigner attempting to pronounce the word *croissant* are likely to be understood. Many other nations besides France offers local foods that the cautious traveller will want to avoid. Pizza Hut, McDonald's, and Holiday Inn provides familiar food, and every wary traveller are advised to eat only in these locations.

Another problem for the unadventurous is that foreigners insist on speaking languages with which no one (other than the natives) are familiar. Neither speaking loudly nor pronouncing slowly and carefully seem to have any effect on the natives' ability to understand English.

As for foreign customs, every country in the world have traditions that those of us who have led sheltered lives find bizarre or dangerous. Even a few days in foreign lands are enough to spell disaster. Spanish bulls, Italian drivers, German beer drinkers, Japanese subways, Brazilian beaches: each of them are to be avoided by the prudent traveller who want to return safe and sound to loved ones at home. In fact, those who are likely to be made uncomfortable by anything unfamiliar, exotic, or even new, should either stay at home or vacation in the West Edmonton Mall.

13

Keeping Your Tenses Consistent

Verbs are time markers. Changes in tense express changes in time: past, present, or future.

Sometimes, as in the sentence above, it is necessary to use several different tenses in a single sentence to get the meaning across. But most of the time, whether you're writing a sentence or a paragraph, you use one tense throughout. Normally, you choose either the past or the present tense, depending on the nature of your topic. (Few paragraphs are written completely in the future tense.) Here is the rule to follow.

Don't change tense unless the meaning requires it.

Readers like and expect consistency. If you begin a sentence with "I argued, protested, and even appealed to his masculine pride," the reader will tune in to the past tense verbs and expect any other verbs in the sentence to be in the past tense too. So, if you finish the sentence with "... but he looks at me with those big brown eyes and gets me to pay for dinner," your readers will be jolted abruptly out of one time frame into another. This sort of jolting is uncomfortable, and readers don't like it.

Shifting tenses is like shifting gears: it should be done smoothly and when necessary—never abruptly, out of carelessness, or on a whim. Avoid causing verbal whiplash; keep your tenses consistent.

Consider these two examples, both of which mix tenses inappropriately.

Problem: I'm standing right behind Sula when she suddenly screamed.
Solution 1: I was standing right behind Sula when she suddenly screamed.
Solution 2: I'm standing right behind Sula when she suddenly screams.

Problem: Tony delayed until the last possible minute and then begins to write his paper. When he gets halfway through, he decided to change his topic.
Solution 1: Tony delayed until the last possible minute and then began to write his paper. When he got halfway through, he decided to change his topic.
Solution 2: Tony delays until the last possible minute and then begins to write his paper. When he gets halfway through, he decides to change his topic.

Now look at this example, which expresses a more complex idea.

Problem: I handed my paper in just before the deadline. The next day, however, when I see the professor, she says that it was late, so I will lose marks.

This sentence is a hopeless muddle. It begins with the past tense, shifts to the present for no reason, and ends with the future.

Solution: I handed my paper in just before the deadline. The next day, however, when I saw the professor, she said that it was late, so I will lose marks.

Here the past tense is used consistently until the last clause, where the shift to future tense is appropriate to the meaning.

In the following exercises, most—but not all—of the sentences contain unnecessary tense shifts. Use the first verb in each sentence as your time marker and change the tense(s) of the other verb(s) to agree with it. Answers for exercises in this chapter appear on page 500.

Exercise 13.1

1. As we walked through the park, we see some people playing Ultimate Frisbee.

2. Alain went home and tells Gulçan what happened.

3. Gil tried to laugh, but he is too upset even to speak.

4. After his fiancée broke up with him, she refuses to return his ring.

5. Some people believe that, in the future, people will live for 200 years.

6. The rebellion failed because the people do not support it.

7. I enjoy my work, but I was not going to let it take over my life.

8. Prejudice is learned and will be hard to outgrow.

9. A Canadian is someone who thinks that an income tax refund was a gift from the government.

10. Although the sun is shining and the skies are clear, the temperature was bitterly cold.

GO TO WEB

EXERCISE 13.1

Exercise 13.2

1. We need proof that the picture was genuine.

2. The couple living in the apartment next door had a boa constrictor that keeps getting loose.

3. The property next door has been sold; soon a house will be built on it.

4. It was getting dark, but Stanley is not afraid.

5. My deadline is Friday, and I had to submit an outline and a rough draft by then.

6. A person who lacks a sense of humour may not appreciate the numerous jokes in this book.

7. I drank a half litre of milk, then I eat two curry wraps, and I am ready for anything.

8. It was great music for dancing, and it's being played by a super band.

9. I will download about 600 songs this year and paid for all of them.

10. When the weekend paper arrives, we will fight over who gets to read it
    first.

GO TO WEB

EXERCISE 13.2

Exercise 13.3

Correct the 15 faulty time shifts in the following paragraph. Use the italicized
verb as your time marker. Then check your answers.

My most embarrassing moment *occurred* just last month when I meet an
old friend whom I have not seen in years. We greet each other and begin
to chat, and I tell her that I have been reading her daughter's columns in
the newspaper. I congratulate her on her daughter's talent. I tell her that
she must be very proud to see her offspring's name in print. My friend looks
puzzled for a minute, then she laughs and tells me that the writer I am praising so highly isn't her daughter. My friend had divorced long ago; her former husband remarries, and the columnist is her ex-husband's new wife.

GO TO WEB

EXERCISE 13.3

Exercise 13.4

Using the italicized verb as your time marker, correct the 10 faulty tense shifts in the following paragraph.

Two friends *were* in a bank when suddenly someone screams, and armed robbers rush in. Some of the robbers take money from the tellers, while others line the customers up, including the two friends, and begin to take their wallets, watches, and jewellery. While this is going on, one of the girls presses something into her friend's hand. Without looking down, the friend asks in a whisper what it is. Her friend replies, "It's the $50 I owe you."

14

Choosing the Correct Pronoun Form

"Pronoun? That's just a noun used by a professional!" When a character in a television sitcom spoke this line, the audience cracked up. His TV wife corrected him, pointing out that a pronoun is a word that stands in for a noun, replacing it in a sentence so the noun doesn't have to be repeated. His response: "Both answers are acceptable."

Of course, he's wrong, and his wife is right. The audience seemed to know this (or maybe they just knew that in sitcoms, the wife is always right). Generally, pronouns are not well understood. In this chapter and the two following, we will look at the three aspects of pronoun usage that can trip you up if you're not careful: pronoun **form**, **agreement**, and **consistency**. We will also consider the special problem of using pronouns in a way that avoids sexist language.

There are three kinds of pronouns that are likely to cause difficulty for writers:

personal pronouns	I, we, she, they, etc.
relative pronouns	who, which, that, etc.
indefinite pronouns	any, somebody, none, each, etc.

(You will find a complete list of these pronouns on pages 458–59.)

The first thing you need to do is be sure you are using correct pronoun forms. Look at these examples of incorrect pronoun usage:

Her and me offered to pick up a video.
Between you and I, I think Pauli's mother does his homework.

How do you know which form of a pronoun to use? The answer depends on the pronoun's place and function in your sentence.

Subject and Object Pronouns

There are two forms of personal pronouns. One is used for subjects, and one is used for objects. Pronoun errors occur when you confuse the two. In Chapter 5, you learned to identify the subject of a sentence. Keep that information in mind as you learn the following basic rule.

When the subject of a sentence is (or is referred to by) a pronoun, that pronoun must be in **subject form**; otherwise, use the **object form**.

Subject Pronouns

Singular	Plural
I	we
you	you
he, she, it, one	they

She and *I* <u>offered</u> to pick up a video.
(The pronouns are the subject of the sentence.)

The lucky <u>winners</u> of the free tickets to the World Wrestling Championships <u>are</u> *they*.
(The pronoun refers to the subject of the sentence, "winners.")

The only <u>person</u> who got an A in the course <u>was</u> *she*.
(The pronoun refers to the subject of the sentence, "person.")

We serious <u>bikers</u> <u>prefer</u> Harleys to Hondas.
(The pronoun refers to the subject of the sentence, "bikers.")

Object Pronouns

Singular	Plural
me	us
you	you
him, her, it, one	them

Between you and *me*, I <u>think</u> Pauli's mother does his homework.
("Me" is not the subject of the sentence; it is one of the objects of the preposition "between.")

Sasha <u>saw</u> *him* and *me* copying from each other.
("Him" and "me" are not the subject of the verb "saw"; Sasha is, so the pronouns must be in the object form.)

The <u>police</u> <u>are</u> always suspicious of *us* bikers.
("Us" does not refer to the subject of the sentence, "police"; it refers to "bikers," the object of the preposition "of.")

Be especially careful with pronouns that occur in multiple subjects or after prepositions. If you remember the following two rules, you'll be able to eliminate most potential errors in pronoun form.

1. Any pronoun that is part of a multiple subject is *always* in subject form.
2. Any pronoun that comes after a preposition is *always* in object form.

She and *I* <u>have</u> season's tickets.
(The pronouns are used as a multiple subject.)

We are very happy for *you* and *her*.
(The pronouns follow the preposition "for.")

I can't believe Chandra would break up with me after me and her got matching tattoos and navel rings.

When you're dealing with a pair of pronouns and can't decide which form to use, try this test.[1] Mentally cross out one pronoun at a time, then read aloud the sentence you've created. Applying this technique to the first example above, you get "*She* has tickets" and "*I* have tickets," both of which sound right and are correct. In the second sentence, if you try the pronouns separately, you get "We are happy for *you*" and "We are happy for *her*." Again, you know by the sound that these are the correct forms. You would never say "*Her* had tickets," or "*Me* had tickets," or "We are happy for *she*." If you deal with paired pronouns one at a time, you are unlikely to choose the wrong form.

Note, too, that when a pair of pronouns includes "I" or "me," that pronoun comes last. For example, we write "*She* and *I*" (not "*I* and *she*"). There is no grammatical reason for this rule. It's based on courtesy. Good manners require that you speak of others first and yourself last.

Exercise 14.1

Choose the correct pronouns from the words given in parentheses. Answers for exercises in this chapter begin on page 500.

1. The movie that Gina and (I/me) rented was a waste of time and money.

2. Dasha wants to come to the restaurant with Joshi and (I/me).

3. Except for Vikram and (her/she), there's no one else who knows how to enter the data manually.

4. (Me and Sasha/Sasha and I) are best friends.

5. The work will go much faster if (he/him) and Roland do it by themselves.

6. Sami and (he/him) wrote, shot, and edited the entire film.

7. I left my CD in the computer when my friends and (I/me) left the lab.

8. Surely your sister wasn't serious when she said (they/them) and their children were coming to stay with us for three weeks?

9. I can't believe Chandra would break up with me after (her/she) and (I/me) got matching tattoos and navel rings.

---

 [1] This test is reliable only for those who are fluent in English. Until they become fluent, unfortunately, ESL students must rely on memorizing the rules.

10. (Him and me/He and I/I and he) have completely different tastes in music.

Exercise 14.2

Correct the 10 errors in pronoun form in the following sentences.

1. Have you and her ever tried skydiving?

2. My boyfriend and me have completely different tastes in music.

3. It is not up to you or I to discipline your sister's children.

4. She and Xan took the videos back before Tami or me had seen them.

5. Arranging the details and hiring the staff are up to he and his team, because us volunteers have done all the planning.

6. Was it him who served you? Or was it her?

7. Him and Marie finished on time; except for they and their staff, no one else met the deadline.

GO TO WEB

EXERCISES 14.1, 14.2

Using Pronouns in Contrast Constructions

Choosing the correct pronoun form is more than just a matter of not wanting to appear ignorant or careless. Sometimes the form you use determines the meaning of your sentence. Consider these two sentences:

Giesele treats her dog better than *I*.
Giesele treats her dog better than *me*.

There's a world of difference between the meaning of the subject form—"Giesele treats her dog better than *I* [do]"—and the object form—"Giesele treats her dog better than [she treats] *me*."

When using a pronoun after *than, as well as,* or *as,* decide whether you mean to contrast the pronoun with the subject of the sentence. If you do, use the subject form of the pronoun. If not, use the object form.

Meiling would rather listen to an iPod than I.
(*I* is contrasted with *Meiling.*)

Meiling would rather listen to an iPod than me.
(*Me* is contrasted with *iPod.*)

 Here's a quick way to check that you've used the correct pronoun form. If you've used a subject form, insert a verb after it. If you've used an object form, insert a preposition before it. If your sentences make sense, you have chosen correctly. For example,

Meiling would rather listen to an iPod than I [would].
Meiling would rather listen to an iPod than [to] me.

Many writers prefer to leave the clarifying verb or preposition in place.

Exercise 14.3

Correct the errors in the following sentences.

1. The prize is sure to go to Omar and she.

2. No one likes our cooking class more than me.

3. In fact, nobody in the class eats as much as me.

4. It's not surprising that I am much bigger than them.

5. My mother would rather cook for my brother than I because he never complains when dinner is burned or raw.

6. At last I have met someone who loves barbecued eel as much as me!

7. More than me, Yuxiang uses the computer to draft and revise his papers.

8. He doesn't write as well as me, but he does write faster.

9. Only a few Mexican food fanatics can eat as many jalapeño peppers as him.

10. I think you have as much trouble with English as me.

GO TO WEB

EXERCISE 14.3

Exercise 14.4

Revise the following paragraphs to correct the 10 errors in pronoun form.

Us Canadians take pride in being "multicultural" and sharing in one another's traditions, and we are all far richer for this diversity. This richness is perhaps best shown in the wide choice of foods that are available to we food lovers from practically every culture on Earth. Newcomers are often surprised by the enormous variety of dishes and cuisines available to they and their families. Older immigrants, however, sometimes find it difficult to adjust. For example, my grandfather came here from England as an adult, and to he and his sisters, pasta was "foreign muck"; anything cooked with garlic was "offensive"; and curry was "inedible." My siblings and me often think of them when we sit down to our favourite winter meal of garlic ravioli followed by tandoori chicken! When my grandparents were growing up, their daily menu consisted mostly of mutton, Brussels sprouts, turnips, and—a real treat—fish and chips with mushy peas. They missed out on the variety of foods my friends and me enjoyed during our childhood.

I imagine that future generations will be even more fortunate. Canada now trains and attracts great chefs who are accustomed to cooking in a multicultural environment; it is them who are combining some of the surprising elements found in delicious "fusion" dishes. Thai-Italian and Caribbean-Indian fusions are featured in local restaurants where many of we adventurous diners go. The enormously varied African cuisines are also becoming widely available to those of we who delight in new taste sensations. The variety of foods, cuisines, and talented chefs from around the world will ensure that our children and grandchildren can look forward to dining experiences even more varied than the ones we now take for granted. We and them are truly fortunate to be living in a multicultural nation.

15

Mastering Pronoun–Antecedent Agreement

"I am writing in response to your ad for a server and bartender, male or female. Being both, I am applying for the position."

Pronoun confusion can take several forms, and some of the resulting sentences can be unintentionally hilarious. In this chapter, we'll look at how to use pronouns consistently throughout a sentence or paragraph to avoid confusing (and embarrassing) mistakes.

Pronoun–Antecedent Agreement

The name of this pronoun problem may sound difficult, but the idea is simple. Pronouns are words that substitute for or refer to a person, place, or thing mentioned elsewhere in your sentence or paragraph. The word(s) that a pronoun substitutes for or refers to is called the **antecedent**.

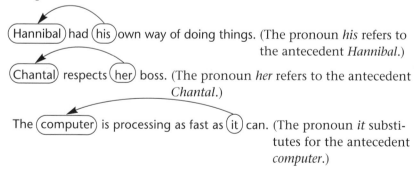

Hannibal had his own way of doing things. (The pronoun *his* refers to the antecedent *Hannibal*.)

Chantal respects her boss. (The pronoun *her* refers to the antecedent *Chantal*.)

The computer is processing as fast as it can. (The pronoun *it* substitutes for the antecedent *computer*.)

Usually, as in these three examples, the antecedent comes before the pronoun[1] that refers to it. Here is the rule to remember:

---

[1] Strictly speaking, possessive words such as *my, his, her, our,* and *their* are pronominal adjectives rather than pronouns. We are dealing with them in this chapter, however, because they follow the same agreement rule that governs pronouns.

A pronoun must agree with its antecedent in
- number (singular or plural)
- person (first, second, or third)
- gender (masculine, feminine, or neuter)

Most of the time, you follow this rule without even realizing that you know it. For example, you would never write

Hannibal had *your* own way of doing things.

Chantal respects *its* boss.

The computer is processing as fast as *she* can.

You know these sentences are incorrect even if you may not know precisely why they are wrong.

There are three kinds of pronoun–antecedent agreement that you need to learn. Unlike the examples above, they are not obvious, and you need to know them so you can watch out for them. The rules you need to learn involve **indefinite pronouns ending in** *-one*, *-body*, **or** *-thing*; **vague references**; and **relative pronouns**.

1. PRONOUNS ENDING IN *-ONE*, *-BODY*, *-THING*

The most common pronoun–antecedent agreement problem involves **indefinite pronouns:**

anyone	anybody	anything
everyone	everybody	everything
no one	nobody	nothing
someone	somebody	something
each (one)		

In Chapter 12, you learned that when these words are used as subjects, they are singular and require singular verbs. So it makes sense that the pronouns that stand for or refer to them must also be singular.

Antecedents ending in *-one*, *-body*, and *-thing* are singular.
They must be referred to by singular pronouns: *he, she, it; his, her, its.*

Everyone deserves a break from *her* children now and then.

Everything has *its* place and should be in it.

Everybody is expected to do *his* share of the work.

No one had the courage to open *his* mouth and protest.

Now take another look at the last two sentences. Until about 30 years ago, the pronouns *he, him,* and *his* were used with singular antecedents to refer to both men and women. In order to appeal to the broadest possible audience, most writers today are careful to avoid this usage and other examples of what might be seen as sexist language.

In informal usage, it has become acceptable to use plural pronouns with *-one, -body,* and *-thing* antecedents. Although they are grammatically singular, they are often plural in meaning, and in conversation we tend to say

Everybody is expected to do *their* share of the work.

No one had the courage to open *their* mouth and protest.

This usage is acceptable in speech, but it is not acceptable in academic or professional writing.

Writers sometimes make errors in pronoun–antecedent agreement because they are trying to write without indicating whether the person referred to is male or female. "Everybody is expected to do *their* share of the work" is incorrect, as we have seen; however, it does avoid making "everybody" male. The writer could replace the plural *their* with the singular and non-sexist *his or her*—"Everybody is expected to do *his or her* share of the work"—but *his or her* sounds clumsy if it is used frequently.

There are two better ways to solve the problem.

1. Revise the sentence to leave out the pronoun.

Everybody is expected to share the work.

No one had the courage to protest.

Such creative avoidance of gender-specific language or incorrect constructions can be an interesting intellectual challenge. The results sometimes sound a little artificial, however. The second solution is easier to accomplish.

2. Revise the sentence to make both the antecedent and the pronoun plural.

We are all expected to do *our* share of the work.

The *staff members* did not have the courage to open *their* mouths and protest.

Here are a couple of examples for you to study:

Problem: Everybody has been given his assignment.
Revision 1: Everybody has been given an assignment.
Revision 2: All of the students have been given their assignments.

Problem: No one wants his copy edited.
Revision 1: No one wants copy-editing.
Revision 2: Most writers object to having their copy edited.

 If you are writing on a word processor, you can use the search function to ensure agreement between pronouns and their antecedents. Search your paper for every occurrence of *their* and *they*, and check each one to be sure its antecedent is not a pronoun ending in *-one*, *-body*, or *-thing*. (This search takes less time than you might think and is well worth it, especially if your instructor has asked for a formal paper or report.)

Exercise 15.1

Identify the most appropriate word(s) from the choices given in parentheses. Check your answers carefully before continuing. Answers for this chapter begin on page 501.

1. Each player on the team has (her/their) strengths.
2. It seemed that everybody in the mall was talking on (his/her/their/a) cellphone.
3. Would someone kindly lend (his/her/their/a) copy of the textbook to Mei Yu?
4. Anything found in the locker room will be returned to (its/their) owner, if possible.
5. A band leader is someone who is not afraid to face (his/her/their/the) music.
6. According to the reviews, not one of the movies at the mall is worth (its/their/the) admission price.

7. So far, no one on the wrestling team has been able to persuade (his/their) parents to host the team party.
8. Everyone is expected to pay (his or her/their/a) share of the expenses.
9. Is there anybody here who can bring (her/their) own car?
10. Anyone who wants a high mark for (his/their/this) essay should see me after class and write out (his/their/a) cheque.

Exercise 15.2

Correct the errors in the following sentences, being careful to avoid awkward repetition and sexist language. Because there is more than one way to correct these errors, your answers may differ from our suggestions.

1. Everyone is a product of their environment as well as heredity.

2. Nobody who is as smart as you needs to have help with their homework.

3. Each car in all categories will be judged on their bodywork, engine, and interior.

4. Every movie-, theatre-, and concert-goer knows how annoying it is to have their evening's enjoyment spoiled by a ringing cellphone.

5. Put the sign at the curb so anyone looking for our yard sale won't have to waste their time driving around the neighbourhood.

6. Everyone who pays their membership fee in advance will receive a free session with a personal trainer.

7. A true geek is somebody who has trouble deciding between buying flowers for their girlfriend and upgrading their RAM.

8. Ultimate is a game in which everyone who participates enjoys themselves, whether their team finishes first or last.

9. No one on the football team has been able to get their parents to donate his or her house for the party.

10. The accident could not have been avoided, and fortunately no one was hurt, so no one should have to say they are sorry.

GO TO WEB

EXERCISE 15.1

2. VAGUE REFERENCE

Avoiding the second potential difficulty with pronoun–antecedent agreement requires common sense and the ability to put yourself in your reader's place. If you look at your writing from your reader's point of view, it is unlikely that you will break the following rule.

> Every pronoun must have a clearly identifiable antecedent.

The mistake that occurs when you fail to follow this rule is called **vague reference**.

> Luc pointed to his brother and said that he had saved his life.

Who saved whom? Here's another:

> Danielle wrote a song about her sister when she was five years old.

Is the song about a five-year-old sister, or was Danielle a musically talented child?

In sentences like these, you can only guess the meaning because you don't know who is being referred to by the pronouns. The antecedents are not clear. You can make such sentences less confusing either by using proper names (Luc, Danielle) more frequently or by changing the sentences around. These solutions aren't difficult; they just take a little time and some imagination. Try them on our examples above.

Another type of vague reference occurs when there is no antecedent for the pronoun to refer to.

> Zoe loves dog shows and is going to enter hers when *it's* old enough. (Enter what? The dog or the show?)

> Snowboarding is Anna's favourite sport, and she's hoping to get *one* for her birthday. (One what?)

3. R

The t
to u
pron
sente

My roommate smokes constantly, *which* I hate. (There is no noun or pronoun for *which* to refer to.)

My sister's work schedule overlaps with her husband's. *This* creates child-
care problems. (What does *this* refer to?)

How would you revise these sentences? Try it, then see our suggestions below.

Us
Us

Th

Th

Th

My

My
ch

Wl
funct

If
Ot
pr

It
Fac

The
pr
pre

A bet
don't

Suggestions: Zoe loves dog shows and is going to enter her *puppy* when it's old enough.

Snowboarding is Anna's favourite sport, and she's hoping to get *a board* for her birthday.

My roommate is constantly smoking, *which* I hate.

My sister's work schedule overlaps with her husband's. *This* conflict creates child-care problems.

Make sure that every pronoun has a clear antecedent and that every pronoun agrees with its antecedent. Both must be singular, or both must be
plural. Once you have mastered this principle, you'll have no trouble with
pronoun–antecedent agreement.

Exercise 15.3

Correct the following sentences where necessary. There are several ways to fix
these sentences. In some cases, the antecedent is missing, and you need to
supply one. In other cases, the antecedent is so vague that the meaning of the
sentence can be interpreted in more than one way; you need to rewrite these
sentences to make the meaning clear.

1. At our college, they strictly enforce the "no smoking" policy.

2. Kara didn't hear my question, which was because she was listening to
   her iPod.

3. Every time David looked at the dog, he barked.

4. In a rage, Max hurled his cellphone at the computer and broke it.

5. The big story on *Entertainment Tonight* was that Cher told Dolly that she
   was losing her looks.

² The
and i

6. My wife was annoyed when I didn't notice she had fallen overboard; this was because I was concentrating on landing my fish.

7. Kevin told Yu to leave his books on the table beside his computer.

8. When I learned that smoking was the cause of my asthma, I gave them up for good.

9. Nell didn't see her son score the winning goal, which was because she was talking on her cellphone at the time.

10. Being on time is a challenge for my girlfriend, so I'm getting her one for her birthday.

GO TO WEB

EXERCISE 15.2

Every time David looked at the dog, he barked.

3. RELATIVE PRONOUNS

The third potential difficulty with pronoun–antecedent agreement is how to use relative pronouns—*who*, *which*, and *that*—correctly. Relative pronouns must refer to someone or something already mentioned in the sentence. Here is the guideline to follow:

> Use *who* and *whom* to refer to people.
> Use *that* and *which* to refer to everything else.

The chef *who* prepared this meal deserves a medal.

The servers *who* presented it deserve to be fired.

The appetizer *that* I ordered was covered with limp cilantro.

My soup, *which* was cold, arrived at the same time as my main course.

My father's meal, *which* was delicious, demonstrated the talent *that* the chef is famous for.

Whether you need *who* or *whom*[2] depends on the pronoun's place and function in your sentence. Apply the basic pronoun rule:

> If the pronoun is, or refers to, the subject of the sentence, use *who*. Otherwise, use *whom*. Or you can revise the sentence to eliminate the pronoun.

It was Lilia *who* drew the winning ticket for a week's holiday in Moose Factory. (The pronoun refers to the subject of the sentence, *Lilia*.)

The trip's promoters were willing to settle for *whom* they could get. (The pronoun does not refer to the subject, *promoters*; it is the object of the preposition *for*.)

A better solution is to solve the problem by rewriting the sentence so you don't need either *who* or *whom*.

---

[2] The distinction between *who* and *whom* has all but disappeared in spoken English and is becoming rarer in written English. Ask your instructor for guidance.

Lilia drew the winning ticket for a week's holiday in Moose Factory.

The trip's promoters were willing to settle for anyone they could get.

 That is required more often than *which.* You should use *which* only in a clause that is separated from the rest of the sentence by commas. (See Comma Rule 4, page 211.)

The moose *that* I met looked hostile.

The moose, *which* was standing right in front of my car, looked hostile.

Exercise 15.4

Correct the pronoun errors in the following sentences. Remember: use *who* to refer to people; use *that* or *which* to refer to everything else.

1. Chi Keung is the technician that can fix your problem.

2. I would have won, except for one judge that placed me fourth.

3. A grouch is a person which knows himself and isn't happy about it.

4. The salesclerk that sold me my DVD player didn't know what he was talking about.

5. Everyone that was at the party had a good time, though a few had more punch than was good for them.

6. The open-office concept sounds good to anyone that has worked in a stuffy little cubicle all day.

7. I wish I could find someone in our class that could help me with my homework.

8. Thanks to the computer, I regularly order supplies from companies which are located in cities all across the country.

9. The tests which we wrote today were designed to discourage anyone that didn't have the knowledge, preparation, and stamina to endure them.

10. My roommate has just started on the term paper, that was assigned a month ago, for her political science course.

GO TO WEB

EXERCISE 15.3

Exercise 15.5

Revise the following paragraphs, which contain 15 errors representing the three different kinds of pronoun–antecedent agreement error. If you change a subject from singular to plural, don't forget to change the verb to agree. Some of your answers may differ from our suggestions and still be correct.

Everyone in North America seems obsessed with showing their grasp of useless information. Trivia games have been hugely popular for decades, and they continue to enjoy large audiences. The trivia player is expected to have at their fingertips all sorts of obscure information, from sports statistics to popular music, from world geography to the film industry. Team trivia contests have become important fund-raising events for charity. Teams of eight to ten players answer trivia questions in competition with other teams. Each member of a team is expected to have their own particular area of expertise and to help their team gain points by answering the questions in that area. At the end of the contest, the winning team will usually have answered correctly more than 80 percent of the questions called out by the quizmaster.

Another forum for trivia is the television shows in which the contestant must demonstrate their knowledge individually in a high-pressure, game show format. Alone, each contestant faces the show's host, who may give him assistance if it's asked for. In other games, the contestant plays against each other and must demonstrate superior knowledge if they want to win. Playing trivia at home is also popular, and many households have one.

Whether you play alone, with friends, on a team, or on television, they should keep the game in perspective. After all, the object of any trivia game is to reward the players that demonstrates that they know more about unimportant and irrelevant facts than anyone else in the game!

Summary

- Every pronoun must agree with its antecedent (a word or phrase mentioned, usually earlier, in the sentence or paragraph). Both must be singular, or both must be plural.
- Antecedents ending in *-one*, *-body*, and *-thing* are singular and must be referred to by singular pronouns: *he, she, it; his, her, its.*
- A pronoun must clearly refer to a specific antecedent.
- Use *who/whom* to refer to people; use *that* and *which* to refer to animals, objects, and ideas.

Exercise 15.6

Correct the 15 errors in the following paragraphs. Part of the challenge in this Mastery Test is to make the paragraphs not only grammatically correct but also free of sexist language.

Everyone that works in retail sales knows that their job has changed in the last decade. A new emphasis on service and satisfaction has changed the way customers and salespeople interact. The salesclerk understands that satisfied customers that are likely to be repeat customers are the best job insurance they can have. Recently, forward-thinking corporations and institutions have begun to apply "customer satisfaction" principles to another sector which has traditionally been ignored: its own employees. Each year, *The Globe and Mail*'s *Report on Business Magazine* publishes a list of the top 50 companies to work for. A few exceptional companies make the list every year, and all have several practices in common.

First, their employee feels recognized and valued for his contribution to corporate or institutional goals. Second, those goals are clear, meaningful, and realistic to the entire work force. Third, every manager maintains communication with their employees through regular meetings that allow them to get to know them. Notice that compensation for the work they do is not on this list of key attributes. Most corporations now recognize competitive pay rates and pay its employees appropriately. More important, the employee feels that they are fairly compensated for the work they do. Even more important than pay is recognition, that may be something as simple as a manager personally congratulating an employee on their fifth-year anniversary with the company, or an e-mail from the CEO recognizing the employee's contribution and commitment. It is no coincidence that every year the list of the top 50 companies to work for includes some of the most successful companies in their fields.

16

Maintaining Person Agreement

So far, we have focussed on using pronouns correctly and clearly within a sentence. Now let's turn to the problem of **person agreement**, which means using pronouns consistently throughout a sentence or a paragraph. There are three categories of person that we use when we write or speak:

	Singular	Plural
first person	I; me	we; us
second person	you	you
third person	she, he, it, one; her, him and all pronouns ending in -one, -body, -thing	they; them

Here is the rule for person agreement:

Do not mix "persons" unless the meaning requires it.

In other words, be consistent. If you begin a sentence using a second-person pronoun, you must use second person all the way through. Look at this sentence:

If *you* wish to succeed, *one* must work hard.

This is the most common error—mixing second-person *you* with third-person *one*.

Here's another example:

At 35, just when you have *your* head together, *one's* body begins to fall apart.

We can correct this error by using the second person throughout:

(1) At 35, just when *you* have *your* head together, *your* body begins to fall apart.

We can also correct it by using the third person throughout:

(2) At 35, just when *one* has *one's* head together, *one's* body begins to fall apart.

or

(3) At 35, just when *one* has *his or her* head together, *one's* body begins to fall apart.

These last two sentences raise two points of style that you should consider.

1. Don't overuse *one*.

All three revised sentences are grammatically correct, but they make different impressions on the reader, and impressions are an important part of communication.

- The first sentence, in the second person, sounds the most informal—like something you would say. It's a bit casual for general writing purposes.
- The second sentence, which uses *one* three times, sounds the most formal—even a little pretentious.
- The third sentence falls between the other two in formality. It is the one you'd be most likely to use in writing for school or business.

Although it is grammatically correct and non-sexist, this third sentence raises another problem. Frequent use of *he or she* in a continuous prose passage, whether that passage is as short as a paragraph or as long as a paper, is guaranteed to irritate your reader.

2. Don't overuse *he or she*.

He or she is inclusive, but it is a wordy construction. If it is used too frequently, the reader cannot help shifting focus from what you're saying to how you're saying it. The best writing is transparent—that is, it doesn't call attention to itself. If your reader becomes distracted by your style, your meaning gets lost. Consider this sentence:

A student can easily pass this course if he or she applies himself or herself to his or her studies.

Readers deserve better than a paper—or even a single paragraph—filled with this clumsy construction.

There are two better solutions to this problem, and they are already familiar to you because they are the same as those for making pronouns ending in -*one*, *body*, or *thing* agree with their antecedents.

- You can change the whole sentence to the plural.

  Students can easily pass this course if they apply themselves to their studies.

- You can rewrite the sentence without using pronouns.

  A student can easily pass this course by applying good study habits.

Exercise 16.1

Choose the correct word(s) from the choices given in parentheses. Answers for exercises in this chapter begin on page 503.

1. You shouldn't annoy the instructor if (one wants/you want/he or she wants) to get an A.
2. A person can succeed at almost anything if (you have/they have/he or she has) enough talent and determination.
3. When we laugh, the world laughs with (you/one/us).
4. You can save a great deal of time if (one fills/you fill/we fill) out the forms before going to the passport office.
5. Clarify the question before beginning to write, or (one/you) may lose focus.
6. Our opinions will never be heard unless (one makes/we make/you make) a serious effort to reach the public.
7. I wish that (one/we) had a few more options to choose from.
8. (One/You) should not question Professor Snapes in class because he loses his temper, and you don't want that to happen.
9. Anyone with a telephone can get (his or her/one's/their/your) voice heard on the radio.
10. Call-in programs give everyone the opportunity to make sure the whole world knows (one's/our/your) ignorance of the issues.

GO TO WEB

EXERCISE 16.1

Exercise 16.2

Correct the errors in pronoun consistency in the following sentences.

1. One is never too old to learn, but you are never too young to know everything.

2. One always removes your shoes when entering a mosque.

3. The speed limit is the speed one goes as soon as you see a police car.

4. You must improve your computer skills if one is to succeed at this job.

5. No one can blame you for trying to do your best, even if one does not always succeed.

6. Experience is that marvellous thing that enables us to recognize a mistake when you make it again. (F.P. Jones)

7. If you can't cope with the pressure, one must be expected to be replaced by someone who can.

8. We all believed his story because you couldn't believe he would lie.

9. I find that unconditional love is most reliably offered by one's dog.

10. One's colleagues and superiors can make us feel stupid and insignificant, but my dog's whole world revolves around me.

GO TO WEB

EXERCISE 16.2

Exercise 16.3

Correct the five consistency errors in the following paragraph. Look for errors in number agreement (singular vs. plural) as well as person agreement.

Those of us who enjoy baseball find it difficult to explain one's enthusiasm to non-fans. We baseball enthusiasts can watch a game of three hours or more as one follows each play with rapt attention. We true fans get excited by a no-hitter—a game in which, by definition, nothing happens. They claim that the game is about much more than mere action, but non-fans must be forgiven if you don't get the point. To them, watching a baseball game is about as exciting as watching paint dry.

Exercise 16.4

Rewrite the following paragraph in the first-person plural, using *we, our,* and *us* as your base pronouns. As you revise, correct the 10 errors in agreement of person and number. Be sure to change verbs, where necessary, to agree with their revised subjects. (The quotation from Robert Frost has been altered to suit the purpose of this exercise.)

When one is at the beginning of our careers, it seems impossible that you may one day wish to work less. The drive to get ahead leads many of us to sacrifice one's leisure, one's community responsibilities, even one's family life for the sake of one's careers. Normally, as you age, one's priorities begin to change, and career success becomes less important than quality of life. Not everyone, however, experiences this shift in priorities. Indeed, some people work themselves to death, while others are so committed to their work throughout their lives that they die within months of retirement—

presumably from stress caused by lack of work. The poet Robert Frost once

observed, "By working faithfully eight hours a day, you may eventually get

to be a boss. Then you can work twelve hours a day." Those of you who are

living and working in the early years of the 21st century would be wise to

take Frost's words to heart.

Exercise 16.5

Find and correct the 15 pronoun agreement errors—in both person and number—in the following paragraph.

Canadians who complain about winter might just as well complain

about your height or hair colour. The experience of winter is part of being

Canadian. In November, we take out of storage your heavy wool socks,

your scarves and mitts and toques. You clean your down-filled coats, fill

the windshield washer reservoir in your cars, and put on your snow tires.

All this preparation is as much a part of being Canadian as strapping on

one's skis, cheering for one's hockey team, or complaining about your gov-

ernment. While most of the world is paralyzed by a few centimetres of

snow that brings traffic to a halt and closes schools and businesses, we

Canadians just get up a few minutes earlier to shovel out one's driveways,

scrape the snow off the car, and chip the ice from the windshield with that specially designed scraper that they always carry in our cars between October and April. As comedian Rick Mercer once observed, very little unites Canadians, but they all know how to pull up your heavy wool socks and pump your brakes.

The paragraphs below contain a total of 15 errors in verb form, subject–verb agreement, pronoun form, pronoun–antecedent agreement, and verb and pronoun consistency. When you've made your corrections, turn to pages 504–05 and compare your answers with ours. For each error you miss, the key directs you to the chapter you need to review.

¹Police officers in a small Manitoba town had saw too many people that were driving on the local roads while drunk, and they decided to make an example of one drunk driver to publicize the problem. ²An officer, together with two reporters from the local newspaper, were stationed outside the town's most notorious bar in order to catch the worst drunk driver they can find. ³As closing time neared, a man who clearly had drank too much come out of the bar and tripped on the curb, staggered to the parking lot, and begun trying to open car doors with his keys. ⁴As the officer and the reporters watch, he tried 30 cars before his key worked. ⁵Once he had succeeded in opening the car door, he stumbles to the front of the car and collapsed on the hood. ⁶Meanwhile, the rest of the patrons that had been in

the bar began to leave, but neither the reporters nor the officer were interested in anyone but the drunk on the hood of his car. [7]As the last car pulled out of the parking lot, the man rolled himself from the hood of his car, gets in, and drove away. [8]The officer immediately pulled him over and, as the reporters watched, gave him a breathalyzer test. [9]"You should not be driving when one is inebriated," the policeman said. [10]"Everyone will read about you when they get their newspapers tomorrow morning."

[11]However, to the officer's surprise, the breathalyzer test showed a reading of 0.0. [12]When him and the reporters asked the man how it could be possible that the breathalyzer showed him to be sober, the man answered, "Tonight was my turn to be the decoy driver!"

UNIT 4

Punctuation

Quick Quiz

17 The Comma
Five Comma Rules

18 The Semicolon

19 The Colon

20 Quotation Marks
Quoted Material
Titles

21 Question Marks, Exclamation Marks, and Punctuation Review
The Question Mark
The Exclamation Mark
Punctuation Review

Rapid Review

QUICK QUIZ

The following quick quiz will let you see at a glance which chapters of Unit 4 you need to concentrate on. The passage below contains 15 errors in punctuation, missing or misused commas, semicolons, colons, quotation marks, question marks, and exclamation marks. (*Note*: Each pair of quotation marks counts as one punctuation mark.) When you've finished your corrections, turn to page 505 and compare your answers with ours. For each error you miss, the Answer Key at the end of the answer directs you to the chapter you need to work on.

[1]When we go to a movie most of us like to sit back, munch away on a bucket of popcorn, and get lost in a good story. [2]Some people however delight in examining each frame to see if the producers of the film have made mistakes called "bloopers." [3]One kind of blooper is anachronisms. [4]An anachronism is something that is inconsistent with the time period in which the movie is set. [5]For example in *Troy* when Brad Pitt is involved in a fight scene a jumbo jet is clearly visible in the sky. [6]In *Gladiator*, Russell Crowe walks past a field marked with tractor-tire tracks. [7]Filter-tipped cigarettes in *Titanic* a Volkswagen Beetle in *The Godfather*, and white, canvas

sneakers in *The Ten Commandments* are other glaring examples of anachro-nisms. [8]Whoops.

[9]Another kind of blooper is: the "continuity" mistake. [10]This kind of slip-up involves inconsistencies from one film sequence to the next. [11]For exam-ple, if a character drinks from a glass in one shot, the glass must contain less liquid, not more, in the next. [12]Continuity problems abound; cigarettes get longer instead of shorter or appear and disappear from an actor's hand, hair changes style or length, and jewellery changes location. [13]Did you notice any of these bloopers when you watched the following films. [14]In *The*

Aviator, the canopy on Leonardo DiCaprio's airplane pops on and off from sequence to sequence. [15]In *Lord of the Rings*: *Return of the King*, Frodo's scar moves several times from the right side of his face to the left and back again. [16]In *The Bourne Identity*, Matt Damon's watch changes from his right wrist to his left, and back while he is cutting Franka Potente's hair.

[17]When we encounter a work of art, we want to experience what the poet Coleridge called the willing suspension of disbelief. [18]We need to believe because getting lost in the story is the essence of a great movie. [19]Bloopers can interfere with this belief but so can looking too hard for mistakes!

17

The Comma

Many writers-in-training tend to scatter punctuation like pepper over their pages. Do not use punctuation either to spice up or to decorate your writing. Punctuation marks are functional: they indicate to the reader how the various parts of a sentence relate to one another. By changing the punctuation, you can change the meaning of a sentence. Here are two examples to prove the point.

1. An instructor wrote the following sentence on the board and asked the class to punctuate it appropriately: "woman without her man is nothing."

   The men wrote, "Woman, without her man, is nothing."
   The women wrote, "Woman! Without her, man is nothing."

2. Now it's your turn. Punctuate this sentence: "I think there is only one person to blame myself."
   If you wrote, "I think there is only one person to blame, myself." the reader will understand that you believe only one person—who may or may not be known to you—is to blame.
   If you wrote, "I think there is only one person to blame: myself." the reader will understand that you are personally accepting responsibility for the blame.

The comma is the most frequently used—and misused—punctuation mark in English. Perhaps nothing is so sure a sign of a competent writer as the correct use of commas, so it is very important that you master them. This chapter presents five comma rules that cover most instances in which you need to use commas. If you apply these five rules faithfully, your reader will never be confused by missing or misplaced commas in your writing.

And if, as occasionally happens, the sentence you are writing is not covered by one of our five rules, remember the first commandment of comma usage: when in doubt, leave it out.

Five Comma Rules

> 1. Use commas to separate three or more items in a series. The items may be words, phrases, or clauses.

Words: The required subjects in this program are math, physics, and English.

Phrases: Punctuation marks are the traffic signals of prose: they tell us to slow down, notice this, take a detour, and stop. (Lynne Truss)

Clauses: Wing-Kee went to the movies, Jan and Yasmin went to play pool, and I went to bed.

The comma before the *and* at the end of the list is optional, but we advise you to use it. Occasionally, misunderstandings can occur if it is left out.

Exercise 17.1

Insert commas where necessary in the following sentences. Answers for exercises in this chapter begin on page 506.

1. Hirako held two aces a King a Queen and a Jack in her hand.
2. Cambodian food is spicy colourful nourishing and delicious.
3. In Canada, the seasons are spring summer fall winter winter and winter.
4. We'll have a hamburger and French fries to begin with.
5. Fax machines are almost as outmoded as typewriters black-and-white TV and record players.
6. You need woollen underwear snowshoes and Arctic boots but very little money to go winter camping.
7. Sleeping through my alarm dozing during sociology napping in the library after lunch and snoozing in front of the TV all are symptoms of my overactive nightlife.

8. Once you have finished your homework taken out the garbage and done the dishes, you can feed the cat clean your room and do your laundry.
9. Of Paris Moscow Sydney Madrid and Beijing, which is not a national capital?
10. Both my doctor and my nutritionist agree that I should eat better exercise more and give up smoking.

The second comma rule is already familiar to you. You encountered it in Chapter 7, "Solving Run-On Sentence Problems."

2. Put a comma between independent clauses when they are joined by

for	but	so
and	or	
nor	yet	

(You can remember these words easily if you notice that their first letters spell "fanboys.")

I hope I do well in the interview, for I really want this job.

I like James Bond, but I prefer Austin Powers.

"We shape our tools, and our tools shape us." (Marshall McLuhan)

I knew I was going to be late, so I went back to sleep.

Be sure that the sentence you are punctuating contains two independent clauses rather than one clause with a single subject and a multiple verb.

<u>We</u> <u>loved</u> the book but <u>hated</u> the movie.
(<u>We</u> is the subject, and there are two verbs, <u>loved</u> and <u>hated</u>. Do not put a comma between two or more verbs that share a single subject.)

<u>We</u> both <u>loved</u> the book, but <u>Kim</u> <u>hated</u> the movie.
(This sentence contains two independent clauses — <u>We</u> <u>loved</u> and <u>Kim</u> <u>hated</u> — joined by *but*. The comma is required here.)

Exercise 17.2

Insert commas where they are needed in the following sentences. Check your answers when you're done.

1. Pierre and I are good friends yet we often disagree.
2. I wonder why the sun lightens our hair but darkens our skin.
3. Please pay close attention for the instructions are a little complicated.
4. Money can't buy happiness but it makes misery easier to live with.
5. The car swerved wildly and just missed the police cruiser.
6. Canadians are proud of their country but don't approve of too much flag-waving.
7. Flying may be the safest form of transportation but why is the place where planes land called a "terminal"?
8. Pack an extra jacket or sweater for evenings in September can be cold.
9. The phone hasn't worked for days and the television has been broken for a month but I haven't missed either of them.
10. Noah had the last two of every creature on his ark so why didn't he swat those mosquitoes?

---

3. Put a comma after an introductory word, phrase, or dependent clause that comes BEFORE an independent clause.

Word: Rob, you aren't paying attention.

Phrase: Exhausted and cranky from staying up all night, I staggered into class.

Clause: If that's their idea of a large pizza, we'd better order two.

Clause: Until she got her promotion, she was quite friendly.

But note: If a subordinate clause FOLLOWS a main clause, no comma is needed (e.g., She was quite friendly until she got her promotion).

Exercise 17.3

Insert commas where they are needed in the following sentences. Check your answers when you have finished all 10.

1. First we need to understand what an independent clause is.
2. In the end we will be judged by how much happiness we have given others.
3. Driving 50 kph over the speed limit Amin was soon pulled over.
4. According to company policy you may not collect air mile points for business-related travel.
5. If you live by the calendar your days are numbered.
6. According to my stomach lunchtime came and went about an hour ago.
7. In most newspaper and magazine advertisements the time shown on a watch is 10:10.
8. When you are right about something it's considered polite not to gloat.
9. As her fortieth birthday approached Eva met the challenge by trading in her minivan for a sports car and her husband for a boyfriend 20 years younger.
10. When the leaves turn colour and the weather turns cold I know it's time to put the snow tires on the car.

4. Use commas to set off any word, phrase, or dependent clause that is NOT ESSENTIAL to the main idea of the sentence.

Following this rule can make the difference between your reader understanding and misunderstanding what you write. For example, the following two sentences are identical, except for a pair of commas. But notice what a difference those two tiny marks make to meaning:

The children who were dressed in clown costumes had ice cream. (Only the children wearing costumes ate ice cream.)

The children, who were dressed in clown costumes, had ice cream. (All the children wore costumes and had ice cream.)

To test whether a word, phrase, or clause is essential to the meaning of your sentence, mentally put parentheses around it. If the sentence still makes complete sense (i.e., the main idea is unchanged; the sentence just delivers less information), the material in parentheses is *not essential* and should be set off from the rest of the sentence by a comma or commas.

Non-essential information can appear at the beginning of a sentence,[1] in the middle, or at the end of a sentence. Study the following examples.

Alice Munro (one of Canada's best-known novelists) spends the summer in Clinton and the winter in Comox.

Most readers would be puzzled the first time they read this sentence because all the information is presented without punctuation, so the reader assumes it is all equally important. In fact, the material in broken parentheses is extra information, a supplementary detail. It can be deleted without changing the sentence's meaning, and so it should be separated from the rest of the sentence by commas:

Alice Munro, one of Canada's best-known novelists, spends the summer in Clinton and the winter in Comox.

Here's another example to consider:

The Queen (who has twice as many birthdays as anyone else) officially celebrates her birthday on May 24.

Again, the sentence is hard to read. You can't count on your readers to go back and re-read every sentence they don't understand at first glance. As a writer, your responsibility is to give readers the clues they need as to what is crucial information and what isn't. In the example above, the information in broken parentheses is not essential to the meaning of the sentence, so it should be set off by commas:

The Queen, who has twice as many birthdays as anyone else, officially celebrates her birthday on May 24.

In this next sentence, the non-essential information comes at the end.

Writing a good letter of application isn't difficult (if you're careful) .

---

[1] Rule 3 covers non-essential information at the beginning of a sentence.

The phrase "if you're careful" is not essential to the main idea, so it should be separated from the rest of the sentence by a comma:

Writing a good letter of application isn't difficult, if you're careful.

And finally, consider this sentence:

Writing a letter of application ⸜ that is clear, complete, and concise ⸝ is a challenge.

If you take out "that is clear, complete, and concise," you change the meaning of the sentence. Not all letters of application are a challenge to write. Writing vague and wordy letters is easy; anyone can do it. The words "that is clear, complete, and concise" are essential to the meaning of the sentence, and so they are not set off by commas.

Writing a letter of application that is clear, complete, and concise is a challenge.

Exercise 17.4

Insert commas where they are missing in the following sentences. Check your answers on page 507.

1. Commas like capitals are clues to meaning.
2. Our hope of course is that the terrorists will be caught and punished.
3. Our family doctor like our family dog never comes when we call.
4. Our adventure began in Barcelona which is the site of a famous unfinished cathedral designed by Gaudi.
5. Gaudi who was killed by a bus in his 50s began the cathedral as an atonement for the sins of mankind.
6. An opportunist is someone who goes ahead and does what the rest of us wish we had the courage to do.
7. A compliment like a good perfume should be pleasing but not overpowering.
8. Our car made it all the way from Thunder Bay to Saskatoon a piece of good luck that surprised us all.
9. Anyone who arrives during July or August will have to adjust to the overwhelming heat and humidity before trying to do any work.

10. The new office manager now in her second month on the job has made many changes to our procedures not all of them welcome.

---

5. Use commas to separate coordinate adjectives but not between cumulative adjectives.

Coordinate adjectives are those whose order can be changed, and the word *and* can be inserted between them without changing the meaning of the sentence.

Our company is looking for energetic, courteous salespeople.

The adjectives *energetic* and *courteous* could appear in reverse order, and you could put *and* between them: "Our company is looking for courteous and energetic salespeople."

In a series of **cumulative adjectives**, however, each adjective modifies the word that follows it. You cannot change their order, nor can you insert *and* between them.

The bride wore a pale pink silk dress, and the groom wore a navy wool suit.

You cannot say "The bride wore a silk pink pale dress" or "The groom wore a navy and wool suit," so no commas are used with these adjectives.

Exercise 17.5

Insert commas where they are needed in the following sentences. Check your answers before continuing.

1. The pen you bought for me leaked dark green ink onto my white shirt.
2. Do you want your portrait in a glossy finish or a matte finish?
3. Bright yellow fabric that repels stains is ideal for rain gear.
4. Toronto in the summer is hot smoggy and humid.
5. Today's paper has an article about a new car made of lightweight durable aluminum.
6. I think you'll like the new improved model that has been assigned to all employees in your category.

7. This ergonomic efficient full-function keyboard comes in a variety of pastel shades.
8. We ordered a large nutritious salad for lunch, then indulged ourselves with apple pie topped with vanilla ice cream.
9. When he retired, my father bought himself a large comfortable leather reclining chair.
10. We survived the long high-velocity descent but almost didn't survive the sudden unexpected crash landing.

The rest of the exercises in this chapter require you to apply all five comma rules. Before you start, write out the five rules and keep them in front of you as you work through the exercises. Refer to the rules frequently as you punctuate the sentences. After you've finished each exercise, check your answers and make sure you understand any mistakes you've made.

Exercise 17.6

1. I call my salary "take-home pay" for home is the only place I can afford to go on what I make.
2. Madalena won my heart by laughing at my jokes admiring my car and tolerating my obsession with sports.
3. Though I try to remember my password I forget it at least once a month.
4. Leo went to the bank to withdraw enough money to pay for his tuition books and the student activity fee.
5. In a moment of foolish optimism I invested my life savings in a software development company.
6. The happiest years of my life in my opinion were the years I spent in college.
7. Sabina spends all day sleeping in bed so she can spend all night dancing in the clubs.
8. Doing punctuation exercises is not very exciting but it's cleaner than tuning your car.
9. This year instead of the traditional gold watch we will be giving retiring employees a framed photograph of our company's president.
10. Iqaluit which was called Frobisher Bay until 1987 is a major centre on Baffin Island in Canada's eastern Arctic region.

GO TO WEB

EXERCISES 17.1, 17.2

Exercise 17.7

Insert the 15 commas that are missing in the following passage.

As long as you are prepared and confident you'll find that an employment interview need not be a terrifying experience. Some people actually enjoy employment interviews and attend them with enthusiasm. Most of us however are intimidated by the prospect of being interrogated by an interviewer or (even worse) a team of interviewers.

To prepare for an interview the first thing you should do is to find out as much as you can about the company. Among the things you need to know are the title of the job you are applying for approximately how much it pays the name of the person or persons who will conduct the interview the address of the company how long it will take you to get there and the location of the washrooms. Employment consultants usually recommend that you make an advance visit to confirm how long it takes to get there and where the interview room is. While on your scouting mission you can learn valuable information about the company's working conditions employee attitudes and even dress code.

On the day of the interview be sure to show up 10 or 15 minutes in advance of your scheduled appointment. When the interviewer greets you you should do three things: memorize his or her name identify yourself and extend your hand. Your handshake should be brief and firm, not limply passive or bone-crushingly aggressive. Practise! Now all you have to do is relax and enjoy the interview.

GO TO WEB

EXERCISES 17.3, 17.4

Summary

The Five Comma Rules

1. Use commas to separate three or more items in a series. The items may be expressed as words, phrases, or clauses.
2. Put a comma between independent clauses when they are joined by *for, and, nor, but, or, yet,* or *so.*
3. Put a comma after an introductory word, phrase, or dependent clause that comes BEFORE an independent clause.
4. Use commas to set off any word, phrase, or dependent clause that is NOT ESSENTIAL to the main idea of the sentence.
5. Use commas to separate coordinate adjectives but not between cumulative adjectives.

Exercise 17.8

Insert the 15 commas that are missing from the following paragraphs.

One of Canada's former prime ministers was John Diefenbaker. According to John Robert Colombo, author of many books about Canada, this was Diefenbaker's favourite story:

Two English ladies were travelling across Canada by train. They admired the Maritime provinces loved Quebec and Ontario and were fascinated by the Prairies. As they travelled across the Prairie provinces they were amazed by the vast openness of the landscape. The bright red sunsets and endless hectares of golden wheat impressed and moved them. Eventually however they began to wonder where they were. One of them decided to ask the conductor so she left the compartment to find him. Having checked the bar car the baggage car and the observation car she finally found him in the dining car and asked for the name of the nearest town. He replied "Saskatoon Saskatchewan." When she returned to her compartment her companion asked her if she had learned where they were. She replied, "No I still don't know where we are but wherever it is they don't speak English!"

18

The Semicolon

The semicolon and the colon are often confused and used as if they were interchangeable. They have distinct purposes, however, and their correct use can dramatically improve a reader's understanding of your writing. The semicolon has three functions.

1. A semicolon can replace a period; in other words, it can appear between two independent clauses.

You should use a semicolon when the two clauses (sentences) you are joining are closely connected in meaning, or when there is a cause-and-effect relationship between them.

I'm too tired; I can't stay awake any longer.

Montreal is not the city's original name; it was once called Ville Marie.

A period could have been used instead of a semicolon in either of these sentences, but the close connection between the clauses makes a semicolon more effective in communicating the writer's meaning.

2. Certain transitional words or phrases can be put between independent clauses to show a cause-and-effect relationship or the continuation of an idea.

Words or phrases used in this way are usually preceded by a semicolon and followed by a comma:

; also,	; furthermore,	; nevertheless,
; as a result,	; however,	; on the other hand,
; besides,	; in addition,	; otherwise,
; consequently,	; in fact,	; then,
; finally,	; instead,	; therefore,
; for example,	; moreover,	; thus,
		; unfortunately,

The forecast called for sun; instead, we got snow.

My monitor went blank; nevertheless, I kept on typing.

"I'm not offended by dumb blonde jokes because I know I'm not dumb; besides, I also know I'm not blonde." (Dolly Parton)

In other words, *a semicolon + a transitional word/phrase + a comma =* a link strong enough to come between two related independent clauses.

Note, however, that, when these transitional words and phrases are used as non-essential expressions rather than as connecting words, they are separated from the rest of the sentence by commas (Chapter 17, Rule 4, page 211).

Your application form, unfortunately, was not completed correctly.

The emissions test, moreover, will ensure that your car is running well.

3. To make a COMPLEX LIST easier to read and understand, put semicolons between the items instead of commas.

A complex list is one in which at least one component part already contains commas. Here are two examples:

I grew up in a series of small towns: Cumberland, British Columbia; Red Deer, Alberta; and Timmins, Ontario.

When we opened the refrigerator, we found a limp, brown head of lettuce; two small containers of yogurt, whose "best before" dates had long since passed; and a hard, dried-up piece of cheddar cheese.

Put a check mark (✓) before the sentences that are correctly punctuated. Answers for exercises in this chapter begin on page 508.

1. _____ We'll have to go soon; for it's getting late.

2. _____ Truth is often stranger than fiction; my experience this morning proves it.

3. _____ I don't remember if my childhood was happy or not; I was only a kid at the time.

4. _____ Here's a book you should read; it's about improving your manners.

5. _____ Make good notes on this topic; for it could be on the exam.

6. _____ If a tree falls in the woods where no one can hear it; does it make a noise?

7. _____ Cooking tasty food is easy; anything with enough garlic in it will be delicious.

8. _____ Invented by a Canadian in the late 19th century; basketball is one of the world's most popular sports.

9. _____ My neighbour works for a high-tech company; but he can't program his own VCR.

10. _____ I think; therefore, I'm single. (Lizz Winstead)

Correct the faulty punctuation in Exercise 18.1.

Insert commas and semicolons where necessary in these sentences, then check your answers.

1. We're late again, this is the third time this week.

2. Kiki is always late, however, she is worth waiting for.

3. The sun is shining, and the temperature has risen 10 degrees; we can finally go to the beach.

4. I've found a delicious-sounding recipe for our dinner party; but you are allergic to two of the ingredients.

5. If you ever need a loan or a helping hand; just call Michel.

6. Travelling in Italy broadens the mind, eating Italian food broadens the behind.

7. North America's oldest continuously run horse race; the Queen's Plate, pre-dates the Kentucky Derby by 15 years.

8. We can't afford dinner at an expensive restaurant, instead, let's have spaghetti and meatballs at home.

9. I am a marvellous housekeeper, every time I leave a man I keep his house. (Zsa Zsa Gabor)

10. A man has to do what a man has to do, a woman must do what he can't. (Feminist saying)

GO TO WEB

EXERCISE 18.1

Exercise 18.4

Correct the punctuation in these sentences by deleting or inserting commas and semicolons where necessary. Check your answers carefully before continuing.

1. An apple a day keeps the doctor away, however an onion a day keeps everyone away.

2. Cash your paycheque right away, this company might be out of business by morning.

3. The telephone has been ringing all day; but there's no one home to take the call.

4. This note says that we are supposed to be at the interview by 9:00 a.m., consequently we'll have to leave home by 7:30.

5. Some people are skilled in many fields, Kumari for example is both a good plumber and a great cook.

6. After staring at a blank screen for half an hour; I decided to play solitaire.

7. The school counsellors maintain that to succeed at this level, you need excellent note-taking skills, organized study habits, and, most of all, good time-management strategies.

8. I know you need this report urgently; but until my computer is fixed, there's nothing I can do.

9. In 1813, Laura Secord trekked 25 km to warn the British and the Canadians of an American attack, her information resulted in victory at the Battle of Beaverdams.

10. Many years later, her name became famous; and a chocolate company was named after her.

Some people are skilled in many fields; Kumari, for example, is both a good plumber and a great cook.

GO TO WEB

EXERCISE 18.2

Exercise 18.5

Have you mastered the semicolon? Try this exercise and find out. Insert semi-colons and change commas to semicolons and semicolons to commas where necessary in the following sentences.

1. Concluding that we weren't really welcome; we left and went to Tim Hortons for coffee.

2. Horton was a native of Cochrane, Ontario, there's a very popular Tim Hortons shop in his home town.

3. He played hockey for the Toronto Maple Leafs at a time when they were league champions, he was a key player on their defensive line.

4. Sadly, Horton was killed in a car accident near St. Catharines, Ontario, while commuting from Toronto to Buffalo.

5. Horton ended his career playing for the Buffalo Sabres, neverthe-less it is as a member of the Toronto Maple Leafs that he is best remembered.

6. The doughnut chain that he started has made his name a household word in Canada and even in parts of the United States.

7. The word "doughnut" is an abbreviated form of the original "dough nought," which means a zero made from dough.

8. Deep-fried in fat and made from starch and sugar, doughnuts tend to pack on the pounds, some Tim Hortons outlets have been obliged to install reinforced seating for their customers.

9. When Tim Hortons became smoke-free, long-time patrons fumed since cigarettes and coffee were thought to go together as naturally as Don

Cherry and bad suits, however, the concept actually increased the chain's popularity.

10. It's sad but true that this icon of the Canadian way of life, named for one of Canada's hockey heroes, is no longer a Canadian corporation, Wendy's bought it in 1995.

19

The Colon

The **colon** functions as an introducer. When a statement is followed by a list, one or more examples, or a quotation, the colon alerts the reader that some sort of explanatory detail is coming up.

When I travel, I am never without three things: sturdy shoes, a money belt, and my laptop.

There is only one enemy we cannot defeat: time.

We have two choices: to study or to fail.

Early in his career, Robert Fulford did not think very highly of intellectual life in Canada: "My generation of Canadians grew up believing that, if we were very good or very smart, or both, we would someday *graduate* from Canada."

The statement that precedes the colon must be a complete sentence (independent clause).

A colon should never come immediately after *is* or *are*. Here's an example of what *not* to write:

The only things I am violently allergic to are: cats, ragweed, and country music.

This is incorrect because the statement before the colon is not a complete sentence.

NEL

> Use a colon between an independent clause and a LIST or one or more EXAMPLES that define, explain, or illustrate the independent clause.

The information after the colon often answers the question "what?" or "who?"

I am violently allergic to three things: (what?) cats, ragweed, and country music.

Business and industry face a new challenge: (what?) offshore outsourcing.

The president has found the ideal candidate for the position: (who?) her brother.

> Use a colon after a complete sentence introducing a quotation.

Lucille Ball observed that there were three secrets to staying young: "Live honestly, eat slowly, and lie about your age."

> Use a colon to separate the title of a book, film, or television show from a subtitle.

Word Play: What Happens When People Talk

Star Wars Episode III: Revenge of the Sith

Trading Spouses: Meet Your New Mommy

If you remember this summary, you'll have no more trouble with colons: the colon follows an independent clause and introduces an example, a list, or a quotation that amplifies the meaning of that clause.

Exercise 19.1

Put a check mark (✓) next to those sentences that are correctly punctuated. Answers for questions in this chapter begin on page 509.

1. _____ The best way to concentrate on what you are reading is to turn off the TV.

2. _____ I stay fit by: cycling and swimming.

3. _____ I read only one kind of book: technical manuals.

4. _____ We agree on the most important things in life: food and music.

5. _____ My car is so badly built that, instead of a warranty, it came with: an apology.

6. _____ There are many species of fish in this lake, including: pike, bass, and walleye.

7. _____ Two common causes of failure are: poor time management and inadequate preparation.

8. _____ Although the results are not yet conclusive, the experiment proved one thing: we're on the right track.

9. _____ This apartment would be perfect if it had more storage, there aren't enough closets, bookshelves, or even drawers.

10. _____ The difference between Canadians and Americans is that: Canadians know there is a difference.

Exercise 19.2

Correct the faulty punctuation in Exercise 19.1.

GO TO WEB

EXERCISE 19.1

Exercise 19.3

Correct the following sentences as necessary.

1. Our dog knows only one trick, pretending to be deaf.

2. Let me give you an example of a female role model, Adrienne Clarkson.

3. If at first you don't succeed: become a consultant and teach someone else.

4. There is a reason I have always felt my little brother was a mean, spiteful child, he always hit me back.

5. Leila spends too much time: shopping at the malls, talking on the phone, and watching TV.

6. My roommate loved *Kill Bill; Vol. 1* and *Kill Bill; Vol. 2*, and I hated them both.

7. Your research paper lacks three important features; a title page, a Works Cited page, and some content in between.

8. The shortstop on our baseball team caught only one thing all season, a cold.

9. My mother always wanted a successful son, so I did my part, I urged her to have more children.

10. Every time I go to a club, I can hear my mother's warning "Don't pick that up! You don't know where it's been."

GO TO WEB

EXERCISE 19.2

Exercise 19.4

As a test of your ability to use colons and semicolons properly, correct these sentences where necessary. There are 10 errors in this exercise.

1. Born in Owen Sound, Ontario, one of Canada's most famous World War I heroes became the Allies' greatest fighter pilot; Billy Bishop.

2. By the age of 23, Bishop had shot down 47 enemy aircraft and had survived an encounter with the greatest of all German pilots in the war, a man known as: "The Red Baron."

3. Credited with 72 victories in air battles, Bishop was awarded Britain's highest military honour; the Victoria Cross.

4. Bishop won the Victoria Cross for a daring, single-handed raid on a German airfield in: June, 1917.

5. His last victory came a year later when, in a single day, he accomplished an amazing feat he shot down five enemy aircraft.

6. One of his fellow pilots once described him as: "a fantastic shot, but a terrible pilot."

7. During World War II, Bishop was an honorary air marshal in the organization he helped to create; the Royal Canadian Air Force.

8. His daughter and son both served in the RCAF during World War II: in his role as Honorary Air Marshal, Bishop proudly presented them with the medals they had earned during the conflict.

9. In 1982, the National Film Board released a documentary that challenged many of Bishop's claims: it even suggested that he didn't make the famous attack on the German airfield for which he had been awarded the Victoria Cross.

10. So what was the real Billy Bishop; hero or fraud? Only time will tell.

Exercise 19.5

The following paragraph will test all you have learned in the last three chapters. Insert commas, semicolons, and colons where appropriate in this passage. There are 15 errors.

Imagine if you can Mario's surprise on being told that he had won a big prize in the lottery, one million dollars. At first he didn't believe it it was simply too good to be true. Once the reality had sunk in however he began to make plans for his fortune. As he thought about how to spend the money he kept one goal in mind "I want to help others as well as myself." He talked to the counsellors at the college who advised him that setting up a scholarship would be a good use of his funds. Every year five thousand dollars would go to three students who were doing well in school but who couldn't afford to continue with their education without assistance. It was a perfect way for Mario to share his good fortune with others. Of course he also bought himself the car of his dreams a sleek silver Porsche.

20

Quotation Marks

Quotation marks (" ") are used to set off short passages of quoted material and some titles. They are a signal to the reader that the words in quotation marks are not yours but someone else's. Quotation marks come in pairs; there must be a set to show where the quotation or title begins and a set to show where it ends. You must be certain that whatever appears in quotation marks is stated *exactly* as it is in the source you are using.[1] The only other thing you need to know about quotation marks is the punctuation needed to introduce and conclude them.

Quoted Material

When you quote a **short passage** (three lines of print or less), you can work it into your own sentence using appropriate punctuation.[2]

---

[1] If you wish to omit a word or words and can do so without changing the meaning of the original, use ellipses (three spaced dots: . . .) to indicate the omission. If you need to add or change a word (e.g., to maintain tense consistency), put square brackets [ ] around the change. See www.essentialsplus3e.nelson.com for information on how to format and document a research paper in MLA and APA styles.

[2] Please note that quotations cannot simply be dropped into your paragraphs. Every quotation must be introduced, usually in a phrase or clause that identifies the author. The examples on pages 233–34 demonstrate several different ways to introduce a quotation.

1. Normally, you use a short phrase and a comma to mark off a quotation of one or more sentences. Put your quotation marks at the beginning and end of the passage you are quoting, including the end punctuation mark.

   > According to Margaret Atwood, "If you like men, you can like Americans. Cautiously. Selectively. Beginning with the feet. One at a time."

   > "As you grow old," wrote Richard Needham, "you lose your interest in sex, your friends drift away, your children ignore you. There are other advantages, of course, but these would seem to me the outstanding ones."

   > "My idea of long-range planning is lunch," confesses Frank Ogden, Canada's foremost futurist.

2. If your own introductory words form a complete sentence, use a colon to introduce the quotation.

   > Frank Ogden, Canada's foremost futurist, confesses that he has little respect for traditional business-planning cycles: "My idea of long-range planning is lunch."

This year's winner of the Wacky Warning Label Contest is "Never iron clothes while they are being worn."

3. If the passage you are quoting is a couple of words, a phrase, or anything less than a complete sentence, do not use any punctuation to introduce it.

> Woody Allen claims his one regret in life is that he is "not someone else."

> Neil Bissoondath argues that racism is based on "willful ignorance and an acceptance of—and comfort with—stereotype."

4. A quotation *within* a quotation is punctuated by single quotation marks.

> According to John Robert Colombo, "the most widely quoted Canadian aphorism of all time is Marshall McLuhan's 'The medium is the message.' "

All lines of a **long quotation** (more than three lines of print) should be indented 10 spaces from the left margin. (Long quotations are NOT enclosed in quotation marks.)

The block indentation indicates to the reader that the words set off in this way are not yours but some other writer's. (Turn to page 435 for an example of how to treat a long quotation.)

College writing normally requires that you indicate the source of any material you quote. The easiest way to do this is to give the author's surname (if it's not already included in your sentence) and the page reference in parentheses at the end of the quotation.

For example:

> An American humorist once noted, "I never let schooling interfere with my education" (Twain 97).

> American humorist Mark Twain once observed, "I never let schooling interfere with my education" (97).

These source identifications are called *parenthetical citations*. For further information on format and documentation, see our Web site at www.essentialsplus3e.nelson.com.

Some instructors prefer footnotes or endnotes to parenthetical citations. Find out what format your instructor requires and follow it. Some institutions are very particular about documentation, so you would be wise to ask your instructor which style to use.

As a general rule, if you are writing a paper for a humanities course and need more details than we provide on our Web site, we suggest you consult Joseph Gibaldi, *MLA Handbook for Writers of Research Papers*, 6th ed. (New York: MLA, 2003), available in paperback, or access the MLA Web site at www.mla.org. You can also check out www.ccc.commnet.edu/mla, which includes a link to an online book that provides guidance on how to cite electronic sources.

For papers in the social sciences, the standard source is the *Publication Manual of the American Psychological Association*, 5th ed. (Washington, DC: APA, 2001) available in paperback. Check www.apastyle.org or www.ccc.commnet.edu/apa for specific details on using APA style, including instruction on citing electronic and online information.

The information and exercises that follow are based on MLA format.

Exercise 20.1

In the following sentences, place quotation marks where they are needed and insert any necessary punctuation before and after each quotation. Answers for this chapter begin on page 510.

1. The most famous quotation in the history of Canadian sports is Foster Hewitt's He shoots! He scores!

2. The beaver, Canada's national animal, was once described by Michael Kesterton as a distant relative of the sewer rat.

3. In the opinion of writer Barry Callaghan We Canadians have raised being boring to an art form.

4. All we want, said Yvon Deschamps, is an independent Quebec within a strong and united Canada.

5. Pierre Berton summed up the difference between Canadians and Americans as follows You ask an American how he's feeling, and he cries Great! You ask a Canadian, and he answers Not bad, or Pas mal.

Titles

Titles of books or other entire works should be *italicized* or <u>underlined</u>.

Titles of parts of books or other works should be put in quotation marks.

The title of anything that is published or produced as a separate entity (e.g., books, magazines, newspapers, pamphlets, plays, films, TV shows, albums) should be italicized or underlined. The title of anything that has been published or produced as part of a separate entity (e.g., articles, essays, stories, poems, a single episode of a TV series, songs) should be placed in quotation marks.

Why the difference? The way you punctuate a title tells your reader what sort of document you are quoting from or referring to: it may be a complete work that the reader can find listed by title, author, or subject in a library, or it may be an excerpt that the reader can find only by looking up the name of the work in which it was published.

Below is an example of a bibliography—a list of works consulted or cited (referred to) in a research paper—showing how titles of different kinds of publications are punctuated.

Works Cited

Book	Baldassare, Angela. *Reel Canadians: Interviews from the Canadian Film World.* Toronto: Guernica Editions, 2003.
Newspaper article in an online database	Craven, Aaron. "Terrific Canadian Films Deserve Bigger Audiences." *Vancouver Sun* 24 July 2004. Online: eLibrary Canada. 30 August 2004.
Article in an online journal	Globerman, Steven. "Foreign Ownership of Feature Film Distribution and the Canadian Film Industry." *Canadian Journal of Communication* 16.2 (1991). 1 Sept. 2004 <http://www.wlu.ca/~wwwpress/jrls/cjc/BackIssues/16.2/glober.html>.
CD-ROM citation	Handling, Piers. "Denys Arcand." *The Canadian Encyclopedia Plus.* CD-ROM. Toronto: McClelland & Stewart, 1996.

Newspaper article	Natali, Vincenzo. "Canadian Film Industry Blues Series: Summer Diaries." *National Post* 5 August 2004: AL5.
Article in a magazine from an online database	Seguin, Denis. "I Think I Cannes." *Canadian Business* 8 July 2002: 102. Online: EBSCO. Canadian Reference Centre. 10 Sept. 2004.
Government Web site	"Through the Lens: Exporting Canadian Film and Animation." 15 Oct. 2004 <http://www.dfait-maeci.gc.ca/latinamerica/wn-04-canadian-films-en.asp>.
Television program	"What Border? The Americanization of Canada, Part IV: Battle at the Box Office." *The National Magazine.* Prod. Jill Offman. CBC. 26 Sept. 2003.

Exercise 20.2

Insert the necessary punctuation (quotation marks or italics or underlining) in the following sentences. Check your answers before continuing.

1. My favourite chapter in William Safire's book How Not to Write is Chapter 14, Don't Use No Double Negatives.

2. Canada's national anthem is derived from a French song, Chant national, which was first performed in Quebec City in 1880.

3. O Canada, the English version of Chant national, was written by R. Stanley Weir, a Montreal judge and poet, and was first performed in 1908.

4. In Shakespeare's play The Winter's Tale, there is a peculiar stage direction that has baffled scholars for 400 years: Exit, pursued by a bear.

5. Crouching Toad, Hidden Lizard, a humorous documentary made by our college's television students, was shown on the CBC program Short Shots.

6. The video documentary A War of Their Own is the story of the Canadian troops in World War II who fought in the long, bloody Italian campaign.

7. The CD Sparkjiver features some great blues songs, such as Harlem Nocturne and Try a Little Tenderness, performed by an unusual trio of electric organ, sax, and drums.

8. Go to The Globe and Mail's Web page if you want to follow the links to Steve Galea's article Thunder in the Snow, which describes the appeal and the dangers of snowmobiling.

9. The Diana Krall album When I Look in Your Eyes has three of my favourite jazz vocals: Devil May Care, I Can't Give You Anything But Love, and Do It Again.

10. The Outdoors Channel is playing reruns of old Survivor episodes to show viewers, as TV Guide puts it, how to live off the land while surrounded by cameras, microphones, TV technicians, and an obnoxious host.

GO TO WEB

EXERCISES 20.1, 20.2

Exercise 20.3

This exercise is designed to test your understanding of how to punctuate short quotations and titles in your writing. When and where do you use quotation marks? Italics (or underlining)? Which punctuation marks precede and follow a quotation?

1. For me, the most helpful chapter of The Bare Essentials Plus is Cracking the Sentence Code.

2. In their book How to Be a Canadian, Will and Ian Ferguson have a chapter entitled How the Canadian Government Works. The chapter consists of only two words: It doesn't.

3. One of Pierre Trudeau's lesser-known statements describes the Liberal Party We are the extreme centre, the radical middle. That is our position.

4. We are all immigrants to this place wrote Margaret Atwood even if we were born here.

5. A jury, in the words of the great American poet, Robert Frost, consists of 12 persons chosen to decide who has the better lawyer.

6. My current favourite pop single is Natasha Gnostic's hit, So Many Men, So Few Who Can Afford Me from her CD Coffee, Chocolate, Men . . . Some Things Are Just Better Rich.

7. An article on overcrowding in Canada's colleges and universities, called The University Crunch, can be found on Maclean's magazine Web site: www.macleans.ca.

8. A few years ago, on CBC Television's program Hockey Night in Canada, Don Cherry informed his audience Most guys that wear visors are Europeans and French guys.

9. In the film Bowling for Columbine, one of the funniest moments occurred when Michael Moore asked a young Sarnia resident what he would do if he was really angry with someone, and the teenager replied I dunno. I guess we'd tease him or something.

10. The last word on growing up goes to American humorist Mark Twain, in this famous observation When I was a boy of 14, my father was so ignorant. When I got to be 21, I was amazed to see how much he'd learned in seven years.

21

Question Marks, Exclamation Marks, and Punctuation Review

The Question Mark

Everyone knows that a **question mark** follows an interrogative, or asking, sentence, but we all sometimes forget to include it. Let this chapter serve as a reminder not to forget!

Put a question mark at the end of every interrogative sentence.

The question mark gives your readers an important clue to the meaning of your sentence. "There's more?" (interrogative) means something quite different from "There's more!"(exclamatory), and both are different from "There's more."(declarative). When you speak, your tone of voice conveys the meaning you intend; when you write, your punctuation tells your reader what you mean.

The only time you don't end a question with a question mark is when the question is part of a statement.

Question	Statement
Are you going?	I asked whether you were going.
Do you know them?	I wonder if you know them.
Is there enough evidence to convict him?	The jury deliberated whether there was enough evidence to convict him.

Exercise 21.1

Put a check mark (✓) before each sentence that is correctly punctuated. Answers for exercises in this chapter begin on page 511.

1. _____ Who's on first?

2. _____ I want to know what's going on?

3. _____ Why do they bother to report power outages on TV.

4. _____ Were you aware that half of the population is below average?

5. _____ If corn oil comes from corn, I wonder where baby oil comes from?

6. _____ We question your conclusions.

7. _____ I'm curious about where you plan to go for your vacation?

8. _____ Theo wanted to know if Maria was going to the concert?

9. _____ Do you know another word for *thesaurus*.

10. _____ As a Canadian, I often wonder if God ever considered having snow fall up?

GO TO WEB

EXERCISE 21.1

Exercise 21.2

Revise the sentences in Exercise 21.1 that were incorrect.

The Exclamation Mark

Consider the difference in tone between these two sentences:

There's a man behind you.
There's a man behind you!

In the first sentence, information is being supplied, perhaps about the line of people waiting their turn at a grocery store checkout counter. The second sentence might be a shouted warning about a mugger.

Use an **exclamation mark** as end punctuation only in sentences requiring extreme emphasis or dramatic effect.

Note that the exclamation mark will have "punch" (dramatic effect) only if you use it sparingly. If you use an exclamation mark after every other sentence, how will your readers know when you really mean to indicate excitement? Overuse of exclamation marks is a technique used by comic book writers to try to heighten the impact of their characters' words. Ironically, the effect is to neutralize the impact. You will seldom find exclamation marks in academic or business writing.

Practically any sentence could have an exclamation mark after it, but remember that the punctuation changes the meaning of the sentence. Read the following sentences with and without an exclamation mark, and picture the situation that would call for each reading.

They've moved   Don't touch that button
The file was empty   Listen to that noise

Exercise 21.3

Supply the necessary punctuation in the following sentences. Then compare your answers with our suggestions. (Answers will vary, depending on the tone and impact the writer wants to convey.)

1. I quit
2. Stop thief
3. Don't you dare
4. He's on the stairway right behind you
5. We won I can't believe it
6. Brandishing her new credit card, Tessa marched through the mall shouting, "Charge it "
7. Take the money and run
8. I can't believe it's over

Exercise 21.4

Using a variety of punctuation marks (periods, question marks, and exclamation marks), supply appropriate end punctuation in the following sentences. Then compare your answers with our suggestions.

1. The question was whether it would be better to stay in bed or to go to the clinic
2. Gregory asked Nell if she had ever been to Nanaimo
3. Hurry, or we'll be late
4. Did you ever notice that the early bird gets the worm, but the second mouse gets the cheese
5. Just imagine   In only three hours, they are going to draw my ticket number in the lottery
6. Is it true that those who live by the sword get shot by those who don't
7. Stop Do you want to be arrested for running a red light
8. Shoot the puck   Why won't he shoot the puck

Exercise 21.5

Supply appropriate punctuation for the 15 sentences in the following paragraph.

(1) I wonder why it is that I cannot dance (2) My girlfriend would go out dancing every night of the week if she didn't have morning classes (3) And can she ever dance (4) When she is really into the music, I've seen her

receive applause from an entire club as she leaves the dance floor (5) They applaud me, too, but it's because they're glad to see me sit down (6) Why is it that every part of my body moves to a different rhythm (7) When my hips find the beat, my feet are half a beat behind, and my shoulders move around on their own as if I had some horrible nervous disorder (8) Is it because I'm tall, and nerve impulses have to travel a long way to get from one part of my frame to another (9) I've been told that, when dancing, I look like a stork with an uncontrollable itch in a vital part of its anatomy (10) Talk about embarrassing (11) "What can I do " I ask myself (12) Should I subject myself to weeks of torture and take dancing lessons when I suspect they wouldn't help in the least (13) Is there no medical cure for my condition (14) I must have been born without a rhythm gene (15) I wonder if it's too late to get a transplant

Punctuation Review

The exercises that follow are designed to test your knowledge of the punctuation marks you have studied in Unit 4. All of the sentences below contain errors: punctuation is either missing or misused. Work through the exercises slowly and carefully. Check your answers before continuing. If you make a mistake, go back to the chapter that deals with the punctuation mark you missed, and review the explanation and examples. If you're still confused, log on to the Web site for *Bare Essentials Plus* and ask the authors to help you solve your problem.

Exercise 21.6

There are 30 errors in this exercise. (Each incorrect punctuation mark counts as one error; each incorrect set of quotation marks also counts as one error.)

1. If you want to make your living as a comedian you must: remember the punch line.

2. Good health, according to my doctor, should be defined as: the slowest possible rate at which one can die.

3. The fast pace of life doesn't bother me, it's the sudden stop at the end that has me worried.

4. This new fad diet can be summed up in a single sentence If it tastes good, don't eat it.

5. Many years ago Mark Twain warned us Be careful about reading health books, you may die of a misprint.

6. My brother doesn't think much of a healthy lifestyle; he often says, Eat well, exercise regularly and die anyway.

7. Don't worry about avoiding temptation advised Winston Churchill. As you grow older, it will avoid you.

8. Did you know that Irish coffee is the perfect food. It provides in a single glass all four essential food groups; alcohol caffeine sugar and fat.

9. The prescription for a healthy life is well known eat a balanced diet, get regular exercise, even if it's just a five-minute walk each day, get regular checkups, and avoid stress.

10. Columbus first encountered turkeys, which were unknown in Europe at that time, on an island off the coast of Honduras, he was served roast turkey by the Native peoples. According to Margaret Visser author of The Rituals of Dinner At ceremonial feasts, the Spaniards were served huge tamales containing a whole turkey each.

GO TO WEB

EXERCISE 21.2

Exercise 21.7

Insert the 25 punctuation marks that are missing in the following passage. You will need to use at least one colon, semicolon, question mark, and exclamation mark in addition to quotation marks and numerous commas.

Comparing the computer industry and the auto industry Bill Gates once said If GM had kept up with technology [the way] the computer industry has, we would all be driving $25 cars that got 1,000 miles to the gallon. In response to Mr. Gates' comment General Motors issued the following press release

• If GM had developed technology like Microsoft your car would crash twice daily.

• Every time the lines on the road were repainted you would have to buy a new car.

• Occasionally, executing a manoeuvre such as a left turn would cause your car to shut down and refuse to start you would then have to reinstall the engine.

• Only one person could use the car unless you bought Car XP and then you would have to buy more seats.

• Macintosh would make a car that was reliable solar-powered five times as fast and twice as easy to drive.

• The oil temperature and alternator warning lights would be replaced by one "general car default" warning light.

• The air bag system would ask Are you sure before going off.

• Occasionally for no reason whatsoever your car would lock you out and refuse to let you in until you simultaneously lifted the door handle turned the key and grabbed hold of the radio antenna.

- Every time GM introduced a new model buyers would have to learn how to drive all over again because none of the controls would operate the way they did on the previous model.
- And finally to shut off the engine you'd have to press the "start" button.

Adapted from *MUFA Newsletter*, October 2003.

Supply the 15 punctuation marks that are missing in the following passage. (*Note*: Each pair of quotation marks counts as one punctuation mark.)

[1]A well-known Canadian politician was asked to make a major speech to the executives of Canada's major banks. [2]Since his staff included a professional speechwriter he called her into his office and outlined for her the background of his audience the policies and programs he wanted to talk about and the tone and approach he thought were appropriate for the occasion. [3]The speechwriter asked only one question she wanted to know how long the speech should be. [4]The politician told her that the speech should be exactly 20 minutes long. [5]Knowing how important this address would be for her boss the writer went right to work she stayed late to draft what she thought was a masterpiece.

[6]On the day after the big speech the writer was at her desk early she was curious to learn how her speech had been received. [7]When her boss called she could tell from the tone of his voice that he was very angry. [8]The speech

was a disaster he bellowed. [9]I asked for a 20-minute speech, not a 60-minute speech. [10]Before I was finished half the audience had left the hall, and most of the others were asleep. [11]The writer replied that she had given him exactly what he had asked for notes for a 20-minute speech and two copies.

Paragraphs and Essays

22 Finding Something to Write About

Choose a Satisfactory Subject

Discover Your Thesis and Main Points

Testing Your Main Points

Organizing Your Main Points

23 The Thesis Statement

24 The Outline

Scratch Outline

Informal Outline

Formal Outline

25 Paragraphs

Developing Your Paragraphs

Writing Introductions and Conclusions

Keeping Your Reader with You

Transitions

Tone

26 Revising Your Paper

What Is Revision?

Step 1: Revise Content and Organization

Step 2: Revise Paragraphs and Sentences

Step 3: Edit and Proofread

Tips for Effective Proofreading

22

Finding Something to Write About

Every writer knows that content is important. Not as many seem to know that form is just as important. In fact, you can't really separate the two: *what you say is how you say it.* Writing a paper (or an essay, a report, a letter, or anything else) is like doing a chemistry experiment: you need the right amount of the right ingredients put together in the right proportions and in the right order. There are five steps to follow.

1. Choose a satisfactory subject.
2. Discover your thesis and main points.
3. Write a thesis statement and/or an outline.
4. Write the paragraphs.
5. Revise the paper.

If you follow these steps faithfully, in order, we guarantee that you will write clear, organized papers.

Note that, when you get to step 3, you have a choice. You can choose to plan your paper with a thesis statement, or with an outline, or with both. The thesis statement approach works well for short papers—about 500 words or less. An outline is necessary for longer papers. Ideally, you should learn to use both methods of organizing your writing. In fact, your teacher may require that you do so.

Steps 1, 2, and 3 make up the planning stage of the writing process. Be warned: done properly, these three steps will take you at least as long as steps 4 and 5, which involve the actual writing. The longer you spend on planning, the less time you'll spend on drafting and revising, and the better your paper will be.

Choose a Satisfactory Subject

Unless you are assigned a specific subject by a teacher or supervisor, choosing your subject can be the most difficult part of writing a paper. Apply the following guidelines carefully, because no amount of instruction can help you to write a good paper on something you don't know anything about or on something that is inappropriate for your audience or purpose. Your subject should satisfy the **4-S test**.

A satisfactory subject is SIGNIFICANT, SINGLE, SPECIFIC, and SUPPORTABLE.

1. Your subject should be **significant**. Write about something that your reader needs or might want to know. Consider your audience and choose a subject that they will find significant. This doesn't mean that you can't ever be humorous, but, unless you're another Stephen Leacock, an essay on "How I Deposit Money in My Bank" will probably be of little significance to your readers. The subject you choose must be worthy of the time and attention you expect your readers to give to your paper.

2. Your subject should be **single**. Don't try to cover too much in your paper. A thorough discussion of one topic is more satisfying to a reader than a skimpy, superficial treatment of several topics. A subject such as "The challenge of government funding cutbacks to colleges and universities" includes too much to deal with in one paper. Limit yourself to a single topic, such as "How private sector donations are helping our college meet the challenge of funding cutbacks."

3. Your subject should be **specific**. This requirement is closely tied to the "single" requirement. Given a choice between a general topic and a specific one, you should choose the latter. In a short paper, you can't hope to say anything new or significant about a large topic: "Employment opportunities in Canada," for example. But you could write an interesting, detailed discussion on a more specific topic, such as "Employment opportunities in Quebec's hospitality industry."

   You can narrow a broad subject by applying one or more **limiting factors** to it. Try thinking of your subject in terms of a specific *kind*, or *time*, or *place*, or *number*, or *person* associated with it. To come up with the hospitality topic, for example, we limited the subject of employment opportunities in Canada in terms of both place and kind.

4. Your subject must be **supportable**. You must know something about the subject (preferably, more than your reader does), or you must be able to find out about it. Your discussion of your subject will be clear and convincing only if you can include examples, facts, quotations, descriptions, anecdotes, and other details. Supporting evidence can be taken from your own experience or from the experience of other people. In other words, your topic may require you to do some research.[1]

Exercise 22.1

Imagine that you have been asked to write a 500-word paper and given this list of subjects to choose from. Test each subject against the 4-S guidelines and identify what's wrong with it. Answers for exercises in this chapter begin on page 513.

1. The theory of evolution
2. The five senses
3. Caring for your cuticles
4. The positive and negative effects of TV on children under 12
5. My best friend: my dog
6. Career opportunities in banking and financial advising
7. Democracy is good
8. Problems our children will face as parents
9. How to parachute or bungee-jump safely
10. On-the-job training

Exercise 22.2

Apply the 4-S guidelines to the following subjects. Some are possibilities for short papers (300 to 500 words) but fail to satisfy one or more of the guidelines. Others are hopeless. Revise the "possible" subjects to make them significant, single, specific, and supportable.

1. Water is necessary to life
2. Some people are very attractive
3. The proper way to stack the dishwasher

---

[1] Many colleges and most universities require students to write formal research papers in their first year. The five steps to essay writing that we outline in this unit apply to research papers as well as to informal and in-class essays. In addition, a research paper requires that you find and use information from sources in your essay, and that you format and document your paper according to specific guidelines. Go to www.essentialsplus3e.nelson.com to find out how to produce a paper in MLA or APA documentation style—the two styles most frequently required in courses at the undergraduate level.

4. The Russian economy
5. Canadian women worth knowing
6. How to mix paint
7. Predicting the future
8. The challenges facing Canada's immigrants

Exercise 22.3

List three subjects that you might choose to write about. Be sure each subject is SIGNIFICANT, SINGLE, SPECIFIC, and SUPPORTABLE.

Discover Your Thesis and Main Points

Once you've chosen a suitable subject for your paper, you need to decide what you want to say about it. There are many possible ways of thinking and writing about any subject. In a short paper, you can deal effectively with only a few aspects of your topic. How do you decide what approach to take?

The approach to your subject that you choose is your **thesis**: a thesis is an *idea about a limited subject*. It is an opinion or point of view that needs to be explained or proved. A thesis is not a statement of fact. Compare the examples that follow.

Fact	Thesis
Most people experience some anxiety when they begin a first job.	The stress I experienced in my first job was caused by my employer, my co-workers, and—surprisingly—myself. (Needs to be explained.)
For several years, Canada ranked first on the UN's list of the world's best countries to live in.	Canadians don't know how lucky they are. (Needs to be explained.)
Some universities do not require students to demonstrate writing before graduation.	All universities should require students to demonstrate writing competence before graduation. (Needs to be proved.)

| Among the G8 countries, Canadians pay the highest percentage of their income in taxes. | Canadians are overtaxed. (Needs to be proved.) |

A thesis can be discovered in several ways. Brainstorming, freewriting, listing, and clustering are strategies that many college students are familiar with from high school. You should continue to use any technique you've learned that produces results. Some students, however, need a more structured approach to discovering what it is they can and want to say about a subject.

If none of the informal approaches you've experimented with works for you, you can try questioning—asking lead-in questions about your subject. A lead-in question is one that guides you into your subject by pointing to an angle or viewpoint—a thesis—that you can explore in your paper. The answers to your lead-in question become the main points your paper will explain.

Six Questions to Ask about Your Subject

1. How can my subject be defined or explained? What are its significant features or characteristics? Examples: "Anorexia," "HD-TV," "The Canadian personality"
2. How is my subject made or done? How does it work? Examples: "How to choose the right college," "Detailing a car," "How to install a motherboard"
3. What are the main kinds, components, or functions of my subject? Examples: "Internet addicts," "An affordable home theatre system," "What does a floor director do?"
4. What are the main similarities and/or differences between my subject and _____? Examples: "Toyota and Honda hybrid systems," "A fan's view of professional vs. amateur hockey," "The major differences between a diploma and an apprenticeship program"
5. What are the causes or effects of my subject? Examples: "Why parents and teenagers disagree," "The causes of ADD," "The effects of coal-burning power generation"
6. What are the advantages or disadvantages of my subject? What are the reasons for or against it? Examples: "Our city's new recycling program," "SUVs should be banned from our highways," "My home is a TV-free zone"

These questions suggest some common ways of looking at or thinking about a subject. Some questions will yield better results than others, and most subjects will produce answers to more than one of the questions. Choose the question that produces the answers you can or want to write most about for your subject.

Here's an example of how the process works. Let's assume you've been asked to write a paper on the topic "A satisfying career."[2] Apply each question to your subject and make notes of the answers.

1. "What is a satisfying career?" What are its significant features or characteristics?
   This question produces useful answers. Answers might include a career that is interesting, highly paid, respected, and provides opportunities for advancement.

2. "How is a satisfying career made or chosen?"
   This question would also work. Some answers might include self-analysis, career counselling, experience (perhaps through part-time work), research, or taking aptitude tests.

3. "What are the main parts or components of a satisfying career?"
   We could use this question, too. The components of a satisfying career might include good pay, compatible co-workers, respect in the community, and challenging work.

4. "How is a satisfying career different from something else?"
   This question has limited possibilities. We could develop a contrast between a satisfying career and an unsatisfying one, but there isn't much new to say. The main points are fairly obvious and could be explained more easily in response to question 1 than question 4.

5. "Does a satisfying career have causes or effects?"
   It has both.

   "What causes a satisfying career?"
   Preparation, planning, self-analysis.

   "What are the effects of a satisfying career?"
   Confidence, stability, recognition, happiness.

---

[2] If your subject has been assigned, don't grumble—be grateful. The way your instructor has worded the assignment may contain information that will help you decide what approach to take. Assignment instructions usually contain "direction words," which are reliable clues to the kind of paper your instructor is looking for. For example, *define* points you to question 1; *describe* means you should apply questions 1 and 2; *discuss* and *explain* tell you to apply questions 3, 4, 5, and possibly 6; and *evaluate* points you to question 6.

6. "What are the advantages or disadvantages of a satisfying career?" Unless you can think of some unusual advantages (i.e., ones that are not covered by the answers to question 3), this question doesn't produce answers that are worth spending your or your readers' time on. We've already discovered the advantages in answering question 3, and there aren't many disadvantages to a satisfying career!

Asking these six questions about your subject will help you decide what approach would be best for your paper. The "best" approach is the one that is most original and most logical: the main points your paper discusses should not only seem fresh to your readers but also sound reasonable to an educated audience. The questioning strategy we've outlined above will (1) help you define your thesis by identifying the point of view you can best explain or defend and (2) put you on the path to drafting your paper by providing some solid main points to work with. Don't rush this process. The more time you spend exploring your subject in the planning stage, the easier the actual drafting of the paper will be.

Below you will find eight sample subjects, together with main points that were discovered by applying the questions on page 256. Study these examples carefully. Figure out the logic that leads from subject to question to main points in each case. When you're finished, you should have a good understanding of how the questioning process can work for you.

Subject	Selected Question	Main Points
A good teacher	1. What are the characteristics of a good teacher?	• knowledge of subject • ability to communicate • respect for students
The hybrid automobile	1. What are the features of a hybrid car?	• gas engine for high speeds • electric engine for low speeds • momentum from gas engine and brakes to recharge batteries
A successful party	2. How do you give a successful party?	• invite the right mix of people • plan the entertainment • prepare the food in advance • provide a relaxed, friendly atmosphere

Subject	Selected Question	Main Points
Internet users	3. What are the main categories of Internet users?	• dabblers • regulars • addicts
Quitting smoking	3. What are the main ways to quit smoking?	• cold turkey • taper off gradually • medical/chemical support (pills, gum, patch)
Refugees in Canada	5. What are the main causes of refugees coming to Canada?	• persecution in homeland • war in homeland • poverty in homeland
Nursing as a career	6. What are the main advantages of a career in nursing?	• opportunities to help people • opportunities for travel • career security
Cellphones	6. What are the main disadvantages of using cellphones?	• prevent escape from work • create disturbance in theatres, restaurants, etc. • put drivers at risk • possible medical hazard

As a general rule, you should try to identify between *two* (the absolute minimum) and *five* main ideas to support your subject. If you have only one main idea, your subject is suitable for a paragraph or two, not for an essay. If you have discovered more than five main ideas that require discussion, you have too much material for a short paper. Either select the most important aspects of the subject, or take another look at it to see how you can focus it more specifically.

Exercise 22.4

In this exercise, select a question from the highlighted list on page 256 and generate good main points for each subject.

Subject	Selected Question	Main Points
1. Internet search engines	•	• • •

Subject	Selected Question	Main Points
2. Owning a car vs. using public transit	•	• • •
3. My family's (or my ancestor's) immigration to Canada	•	• • •
4. Leaving home	•	• • •
5. Holding a part-time job while going to college	•	• • •
6. Hip hop (or another kind of music)	•	• • •
7. Blogs (Web logs)	•	• • •
8. Co-op programs	•	• • •

Exercise 22.5

For each of the three subjects you chose in Exercise 22.3, list two to five main points. To discover suitable main points, apply to your subject the six questions highlighted on page 256, one at a time, until you find the question that fits best. The answers to that question are your main points.

TESTING YOUR MAIN POINTS

Now take a close look at the main points you've chosen for each subject in Exercise 22.5. It may be necessary to revise some of them before going any further. Are some points too trivial to bother with? Do any of the points overlap in meaning? Are there any points that are not directly related to the subject?

Main points must be SIGNIFICANT, DISTINCT, and RELEVANT.

To be satisfactory, the main points you have chosen to write about must all be **significant**: they must require a paragraph or more of explanation. If you have any trivial ideas mixed in with the important ones, now is the time to discard them.

Each of the main points you've chosen must also be **distinct**. That is, each must be different from all the others. There must be no overlap in meaning. Check to be sure you haven't given two different labels to what is really one aspect of the subject.

Finally, each main point must be **relevant**: it must be clearly **related** to the subject. It must be an aspect of the subject you are writing about, not some other subject. For example, if you're writing about the advantages of a subject, cross out any disadvantages that may have appeared on your list.

Exercise 22.6

Each of the following subjects is followed by some possible main points. Circle the unsatisfactory point(s) in each group.

1. Popular Canadian sports teams
   - Toronto Blue Jays
   - Winnipeg Blue Bombers
   - Montreal Canadiens
   - Seattle Mariners
   - Hamilton Tiger Cats

2. The advantages of being physically fit
- improved muscle tone
- improved looks
- improved stamina
- improved appearance
- improved social life

3. Problems faced by new immigrants in Canada
- travelling
- finding suitable work
- shovelling snow
- learning a new language
- finding a suitable place to live
- adjusting to the climate

4. Dangerous weather systems
- hurricanes
- blizzards
- tornadoes
- earthquakes
- typhoons

5. Reasons for drug abuse among adolescents
- peer pressure
- school pressure
- alcohol
- boredom

6. The main kinds of daytime television
- talk shows
- quiz shows
- soap operas
- Oprah Winfrey
- game shows

7. Characteristics of sharks
- tiny brains
- white shark
- skeletal system is cartilage
- several sets of needle-sharp teeth
- hammerhead shark
- not all are dangerous to humans

8. Lower taxes stimulate the economy

- businesses have more money to hire workers
- individuals have more money to buy goods and services
- low-tax economic environment attracts foreign investment
- government has less money to spend on social services

GO TO WEB

EXERCISE 22.1

Exercise 22.7

Study the main points you chose in Exercise 22.5 on page 261. Cross out any that are not *significant*, *distinct*, or *relevant* to the subject. If necessary, add new main points so that you end up with at least three main points for each subject.

ORGANIZING YOUR MAIN POINTS

Now that you've decided on three or four main points to discuss, you need to decide on the order in which to present them in your paper. Choose the order that is most appropriate for your particular subject.

There are four basic ways to arrange main points in an essay: CHRONOLOGICAL, CLIMACTIC, LOGICALLY LINKED, and RANDOM order.

In writing, as in life, it's important to do first things first.

1. **Chronological order** means in order of time sequence, from first to last. Here's an example:

Subject	Main Points
The development of a relationship	• attraction • meeting • discovery • intimacy • disillusionment

2. **Climactic order** means presenting your strongest or most important point last. Generally, you would discuss your second-strongest point first and the others in between, like this:

Subject	Main Points
Reasons for the federal government to legislate lower gas emissions	• airborne pollutants put health of individual Canadians at risk • damage to trees hurts the economy • our emissions affect the U.S. individually and collectively • global warming, caused by gas emissions, threatens our existence

3. **Logically linked order** means that the main points are connected in such a way that one point must be explained before the next can be understood. Consider this example:

Subject	Main Points
Main causes of gang involvement	• lack of opportunity for work • lack of recreational facilities • boredom • need for an accepting peer group

The logical link here is this: because of unemployment, recreational facilities are needed, and because of both unemployment and inadequate recreational facilities, boredom becomes a problem. Bored by having nothing to do and nowhere to go, young people need an accepting peer group to bolster their self-esteem. The first three points must be explained before the reader can fully understand the fourth.

4. **Random order** means the points can be satisfactorily explained in any order. A random arrangement of points is acceptable only if the main points are *equally significant* and *not chronologically or causally linked*, as in this example:

Subject	Main Points
Reasons for the garbage disposal crisis	• disposal sites are hard to find • costs are high • new cost-effective technologies have not yet been developed

Exercise 22.8

On pages 266–68, you will find eight subjects, together with several main points that could be used to develop them. For each subject, number the points so that they are arranged in the order suggested.

Subject	Order	Main Points
1. How to start a gas lawn mower	chronological	_____ make sure there is enough gas in tank _____ turn switch to start _____ put lawn mower on flat ground _____ when running, adjust to proper speed _____ pull cord _____ mow!
2. Differences between spoken and written language	climactic	_____ speech is transitory; writing is permanent _____ speech is direct and personal; writing isn't _____ speech can't be revised; writing can
3. How to write a research paper	chronological	_____ read and take notes on selected research sources _____ draft the paper _____ compile a working bibliography of research sources _____ define the subject _____ type and proofread paper _____ prepare footnotes, if needed, and list of works cited _____ revise the paper
4. How colleges benefit society	logical	_____ they provide the individual with a higher level of general education

Subject	Order	Main Points
		_____ society benefits from increased productivity and commitment of an educated populace
		_____ they provide the individual with job skills
5. Effects of malnutrition	logical	_____ malnutrition affects the productivity and prosperity of nations as a whole
		_____ malnutrition impedes the mental and physical development of children
		_____ undernourished children become sickly adults unable to participate fully in their society
6. Why pornography should be banned	chronological	_____ it degrades the people involved in making it
		_____ it brutalizes society as a whole
		_____ it desensitizes the people who view it
7. Why pornography should not be banned	climactic	_____ organized crime benefits from illegal distribution
		_____ censorship violates individual civil rights
		_____ banning pornography would lead to censorship of legitimate art and literature

Subject	Order	Main Points
8. Reasons for student poverty	climactic	_____ lack of parental assistance
		_____ lack of government loan assistance
		_____ inability to manage money effectively
		_____ inability to find part-time work

Exercise 22.9

Using the list of subjects you choose in Exercise 22.3 and the main points you identified in Exercise 22.7, arrange the main points for each subject in the most appropriate order. (*Note:* Keep your answer sheet. You will need it in some of the exercises in the next chapter.)

In this chapter, you've learned how to choose a satisfactory subject; how to discover a thesis; and how to find, test, and arrange main points that support your thesis. Now it's time to think about the best way to develop your paper: by the thesis statement method or by the outline method. We think the former generally works best for short papers and the latter for long papers, but this distinction isn't hard and fast. Your wisest choice is to learn both ways to structure a paper. You will often get the best results if you use them together.

23

The Thesis Statement

Once you have chosen a topic and selected some aspects of it to discuss, your next task is to outline your paper. There are several different methods to choose from, ranging from a sentence or two (a thesis statement) to a formal outline. For short papers, we recommend that you use the method presented in this chapter. For longer papers, or if your teacher requires a more detailed outline, you will find instructions in Chapter 24, "The Outline."

The key to a well-organized paper is a **thesis statement**—a statement near the beginning of your paper that announces its subject and scope. The thesis statement helps both you and your readers because it previews the plan of your paper. It tells your readers exactly what they are going to read about.

In fiction, telling readers in advance what they are going to find would never do. But for practical, everyday kinds of writing, advance notice works well. Term papers, technical reports, research papers, office memoranda, and business letters are no place for suspense or surprises. In these kinds of writing, you're more likely to get and keep your readers' attention if you indicate the subject and scope of your paper at the outset. A thesis statement acts like a table of contents. It's a kind of map of the territory covered in your paper: it keeps your reader (and you) on the right track.[1]

---

[1] Not all thesis statements contain a plan of development (a preview of the main points) in the final draft. Nevertheless, we recommend that you begin the drafting process with a full thesis statement. You can always omit the preview portion at the end of the drafting process if it seems obvious or redundant.

A thesis statement clearly and concisely indicates the SUBJECT of your paper, the MAIN POINTS you will discuss, and the ORDER in which you will discuss them.

To write a thesis statement, you join the **subject** you are going to explain or prove to your **main points**, which you have arranged in an appropriate order. To join the two parts of a thesis statement, you use a **link**. Your link can be a word or a phrase such as *are, include, consist of, because,* or *since,* or it can be a colon.[2] Here is a simple formula for constructing a thesis statement. (S stands for your subject.)

subject   *link*   *main points*

S   consists of   1, 2, 3 . . . n.

Here's an example:

subject   *link*   *main points*

Three kinds of dangerous drivers   (are)   speeders, tailgaters, and cellphone users.

Exercise 23.1

In each of the following thesis statements, underline the subject with a wavy line, circle the link, and underline the main points with a straight line. Answers for this chapter begin on page 515.

1. The essential features of a good novel are interesting characters, a stimulating plot, and exceptional writing.

2. My boss enjoys two hobbies: improving his golf game and tormenting his employees.

3. Well-known stars, stunning technical effects, and a hugely expensive advertising campaign are the requirements for a blockbuster movie.

4. If I were you, I would avoid eating in the cafeteria because the food is expensive, tasteless, and unhealthy.

---

[2] Remember that a colon can be used only after an independent clause. See Chapter 19 if you need a review.

5. The original Volkswagen Beetle, the Citröen CV, and the Morris Minor are three cars that will be remembered for their endearing oddness.

6. The responsibilities of a modern union include protecting the jobs of current employees, seeking to improve their working conditions and compensation, and protecting the pensions and benefits of pensioners.

7. Fad diets are not the quick and easy fixes to weight problems that they may seem to be; in fact, they are often costly, ineffective, and even dangerous.

8. Because they lack basic skills, study skills, or motivation, some students run the risk of failure in college.

9. *The Simpsons* amuses and provokes viewers with its depiction of a smart-aleck, underachieving son; a talented, overachieving daughter; and a hopeless, blundering father.

10. The Canadian political culture differs from the American political culture in terms of attitudes toward universal health care, gun control, and capital punishment.

When you combine your subject with your main points to form a thesis statement, there is an important rule to remember.

Main points must be stated in GRAMMATICALLY PARALLEL FORM.

This rule means that, if main point 1 is a word, then main points 2 and 3 and so on must be words too. If main point 1 is a phrase, then the rest must be phrases. If your first main point is a dependent clause, then the rest must be dependent clauses. Study the model thesis statements you analyzed in Exercise 23.1. In every example, the main points are in grammatically parallel form. For each of those thesis statements, decide whether words, phrases, or dependent clauses were used. If you think your understanding of parallelism is a bit wobbly, review Chapter 9 and do the following Web exercise before continuing.

GO TO WEB

EXERCISE 23.1

Exercise 23.2

Put a check mark (✓) before the sentences that are grammatically parallel. When you have completed the exercise, check your answers on page 515.

1. _____ A good counsellor must have knowledge, insight, patience, and compassion.

2. _____ Good writing involves applying the principles of organization, sentence structure, spelling, and you have to punctuate correctly.

3. _____ Our company requires employees to be knowledgeable, totally honest, disciplined, and we have to be able to rely on them.

4. _____ Hobbies are important because they provide us with recreational activities, stimulation, and they are relaxing.

5. _____ Some of the negative effects of caffeine are nervousness, you have difficulty sleeping, and heart palpitations.

Exercise 23.3

Now revise the incorrect sentences in Exercise 23.2.

GO TO WEB

EXERCISE 23.2

Exercise 23.4

Revise the following draft thesis statements. Be sure that the main points of each statement are significant, distinct, relevant, and grammatically parallel. Some sentences contain more than one kind of error. Make corrections as needed; then compare your revisions with our suggested answers.

1. The four kinds of essay writing are description, narrative, expository, and argumentation.

2. Intramural sports offer students a way to get involved in their school, an opportunity to meet friends, uniforms, and they can keep fit.

3. Increasingly, scientists are finding links between the weather and diseases such as colds, cancer, arthritic ailments, and aging.

4. The most prolific producers of pretentious language are politicians, teachers and administrators, those who write advertising copy, educators, and sportswriters.

5. There are three categories of students whom teachers find difficult: those who skip class, sleeping in class, and those who disrupt class.

Exercise 23.5

For each of the following subjects, consider the potential main points we've provided and decide whether each is appropriate to develop that subject in a short essay. Then, using the points that pass the test, write a grammatically parallel thesis statement. Underline the subject with a wavy line, circle the link, and underline the main points with straight lines. We've done part of the first question for you as an example.

1. **Subject:** Qualities needed to succeed in college

   Choose the main points that support the subject:

   • Motivation? Yes, a student must really want to succeed.

   • Choosing a major? No, that's part of the process of going to college, but not a quality required to succeed.

   • Organizational skills? Yes, good college students are able to set priorities and manage their time to achieve their priorities.

   • Academic skills? Yes, a good student must have solid academic skills to achieve success.

   • Writing ability? Good writing ability is one of the academic skills that students require, so it wouldn't be mentioned separately in the thesis statement.

- Time-management ability? Time management is an organizational skill, so it would be dealt with in that paragraph.
- Achieving a higher income? No. It's true that, over a lifetime, college graduates generally earn more than high school graduates, but higher earning isn't a quality. It's a result.
- Living in residence? No. Why? _____

A. Thesis statement: <u>To succeed in college, a student requires three impor-tant qualities</u>⊙ <u>good academic skills</u>, <u>organizational skills</u>, and <u>motivation</u>.

Now rewrite the thesis statement using *are* as a link.

B. _____

_____

_____

_____

2. Living in Canada has some advantages over living in the United States.
- Universal medical care
- Pleasant climate
- Less crime
- Tundra
- More affordable post-secondary education
- Multicultural environment

A. Three advantages that living in Canada has over living in the United

States are _____

_____

_____

_____

Rewrite the thesis statement using *because* as a link.

B. _____

_____

_____

_____

3. Some forms of electronic communication can improve a person's social life.

- Instant messaging
- iPods
- Blogging
- Expensive gadgets
- Internet dating

A. Some forms of electronic communication can improve a person's social

life; for example, _____

_____

_____

_____

Rewrite the thesis statement using *are* as a link.

B. _____

_____

_____

_____

4. What most immigrant parents encourage their Canadian-born children

to learn

- Their native language
- Their native footwear
- Their cultural history

- Their ethical/religious beliefs
- Canadian tax law
- Nothing about their homeland

A. Most immigrant parents encourage their Canadian-born children to

learn _____

_____

_____

Now rewrite the thesis statement using *include* as a link.

B. _____

_____

_____

_____

5. The subject is "Maintaining a healthy lifestyle." Two satisfactory main
   points are identified below. Choose a third point and write two different
   versions of a thesis statement on this subject. Thesis statement A should
   put the main points first.
   - Balanced diet
   - Adequate exercise
   -

A. (Main points first) _____

_____

_____

_____

B. Maintaining a healthy lifestyle involves _____

_____

_____

_____

Exercise 23.6

Exchange with another student the thesis statements you created for Exercise 23.5. Look carefully at each other's work. Check each thesis statement for completeness and grammatical parallelism. Suggest revisions, if they are needed. When you are both satisfied with your thesis statements, decide which one you prefer for each question and why.

Exercise 23.7

For each of the topics below, provide main points and write a thesis statement. Then exchange papers with a partner and check each other's work.

1. Learning a new language

•

•

•

Thesis statement: _____

_____

_____

_____

2. What I've learned from my family since I became an adult

•

•

•

Thesis statement: _____

_____

_____

_____

3. What a college education means to me

•

•

•

Thesis statement: _____

_____

_____

_____

4. What makes us laugh

- •

- •

- •

Thesis statement: _____

_____

_____

_____

5. How to save money

- •

- •

- •

Thesis statement: _____

_____

_____

_____

_____

Exercise 23.8

Find the subjects and main points you produced for Exercise 22.9 in Chapter 22. Combine each subject with its main points to make a thesis statement. Be sure the main points are expressed in parallel form. Then trade papers with another student and check each other's work.

We said at the beginning of this chapter that a thesis statement outlines your paper for you. Before we turn to the actual writing of the paper, you should have a general idea of what the finished product will look like.

In a short paper, each main point can be explained in a single paragraph. The main points of your subject become the topics of the paragraphs,[3] as shown in the following model format for a paper with three main points. Once you've mastered this basic structure, you can modify, expand, and develop it to suit papers of any length or kind.

_____

[3] Chapter 25 will show you how to develop your paragraphs fully and convincingly.

Paragraph 1:
contains your
introduction
and thesis
statement

> _____ Title _____
> _____
> _____
> _____
> _____
> S consists of 1, 2, and 3.

Paragraph 2:
explains your
first main
point

> Topic sentence identifying main point 1. ____
> _____
> _____
> _____
> _____
> _____
> _____ .

Paragraph 3:
explains your
second main
point

> Topic sentence identifying main point 2. ____
> _____
> _____
> _____
> _____
> _____
> _____ .

Paragraph 4:
explains your
third main
point

> Topic sentence identifying main point 3. ____
> _____
> _____
> _____
> _____
> _____
> _____ .

Paragraph 5:
states your
conclusion

> _____
> _____
> _____
> _____ .

Notice the proportions of the paragraphs in the model format. This format is for a paper whose main points are approximately equal in significance, so the body paragraphs are approximately equal in length. (In a paper in which your last main point is more important than the other points, however, the paragraph that explains it will probably be longer than the other paragraphs.)

Notice, too, that the introductory and concluding paragraphs are shorter than the ones that explain the main points. Your introduction should not ramble on, and your conclusion should not trail off. Get to your main points as quickly as you can, and end with a bang, not a whimper.

Exercise 23.9

An example of a paper that follows the model format exactly is Brian Green's "Career Consciousness" on pages 412–13 in Unit 7, Readings. Read it through; then go back and underline the thesis statement and the topic sentences.

24

The Outline

For longer compositions—business and technical reports, research papers, and the like—an outline is often necessary. A good outline maps out your paper from beginning to end. It shows you what you have to say about each of your main points before you begin drafting. Outlining spares you the agony of discovering too late that you have too much information about one point and little or nothing to say about another.

Once you've chosen a satisfactory subject and main points to discuss, the next step is to expand this material into an organized plan for your finished paper. To do this, you may need to do some more thinking or reading to gather additional information and supporting details. (For ideas about what kinds of information you might use, see "Developing Your Paragraphs" in Chapter 25.) After you've assembled all the information you think you'll need, prepare the outline.

There are as many different kinds of outline as there are writers. The kind of outline you prepare for a paper will vary depending on your approach to the topic, the amount of time before the due date, and your instructor's preference (or requirement). Here are a few of the strategies you can choose from:

- People who like to begin the writing process with brainstorming, freewriting, or another inductive technique often choose to postpone outlining until after they see what their creative juices produce on paper.
- Some writers prefer to start with a "scratch" outline, which consists of one- or two-word points that act as a bare-bones guide.
- Other writers like an informal outline that sketches out the parts of the paper in more detail, showing major headings and supporting points.
- Some writers do best with a full, formal outline with numbered points and subheadings.

Whatever approach is right for you, your topic, and your instructor, the time you spend outlining is invested, not wasted. The more time you spend at this stage of the process, the less time you'll need to devote to drafting and revising.

Scratch Outline

As we've seen in Chapters 22 and 23, after choosing a thesis, your next steps are to come up with main points and to arrange them in an order that will make sense to your reader. A thesis and main points are the beginnings of a scratch outline. Write these down, leaving enough space between them to jot down a few of the things you might say as you expand on each of the main points. Now you have a bare-bones outline to guide you as you draft the body of your paper. Here's an example:

Thesis: A satisfying career—interesting, rewarding, productive
- Interesting
  - enjoyable
  - like hobbies
  - Clive Beddoe
- Rewarding
  - financial
  - emotional rewards
- Productive
  - need to contribute
  - unproductive jobs

This is the skeleton of a paper. Put some meat on the bones, add an introduction and a conclusion, and you'll have a good first draft.

Informal Outline

An informal outline carries the scratch outline a step further, adding notes and ideas that will form the content of each paragraph. If whole sentences occur to you, write them down, but generally the informal outline is in point form.

Introduction
Thesis: "A satisfying career should be interesting, rewarding, and productive"

- Interesting
  1. Look forward to going to work
  2. Leisure activities are stimulating, why not your career?
     Examples: artists, Clive Beddoe
  3. Important not to spend rest of your life doing something you hate
- Rewarding
  1. Know yourself: What do you need?
     Are you ambitious? Do you need status, high salary?
     Low stress?
  2. Success is what it means to you
     Examples: technician, news director—which one is "successful"?
- Productive
  1. People want to contribute, to make a difference
  2. Some jobs are easy but meaningless
     Examples: factory job, night shift

Conclusion
  The need to understand yourself is key.
  Don't be swayed by opinions of others.
  Keep working at it. Strive to improve for your own sake, not your employer's.

Formal Outline

A formal outline is more detailed than a scratch or an informal outline. It may be drafted in point form, but the finished outline usually consists of complete sentences.

First, write down your main points in the order you've decided is best for your presentation. Leave at least half a page between points. Using Roman numerals (I, II, III, and so on), number your main points. Now, under each main point, indent and list the examples, facts, quotations, or other supporting information you're going to use to explain it. Again, leave lots of space. Check to be sure these items are arranged in an order that will be clear to your reader.[1] Label your supporting points *A, B, C,* and so on.

If some of these supporting points need to be explained or developed, indent again and list the second level of supporting points, numbering

---

[1] The four kinds of order explained in Chapter 22 (chronological, climactic, logically linked, and random order) apply to the arrangement of ideas within a paragraph as well as to the arrangement of main points in a paper.

them *1, 2, 3,* and so on. Third-level supporting details, if there are any, should be indented under the points to which they relate and labelled *a, b, c,* and so on. Add the introduction and the conclusion, and you're done. Your outline might look something like this:

Introduction
    Attention-getter
    Thesis statement/statement of subject

I. First main point
  A. Item that develops first main point
  B. Item that develops first main point
      1. Supporting material that develops item B
      2. Supporting material that develops item B

II. Second main point
  A. Item that develops second main point
  B. Item that develops second main point
  C. Item that develops second main point

III. Third main point
  A. Item that develops third main point
      1. Supporting material that develops item A
        a. Detail
        b. Detail
      2. Supporting material that develops item A
  B. Item that develops third main point

Conclusion
    Summary
    Memorable statement

The outline stage is the time to consider questions about how to arrange the information under each main point and how much time to spend on a particular point. If, for example, you find you have six subheadings under main point I and only one under main point II, you need to do some rethinking to balance your paper. Main points should be supported by approximately equal amounts of information.

Preparing a satisfactory outline takes time. Be prepared to spend time adding, deleting, and rearranging your ideas and supporting details until you're completely satisfied with the arrangement and proportions of your outline.

If you have access to a word-processing program with an outline feature, try it out. These programs can be very helpful to an inexperienced writer with little knowledge of how to organize a writing assignment.

When you have written and revised your outline, you are ready to draft the paper. Make the main points into paragraph divisions, develop the supporting points, and add an introduction and a conclusion. Chapter 25 explains how.

To show you the relationship between an outline and the final product, we've re-created the outline that was used to write "Career Consciousness," which you will find on pages 412–13.

Introduction

    Attention-getter: Choosing a life's vocation is not a decision to be taken lightly.

    Thesis statement: A satisfying career is one that is stimulating, rewarding, and productive.

I. A satisfying career is stimulating.

    A. When you get up in the morning, you look forward to your day.

        1. While not the image most people have of work, it is achievable.

        2. Most people can enjoy work just as they enjoy leisure activities.

    B. Many successful people have turned their interests into careers.

        1. Career professionals in the arts get paid for what they love to do.

            a. write, compose, paint, sculpt, etc.

            b. act, dance, sing, etc.

        2. Clive Beddoe turned his love of flying into the development of WestJet.

    C. If you deny yourself the chance to do what you love, you will spend most of your life wishing you were doing something else.

II. A satisfying career is rewarding, both financially and emotionally.

    A. To choose the right career, you must know yourself.

        1. Do you seek power and status?

        2. Or would you prefer a lower-profile position with less stress?

    B. Success is a state of mind.

        1. Contrast the careers of a small-town TV tech and a big-city news director.

            a. TV tech loves his job, family, community, and volunteer activities.

            b. News director thrives on deadlines, big-city life, money, and recognition her job provides.

        2. Both feel they are successful in their careers.

III. A satisfying career is productive.

   A. People need meaningful work.

      1. People need to feel they make a difference.

      2. Friendly co-workers, a pleasant routine, and money do not make up for lack of appreciation.

   B. Many people go unnoticed in their working lives.

      1. Some boast about reading paperbacks on the job.

      2. Some sleep through the night shift and fish or golf during the day.

   C. Knowing that you are doing something worthwhile is essential to your sense of well-being.

Conclusion

   Summary: It's not easy to find a career that provides stimulating, enjoyable, and meaningful work.

   A. You need to understand yourself.

   B. Make career decisions consistent with your values and goals.

   C. Once you have found a satisfying career, keep working at it.

      1. Seek challenges and opportunities that stimulate you.

      2. Enjoy the rewards of doing your job well.

      3. Strive for improvement for your own sake, not your employer's.

   Memorable Statement: Your career will occupy three-quarters of your life, so make the most of it!

Once you've mapped out your plan in an outline, the task of writing the essay is much easier. You can see at a glance where you're going and how to get there.

Exercise 24.1

Turn to "Career Consciousness" on pages 412–13. Find the paragraphs that correspond to the various headings and subheadings in the outline on pages 285–86. In the margins of the essay, label the paragraphs and sentences to show where they fit into the outline: I, A, 1, 2, and so on.

Exercise 24.2

1. With a partner, choose an essay in Unit 7 that interests you. Read the essay carefully, and create for it
   - a scratch outline
   - an informal outline
   - a formal outline

2. Exchange your work with another team that selected the same reading, and compare outlines. Are there significant differences between the two teams' outlines? If so, which set of outlines best captures the essence of the reading selection?

Exercise 24.3

Turn to the subjects and main points you developed for Exercise 22.9 in Chapter 22 and create scratch, informal, and formal outlines for a paper on one of those subjects.

25

Paragraphs

Armed with your thesis statement and outline, you are ready to turn your main points into paragraphs. Does that sound like a magician's trick? It isn't. All you need to know is what a paragraph looks like and how to put one together.

A paragraph looks like this:

Three or more sentences that specifically support or explain the topic go in here.

A sentence that introduces the **topic** (or main idea) of the paragraph goes here.

_____
_____
_____
_____
_____
_____

A sentence that concludes your explanation of the topic goes here.

Sometimes you can explain a main point satisfactorily in a single paragraph. If the main point is complicated and requires lots of support, you will need two or more paragraphs. Nevertheless, whether it is explaining a main point or a supporting point, every paragraph must contain two things: a **topic sentence** (usually the first sentence in the paragraph) and several sentences that develop the topic.

A sentence clearly stating your main idea is a good way to start a paragraph. The sentences that follow should support or expand on the topic. The key to making the paragraph *unified* (an important quality of paragraphs) is to make sure that each of your supporting sentences relates directly to the main idea introduced in the topic sentence.

Exercise 25.1

Turn to page 416 in Unit 7, Readings, and read Eva Tihanyi's "Resolving Conflict in the Workplace." Study the third, fourth, and fifth paragraphs and find in each the three basic components of a paragraph: the topic sentence, the supporting sentences, and the conclusion. Then compare your answer with ours. Answers for exercises in this chapter begin on page 517.

Developing Your Paragraphs

How do you put a paragraph together? First, write your topic sentence, telling your reader what topic (main point or key idea) you're going to discuss in the paragraph. Next, develop the topic. An adequately developed paragraph gives enough supporting information to make the topic completely clear to the reader. An average paragraph runs between 75 and 200 words (except for introductions and conclusions, which often are shorter), so you will need lots of supporting information for each point.

Unless you are writing from a detailed outline and have all the supporting material you require listed in front of you, you need to do some more thinking at this point. Put yourself in your reader's place. What does your reader need to know in order to understand your point clearly? If you ask yourself the six questions discussed below, you'll be able to decide what kind(s) of development to use to support a particular topic sentence. The kind of development you choose is up to you. Decide on the basis of your topic and what the reader needs to know about it.

1.   Is a **definition** necessary?

If you're using a term that may be unfamiliar to your reader, you should define it. Use your own words in the definition. Your reader needs to know what *you* mean by the term—and, besides, quoting from the dictionary is a boring way to develop a paragraph. In the following paragraph, Jeffrey Moussaieff Masson, author of "Dear Dad" (see pages 427–30), defines and describes a penguin *tortue*, a term with which few readers would be familiar.[1]

---

[1] The page numbers in parentheses at the end of each block quotation in this chapter indicate either the page number in the book or article from which the quotation was derived or the page number in Unit 7, Readings, where you will find the quotation in its context.

. . . [As] soon as the bad weather starts, generally in June, the males need some protection from the bitter cold, and nearly all of them find it by forming a *tortue*, which is a throng of very densely packed penguins. When the storms come they move in close to one another, shoulder to shoulder, and form a circle. The middle of the tortue is unusually warm and one would think that every penguin fights to be at the epicentre of warmth. But in fact what looks like an immobile mass is really a very slowly revolving spiral. The constantly shifting formation is such that every penguin, all the while balancing [a] single precious egg on his feet, eventually winds up in the middle of the tortue, only to find himself later at the periphery. (428)

You should also include a definition if you're using a familiar term in a specific or unusual way. In the following paragraph, Andrew Nikiforuk defines how he interprets the familiar phrase "back to the basics":

Let me reiterate what "back to the basics" means. It means teaching subjects that matter—such as English, math, history, geography, and science—because they contain the codes for power in a technological society as well as the only tools for criticizing and analyzing it. It means giving teachers more control over how their classrooms are organized and taught as well as making them more accountable for the results. It means skills in the context of disciplines (that's critical thinking) with the honest realization that not all students will become critical thinkers. It means fair tests and even standardized tests, because product matters in this culture. And finally, it means using the varied cultural backgrounds of students to explore common ground and Canadian realities. (106)

Exercise 25.2

Write a paragraph in which you define one of the following terms:

a good (or bad) parent	a good (or bad) friend	success
community	creativity	boredom
racism	a good (or bad) job	a good (or bad) marriage

2. Would **examples** help to clarify the point?

Listing a number of examples is probably the most common method of developing a topic. Readers become confused, even suspicious, when they read unsupported generalizations or statements of opinion. One of the most effective ways of communicating your idea is by providing clear, relevant examples. In the following paragraph, excerpted from a reading in Unit 7, Sun-Kyung Yi uses examples to explain why her job with a Korean company proved to be a "painful and frustrating experience."

> When the president of the company boasted that he "operated a little Korea," he meant it literally. A Canadianized Korean was not tolerated. I looked like a Korean; therefore, I had to talk, act, and think like one, too. Being accepted meant a total surrender to ancient codes of behaviour rooted in Confucian thought, while leaving the "Canadian" part of me out in the parking lot with my '86 Buick. In the first few days at work, I was bombarded with inquiries about my marital status. When I told them I was single, they spent the following days trying to match me up with available bachelors in the company and the community. I was expected to accept my inferior position as a woman and had to behave accordingly. It was not a place to practice my feminist views, or be an individual without being condemned. Little Korea is a place for men (who filled all the senior positions) and women don't dare to speak up or disagree with their male counterparts. The president (all employees bow to him and call him Mr. President) asked me to act more like a lady and smile. I was openly scorned by a senior employee because I spoke more fluent English than Korean. The cook in the kitchen shook her head in disbelief upon discovering that my cooking skills were limited to boiling a package of instant noodles. "You want a good husband, learn to cook," she advised me. (415)

Sometimes one or two examples developed in detail are enough to allow the reader to understand what you mean. In the following paragraph, Brian Green first defines what he means by "a rewarding career," and then he provides two different examples to illlustrate his definition.

> If your career is stimulating, then chances are good that it can also be rewarding. A good career offers two kinds of rewards: financial and emotional. Rewarding work doesn't just happen; it's something you need to plan for. The first and most important step is to know yourself. Only if you know who you are and what you need to be happy can you consciously seek out career experiences that will bring you satisfaction and steer clear of those that will annoy or stress you. Are you genuinely ambitious, or is power something you seek because you think it is expected of you? The pursuit of status and a high salary brings some people pure pleasure. Many people, however, find leadership positions excruciatingly stressful. Career

enjoyment depends to some extent on whether or not you are successful, and success is a state of mind. Consider two graduates from the same college program. One is a technician in a small-town television station who loves his work, takes pride in keeping the station on the air, and delights in raising his family in a community where he is involved in volunteer activities ranging from sports to fire-fighting. The other is a news director at one of Canada's major television networks. Her work is highly stressful, full of risks, and continually scrutinized by viewers, competitors, and her supervisors. She thrives on the adrenaline rush of nightly production, and loves the big-city life, the financial rewards of her position, and the national recognition she receives. Which graduate is "successful"? Certainly, both feel their careers are rewarding, according to their individual definitions of the term. (412–13)

Exercise 25.3

Write a six- to ten-sentence paragraph based on one of the topic sentences below, using examples to develop it.

Life in the big city is not for me.
Living away from home is hard to adjust to.
Recent movies aren't worth the price of admission.
Outside its own borders, the United States is probably the world's most disliked country.

3. Is a **series of steps** or **stages** involved?

Sometimes the most effective way to develop the main idea of your paragraph is by explaining how to do it—that is, by relating the process or series of steps involved. Make sure you break the process down into its component parts and explain the steps logically and precisely. Below, Sarah Norton outlines the first stage of language development. As you read through this paragraph, number the steps the author identifies as the parts of the process.

Infancy, the first stage of language development, literally means "unable to speak." For the first six months of her life, Jeanie isn't able to talk, but she can respond to speech. Shortly after birth, she'll turn her head toward the sound of a voice. By two weeks of age, she will prefer the sound of a human voice to non-human sounds. Between two and four months, she will learn to distinguish the voices of her caregivers from those of strangers, and she knows whether those voices are speaking soothingly or angrily. By the time she is two months old, Jeanie will have learned to coo as well as cry, and she coos happily when people smile and talk to her. Now she can express contentment as well as discomfort. At around four months of age, Jeanie's happy sounds become more varied and sophisticated: she registers delight on a scale ranging from throaty chuckles to belly laughs. All this vocal activity is actually a rehearsal for speech. As Jeanie cries and coos and laughs, her vocal cords, tongue, lips, and brain are developing the co-ordination required for her to speak her first words. (425)

Exercise 25.4

Write a paragraph developed as a series of steps telling your reader how to make or do something you are good at. (Choose a significant topic, not a trivial one.)

4. Would **specific details** be useful?

Providing your reader with concrete, specific, descriptive details can be an effective way of developing your main point. In the following paragraph, underline the specific details that help to bring alive the attractions that make Montreal a special place for students to live in:

> Pedestrian-friendly urban planning plays a large part in Montreal's reputation as a festival city that hosts over 40 events annually. In the sultry summer months, streets shut down for the Jazz Festival, the Montreal Grand Prix, and Just for Laughs, while the Fête des Neiges and the Montreal High Lights Festival provide outdoor activities and culinary delight in the winter. Students find plenty of ways to keep active—cycling, jogging, skating, skiing, dancing and drumming at Montreal's sexy Tam-Tams in Mount Royal Park—and gain an appreciation of the city's vibrant arts scene, from the numerous galleries in Old Montreal to fine art cinemas such as Cinema du Parc and Ex-Centris. Students can argue the merits of the latest Denys Arcand film in one of the many cafés along St. Denis frequented by their compatriots from Concordia, McGill, Université de Montréal, and Université du Québec à Montréal. As for ambience, the eclectic mix of old European limestone mansions and North American glass towers lends this oldest of Canadian cities a unique architectural allure. (Tryphonopoulos 439–40)

In some paragraphs, numerical facts or statistics can be used to support your point effectively. Ever since Benjamin Disraeli's immortal comment that the media publish "lies, damned lies, and statistics," however, critical readers tend to be suspicious of statistics, so be very sure that your facts are correct and that your statistics are current.

[Mated penguins] stay together afterward constantly, leaning against one another when they are standing up, or if they lie down, the female will glide her head under that of her mate. About a month later, between May 1 and June 12, the female lays a single greenish-white egg. French researchers noted that the annual dates on which the colony's first egg was laid varied by only eight days in 16 years of observation. Weighing almost a pound, and measuring up to 131 millimetres long and 86 millimetres wide, this is one of the largest eggs of any bird. The male stays by the female's side, his eyes fixed on her pouch. As soon as he sees the egg, he sings a variation of what has been called the "ecstatic" display by early observers, and she too takes up the melody. (Masson 427)

Exercise 25.5

Write an eight- to ten-sentence paragraph describing one of the following topics. Include details that involve several of the physical senses: sight, hearing, touch, smell, and taste. Be sure to begin with a clearly identifiable topic sentence.

A restaurant (store, workplace, city, etc.) you will never go back to
A place where you feel at ease
A new car (baby, pair of shoes, etc.)
Your favourite club/coffee shop
An embarrassing incident
A locker room after a game
A classroom during an exam
Your first day at a new school/job

5. Would a **comparison** or **contrast** help to clarify your point?

A **comparison** points out similarities between objects, people, or ideas; it shows how two different things are alike. A **contrast** points out dissimilarities between things; it shows how two objects, people, or ideas are different. A **comparison and contrast** identifies both similarities and differences. In the paragraph below, Sun-Kyung Yi contrasts the two sides of her "split personality."

When I was younger, toying with the idea of entertaining two separate identities was a real treat, like a secret game for which no one knew the rules but me. I was known as Angela to the outside world, and as

Sun-Kyung at home. I ate bologna sandwiches in the school lunch room and rice and kimchee for dinner. I chatted about teen idols and giggled with my girlfriends during my classes, and ambitiously practiced piano and studied in the evenings, planning to become a doctor when I grew up. I waved hellos and goodbyes to my teachers, but bowed to my parents' friends visiting our home. I could also look straight in the eyes of my teachers and friends and talk frankly with them instead of staring at my feet with my mouth shut when Koreans talked to me. Going outside the home meant I was able to relax from the constraints of my cultural conditioning, until I walked back in the door and had to return to being an obedient and submissive daughter. (414)

In the following paragraph, Germaine Greer summarizes her essay by contrasting Ottawa and New York.

Though I love New York, I disapprove of it. Dreary as Ottawa was, it was in the end a better place than New York. Canadians believe that happiness is living in a just society; they will not sing the Yankee song that capitalism is happiness, capitalism is freedom. Canadians have a lively sense of decency and human dignity. Though no Canadian can afford freshly squeezed orange juice, every Canadian can have juice made from concentrate. The lack of luxury is meant to coincide with the absence of misery. It doesn't work altogether, but the idea is worth defending. (424)

Exercise 25.6

Write a paragraph comparing or contrasting two cities (or countries, co-workers, instructors, careers, or employers). Begin your paragraph with a clearly identifiable topic sentence and support it with fresh, original points. The differences in size, climate, and world status between London, England, and London, Ontario, will not grab a reader's attention; the differences in the cities' ethnic mixes, employment possibilities, and cultural opportunities might intrigue a Canadian reader, at least.

6. Would a **paraphrase** or **quotation** be appropriate?

A **paraphrase** is a summary in your own words of someone else's idea. Remember to indicate whose idea you are paraphrasing, the way the unnamed editor who wrote "The Myth of Canadian Diversity" does in the following paragraph.

> . . . [O]ur much-discussed ethnic differences are overstated. Although Canada is an immigrant nation and Canadians spring from a variety of backgrounds, a recent study from the C.D. Howe Institute says that the idea of a "Canadian mosaic"—as distinct from the American "melting pot"—is a fallacy. In *The Illusion of Difference*, University of Toronto sociologists Jeffrey Reitz and Raymond Breton show that immigrants to Canada assimilate as quickly into the mainstream society as immigrants to the United States do. In fact, Canadians are less likely than Americans to favour holding on to cultural differences based on ethnic background. If you don't believe Mr. Reitz and Mr. Breton, visit any big-city high school, where the speech and behaviour of immigrant students just a few years in Canada is indistinguishable from that of any fifth-generation classmate.

Occasionally, you will find that someone else—an expert in a particular field, a well-known author, or a respected public figure—has said what you want to say better or more convincingly than you could ever hope to say it. In these cases, quotations—as long as they are kept short and not used too frequently—are useful in developing your topic. In the following paragraph, Nell Waldman uses first a paraphrase, and second, a quotation from experts to explain one of the reasons why it is so difficult for adults to learn a second language.

> An adult has intellectual and cognitive skills that a child lacks. An adult can think abstractly and is able to memorize and use dictionaries (Crystal 373). These skills might seem to make it easier to learn a new language. However, an adult already has a firmly established first language in his intellectual repertoire, and the native language actually interferes with mastering the second language. H. Douglas Brown describes the process whereby remnants of the native language collide with the new language: "The relatively permanent incorporation of incorrect linguistic forms into a person's second language competence . . . [is] referred to as *fossilization*" (217). The fossils of our native language tend to keep turning up as errors in the new language we are struggling to learn. (435)

College writing normally requires that you indicate the source of any material you quote. The easiest way to do this is to give a reference in parentheses at the end of your quotation; the "Works Cited" or "References" list at the end of your paper will give full publication details. If the author's name is already mentioned in your introduction to the quotation, you need give only the page number(s) on which you found the quotation. If the author's name is not given in your introduction to the quotation, you need to include it along with the page number(s). If your quotation is short and included in your sentence, you use the same citation format, but you insert the parenthetical reference—author's name (if not already mentioned) and page number—before the end punctuation. For example:

> According to Germaine Greer, "Ottawa coffee is perhaps the worst in Canada and Canadian coffee on the whole is the bitterest and weakest you will ever encounter" (421).

> An internationally known writer and speaker who, for the most part, likes Canada, deplores our coffee: "Ottawa coffee is perhaps the worst in Canada and Canadian coffee on the whole is the bitterest and weakest you will ever encounter" (Greer 421).

At the end of your paper, include a "Works Cited" or "References" list: a list in alphabetical order by authors' surnames of all the books, articles, and other publications from which you have quoted in your paper. See pages 434–36 for an example of an essay written in MLA format. Follow the instructions given in whatever style guide your instructor recommends, or go to "More Information" on the Student Resources page of our Web site at www.essentialsplus3e.nelson.com for details of MLA and APA style requirements.

When you plan the paragraphs of your essay, remember that you will often need to use more than one method of development to explain each point. The six methods outlined above can be used in any combination. Choose whichever kinds of development will best help your reader understand what you have to say.

Exercise 25.7

Working with a partner, identify the kinds of development used in the following paragraphs from essays in Unit 7. (More than one kind of development may be present in each.) Then check your answers.

1. "Metamorphosis," paragraph 4
2. "The Second-Language Struggle," paragraph 2
3. "Baba and Me," paragraph 5
4. "Dear Dad," paragraph 12
5. "Career Consciousness," paragraph 4
6. "Labouring the Wal-Mart Way" paragraph 2
7. "Ottawa vs. New York," paragraph 6
8. "Baba and Me," paragraph 13
9. "An Immigrant's Split Personality," paragraph 4
10. "An Immigrant's Split Personality," paragraph 10

Exercise 25.8

Choose one of the following topic sentences (or make up one of your own) and write a paragraph of approximately 100–150 words using one or more of the methods of paragraph development we have discussed in this chapter. When you've completed your paragraph, exchange your work with another student and see if you can identify the method(s) of development your partner has chosen. Were you given enough information to understand the topic completely? If not, what additional information do you need?

1. The world's worst date
2. Life is like a game of _____.
3. How to succeed (*or* fail) as a parent
4. Our choice of clothes reveals who we are.
5. How to make a good (*or* bad) impression on your boss
6. _____ is a profession with a future.
7. Yesterday's music is (not) better than today's.
8. How to assess a potential mate
9. Canadians don't appreciate how lucky they are.
10. Few Canadians understand the experience of being a refugee.

Writing Introductions and Conclusions

Two paragraphs in your paper are not developed in the way we've just outlined: the **introduction** and the **conclusion**. All too often, these paragraphs are dull or clumsy and detract from a paper's effectiveness. But they needn't. Here's how to write good ones.

The introduction is worth special attention because that's where your reader either sits up and takes notice of your paper or sighs and pitches it into the wastebasket. Occasionally, for a short paper, you can begin by simply stating your thesis. More usually, though, an **attention-getter** comes before the thesis statement. An attention-getter is a sentence or two designed to get the reader interested in what you have to say.

There are several kinds of attention-getters to choose from, as these examples from the Unit 7 "Readings" section illustrate.

1. A question (see "The Second-Language Struggle")
2. A little-known or striking fact (see "An Immigrant's Split Personality")
3. A comparison/contrast that will intrigue your reader (see "Dear Dad")
4. An interesting incident or anecdote related to your subject (see "Resolving Conflict in the Workplace")
5. A definition (see "Career Consciousness")

Add your thesis statement to the attention-getter and your introduction is complete.

The closing paragraph, too, usually has two parts: a **summary** of the main points of your paper (phrased differently, please—not a word-for-word repetition of your thesis statement or topic sentences) and a **memorable statement**. Your memorable statement may take several forms.

1. Refer to the content of your opening paragraph (see "Career Consciousness").
2. Include a relevant or thought-provoking quotation, statement, or question (see "The Second-Language Struggle").
3. Emphasize the value or significance of your subject (see "A City for Students").
4. Make a suggestion for change (see "An Immigrant's Split Personality").
5. Offer a solution, make a prediction, or invite the reader to get involved (see "Labouring the Wal-Mart Way").

Exercise 25.9

Using as many of the different kinds as you can, write an attention-getter and a memorable statement for each of the following topics.

1. Television is (not) a waste of time.
2. I love (hate) hockey (baseball, basketball, football, etc.).
3. Honesty is (not) always the best policy.
4. College professors should (not) be required to take courses in how to teach.
5. Travel is the best form of education.
6. The experience of war changes one in unexpected ways.
7. It's not easy being a man (woman).

8. Canada's new immigration policy will (not) benefit the country over time.
9. The notion of lifelong learning (i.e., continual retraining throughout my career) is (not) appealing to me.
10. We can learn much from our grandparents/children.

Keeping Your Reader with You

As you write your paragraphs, keep in mind that you want to make it as easy as possible for your reader to follow you through your paper. Clear transitions and an appropriate tone can make the difference between a paper that confuses or annoys readers and one that enlightens and pleases them.

TRANSITIONS

Transitions are those words or phrases that show the relationship between one point and the next, helping a paragraph or a paper to read smoothly. Like turn signals on a car, they tell the person following you where you're going. Here are some common transitions you can use to keep your reader on track.

1. *To show a time relation:* first, second, third, next, before, during, after, now, then, finally, last
2. *To add an idea or example:* in addition, also, another, furthermore, similarly, for example, for instance
3. *To show contrast:* although, but, however, instead, nevertheless, on the other hand, in contrast, on the contrary
4. *To show a cause–effect relation:* as a result, consequently, because, since, therefore, thus

Here is a paragraph that has adequate development but no transitions:

> There are several good reasons why you should not smoke. Smoking is harmful to your lungs and heart. It is annoying and dangerous to those around you who do not smoke. Smoking is an unattractive and dirty habit. It is difficult to quit. Most worthwhile things in life are hard to achieve.

Not very easy to read, is it? Readers are jerked from point to point until, battered and bruised, they reach the end. This kind of writing is unfair to readers. It makes them do too much of the work. The ideas may all be there, but the readers have to figure out for themselves how they fit together. After a couple of paragraphs like this one, even a patient reader can become annoyed.

Now read the same paragraph with the transitions added:

> There are several good reasons why you should not smoke. Among them, three stand out as the most persuasive. First, smoking is harmful to your lungs and heart. Second, it is both annoying and dangerous to those around you who do not smoke. In addition to these compelling facts, smoking is an unattractive and dirty habit. Furthermore, once you begin, it is difficult to quit; but then, most worthwhile things in life are hard to achieve.

In the revised paragraph, readers are gently guided from one point to the next. By the time they reach the conclusion, they know not only what ideas the writer had in mind but also how they fit together. Transitions make the reader's job easier and more rewarding.

TONE

One final point. As you write the paragraphs of your paper, be conscious of your **tone.** Your audience, purpose, and subject will all influence the tone you choose, which must be appropriate to all three. The words you use, the examples, quotations, and other supporting materials you choose to help explain your main points—all these contribute to your tone.

When you are trying to explain something to someone, particularly if it's something you feel strongly about, you may be tempted to be highly emotional in your discussion. If you allow yourself to get emotional, chances are you won't be convincing. What will be communicated is the strength of your feelings, not the depth of your understanding or the validity of your opinion. To be clear and credible, you need to restrain your enthusiasm or anger and present your points in a calm, reasonable way.

Here are a few suggestions to help you find and maintain the right tone.

- Be tactful. Avoid phrases such as "Any idiot can see," "No sane person could believe," and "It is obvious that. . . . " What is obvious to you isn't necessarily obvious to someone who has a limited understanding of your subject or who disagrees with your opinion.

- Don't talk down to your readers as though they were children or hopelessly ignorant. Don't use sarcasm, profanity, or slang.

- Don't apologize for your interpretation of your subject. Have confidence in yourself. You've thought long and hard about your subject, you've found good supporting material to help explain it, and you believe in its significance. State your thesis confidently. If you hang back, using phrases such as "I may be wrong, but . . . " or "I tend to feel that . . . ", your reader won't be inclined to give your points the consideration they deserve. Keep your reader in mind as you write, and your writing will be both clear and convincing.

The following paragraph is an example of inappropriate tone. The writer is enthusiastic about the topic, but the tone is arrogant, bossy, and tactless rather than persuasive.

> It is time that governments at all levels did something useful: take action. We need laws requiring the addition of 10 percent ethanol to gasoline. Ethanol burns cleaner than gas and also boosts octane, so it's obvious that the oil companies don't have to put so many poisons in the gas to make our already too powerful cars go even faster. For another thing, everybody knows that ethanol is made out of corn, which is grown on farms and is a renewable resource. Growing it will make farmers happy, and drivers should also be pleased because it can be produced for less than the outrageous prices we pay for conventional gasoline. Adding 10 percent of the cheaper fuel should bring pump prices down, although I'm sure the oil companies will find a way to gouge us consumers. Obviously, the government is going to have to pass laws forcing the oil companies to add ethanol because there's no way they're going to do what is good for the environment and the economy at the expense of their profits. However, relying on government to do the right thing is about as likely as big business doing the right thing.

Now read the paragraph below, which argues the same point but in a courteous, more tactful way.

> Legislation requiring the addition of ethanol to gasoline is both sensible and overdue. The addition of 10 percent ethanol to gasoline sold at the pump is sensible for two reasons. First, it makes the fuel that we burn in our cars and trucks cleaner. Ethanol burns hotter than gasoline, thus destroying pollutants rather than sending them out of the tailpipe. Second, ethanol is a renewable source of energy that will provide jobs in rural Canada because it is made from corn. At current oil prices, ethanol is cheaper than gasoline, so its addition to our fuel will help to reduce costs for consumers. Why should governments have to legislate such a sensible course of action? The petroleum industry, from exploration to retail, is not

about to voluntarily dilute its product—or its profits—by any amount, let alone 10 percent!

The following paragraph is a draft written for a general reader. The writer's purpose is to persuade her audience that city dwellers should be more aware of the labour that lies behind every packaged product we eat. Revise the paragraph to make it appropriate to its audience and purpose by deleting or rewording any lapses in tone. Then compare your answer with ours on page 518.

I'm from the city, so I may not know much about the subject, but it seems to me that we urban dwellers have lost touch with the food we eat. By this I mean, obviously, that we no longer appreciate the farmers and farm workers who supply the food that we enjoy every day. Anyone with half a brain should realize that most of the food we buy is prepackaged in Styrofoam, wrapped in plastic, or precooked and frozen by huge corporations whose goal is to make humongous profits by selling us the packaging, not the contents. Do any urban consumers understand that their ketchup is made from farm-grown tomatoes? Do any advertising-driven supermarket shoppers really think about the fact that those overpackaged frozen pork chops, so irresistible with their sprig of parsley, were once a pig, raised by a farmer? Not only are we ignorant, but also we could care less about the journey our food makes from farm to fridge. My guess is that if you asked most city kids where their food comes from, they'd say, "the food factory."

Exercise 25.11

Do either A or B.

A. Using one of the thesis statements you prepared in Chapter 23, Exercise 23.7, write a paper of approximately 400 words.

B. Using one of the outlines you prepared in Chapter 24, Exercise 24.3, write a paper of approximately 500 words.

26

Revising Your Paper

No one other than a seasoned professional writer can write in a single draft an essay that is perfectly organized and developed, let alone one that is free of errors. The purpose of the first draft is to get down on paper something you can work with until it meets your reader's needs and expectations. Planning and drafting should take about half the time you devote to writing a paper. The rest should be devoted to revision.

Revision is the process of refining your message until

- it says what you want it to say
- your reader(s) will understand it and
- your reader(s) will receive it favourably

These three goals are the essentials of good communication. You can achieve them only if you keep your readers in mind as you revise. Because a first draft reflects the contents of the writer's mind, it often seems all right to the writer. But in order to transfer an idea as clearly as possible from the mind of the writer to the mind of the reader, revision is necessary. The idea needs to be honed and refined until it is as clear to your reader as it is to you. By revising from your reader's point of view, you can avoid misunderstandings before they happen.

What Is Revision?

Revision means "to see again." It does *not* mean "to *re-copy*." The aim of revision is to improve your writing's organization, accuracy, and style. Revising is a three-stage process. Each step requires that you read through your entire essay, painful though this may be. The goal of your first reading is to ensure that you've said what you want to say in language your reader will understand. In your second reading, you focus on structure. Your third reading concentrates on correctness. Here are the steps to follow in revising a paper.

1. Improve the whole paper by revising its content and organization.
2. Refine paragraph and sentence structure, and correct any errors in grammar.
3. Edit and proofread to catch errors in word choice, spelling, and punctuation.

Inexperienced writers often skip the first two stages and concentrate on the third, thinking they will save time. This is a mistake. In fact, they waste time—both theirs and their readers'—because the result is writing that doesn't communicate clearly and won't make a positive impression.

The best way to begin revising is to do nothing to the early version of your paper for several days. Allow as much time as possible between completing your first draft and re-reading it. Ten minutes, or even half a day, is not enough. The danger in re-reading too soon is that you're likely to "read" what you *think* you've written—what exists only in your head, not on the page.

If you haven't allowed enough time for this cooling-off period, don't despair. There are two other things you can do to help you get some distance from your draft. If your first draft is handwritten, type it out. Reading your essay in a different form helps you to see its content in a different way. Alternatively, read your paper aloud and listen to it from the point of view of your reader. Hear how your explanation unfolds, and mark every place you find something unclear, irrelevant, inadequately developed, or out of order.

Step 1
Revise Content and Organization

As you read your paper aloud, keep in mind the three possible kinds of changes you can make at this stage:

1. You can *rearrange* information. This is the kind of revision that is most often needed but least often done. Consider the order in which you've arranged your paragraphs. From your reader's point of view, is this the most effective order in which to present your ideas? If you are not already using a word-processing program, now is the time to begin.

With a good word processor, moving blocks of text around is as easy as dealing a deck of cards.

2. You can *add* information. Adding new main ideas or more development is often necessary to make your message interesting and convincing as well as clear. It's a good idea to ask a friend to read your draft and identify what needs to be expanded or clarified. (Be sure to return the favour. You can learn a great deal by critiquing other people's writing.)

3. You can *delete* information. Now is the time to cut out anything that is repetitious, insignificant, or irrelevant to your subject and reader.

Use the checklist that follows to guide you as you review your paper's form and content.

Content and Organization Checklist

ACCURACY

Is everything you have said accurate?

- Is your information consistent with your own experience and observations or with what you have discovered through research?
- Are all your facts and evidence up to date?

COMPLETENESS

Have you included enough main ideas and development to explain your subject and convince your reader? Remember that "enough" means from the reader's point of view, not the writer's.

SUBJECT

Is your subject

- significant? Does it avoid the trivial or the obvious?
- single? Does it avoid double or combined subjects?
- specific? Is it focussed and precise?
- supportable? Have you provided enough evidence to make your meaning clear?

MAIN POINTS

Are your main points

- significant? Have you deleted any unimportant ones?
- distinct? Are they all different from one another, or is there an overlap in content?
- relevant? Do all points relate directly to your subject?
- arranged in the most appropriate order? Again, "appropriate" means from the reader's perspective. Choose chronological, climactic, logical, or random order, depending on which is most likely to help the reader make sense of your information.

INTRODUCTION

Does your introduction

- catch attention and make the reader want to read on?
- contain a clearly identifiable thesis statement?
- identify the main points that your paper will explain?

CONCLUSION

Does your conclusion

- contain a summary or reinforcement of your main points, rephrased to avoid word-for-word repetition?
- contain a statement that effectively clinches your argument and leaves the reader with something to think about?

TONE

Is your tone consistent, reasonable, courteous, and confident throughout your essay?

When you have carefully considered these questions, it's time to move on to the second stage of the revision process.

Exercise 26.1

Read the following draft outline for a short essay on how to write effective e-mails in a business environment. Working with a partner, rearrange the main points in chronological order, delete any unnecessary supporting points, and write a thesis statement to produce a working outline for the essay. Then compare your answer with our suggestion. Answers for exercises in this chapter begin on page 518.

E-Mail Excellence

Attention-getter: As the recipient of approximately 1,000 business-related e-mail messages every month, I am something of an expert on what is effective and what is not in e-mail correspondence.

Thesis statement: _____

_____

_____

_____

Main points:

I. Subject line

    A. always include one

    B. make sure it states clearly what the message is about

    C. never use vague subject lines such as "hello," or "message," or "Are you there?"

    D. never leave the subject line blank

II. Attachments

    A. use sparingly

    B. may carry viruses

    C. take time to transfer and to open

    D. attach text-only files unless a graphic is absolutely necessary

    E. use only if necessary

III. Message

    A. Content

        1. be concise and to the point

        2. tell the reader what action is needed, by whom, and when

        3. don't be a novelist or a "Chatty Cathy"

        4. use plain English, not "cyberspeak"

        5. use an appropriate level of language in your message as well as in your salutation and signature

    B. Format

        1. use bullets to identify points you want to emphasize

        2. leave white space between points

        3. avoid sending your message in upper-case letters (shouting)

        4. avoid smilies and other "cute" computer shorthand symbols

Summary: If you follow my recommendations on these three points whenever you write an e-mail, you will make the recipient of your
message very happy.

Memorable statement: Especially if you're writing to me.

Step 2
Revise Paragraphs and Sentences

Here, too, you should allow time—at least a couple of days—between your
first revision and your second. Enough time must elapse to allow you to
approach your paper as if you were seeing it for the first time. Once again,
read your draft aloud, and use this list of questions to help you improve it.

Paragraph and Sentence Checklist

PARAGRAPHS

Does each paragraph
- begin with a clear, identifiable topic sentence?
- develop one—and only one—main idea?
- present one or more kinds of development appropriate to the main idea?
- contain clear and effective transitions to signal the relationship between
  sentences? Between paragraphs?

SENTENCES

Sentence Structure
1. Is each sentence clear and complete?
   - Are there any fragments or run-ons?
   - Are there any misplaced or dangling modifiers?
   - Are all lists (whether words, phrases, or clauses) expressed in parallel
     form?
2. Are your sentences varied in length? Could some be combined to
   improve the clarity and impact of your message?

Grammar
1. Have you used verbs correctly?
   - Are all verbs in the correct form?
   - Do all verbs agree with their subjects?

- Are all verbs in the correct tense?
- Are there any confusing shifts in verb tense within a paragraph?
2. Have you used pronouns correctly?
    - Are all pronouns in the correct form?
    - Do all pronouns agree with their antecedents?
    - Have any vague pronoun references been eliminated?

When you're sure you've answered these questions satisfactorily, go to the third and last stage of the revision process.

Exercise 26.2

Here is the first draft of the essay on e-mails. Revise it to correct errors in paragraph structure, sentence structure, and grammar. (Don't worry about spelling and punctuation errors at this stage. You'll correct them later, in Exercise 26.3.) Then compare your answer with our suggestion on pages 519–20.

1   As the recipient of approximately 1,000 business-related e-mail messages every month, I am something of an expert on what is effective and what is not in e-mail correspondence. The three areas that need attention in most e-mail messages are the subject line, the content, and format of the message and the use of attachments.

2   Some people leave the subject line blank, this is a mistake. I want to know what the message is about before I open it so I can decide if it needs my immediate attention. Or can wait until later. A message with no subject line or with a line that didn't tell me nothing about the content of the e-mail get sent to the bottom of my "to-do" list. There are lots of readers like me busy people who receive tons of e-mail, much of it unsolicited advertising that clutter up their in-boxes. For this reason the subject line should always clearly state the subject of the message and should never be vague or cute like "hello" or "message" or "are you there?"

3   As for the message itself, it's function should be to tell the reader what action one wants, you need to be clear about this and be as brief as possible. What is it that you want the recipient to do. Who else needs to be involved. By when does the action need to take place. Communicate your message in plain English, not in "cyberspeak" Not everyone knows Net lingo, and even some who are famliar with it find it irritating not charming. Use an appropriate level of language (general-level Standard English will always be appropriate) to convey you're message. Use the same level of language in you're salutation and closing or "signature." One should definitely not sign off a message to you're client or you're boss with "love and kisses." Format you're message so that the recipient will be able to read it quickly and understanding it easily. Use bullets to identify points you want to emphasize, separate the bullets with white space so they can be read at a glance and reviewed individually if necessary. There are some important points of e-mail etiquette that you should observe. Don't type you're message in upper-case letters, that's considered "shouting." Do avoid "smilies" and other "cute" computer shorthand symbols. Some of you're readers won't understand them others will have seen them so often they will be turned off.

4   Attachments should be included only if they are really necessary, for one thing, they may carry virruses and some people won't open them.

Another disadvantage is that they take time to send download and open. Unless I am sure that an attachment is both urgent and vitally important—the agenda of tomorrow's meeting, for example—I don't bother to open it, for all I know, it might contain not only a virus but also footage of the sender's toddler doing her latest photogenic trick. As a general rule attach only what you must and attach text-only files. Try to include everything you need to say in the message itself and use attachments only as a last resort. Think of them as equivalent to footnotes supplementary to the message not an essential part of it.

5   If you follow my recommendations on these three points whenever you write an e-mail, you will make the recipient of your message very happy, especially if you're writing to me.

Step 3
Edit and Proofread

By now you're probably so tired of refining your paper that you may be tempted to skip **editing**—correcting errors in word choice, spelling, and punctuation—and **proofreading**—correcting errors in typing or writing that appear in the final draft. But these final tasks are essential if you want your paper to make a positive impression.

Misspellings, faulty punctuation, and messiness don't always create misunderstandings, but they do cause the reader to form a lower opinion of you and your work. Careful editing and proofreading are necessary if you want your writing to be favourably received.

Most word-processing programs include a grammar checker and a spell checker. It is worthwhile running your writing through these programs at

the editing stage. The newer programs have some useful features. For example, they will question (but not correct) your use of apostrophes; they will sometimes catch errors in subject–verb agreement; and they will catch obvious misspellings and typos.

But don't make the mistake of assuming these programs will do all your editing for you. Many errors slip past a computer's database, no matter how comprehensive the salesperson told you it is. Only you or a knowledgeable and patient friend can find and correct all errors.

If spelling is a particular problem for you, you should first run your paper through a spell checker. After that, you're on your own. Read your paper backward word by word, from the end to the beginning. Reading backward forces you to look at each word by itself and helps you to spot those that look suspicious. Whenever you're in doubt about the spelling of a word, look it up! If you find this task too tedious, ask a good speller to read through your paper for you and identify any errors. (Then take this person out for dinner. If you get an A, add a show.)

Here are the questions to ask yourself when you are editing.

Editing Checklist

WORDS

Usage
Have you used words to "mean" rather than to "impress"?
- Have you eliminated any slang, pretentious language, or offensive language?
- Have you cut out any unnecessary words?
- Have you corrected any "abusages"?

Spelling
Are all words spelled correctly?
- Have you double-checked any homonyms?
- Have you used capital letters where they are needed?
- Have you used apostrophes correctly for possessives and omitted them from plurals?

PUNCTUATION

Within Sentences
- Have you eliminated any unnecessary commas and included commas where needed? (Refer to the four comma rules as you consider this question.)
- Have you used colons and semicolons where appropriate?
- Are all quotations appropriately marked?

Beginnings and Endings
- Does each sentence begin with a capital letter?
- Do all questions—and only questions—end with a question mark?
- Are all quotation marks correctly placed?

Exercise 26.3

Now go through the revised first draft of the e-mail essay that you produced in Exercise 26.2. This is your last chance to make this essay error-free. Use the "Editing Checklist" above and the "Tips for Effective Proofreading" below to guide you as you make your final pass through this document. Then compare your answer with our suggestion on page 520.

TIPS FOR EFFECTIVE PROOFREADING

By the time you have finished editing, you will have gone over your paper so many times you may have practically memorized it. When you are very familiar with a piece of writing, it's hard to spot the small mistakes that may have slipped in as you produced your final copy. Here are some tips to help you find those tiny, elusive errors:

1. Read through your essay line by line, using a ruler to guide you.
2. If you've been keeping a list of your most frequent errors in this course, scan your essay for the mistakes you are most likely to make.
3. Use the "Quick Revision Guide" on the inside front cover of this book to make a final check of all aspects of your paper.
4. Use the list of correction marks on the page facing inside the back cover to check for errors your instructor has identified in your writing.

Your "last" draft may need further revision after your proofreading review. If so, take the time to rewrite the paper so that the version you hand in is clean and easy to read. If a word processor is available to you, use it. Computers make editing and proofreading almost painless, since errors are so easy to correct.

At long last, you're ready to submit your paper. If you've followed the three steps to revision conscientiously, you can hand it in with confidence that it says what you want it to say, both about your subject and about you. One last word of advice:

DON'T FORGET TO KEEP A COPY FOR YOUR FILES!

GO TO WEB

EXERCISE 26.1

Exercise 26.4

Turn to the draft paper you wrote for Exercise 25.11 in Chapter 25. Revise the paper by applying to it the three steps of the revision process.

For ESL Learners: A Review of the Basics

Introduction

Quick Quiz

27 Choosing the Correct Verb Tense
Verb Tense Formation
The Present Tenses
The Past Tenses
The Future Tenses
Using Present Tenses to Indicate Future Time

28 More about Verbs
Forming Negatives
Participial Adjectives
Modal Auxiliaries

29 Solving Plural Problems
Singular vs. Plural Nouns
Count vs. Non-Count Nouns
Quantity Expressions

30 Using Articles Accurately
The Indefinite Article: *A/An*
The Definite Article: *The*
No Article (Zero Article)
Using *The* or No Article in Geographical Names

31 Practising with Prepositions
Prepositions That Indicate Time Relationships
Prepositions That Indicate Place or Position
Prepositions That Indicate Direction or Movement
Other Prepositional Relationships

Rapid Review

Introduction

As a college student, you are preparing for a meaningful and rewarding career. If you are preparing for this career in a language that is not native to you, English, we acknowledge your accomplishment. Your hard work and your ability to use two (or more) languages suggest that you are able to achieve a high level of success.

However, you may feel that your communication skills in English are holding you back. Even if your command of spoken English is good, you may lack fluency with standard written English (SWE), and poor writing skills can hinder your opportunities for academic and career success.

The ability to use SWE confidently helps you in three ways. First, it gives you the power to express your ideas clearly. Second, it helps you win the respect of your readers. And third, it increases the number of people with whom you can communicate. That's why employers look for people who can use SWE effectively.

This unit of *The Bare Essentials Plus* is designed specifically to help the second-language writer master the conventions of SWE. It focusses on the most common problems that ESL students experience when they write English. These include verb tense and formation, plural forms/quantity expressions, articles, and prepositions. Even highly sophisticated ESL writers occasionally make mistakes in these constructions, mistakes that are evident to native speakers. Working on these problem areas will develop and improve your ability to write in English.

These chapters provide concise explanation, likely less explanation than you have come to expect in advanced grammar texts. But there are many exercises and much opportunity for you to practise specific writing skills. Grammatical explanation can certainly help you to understand what constitutes correct English, but ultimately you must gain confidence in your ability to write correctly without constant reference to grammar rules. This confidence is what will make you a fluent writer of English.

The following quick quiz will let you see at a glance which chapters of Unit 6 you need to focus on. The paragraphs below contain 15 errors: verb tense, negative verb formation, participial adjectives, modal auxiliaries, singular and plural forms, articles, and prepositions. When you've made your corrections, turn to page 521 and compare your version with ours. For each error you miss, the answer key directs you to the chapter you need to work on.

¹People learn their first langauge very early and very easily. ²Most of us understand spoken words and respond to them since the time we are two or three years old. ³It takes another few years for us to learn how to read and write, but we acquire our first language fairly easily. ⁴By most of us, however, learning a second language is a slow and exasperating process. ⁵Most people who study English as a second language are especially frustrating by three of its peculiarities: its unsystematic pronunciation, its inconsistent spelling, and its enormous vocabulary.

⁶English is having sounds that are difficult for speakers of other languages. ⁷The *th* sound is one of them. ⁸Why is it pronounced differently in words such as *this* and *think*? ⁹The consonant sounds *l*, *r*, and *w* also present problems. ¹⁰Many new English speakers don't hear the differences between *light*, *right*, and *white*, and so they don't pronounce them. ¹¹There are also more vowel sounds in English than in most other language. ¹²The *a* sound in the words *bat* and *mat* is peculiar to English, so second-language

learners often pronounce *bet*, *bat*, and *but* identically. [13]To native speakers of English, these words are having quite distinct sounds that many second-language learners do not hear and so cannot pronounce. [14]Many ESL speaker find it difficult to pronounce the unusual vowel sounds that occur in the words *bird*, *word*, and *nurse*. [15]The fact that the same sound occurs in words with three different vowels—*i*, *o*, and *u*—is example of second major difficulty with English: its inconsistent spelling system.

[16]Most native speakers would agree that English spelling is challenging. [17]Why do *tough* and *stuff* rhyme when their spelling is so different? [18]Shouldn't *tough* rhyme with *cough*? [19]But *cough* rhymes with *off*. [20]Why does *clamour* rhyme with *hammer* while *worm* and *storm*—which should rhyme—don't? [21]There isn't no single answer, but part of the reason is that English is a language that has absorbed many words and sounds from other languages, along with their spellings. [22]Almost 75% of English words have regular spellings, but, unfortunately, the most frequently used words in English are the irregular one. [23]All of us, second-language learners and native speakers alike, simply have to learn to cope.

[24]English also has a huge vocabulary, in part because it borrows freely from other languages. [25]The roots of English are Germanic, but the Celts, Romans, French, and many others have contributed heavily to the language. [26]The gigantic *Oxford English Dictionary* lists about 500,000 words and does not include about another half million technical and scientific word.

[27]English is difficult language for all of these reason, but it's a rich and satisfied one that is well worth the effort to learn.

27

Choosing the Correct Verb Tense

In English, the tense of a verb signals the time of an action: present, past, or future.

> I *work* hard every day.
> I *worked* at the library yesterday.
> I *will work* at the library next summer.

Of course, as you know, there is more to the English tense system than this simple example suggests. English verbs change in complicated and subtle ways to describe complex time relations.

> I *am working* at the library now, but I *have worked* at a number of different jobs in the past. I *will be working* for most of my life, so it *is* important that I *develop* more skills than I *have developed* so far.

Trying to sort out the tenses of the verbs in these sentences is a real headache for second-language learners. Another headache is the fact that some verb tenses have the same meaning, or close to the same meaning. Most native speakers will not hear a difference in meaning between *I am working at the library now* and *I work at the library now*. However, native speakers will certainly pick up the mistake if you say or write *I am been working at the library now* or *I will work at a number of different jobs in the past*. To write clearly, you require a thorough understanding of—and lots of practice with—the English verb tense system. This chapter will provide you with both.

To see at a glance how the English tense system expresses past, present, and future time, study "The Time Line" on the inside of the back cover of this book. The symbol key below explains how to interpret the time line and also the graphic illustrations of tenses covered in this chapter.

▲ indicates *now*, the present moment.

● represents *a completed action or state of being.*

○ indicates *an event that occurred or will occur sometime after the action represented by the black dot took place.*

〰〰 represents *a continuing action or condition*, both of which are expressed by the progressive forms of a verb.

------- indicates that *the action or condition may continue* into the future.

Now that you have an overview of the six basic tenses and the "times" they represent, let's look at how the various tenses are formed. Then we will focus on how to use each one.

Verb Tense Formation

The chart below shows how the different tenses are formed. It provides two examples, *work* (a regular verb) and *grow* (an irregular verb), to illustrate the changes. The principal parts of the verbs are presented first because all tenses are formed from them. (See pages 137–42 for more information about principal parts of verbs.)

Principal parts

Base/ Infinitive	Present Participle	Past	Past Participle
(to) work	*working*	*worked*	*(has) worked*
(to) grow	*growing*	*grew*	*(has) grown*

Tense	Example *(work)*	Example *(grow)*
Simple present (*base; base + s* for third-person singular)	work/works	grow/grows
Present progressive (*am/is/are + present participle*)	am/is/are working	am/is/are growing
Present perfect (*has/have + past participle*)	has/have worked	has/have grown
Present perfect progressive (*has/have + been + present participle*)	has/have been working	has/have been growing

Tense	Example *(work)*	Example *(grow)*
Simple past (*past form*)	worked	grew
Past progressive (*was/were + present participle*)	was/were working	was/were growing
Past perfect (*had + past participle*)	had worked	had grown
Past perfect progressive (*had + been + present participle*)	had been working	had been growing
Simple future (*will + base*) OR (*am/is/are going to + base*)	will work am/is/are going to work	will grow am/is/are going to grow
Future progressive (*will be + present participle*)	will be working	will be growing
Future perfect (*will + have + past participle*)	will have worked	will have grown
Future perfect progressive (*will + have been + present participle*)	will have been working	will have been growing

The chart above shows how to form all the English tenses. Some tenses, however, such as the future perfect progressive, are rarely used because the same meaning can usually be expressed in a less complicated manner. So while this chapter will provide an overview of all tenses, we will concentrate on the most commonly used ones in order to make sure that you understand how to form them correctly and use them appropriately.

Exercise 27.1

Practise by filling in the "missing pieces" (either a principal part or an auxiliary) to form the required verb tense. Use the verb *go* and then use the verb *see*. The first one is done for you. Answers to exercises for this chapter begin on page 522.

	GO	SEE
1. present perfect progressive:	He <u>has</u> been <u>going</u>.	He <u>has</u> been <u>seeing</u>.
2. past progressive:	I was _____.	I was _____.
3. simple present:	He _____. They _____.	He _____. They _____.
4. present progressive:	You _____ _____.	You _____ _____.
5. simple past:	We _____.	We _____.
6. future progressive:	She _____ be _____.	She _____ be _____.
7. present perfect progressive:	He _____ been _____ .	He _____ been _____.
8. past perfect:	We had _____.	We had _____.
9. simple future:	You _____ _____.	You _____ _____.
10. past perfect progressive:	Someone had _____ _____.	Someone had _____ _____.

Exercise 27.2

This exercise requires you to practise with the "pieces" (auxiliaries and principal parts) that are used to form various verb tenses. Use only one word for each blank. Identify the verb tense you used after you have filled in each blank.

1. He will _____ going with us. (Tense: _____)

2. The new year _____ on January 1. (Tense: _____)

3. My parents _____ always _____ good to me. (Tense: _____)

4. Linda and Joy _____ leaving for China a week from now.
   (Tense: _____)

5. My friend _____ lived in Canada for two years, but he returned to Poland last week. (Tense: _____)

6. You _____ _____ working very hard, so why not take a break?
   (Tense: _____)

7. The movie _____ _____ playing for 30 minutes by the time we got there. (Tense: _____)

8. I _____ all the stories last night to prepare for the quiz.
(Tense: _____)

9. I _____ taking off my running shoes right now because they

_____ killing my feet. (Tense: _____)

10. He _____ watching TV when I _____ him last night.

(Tense: _____ ; _____)

The Present Tenses

A. THE SIMPLE PRESENT TENSE

The simple present is used to express present time (especially with non-action linking verbs), general truths, and regular or habitual activity.

> Gianni *is* a handsome man.
> I *hope* that you *are* happy now.
> People *need* food and water to survive.
> Sarah *swims* every day.

B. THE PRESENT PROGRESSIVE TENSE

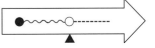

The present progressive is used to express an activity that is *in progress now* or one that is ongoing. Sometimes the activity is in progress over a period of time such as *this week*, *month*, or even *year*.

> I *am talking* on my cellphone.
> They *are driving* home right now.
> Everyone *is learning* verb tenses this week.

It is important to know that some English verbs are not used in any of the progressive tenses. "Non-progressive" verbs describe conditions or states of being, not actions in progress. Often, non-progressive verbs express mental (cognitive) or emotional states, possession, or sense perception. Study the following list. (We will come back to the asterisked words later.)

States of being: appear*, be*, cost, exist, look, seem, weigh*

Mental (cognitive) or emotional states: appreciate, believe, care, dislike, doubt, envy, fear, feel, forget, hate, imagine, know, like, love, mean, mind, need, prefer, realize, recognize, remember, suppose, think*, understand, want

Possession: belong, have*, own, possess

Sense perception: appear*, be, feel*, hear, see*, smell*, taste*

To repeat, these "states of being" verbs are not used in the progressive tenses. You wouldn't say "I am liking her very much." You would use the simple present: "I like her very much." Revise the following sentences by replacing the incorrect verbs with correct ones.

I *am hearing* that you *are owning* a laptop computer. I *am needing* to bor-

row one for today's class. I *am knowing* that you *are hating* to lend your

things, but I *am promising* to return it this evening.

Note that 10 of the verbs on the list—the ones marked with an asterisk (*)—can be used to describe actions as well as states of being or conditions.

State of Being	Action
Solaya *weighs* 65 kg.	Solaya *is weighing* herself to see how much she has gained.
Tom *appears* old and tired.	Tom *is appearing* on a reality TV show.
The food *tastes* good.	We *are tasting* the soup to see if it's good.

Often, you have to decide whether the verb is expressing a state of being or an action before you can decide whether or not to use a progressive tense.

Incorrect:	He *is having* a car. She *is smelling* of cigarette smoke. I *am knowing* you for a long time.
Correct:	He *has a* car. She *smells* of cigarette smoke. I *have known* you for a long time.

Exercise 27.3

Fill in each blank with the appropriate tense—simple present or present progressive—of the verb given in parentheses. Then check your answers.

1. It (snow) _____ again today. In my country, it often (rain)

   _____ , but it never (snow) _____.

2. My father usually (come) _____ to see my games, but tonight

   he (work) _____ a late shift.

3. I (study) _____ almost every night, but tonight I (go)

   _____ to visit some friends.

4. A ticket home (cost) _____ so much that I (doubt)

   _____ that I can afford the trip.

5. We still (believe) _____ we have a good team, and now we

   (try) _____ to develop a winning strategy.

6. My mother usually (phone) _____ me every day at 6:00, but it

   is now 6:30 and I am (wait, still) _____ for her call. I wonder

   what she (do) _____.

7. The baby (cry) _____ again. He always (cry) _____

   when his mother (leave) _____.

8. What (do, you) _____ right now? I (learn) _____

   English verb tenses.

9. The little girl (look) _____ tired, but right now she (look)

   _____ at her favourite storybook.

10. Wanda (want) _____ to get a good job, but she (have)

    _____ to finish her college education first.

GO TO WEB

EXERCISES 27.1, 27.2

C. THE PRESENT PERFECT TENSE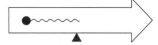

The present perfect tense is used to express three different meanings.

1. Events that occurred (or didn't occur) at some unspecified time in the past, the consequences of which persist in the present.

>   The rain *has stopped.*
>   I *have*n't *voted* yet.

2. Events that were repeated several or many unspecified times in the past and are likely to occur again in the present and future.

>   It *has rained* practically every day this month.
>   I *have* always *voted* for the best person.

3. Events that began at some unspecified time in the past and continue into the present.

>   Yu *has lived* in Canada for a long time.
>   Alessandro *has been* a good boy.

Sentences requiring the present perfect tense frequently contain words or phrases that suggest action beginning in the past and persisting into the present; e.g., *for, since, for a long time, already, so far, always, often, during, recently, this year.*
  Note that *for* is used with a period of time and *since* is used with a specific time.

>   I have lived in Canada *for* a long time.
>   I have lived in Canada *since* 1979.

Exercise 27.4

Answer the questions using the present perfect tense and completing the time phrases correctly.

1. Does Rahim like to travel?

  Yes, he does. He (go) _____ to many different places during his

  life. He (visit) _____ both Asia and Africa (since/for) 2002.

2. Are you taking an ESL course this semester?

No, I (take, already) _____ it. I (study) _____ English

(since/for) 11 years.

3. Do you love me?

Yes, I (love, always) _____ you. I (know) _____ you

(since/for) I was a little girl, and I (love, never) _____ anyone

but you.

4. Does Mira like to shop?

Yes, she loves to shop. She (buy) _____ four pairs of shoes last

week. She already (have) _____ dozens of pairs of shoes in her

closet.

5. When did you move here?

I moved here in _____ . I (be) _____ here (since/for)

_____ years.

D. THE PRESENT PERFECT PROGRESSIVE TENSE

The present perfect progressive tense puts more emphasis on the duration of an action than the present perfect tense does, but other than that subtle difference, the two tenses are practically equivalent in meaning. The present perfect progressive is used to express actions that began at some unspecified time in the past and continue in the present moment or to emphasize the duration of a single past-to-present action. Time phrases such as *for, since, all afternoon, all day, all year* are often used with the present perfect progressive tense to emphasize the period of time over which the action has been taking place.

The class *has been working* on verb tenses. (And they are still working on them.)

I *have been sitting* here all day. (And I am still sitting here.)

Your husband *has been waiting* for you for over an hour. (And he is still waiting.)

The present perfect progressive and present perfect tenses often express the same meaning, especially when the sentence contains *since* or *for*.

Juan *has been living* here since 1997.   Juan *has lived* here since 1997.

I *have been working* here for 20 years.   I *have worked* here for 20 years.

Exercise 27.5

Fill in the blanks with the correct form of the present perfect progressive.

1. (snow) It _____ all day.

2. (study) They _____ physics for three days straight.

3. (work) We _____ hard on our grammar.

4. (answer) She _____ all of the e-mail messages.

5. (ring) The phone _____ all morning.

Exercise 27.6

Fill in the blanks in the sentences below with either the present perfect or the present perfect progressive form of the verb provided. In some sentences, either tense may be used. Compare your answers with ours on page 523.

1. It (rain) _____ all night, and the basement is flooded.

2. There (be) _____ four big rainstorms already this week.

3. I always (do) _____ my homework carefully, and I also (work)

    _____ with a tutor right now.

4. Marty (know) _____ the man for many years.

5. How long (you/live) _____ in Canada?

GO TO WEB

EXERCISES 27.3, 27.4

The Past Tenses

A. THE SIMPLE PAST TENSE

The simple past tense indicates an action or a state that began and ended in the past. It can be used to refer to one event completed in the past or to repeated events completed in the past.

> I *ate* too much last night.
> The weather *was* horrible last winter.
> Binh *lived* in Hong Kong before he *moved* to Montreal.

B. THE PAST PROGRESSIVE TENSE

The past progressive tense is used to express an action or condition that began and ended sometime in the past. It emphasizes the duration—or ongoing quality—of an event that is now completed.

> The boys *were watching* television all morning.
> I *was flying* home from Halifax.
> What *were* you *doing* in Halifax?

The past progressive is also used to indicate an action that was taking place when another occurred. It is often used with time words such as *for* or *since*, or with a clause that uses *when* or *while* to denote simultaneous occurrences.

> Julieta *was driving* to school when the accident happened.
> While I *was cooking* dinner, the power went off.

Sometimes there is little difference in meaning between the past and the past progressive: "It snowed last night" and "It was snowing last night" mean the same thing, and both are correct.

Exercise 27.7

Fill in each blank with the appropriate tense—simple past or past progressive—of the verb given in parentheses. Then check your answers on page 523.

1. Three of us (smoke) _____ in the upstairs washroom when the

   boss (walk) _____ in.

2. The cat (hide) _____ behind the fish tank when I (see) _____ his tail twitch and (catch) _____ him.

3. While their sister (prepare) _____ their lunch, the children (run) _____ into the house and (turn) _____ on the television.

4. When we (work) _____ outside in the yard last night, we (feel) _____ the jolt of a small earthquake.

5. Marco (try) _____ to park his new SUV in the narrow driveway when he (hit) _____ the neighbour's hedge. The branches (make) _____ deep scratches in the paint.

6. As Julio (tell) _____ his friends about his new job, one of them (ask) _____ how he (find) _____ the position.

7. The professor (teach) _____ an important lesson when two men (come) in late and (disturb) _____ the class.

8. I (hear, not) _____ you arrive last night because I (sleep) _____ .

9. (eat) _____ you _____ breakfast this morning when I (phone) _____?

10. I (study) _____ in the college library when I (become) _____ ferociously hungry and (know) _____ that I (have) _____ to eat.

C. THE PAST PERFECT TENSE

Sometimes two different actions or conditions that occurred in the past are included in the same sentence. The past perfect tense is used to depict an action that was completed before another event (or time) in the past. It is the "further-back-in-the-past" tense. In other words, the action that happened first chronologically is expressed by the past perfect; the action that occurred after it is expressed in the simple past.

I *had left* the building before the bomb *exploded*.

Obviously the "leaving" happened first (and is in the past perfect tense)—before the explosion (in the simple past tense)—or I wouldn't be around to tell the story.

The past perfect tense is frequently used with time expressions such as *after*, *before*, and *when*.

Kareem realized his mistake after he *had spoken*.
The class *had left* before the instructor found the room.

To be fair, however, we should acknowledge that if the time sequence is clear from other elements in the sentence, the past perfect is often not necessary. Most native speakers would not hear an error in the following sentences:

I *left* the building before the bomb *exploded*.
The class *left* before the instructor *found* the room.
Kareem *realized* his mistake after he *spoke*.

However, in sentences with *just, already, scarcely, hardly,* and *no sooner than,* the past perfect is required.

My boyfriend *had already gone* home when I *arrived*.
We *had hardly unpacked* our suitcases when the fun *began*.

In these sentences, using the simple past (*already went* and *hardly unpacked*) would be incorrect.

Exercise 27.8

Fill in the blanks with the appropriate tense—simple past or past perfect—of the verbs in parentheses.

1. Dick was late for class. The professor (give, just) _____ a quiz when

   he (get) _____ there.

2. Yesterday my friend Ronit (see) _____ an old friend whom she

   (see, not) _____ in years.

3. I almost missed my flight. Everyone (board, already) _____ the

   plane by the time I (rush) _____ in.

4. We (begin) _____ scarcely _____ the test when the fire alarm

(ring) _____.

5. The movie (start) _____ hardly _____ when the audience

(walk) _____ out.

D. THE PAST PERFECT PROGRESSIVE TENSE

The past perfect progressive tense emphasizes the duration of a past event that took place before another event. Often it is used to refer to a past event that was in progress before being interrupted by another event.

He *had been waiting* in the doctor's office for an hour before she arrived. They *had been talking* about Carol when she walked in.

The exercise below will help you with the time sequencing of English verbs by reminding you of the difference between the present perfect progressive (*has/have + been + present participle*) and the past perfect progressive (*had + been + present participle*).

Exercise 27.9

Fill in the blanks in the sentences below with the present perfect progressive tense or the past perfect progressive tense as appropriate.

1. It is 6:00 p.m. I (work) _____ for 10 hours straight, so it is time to

go home.

2. It was 6:00 p.m. I (work) _____ for 10 hours straight, so it was time

to go home.

3. I woke up feeling strange this morning because I (dream) _____

about dinosaurs all night.

4. Sam is tired because he (work) _____ all morning.

5. They (date) _____ for a year when they got engaged.

Exercise 27.10

Fill in each blank with the most appropriate tense—simple past, past perfect, or past perfect progressive—of the verb in parentheses. In some sentences, more than one answer is possible. Compare your answers with ours on page 524.

1. By the time I (realize) _____ that I needed an elective to graduate, I (drop, already) _____ my history course.

2. He (live) _____ in Beijing until he (be) _____ 20.

3. Karin's sister (arrive) _____ about 10 minutes after Karin (leave) _____ .

4. I (listen, not) _____ when they (make) _____ the announcement.

5. By the time Kim (work) _____ the night shift for three months, she (think) _____ that she would never have a social life again.

6. We (look) _____ forward to our vacation for months when my wife (get) _____ a promotion, and we (have) _____ to cancel our plans.

7. If I (know) _____ how difficult this course (be) _____, I would have signed up for something easier.

8. When he (retire) _____, Professor Green (teach) _____ creative writing for 30 years.

9. We (decide) _____ to sell our condominium, but we (change) _____ our minds when the real estate agent (tell) _____ us the low price we would get.

10. Kim (think, never) _____ about her friend's feelings; she (be) _____ very selfish when she made the decision.

GO TO WEB

EXERCISES 27.5, 27.6

Exercise 27.11

Review the present and past tenses by filling in the blanks using any of the tenses we have studied so far.

1. When I (get) _____ home last night, everyone (eat, already)

   _____ dinner.

2. I (see, never) _____ any of Monet's paintings until I (go)

   _____ to the Museum of Modern Art in New York last year.

3. We (plan) _____ to renovate our house for a long time, but we

   (decide) _____ on a contractor only last week.

4. Hockey (be, always) _____ Canadians' favourite sport; we (play)

   _____ the game for more than 150 years.

5. Although Ali (live) _____ in Toronto since he was 10, he (visit,

   never) _____ the CN Tower.

6. While Igor (talk) _____ on the phone, the bathtub (overflow)

   _____.

7. For six weeks, I (wait) _____ for my transcript to come in the mail.

   I wonder if the Registrar's Office (go) _____ on strike.

8. (you, finish) _____ your homework yet?

9. Yesterday my father (make) _____ me go to the barber who (cut)

   _____ his hair for the past 20 years.

10. While I (wait) _____ for my turn, I (notice) _____ that I (be)

    _____ the only person in the shop under 50.

The Future Tenses

A. THE SIMPLE FUTURE TENSE

There are two ways to express the simple future tense:

1. *will + base form*:   I *will go* home. They *will see* you tomorrow.

2. *(be) + going to + base form*: I *am going to go* home. They *are going to see* you tomorrow.

Both constructions have the same meaning. In informal English, especially speech, *will* is usually contracted to *'ll* in the future tense:

I *'ll go* home. They *'ll see* you tomorrow.
You *'ll go* home. We *'ll see* them tomorrow.

Won't is the contraction for *will not*: You *won't see* me tomorrow.

The *(be) + going to + base form* is usually used when the sentence expresses a prior plan or decision. The *will + base form* is more likely to be used to express willingness or ability. The following examples illustrate the difference.

Prior plan: *(be) + going to + base*

Why did you buy these flippers?
I *am going to learn* how to snorkel. (Not "I *will learn* how to snorkel.")

Willingness: *will + base*

Help me! I'm broke, and my rent is due today.
Ask Roderigo. Maybe he *'ll lend* you some money. (Not "Ask Roderigo. Maybe he *is going to lend* you some money.")

Traditional grammar texts often describe different (and very subtle) changes in meanings expressed by the future tense—e.g., promise, prediction, permission, volition, supposition, concession—and prescribe using a specific form with each purpose. However, these meanings are often difficult to separate from futurity, and native speakers rarely hear lapses in these distinctions as grammar errors. Traditional grammar texts also teach that *shall* is used for first-person subjects (*I shall go home*) and *will* is used with second- and third-person subjects (*You/They will go home*). In North American English, this distinction is obsolete. In short, don't spend a lot of time worrying about the difference between *will/is going* to or *shall/will*.

Fill in the blanks with the appropriate form of the future: *will + base form* or *(be) + going to + base form* of the verbs in parentheses. Check your answers on page 524.

1. He (arrive) _____ tonight, but I (be, not) _____ here.

2. Tomorrow is his birthday, so he (have) _____ dinner with friends.

3. Since you (take) _____ an elective course next semester, I suggest you sign up for sociology. You (enjoy) _____ Professor Singh's sense of humour.

4. Our neighbours (build) _____ an addition onto their home next summer. I hope we (be) _____ on vacation when the construction begins.

5. I (buy) _____ a daytimer schedule because my counsellor says that it (help) _____ me put some order into my life.

B. THE FUTURE PROGRESSIVE TENSE

The future progressive tense expresses an action that will be in progress at a time in the future. There is often little difference in meaning between the future progressive and the simple future.

I *will be seeing* him later tonight.   I *will see* him later tonight.
Tomorrow you *will be dining* with us.   Tomorrow *you will dine* with us.

Exercise 27.13

Use the appropriate verb form—future or future progressive—to fill in the blanks in these sentences.

1. I have no idea where I (work) _____ next week, but I (let) _____ you know as soon as I found out.

2. My fiancée insists that I buy her a diamond ring before she (marry) _____ me, so I (buy) _____ a lot of lottery tickets.

3. I (have, not) _____ time to talk on the phone this afternoon because I (cook) _____ a traditional dinner for 14 people.

4. Ravi says that he (teach) _____ in Tokyo next year.

5. We (stay, not) _____ at this hotel again.

C. THE FUTURE PERFECT TENSE

The future perfect expresses an action that will be completed before another time or action in the future.

> By next June, we *will have graduated* from college.
> Before the end of the semester, we *will have covered* a lot of grammar.
> Before we *leave* Quebec City, we *will have seen* all of the tourist attractions.
> (Note that the verb in the time clause is in the simple present tense.)

Often, use of the future perfect tense is not absolutely necessary. For instance, the simple future could be used in these sentences:

> By next June, we *will graduate* from college.
> Before the end of the semester, we *will cover* a lot of grammar.
> Before we leave Quebec City, we *will see* all of the tourist attractions.

However, if *already* is used in the sentence, the future perfect is required as it is in this example:

> Correct: I *will already have gone* to bed before you arrive.
> Incorrect: I *will already go* to bed before you arrive.

D. THE FUTURE PERFECT PROGRESSIVE TENSE

This tense is seldom used. It stresses the duration of an action in the future that takes place before another action in the future. Often, the future perfect progressive and the future perfect tenses have the same meaning, as in the examples below:

Our cousins *will have been studying* English for three months before they arrive in Canada.

Our cousins *will have studied* English for three months before they arrive in Canada.

Exercise 27.14

Fill in the blanks with a future tense of the verb in parentheses. More than one correct answer is possible in some of these sentences.

1. I (go) _____ to Florida with Josef next spring because by then he

   (earn) _____ enough money to pay for his share of the trip.

2. We are going to be late because of the terrible traffic. By the time we

   (reach) _____ the airport, Miryam's plane (arrive, already)

   _____. She (worry) _____ that something has happened to

   us.

3. At this pace, we (walk) _____ 30 km by tonight.

4. You were born in _____. By the year 2050, you (live) _____

   for _____ years. You (see) _____ many changes!

5. I (clean, already) _____ the house by the time you get here.

Using Present Tenses to Indicate Future Time

As if distinguishing among all these tenses is not complicated enough, there is another convention you need to know about. In English, the simple present and present progressive tenses are also used to express future time in several circumstances.

1. A few simple present tense verbs—*arrive, begin, close, come, end, finish, leave, open, return, start*—are used with scheduled events to express future time. Usually the sentences contain future time words or phrases; these are underlined in the three examples below.

> Sunil's flight *arrives* <u>at midnight</u>.
> School *begins* <u>on September 8 next year</u>.
> The stores at the mall *close* <u>at 6:00 p.m. today</u>.

2. When the sentence contains a time or condition clause, the simple present tense is required in that clause even though the verb refers to future or conditional time. Consider these examples carefully; the underlined clauses express time or condition and the verbs must be in the simple present.

> Incorrect: I *will take* a vacation <u>after I *will quit*</u> my job.
> <u>If the snow *will continue*</u>, the president *will close* the college.
>
> Correct: I *will take* a vacation <u>after I *quit*</u> my job.
> <u>If the snow *continues*</u>, the president *will close* the college.

3. The present progressive is often used when a time word or phrase in the sentence indicates the future.

> I *am touring* Tuscany <u>next fall</u>.
> Jess *is meeting* Deb and Tamara in New York <u>on the weekend</u>.

Exercise 27.15

Fill in the blanks with the correct form of the verb in parentheses.

1. As soon as Val (graduate) _____, he (leave) _____ for Africa.

2. If the wind (blow) _____ hard, that house (collapse) _____.

3. They (return) _____ to China next year.

4. If it (rain) _____ on the weekend, we (cancel) _____ our

   plans for a beach party.

5. Pierre (be) _____ here in Canada for at least another year before

   he (return) _____ home to Haiti and (get) _____ a job.

GO TO WEB

EXERCISES 27.7, 27.8

Exercise 27.16

Complete the following paragraphs using only the progressive forms of the present, past, and future tenses. The first verb has been converted for you.

Many of us (study) *are studying* computers as part of our college programs.

In fact, computer skills have become essential for success in almost all of the

jobs we (do) _____ in the next decade. Most Canadians take the pres-

ence of a computer in the home, at work, and at school for granted. It is

astonishing, therefore, to reflect that not that many years ago, many people

(treat) _____ computers as a mere fad. During the 1940s, for example,

engineers (predict) _____ that computers in the future would weigh

over a tonne. In the same decade, the chairman of IBM told his company,

"We (lose, not) _____ sleep over these machines." He thought there

would be a world market for "maybe five computers." A decade later, book

publishers (assure) _____ their employees that data processing was a

fad that wouldn't last a year. In 1977, the president of Digital Equipment

Corporation (tell) _____ the company's shareholders that there was no

reason for anyone to want a computer in the home.

Today, all of us who (use) _____ computers know about Bill Gates, the president of Microsoft. In the years to come, his company (produce) _____ many of the programs and applications that will become the standard of the future. These programs will use gigabytes of memory. It is hard to believe that in 1981 Bill Gates (tell) _____ anyone who would listen, "640K ought to be enough for anybody."

Exercise 27.17

Go through Exercise 27.16 again. This time, assume that the writer wishes to emphasize the events themselves, not the time over which they took place. Fill in the blanks with the appropriate simple tenses (past, present, and future). Avoid using any progressives. When you have finished, compare your two sets of paragraphs. Which version do you prefer? Why?

Exercise 27.18

In the following paragraphs, fill in the blanks with the most appropriate verb tenses, choosing from the 12 tenses you have reviewed.

The patriarch of my family (be) _____ my late grandfather Sergei, who was born in 1935 near the Russian city of Moscow. Sergei's parents, Boris and Natasha, (work) _____ hard all their lives, but they never (earn) _____ much money. Sergei (have) _____ two younger sisters and a younger brother, but his sisters (die) _____ during the terrible years of World War II. In 1955, Sergei (come) _____ to Canada as a refugee. Soon he (work) _____ hard at a small furniture factory in Toronto. He (meet) _____ a young Ukrainian woman named Irena, and they (get + marry) _____ in 1958. They (buy) _____ a small house in Toronto after their son, my father Yuri, was born in 1960. Later, three more children were born. My grandfather always loved music; in fact, he (play) _____ his balalaika (a Russian stringed instrument) when he (pass) _____ away suddenly in 1997. My grandparents (create) _____ a loving and musical family, and I (feel) _____ lucky to (know) _____ them both.

My father Yuri (be) _____ a professional musician. He (learn) _____ to play the balalaika from his father when he (be) _____ a child. Now he (play) _____ guitar, and he (make) _____ his living as a rock musician. My father (marry) _____ my mother Alice in 1980, but they (divorce) _____ since 1985, the year I was born. My father (travel) _____ a lot because of his work, and I think that it (be) _____ difficult for him to maintain relationships. Nevertheless, he (be + always) _____ a very good father to me. He (teach) _____ me music since I was a little girl. Sometimes I (go) _____ with him on the road when I'm not in school.

I (study) _____ at Humber College in the music program for the past two years. Like my father and grandfather, I focus on stringed instruments, mainly the bass. My father (play) _____ rock music, but I (concentrate) _____ on jazz. In the future, I (go) _____ to study and work in New York, and I (hope) _____ to learn from some of the great jazz musicians whom I (admire + always) _____. With my musical heritage, my talent, and my ambition, I (think) _____ that I (be) _____ a great musician some day.

28

More about Verbs

In addition to verb formation and tense, there are three verbal constructions that present problems for second-language writers: negatives, participial adjectives, and modal auxiliaries.

Forming Negatives

Not expresses a negative idea. In a negative sentence, the word *not* comes immediately after the *to be* verb or an auxiliary verb. Auxiliary verbs are forms of *to be*, *to have*, *shall*, *will*, or a modal auxiliary. (Reminder: The forms of *to be* are *am/is/are/was/were/will be*. The forms of *to have* are *have/has/had*.)

Yes, the sun *is* out.	No, the sun *is not* out.
I *have learned* my lesson.	I *have not learned* my lesson.
They *will eat* a whole pizza.	They *will not eat* a whole pizza.
She *might visit* her family.	She *might not visit* her family.

If the main verb in the sentence does not have an auxiliary, the *to do* verb is added before the *not*; the main verb follows.

I *love* him.	I *do not love* him.
He *loves* me.	He *does not love* me.
I *loved* him.	I *did not love* him.

Not can be contracted to *n't*. *Isn't, aren't, wasn't, weren't, won't, doesn't, don't, didn't, hasn't, haven't, hadn't, can't, couldn't*, and *wouldn't* are examples of contracted negative verbs. What are the full forms of these contractions? (Note that *ain't* is not included in the list. Using *ain't* is a grammatical error.)

Grammatically, the word *not* is a negative adverb; it isn't actually part of the verb itself. Other negative adverbs that are used to express negative meanings are *never, rarely, seldom, scarcely (ever), hardly (ever),* and *barely (ever)*. Here are some examples:

My wife and I *rarely* go out.
I *never* understand what my boyfriend really wants.
The train is *hardly ever* late.
My son *seldom* goes to school.

The word *no* can be used as an adjective in front of a noun to provide the same meaning as *not*. Just make sure that you do not use two negatives. If you do, you create a grammatical error known as a "double negative."

Correct: Ali *doesn't have* problems speaking English.
             Ali *has no* problems speaking English.

Incorrect: Ali *doesn't have no* problems speaking English. (Double negative)

Exercise 28.1

Rewrite the following sentences to make them negative. Include both the full form and the contracted form of the verbs. We've completed the first question for you as an example. Answers for exercises in this chapter begin on page 526.

1. The student needs help from the teacher.

   The student *does not* (or *doesn't*) *need* help from the teacher.

   ALSO CORRECT: The student *needs no* help from the teacher.

2. I trust the bank.

3. Everyone trusts the bank.

4. The passengers have their passports in order.

5. You should have given the students a quiz on negatives.

6. The man looks suspicious to me.

7. Ling forgot to pick us up yesterday.

8. We always watch our diet.

9. José and Marta wanted to eat before the movie.

10. The class needs more exercises on verb forms.

Exercise 28.2

Change the following affirmative sentences to negative ones; make any negative clauses affirmative. Pay close attention to verb tense as you make these changes.

1. Mohammed and Hassan have enjoyed the winters in Canada.

2. I certainly want to see you.

3. I certainly wanted to see you.

4 We were sleeping when you called.

5. Most of the class attended the reception for international students.

6. The Montreal Canadiens succeeded in winning many new fans last season.

7. Susana always wants to come to the movies with us, even when we don't want her to join us.

8. The computer is working very well.

9. The computer was working very well.

10. She came to the meeting alone.

GO TO WEB

EXERCISES 28.1, 28.2

Participial Adjectives

Allan and Zeta went out on a date. It didn't go well. The two sentences that follow describe why the evening was not a success, but their meanings are different.

Version 1: Allan was a *boring* date.
Version 2: Allan was a *bored* date.

Boring and *bored* are adjectives that are formed from the participle forms of the verb *to bore*. *Boring* is the present participle; *bored* is the past participle. Choosing the correct participial adjective is often a problem for second-language writers. Let's go back to the story.

In version 1, Allan is a dull fellow. He is shy and has nothing to talk about. He bored Zeta. She found him *boring*. In version 2, Zeta is the dull person with nothing to talk about. Zeta bored Allan, so he was a *bored* date.

Are you *confused*? Is the choice *confusing*? Yes. First, we'll sort it out for you, and then we'll provide some practice with participial adjectives.

The present participle, the *-ing* form, conveys an active meaning. The noun it describes *is* or *does something*. Allan bores Zeta in version 1, so he is *boring*. Participial adjectives often confuse ESL writers, so these words are *confusing*.

The past participle conveys a passive meaning. The noun it describes *has something done to it*. Zeta bores Allan in version 2, so he is *bored*. Participial adjectives confuse ESL writers, so these writers are *confused*. Note that the past participle of irregular verbs may not end in *-ed*. (See Chapter 11, then check your dictionary for the past participle form of any irregular verb not covered in Chapter 11.)

Exercise 28.3

Complete each of the following sentences by filling in the blank with the correct participle of the italicized verb. Then check your answers on page 526.

1. Bob *loves* Mary. He is a _____ man.

2. Bob *loves* Mary. She is a _____ woman.

3. The movie *interests* the children. They are _____ children. They are watching an _____ movie.

4. The news *surprised* my brother. He is a _____ person. The news was quite _____ .

5. The cartoons *amused* me. The cartoons were _____ . I was _____ .

6. The lecture *stimulated* the students. The lecture was _____ . The students were _____ .

7. The task *exhausted* me. I was _____ by this _____ task.

8. The possibility *excites* everyone. The possibility is _____. Everyone is _____.

9. The child's tantrum *embarrassed* his father. The father was _____. The child's tantrum was _____.

10. The test results *shocked* the whole town. The _____ people could hardly believe the _____ test results.

Exercise 28.4

In each of the following sentences, supply the correct present or past participle. The first one has been done for you as an example.

1. If a new friend *fascinates* you, how would you describe the person? *fascinating*

   How would you describe yourself? *fascinated*

2. If your neighbour *annoys* you, how would you describe the neighbour?

   _____

   How would you describe yourself? _____

3. If an accident *horrifies* you, how would you describe the accident?

   _____

   How would you describe yourself? _____

4. If the garbage *disgusts* you, how would you describe yourself?_____
   How would you describe the garbage? _____

5. If a meal *satisfies* you, how would you describe the meal? _____
   How would you describe yourself? _____

6. The test results *disappointed* him. The test results were _____. He was _____.

7. Jan's job doesn't *bore* her. Jan _____. Jan's job _____.

8. If the music *pleases* you, how would you describe yourself? _____

   How would you describe the music?_____

9. If the answer *amazes* you, how would you describe the answer? _____

   How would you describe yourself? _____

10. Your story *inspires* me. I am _____. Your story is _____.

GO TO WEB

EXERCISES 28.3, 28.4

Modal Auxiliaries

As we have seen, the verbs *am, is, are, was, were; do, does, did; has, have,* and *had* can stand alone as the only verb in a sentence. They can also work in an auxiliary capacity; that is, they can combine with the main verb in a sentence to change time zones or to form a negative construction.

There is another kind of auxiliary verb called a "modal" auxiliary. These words provide different shades of meaning to the main verb. The modal auxiliaries are listed below:

can	might	should
could	must	will
may	shall	would

Some common verb phrases also function as modals:

be able to	have to	supposed to
be going to	ought to	used to

We will discuss these and other modal phrases in detail below.

The examples that follow will show you how modals change the meaning of the main verb.

Modal	Interpretation
I *can* work.	I am able to do the job.
I *could* work.	If someone would offer me a job.
I *may* work.	But, then again, maybe I won't.
I *must* work.	My family needs the money.
I *should* work.	My mother is nagging me to get a job.
I *would* work.	If you paid me enough.
I *used to* work.	But I don't anymore.

The good news about modals is that they are always followed by the base form of the verb (e.g., *work*) with no *-s* added to the third-person singular or *-ed* added to the past tense. Unlike *do* and *has*, the modal auxiliaries don't change number and, except for *can/could* and *will/would*, they don't change time.

The bad news about modals is that they often suggest subtle changes in meaning that confuse second-language writers. Traditional grammar texts use a great deal of ink attempting to distinguish "obligation" versus "advisability" and "polite" versus "impolite" requests. The following chart will help you sort out the meanings of modals. But while you're struggling to learn the differences among various modals, keep in mind that native speakers almost never hear a difference between your telling them that you *may work tomorrow* and you *might work tomorrow*.

Single-Word Modal Auxiliaries

Auxiliary	Meaning	Example (Present/Future)	Example (Past)
can	1. ability	I *can swim* well.	I *could swim* when I was two.
	2. informal request	*Can* I *call* you tonight?	
could	1. past tense of *can*		I *could swim* when I was two.
	2. polite request	*Could* I please *speak* to your wife?	
	3. low level of certainty	It *could rain* tonight, or it *could be* clear.	
may	1. polite request	*May* I please *speak* to your wife?	
	2. low level of certainty	It *may rain* tonight, but it *may* not [*rain*].	
	3. possibility	Harvey says he *may go* with us.	

Auxiliary	Meaning	Example (Present/Future)	Example (Past)
might	1. low level of certainty	It *might rain* tonight, but it *might* not [*rain*].	
	2. possibility	I *might visit* Paris this summer.	
	3. past tense of *may*		Harvey said he *might go* with us.
must	1. strong necessity	You *must drink* water.	
	2. high level of certainty	The teacher isn't here, so she *must be* ill.	
shall	1. polite question	*Shall* I *help* you across the street?	
	2. future (with *I/we*)	I *shall see* you tomorrow. (or *will see* . . .)	
should	1. advisable	You *should lose* a few pounds.	
	2. high level of certainty	You study hard, so you *should do* well in the course.	
	3. obligation	He *should support* his children.	
will	1. complete certainty	I'm sure you *will* succeed.	
	2. willingness	I*'ll* be happy to help you.	
	3. polite request	*Will* you please *tell* me what you think?	
would	1. preference (with *rather*)	I *would rather eat* at a restaurant.	
	2. polite request	*Would* you please *tell* me what you think?	
	3. repeated action in past		We *would* always *phone* home on weekends when we lived abroad.
	4. conditional with *if* clause	I *would go* outside if it stopped raining.	

Exercise 28.5

Complete the sentences in the following exercise by using one modal auxiliary together with one main verb from the choices we have provided. We have done the first sentence as an example. Use each modal and main verb only once. Be careful: two of the sentences require negations. When you have completed this exercise, check the answers on page 527.

Modal Auxiliaries		**Main Verbs**	
can	shall	tell	say
could	should	clean	talk
may	will	~~fall~~	eat
~~might~~	would	go	live
must		hand	

1. If you lean out of the window, you <u>might</u> <u>fall</u>.

2. _____ you please _____ me the phone?

3. You _____ _____ Rani about the party because we want it to be a surprise for her.

4. The baby is just learning to talk but he _____ _____ five or six words. A few weeks ago, he _____ _____ at all.

5. Pat _____ _____ at her parents' home, but I'm not sure.

6. _____ we _____ at the new restaurant?

7. I didn't get much sleep last night. I _____ _____ to bed early tonight, but I want to wait up for you.

8. I promise I _____ _____ my room tomorrow.

The chart on page 355 summarizes modal and other auxiliaries that are made up of more than a single word. *Ought to* and *used to* do not require any change in the verb form. Like the single-word modals, they simply precede the base form of the main verb. For example, "She used to (*modal*) love (*base form of verb*) me."

    Be able to, be going to, be supposed to, and *has/have to* present an extra challenge. Because they include the verb *to be*, they require a change in the auxiliary itself to mark tense and number. Study the following examples.

We *were able to* finish the assignment.
You *are going to* have trouble with that car.
I *am supposed to* teach a class at noon today.
She and I *were supposed to* teach a class yesterday.
He *has to* change his clothes.
They *had to* change their clothes.

When you are using past participles such as *supposed to* and *used to*, don't forget to include the *-d* at the end of the word. Omitting the *-d* is one of the most common errors made by student writers.

Incorrect: The show was suppose to begin an hour ago.
             I use to have more money.

Correct: The show was suppose*d* to begin an hour ago.
             I use*d* to have more money.

Phrasal Modal Auxiliaries

Auxiliary	Meaning	Example (Present/Future)	Example (Past)
be able to	ability (can)	He *is able to handle* the truck	He *was able to handle* the truck.
be going to	plan (for the future)	I *am going to help* you.	I *was going to help* you, but I changed my mind.
be supposed to	expectation	We *are supposed to meet* them.	We *were supposed to meet* them, but we forgot.
have/has/had to	necessity (must)	He *has to go* to the bank today.	He *had to go* to the bank on Tuesday.
ought to	1. advisability (should)	We *ought to bring* our raincoats and an umbrella.	
	2. high level of certainty	She studies hard and *ought to do* well in school.	
used to	repeated action		She *used to work* hard in school. He *used to weigh* 100 kg.

Exercise 28.6

Fill in each blank with one of the phrasal modal auxiliaries. More than one modal may be correct, but use each only once. Compare your answers with our suggestions on page 527.

1. It _____ rain later, so you _____ take your umbrella.

2. I _____ go to the United States with just a passport, but now I _____ get a visa.

3. We _____ go to the beach yesterday, but it was too cold. We hope that we _____ go tomorrow.

Exercise 28.7

Use one of the auxiliaries with each verb in parentheses. More than one auxiliary may be possible.

1. (see) The doctor _____ you later this afternoon.

2. (finish) If he works very hard, Paulo _____ the project before the deadline.

3. (complete) He _____ it on time if he wants to get paid.

4. (visit) You _____ your grandmother because she misses you.

5. (run) When Oswaldo was younger, he _____ very fast.

6. (love) Felix bought his girlfriend a beautiful engagement ring; he _____ her very much.

7. (drink) Her parents _____ heavily, but they have stopped entirely since joining Alcoholics Anonymous.

8. (suppose) I _____ to study for the quiz yesterday, but I forgot.

9. (rain) The sky is getting darker; it _____ _____ .

10. (smoke, not) You _____ _____ in public buildings in Canada.

Exercise 28.8

Use a modal auxiliary (one word or a phase) in each of the blanks. Some sentences require negatives.

1. I wonder when the boat will arrive. It _____ be here an hour ago.

2. You _____ answer your cellphone in class.

3. If you have a food processor, you _____ prepare this salad in a few minutes.

4. What did you say? _____ you please repeat it?

5. You _____ be in two places at once.

6. The mayor is not in her office; she _____ be at a meeting.

7. Their whole house is decorated in red; they _____ really love the colour!

8. Jon _____ know better than to call me at midnight.

9. Our instructor _____ give us quizzes every day, but now he gives only three a semester.

10. _____ you _____ come to our party?

Exercise 28.9

Fill in each blank with an appropriate modal auxiliary.

People choose to immigrate to Canada for many reasons. They _____ want to have more economic opportunity. Or they _____ be looking for a better education for their children. Or they _____ want to _____ to practise their beliefs openly. Perhaps the country where they _____ live denied them certain rights that they _____ take for granted in Canada. Whatever their reasons for coming, immigrants to Canada _____ work very hard to adjust to their new country. They _____ find new homes and jobs, and most of them _____ learn a new language. Immigrating is not an easy process, but new immigrants hope that they _____ build a better life in their new home.

GO TO WEB

EXERCISES 28.5, 28.6

Exercise 28.10

Edit these sentences to correct the errors in negative constructions, participial adjectives, and modal auxiliaries.

1. Claude doesn't very interesting in the movie; he found it bored.

2. All the plants in the office are dying. They may be getting enough sunlight.

3. He ought to been more surprising when I told him the shocked news.

4. You hardly never meet a real prince. Was it an excited experience?

5. Cao was disappointing because he was suppose to get a good grade on the test and he failed.

6. They hasn't never been to Europe, but they are suppose to go next year.

7. Neither Amit nor Helene is going to work on the weekend, but they don't have no money to go to the clubs with us.

8. The whole beach was deserting. We couldn't see nothing but sand.

9. Don't a person has to be rich to lead an excited life?

10. Who is knocking on the door? It can be Victoria because she is out of town, so it shall be Marcella or it used to be Brian. Why you don't open the door and found out?

29

Solving Plural Problems

Singular vs. Plural Nouns

Nouns in English are words that name people, places, things, or ideas. For example, *Bart Simpson*, *Quebec*, *alligator*, and *honesty* are all examples of nouns. The first three examples are **concrete** nouns; in other words, they refer to physical objects that we can see or touch. The fourth example, *honesty*, is an **abstract** noun that refers to a concept that exists in our minds; it cannot be seen or touched.

Singular nouns refer to one person, place, thing, or idea: *mother*, *bedroom*, *book*, *justice*. Plural nouns refer to more than one person, place, or thing: *mothers*, *bedrooms*, *books*. Abstract nouns are not usually found in the plural form.

To form the plural of most nouns, you add *-s* to the singular form.

Singular	Plural	Singular	Plural
classroom	classrooms	idea	ideas
cousin	cousins	truck	trucks
friend	friends	umbrella	umbrellas

Exercise 29.1

Rewrite the following sentences in the plural. Make sure that your verbs and pronouns agree with the plural nouns; you may also have to delete an article (*a* or *an*). The first question is done for you. Answers for exercises in this chapter begin on page 528.

1. The book is on her table.

   The books are on their tables.

2. Your little girl loves her new toy.

3. A student learns to take a test.

4. A good doctor listens to her patient.

5. The shark is swimming around the boat.

6. The boy visits his girlfriend every night.

7. This room is very large.

8. An angry dog is a dangerous animal.

9. Should my brother find his own apartment?

10. My house has a swimming pool.

Unfortunately, there are many exceptions to the "add -*s* for plural" rule. The most common exceptions are listed below.

1. Irregular plural forms

Most of these are very common words, but they are based on an older form of English. You need to memorize them and get used to their irregular nature.

Singular	Plural	Singular	Plural
child	children	mouse	mice
foot	feet	ox	oxen
goose	geese	tooth	teeth
man	men	woman	women

2. Nouns ending in "soft" sounds of *-s, -x, -z, -ch, -sh*: add *-es*

Singular	Plural
box	boxes
buzz	buzzes
church	churches
class	classes
dish	dishes
kiss	kisses

If the *-ch* is a "hard" sound—as in *stomach*—add *-s* only: *stomachs*.

3. Nouns ending in *-y* preceded by a consonant: change the *-y* to *-i* and add *-es*

Singular	Plural
country	countries
lady	ladies
penny	pennies
reply	replies

Nouns ending in *-y* preceded by a vowel are regular. Add *-s* to pluralize them.

boys	keys
delays	valleys

4. Nouns ending in *-f* or *-fe*: add *-ves* if the plural is pronounced with a *-v* sound

Note that the word *self* is in this category. This rule has important consequences for the "self" words.

calves	himself → themselves
knives	yourself → yourselves
thieves	herself → themselves
wives	myself → ourselves

5. If the plural noun keeps its -*f* sound, add only -*s*.

beliefs   chiefs
chefs   proofs

6. Some nouns ending in -*o* are pluralized by adding -*es*; other nouns ending in -*o* require only -*s*. Check your dictionary if you're not sure.

echoes	BUT	pianos
heroes		sopranos
potatoes		studios
tomatoes		zoos

7. Some nouns are used in the singular form only, for both singular and plural.

caribou	elk	salmon
carp	moose	sheep
deer	pickerel	trout

8. Some nouns are used in the plural form only, even though they refer to a single unit.

glasses	pyjamas
jeans	scissors
pants	shorts

9. Some foreign language nouns retain their original plural form.

Singular	Plural	Singular	Plural
analysis	analyses	larva	larvae
criterion	criteria	phenomenon	phenomena
fungus	fungi	stimulus	stimuli
hypothesis	hypotheses	thesis	theses

Fill in the blank with the missing form (singular or plural) of the noun or pronoun given in each item below. The first one is done for you.

Singular	**Plural**
1. one movie	two <u>movies</u>
2. look at yourself (one person)	look at _____ (two people)
3. the category	three different _____
4. a _____	the women
5. one moose	many _____
6. my foot	their _____
7. an _____	thick eyelashes
8. one _____	many criteria
9. the man himself	the men _____
10. a photo	several _____
11. the zoo	two _____
12. a _____	many tomatoes
13. one _____	four stimuli
14. the monarch	two _____
15. one thesis	several _____
16. a thief	a pack of _____
17. my husband	my friends' _____
18. his only _____	all your teeth
19. the hero	these _____
20. one chief	two _____

Insert the correct plural forms of the nouns provided before each sentence.

child, class   1. No one would take the _____ to swim

           _____.

mushroom, berry   2. Some wild _____ and _____ might be poisonous, so be careful about eating them.

tree, leaf   3. It is difficult to identify _____ by their bark, but it's easy if you have some _____ from the tree.

course, quiz   4. We are lucky to have only three _____ this semester because each of them has weekly _____.

scissors, knife   5. They had to defend themselves with _____ and _____.

city, community   6. Most Canadian _____ are home to many different ethnic _____.

inquiry, reply   7. Ming mailed out a dozen _____ about jobs, but she received only six _____.

potato, yourself   8. The three of you will have to pick the _____ by _____.

ninety, attorney   9. When my grandmother was in her _____, she hired several _____ to manage her business.

activity, study   10. Marcel has so many after-school _____ that he has no time left for his _____.

GO TO WEB

EXERCISES 29.1, 29.2

Count vs. Non-Count Nouns

Count nouns are words for separate persons, places, or things that can be counted: *one apple, two apples, three apples*. Count nouns can be made plural in one of the ways explained above. Count nouns name individual, distinct items: e.g., *college, job, meal, student, toy*. Note that the *-s* ending makes each of these count nouns plural: *colleges, jobs, meals, students, toys*.

Non-count nouns (also known as "uncountable" nouns) are words that identify things that cannot be counted. Many non-count nouns refer to a "whole" that is made up of different parts. For instance, a room may contain two sofas, three tables, four chairs, and a television. All of these items can be counted—and the words can be made plural. However, all of these items can be considered as a *"whole"* and described as *furniture*, which is a non-count noun that cannot be pluralized.

> Incorrect: two chair, furnitures
> Correct: two chairs, furniture

There are several categories of non-count nouns.

- Abstract nouns (words for concepts that exist as ideas in our minds): e.g., *courage, fun, hatred, health, information*. You acquire data in bits and pieces, but you acquire *information* as a whole. You wouldn't say that you have gathered *informations* as you acquire more of it.
- Words that identify a quantity or mass: e.g., *air, coffee, food, rice, salt, sugar, water*. These words identify substances that are made up of particles too numerous to count. You can count *bottles of water* or *bowls of rice*, but you cannot count *water* or *rice*.
- The names of many sports: e.g., *golf, hockey, tennis*
- The names of some illnesses: e.g., *diabetes, flu, osteoporosis*
- Subjects of study, whether their form is singular (*astronomy, biology, chemistry*) or plural (*economics, mathematics, physics*)
- Weather and other natural phenomena: e.g., *electricity, fire, lightning, sunshine*

The important thing to remember about non-count nouns is that they have only one form, not different forms for singular and plural. The count or non-count quality of a noun also determines the articles and modifiers that are used before the noun. (We will review articles and modifiers in Chapter 30.) For now, keep in mind that you do not add plural endings to non-count nouns, although some of them, such as the academic disciplines listed above, have an *-s* ending.

Incorrect: I should do my homeworks.
Correct: I should do my homework.

Incorrect: We always have funs on our vacations.
Correct: We always have fun on our vacations.

Incorrect: My friends and I are concerned about our healths.
Correct: My friends and I are concerned about our health.

Incorrect: The airline lost our luggages.
Correct: The airline lost our luggage.

Exercise 29.4

Choose the correct word from the list below for the blank in each sentence. Write a C above the word in the sentence if it is a count noun; write NC above the word in the sentence if it is a non-count noun. Make the word plural if necessary. Use each word only once. Check your answers on page 529.

advice	suitcase	coffee
health	sugar	dinner
baggage	problem	water
milk	knowledge	vitamin
math	beef	chemical

1. Put some _____ and _____ in my _____, please.

2. I need your _____ to solve two _____.

3. Your _____ of _____ is better than mine.

4. I love to eat _____ for _____.

5. Please pick up both of my _____ at the _____ claim.

6. The _____ in the lake is full of dangerous _____.

7. You have to take your _____ if you want to regain your

_____.

So far so good, but there is one complication that makes the count/non-count issue very tricky. Some nouns can be both count and non-count, depending on how they are used. If the noun has a general, as-a-whole kind of meaning, it is non-count and is not pluralized; e.g., "We often have chicken for dinner." If the noun has a specific, count-them-up kind of meaning, it is a count noun and can be pluralized; e.g., "Four chickens were running around in the yard." Therefore, some non-count nouns may be used in a countable sense and have a plural form. Study the four examples given below.

Exercise
Non-count (in a general sense): *Exercise* is good for you.
Count (a specific movement or example): Do all of the *exercises* and check your answers.

Food
Non-count (in a general sense): *Food* is an important part of every culture.
Count (specific cuisines): There were *foods* from all over the world at the party.

Experience
Non-count (in a general sense): You need *experience* for this job.
Count (specific happenings): I had some interesting *experiences* in class this semester.

Fire
Non-count (in a general sense): When did humans learn to use the power of *fire*?
Count (specific blazes): We could see several different *fires* on the beach.

Check an advanced learner's dictionary if you are unsure whether a noun is count or non-count. Sometimes non-count nouns are identified as "uncountable" (a *U* in your dictionary). "Non-count" and "Uncountable" mean the same thing.

Exercise 29.5

Write the correct form of the word—either singular or plural—in the blanks below.

money, luck

1. They often win _____ in the lottery, so I guess you could say they have good _____.

luggage, backpack   2. After the _____ arrived at the hotel, we found that two _____ were missing.

piano, furniture   3. Both _____ were too large to fit into the living room because of all the _____.

advice, homework   4. Our teacher gave us good _____ about doing all the _____ he assigns.

cattle, beef   5. At the slaughterhouse, those _____ will be turned into _____.

light   6. As the sun set and the _____ faded, we turned on all the _____ in the cottage.

time   7. How many _____ do I have to tell you that _____ is important?

garbage, work   8. Taking out the _____ every week is not much _____.

history, music   9. Carmine studied the _____ of _____ while he was at university.

jeans, wardrobe   10. Most people have a pair of _____ in their _____.

Exercise 29.6

Correct the errors in the following sentences, then check your answers on page 529.

1. Robert is going bald and wants to know where he can get informations on hairs replacement.

2. I found a couple of hairs in my soup.

3. You can have funs in sports, but the enjoyments disappear if you play too much hockeys or footballs.

4. We want to give you some new cloths to wear as an expression of our thank.

5. The riches get richer, and the poors get poorer.

6. Having two business go bankrupt was a learning experiences.

7. All of my relatives had advices for me when I came to Canada.

8. Did you get any new informations about the computer datas we lost?

9. We didn't hear much laughters coming from the back of the van as we drove through the rush-hour traffics.

10. Why don't you tell us some jokes?

Robert wants informations about hairs replacement.

Exercise 29.7

Rewrite the following paragraph, changing the appropriate nouns from singular to plural. Don't forget to make your verbs and pronouns agree with your plural nouns, and prepare to omit some articles (*a*, *an*)—the subject of Chapter 30. Your paragraph will begin "Sharks are scary animals to most people." Check your answers before continuing.

The shark is a scary animal to most people. It is considered to be a fish that attacks and eats humans from the depths of the ocean. The shark is, in fact, an ancient species. Its ancestor dates back about 350 million years, as the fossil record shows. In size, the shark ranges from a tiny angel shark that is less than a metre in length to the huge 15-metre whale shark that can weigh 700 kilograms.

The shark is a very effective predator in the ocean. It has very good eyesight, and even in total darkness, the shark can sense the movement of its prey by means of special pores in its skin that sense another animal's electrical vibrations. In addition, a shark actually smells its prey from a long way off. These characteristics make the shark a good killing machine as it hunts for food.

Although the shark is high on the food chain, it usually eats smaller fish, crabs, seals, and other sea creatures. A shark does not seek out humans to eat. We may fear the shark, but there are only about 100 shark attacks on humans in the world in a year, and perhaps 25 to 30 of these are fatal. Given our increasing appetite for shark meat, the truth is that we eat many more of them than they eat of us.

GO TO WEB

EXERCISES 29.3, 29.4, 29.5

Quantity Expressions

The English language contains many words and phrases that tell us the quantity or amount of something. For instance, *one prize*, *three prizes*, and *fifty prizes* state the exact number of prizes; *many prizes*, *several prizes*, and *a few prizes* tell us that there is more than one prize, but not exactly how many there are. Whether a noun is count or non-count determines the appropriate expression of quantity that is used with the noun. But before we study the chart that summarizes the correct quantity expressions, there is an important rule to remember.

> When a quantity expression contains the word *of*, any count noun that follows it must be plural.

Incorrect: We ate a couple of pizza.
Correct: We ate a couple of pizzas.

Incorrect: She grew a lot of vegetable in the garden.
Correct: She grew a lot of vegetables in the garden.

Incorrect: Several of the teacher were very kind.
Correct: Several of the teachers were very kind.

Note that it is also correct to omit the *of* in this last sentence, but the noun *teachers* remains plural: *Several teachers were very kind*.

The following chart uses a count noun (*dollars*) and a non-count noun (*money*) to illustrate how quantity expressions are used with count and non-count nouns.

Quantity Expression	Count Noun	Non-Count Noun
Singular	**Dollar(s)**	**Money**
one	one dollar	——
each	each dollar	——
every	every dollar	——
Plural		
a couple of	a couple of dollars	——
a few	a few dollars	——
a number of	a number of dollars	——
both	both dollars	——
few	few dollars	——
many	many dollars	——
several	several dollars	——
two, three, etc.	two dollars	——
a great deal of	——	a great deal of money
a little	——	a little money
much	——	much money
all	all dollars	all money
a lot of	a lot of dollars	a lot of money
hardly any	hardly any dollars	hardly any money
lots of	lots of dollars	lots of money
not any/no	not any/no dollars	not any/no money
most	most dollars	most money
plenty of	plenty of dollars	plenty of money
some	some dollars	some money

Exercise 29.8

Each of the following sentences has a blank indicating where a quantity expression is required. Several choices of quantity expression are given in parentheses following each sentence. Using the information in the chart above, cross out the quantity expressions that *cannot* be appropriately used in the blank. Then check your answers.

1. I will read _____ reports. (*four, several, much, a great deal of, some, few, a lot of, too many, every, most, a little*)

2. I will study _____ information. (*three, each, much, a lot of, several, a great deal of, plenty of, a few, a little, hardly any*)

3. My friend has _____ comfortable chairs on the patio. (*too much, hardly any, four, a few, a great deal of, no, plenty of, some, every*)

4. My friend has _____ comfortable furniture on the patio. (*a few, three, one, some, several, hardly any, much, a lot of, lots of, a couple of*)

Note that *a few* and *few* have different meanings, as do *a little* and *little*. A *few* and *a little* have a positive meaning: for example, "I have a few friends" and "I have a little money" suggest that I have at least some friends and some funds. I'm not completely alone, nor am I completely broke. On the other hand, *few* and *little* have negative connotations. "I have few friends" and "I have little money" suggest that I am a lonely person who has almost no money to spend.

Exercise 29.9

The following sentences require that you fill in each blank either with an appropriate expression of quantity (choose from the list on page 372) or with an appropriate noun. When you've completed this exercise, compare your answers with our suggestions.

1. _____ extra money is good to have.

2. Several _____ lost money.

3. Roberto has _____ friends here in Canada, so he feels very homesick.

4. _____ of the _____ found the course very boring. Only two or three people found it interesting.

5. Very _____ tourists visit the country because of the war.

6. My best friend has _____ good-looking brothers, so I like to spend as _____ time at her house as I can.

7. _____ one of her _____ is tall, dark, handsome, and smart.

8. _____ of my friends will be at my party, so we must have _____ of _____.

9. It takes _____ practice to learn how to ice skate.

10. _____ of us got home from the game quickly because there was _____ traffic.

GO TO WEB

EXERCISES 29.6, 29.7

Exercise 29.10

Correct the 25 errors in plural form in this paragraph. Be sure to revise verbs and pronouns to agree with any nouns you change from singular to plural.

In Canada, we have an abundance of food. Only few people actually starve, and not that much go hungry on a regular basis. The problem Canadians have with food is the opposite. A great deal of us eat too much foods. The government department called Health Canada has prepared *Canada's Food Guide* to try to promote healthy eating for Canadian. It is based on the four food group: grain products, vegetables and fruit, milk products, and meat and its alternatives.

Canada's Food Guide recommends 5 to 12 servings of grain products per day. A servings, for example, may be a slice of breads, a small muffin, or a half-cups (125 mL) of rices or pasta. Grain products provide us with the carbohydrates, fibre, and irons we need for good health. The second food group is vegetables and fruit, and the *Food Guide* recommends 5 to 10 serving per day. A serving could be a medium pieces of fruit, 125mL of vegetables, or 250 mL of salad. Vegetable and fruit help to provide necessary amount of fibre, carbohydrates, and vitamin C and A.

The third food group, milk products, includes milk, soy beverages, cheese, and yoghurt, and the *Food Guide* recommends 2 to 4 serving per day. A serving would be about 250 mL of milk or soy beverage or 50 grams of cheeses. Milk products provide protein, fat, and calciums. The final food groups is meat and its alternatives; the *Food Guide* says we should eat 2 to 3 servings of about 50 to 100 grams per day. However, for people who don't eat meat, there are other alternative; for example, fish such as salmons, tofu, or eggs. Like the milk group, the meat group gives us the protein, fat, and some of vitamin we need to thrive.

Eating according to these food guidelines will help you avoid obesity and maintain your healths!

30

Using Articles Accurately

People who learn English as their first language rarely have problems with these three little words: *a*, *an*, and *the*. But if you learn English as a second language, articles are a potential minefield of trouble for you. One reason is that the use or non-use of articles often depends on meaning that is implied rather than stated. Look at these sentences, for example:

A woman is waiting in your office.
The woman is waiting in your office.

Both sentences are correct, but the meanings they convey are quite different. Whether you choose *a* or *the* is determined by what you know about the woman, not by the grammar of the sentence. If she is an unknown, *indefinite* woman, you use the **indefinite article**, *a*. But if she is a known, *definite* person whom you recognize, you use the **definite article**, *the*. Both articles *can* be used; which one you *should* use depends on what you mean to say. There are few hard-and-fast rules that govern the use of these troublesome little words. You need to take time and practise until you become familiar with them. There are, however, some general guidelines that will help you use articles correctly. In this chapter, we explain the guidelines and give you practice in applying them.

The Indefinite Article: *A/An*

The indefinite article marks a non-specific noun. In other words, *a/an* is used to refer to a common noun in a general way. The following are some examples.

A woman is waiting in your office. (could be any woman)

I ate *an* apple. (any apple, not a specific apple)

A shark is a dangerous creature. (the whole species of shark, not a specific one)

One rule that always applies (no exceptions) tells you whether to use *a* or *an*.

Use *a* if the word that follows it begins with a consonant or the sound of a consonant.

Use *an* if the word that follows it begins with the vowel or the sound of a vowel.

Consonant or Consonant Sound	Vowel or Vowel Sound
a party	an event
a sunset	an umbrella
a great evening	an awful trip
a tiny elf	an oak tree
a university (*university* begins with a vowel, but it sounds like the consonant -*y*)	an honour (*honour* begins with a consonant, but it sounds like the vowel -*o*)

Exercise 30.1

Complete this exercise with the correct indefinite article, *a* or *an*. Don't use *the*. Answers for exercises in this chapter begin on page 530.

1. We saw _____ ugly dog with _____ strange-looking old man.

2. _____ zoologist is _____ scientist who studies animals.

3. You should see _____ dentist about your teeth.

4. He made _____ hasty retreat after realizing his error.

5. The child took _____ bad fall and needed _____ X-ray.

6. Sign me up for _____ half-hour lesson.

7. The teacher gave us _____ extremely difficult test.

8. _____ European man met us at the airport.

9. After high school, you can study at _____ college or you can choose _____ university.

10. You were lucky to get _____ VIP pass to the film festival.

Now let's look at how to use indefinite articles accurately. Study the five guidelines and examples that follow.

1. Use the indefinite article with singular count nouns. (See Chapter 29 for an explanation of count and non-count nouns.)

- *A/an* is never used with plural nouns.
  Incorrect: A women are waiting in your office.
  Correct: Women are waiting in your office.

- *A/an* is never used with non-count nouns.
  Incorrect: We moved a new furniture into the office.
  Correct: We moved new furniture into the office.
  Also correct: We moved a new desk into the office. (count noun)

2. Many nouns have a count meaning as well as a non-count meaning. The indefinite article *a/an* is required if the noun is being used as a singular count noun.

For example, the noun *life* is usually thought to be non-count and is not pluralized; e.g., "Life is good." The noun *life*, though, also has a count sense and can be pluralized; e.g., "Six lives were lost in the earthquake" or "The hurricane did not take a single life." To take another example, consider the difference between these two sentences:

Incorrect: Life of poverty is very difficult.
Correct: A life of poverty is very difficult. (*life* is being used as a singular count noun)

Again, the meaning—as well as the grammar of your sentence—determines whether or not you need the article.

There are other nouns usually considered to be non-count that are also used as count nouns. For example, liquids thought of as contained items (such as *coffee* in a cup) are count nouns and can be used with *a*. These nouns can also be pluralized.

Coffee is grown in South America. (*Coffee* is used as a non-count noun.)

Please bring me *a* coffee. (*Coffee* is used as a singular count noun.)

Please bring us two coffees. (*Coffee* is used as a plural count noun.)

3. The indefinite article is used with certain quantity expressions such as *a few, a little, a couple of* (see page 372).

He has a few friends in Mumbai.

We have *a couple of* questions for you.

4. The indefinite article is used in certain time expressions, such as *half an hour* and *a half-hour*. The phrases *once an hour, twice a day, three times a week, several times a month,* and similar expressions use *a/an* to express frequency.

Can you meet me in *half an hour*?

You should have a checkup *once a year*.

5. Many idioms require the indefinite article.

You should be familiar with the common idioms listed below.

as a rule	lend a hand
do a favour	make a living, make a point of, make a
for a long time	difference, make a fool of
give me a break (informal)	once in a while
have a headache	stand a chance
in a hurry	take a trip, take a break, take a look at
keep an eye on	tell a lie

Exercise 30.2

In the following sentences, fill in the blanks with the correct indefinite article (*a/an*), if it is required. Do not write in the blanks where *a/an* is not required. Do not use the definite article (*the*) in this exercise.

1. _____ veterinarian is _____ doctor who treats _____ animals.

2. _____ child learns affection through the love of _____ parents.

3. Reggie asked for _____ last drink before the bar closed even though he had already drunk _____ half-bottle of whiskey.

4. _____ man with _____ big nose and _____ huge feet stepped into the room.

5. As _____ rule, _____ rich person should be prepared to help others who are less fortunate.

6. I waited for _____ hour and _____ half to see _____ counsellor.

7. Twice _____ year, I take _____ adventure trip with _____ friend or two.

8. _____ baby needs to drink _____ milk.

9. Would you please bring me _____ cup of _____ coffee.

10. The dog ate your homework? Give me _____ break!

GO TO WEB

EXERCISES 30.1, 30.2

The Definite Article: *The*

The is a word that makes a noun specific or definite. It distinguishes the known from the unknown. In the sentence "The woman is waiting in your office," we know something about the woman. She isn't a stranger off the street. She is a definite person. Nouns can be particularized—made definite or specific—in several ways. The following guidelines and examples show how nouns are particularized and will help you figure out how to use the definite article.

> 1. Use the definite article with familiar objects, places, and people in the external environment.

For instance, we speak about *the* Earth, *the* sun, *the* apartment we live in, *the* school we attend, *the* doctor we consult, and *the* TV shows we watch. All of these things are particularized (made definite) because we are familiar with them. We know who or what we have in mind when we use the word, and the reader or listener is going to be thinking about the same thing.

The Earth rotates around *the* sun.

Put *the* computer on *the* desk.

> 2. Nouns can be made definite from the context of the sentence. (This principle is called the anaphoric use—or second mention—of *the*.)

Once you refer to an unknown person, place, or thing using the indefinite article, that person, place, or thing becomes a known—or definite—entity the next time you refer to him, her, or it. Consider this example:

A strange woman is waiting in your office. *The* woman is wearing *an* interesting suit. *The* suit is made of blue silk and is held together with giant safety pins.

The first time we mention the woman, she is unknown and referred to as "*a* woman." This first mention makes her definite, so we refer to her as "*the* woman" in the second sentence. Can you explain the shift in the articles that modify the suit she is wearing?

Exercise 30.3

Complete the exercise below using *a/an* or *the* correctly in the blanks.

When you move to _____ new city, you have to think about your

housing needs. If you are going to be there for only _____ short time,

you can rent _____ furnished apartment. _____ apartment

should be in _____ convenient location. Perhaps you should locate

yourself in _____ downtown area near public transportation.

_____ furnished apartment you rent needs to have _____ decent

kitchen. _____ kitchen should have _____ working stove and

refrigerator. _____ place where you live is _____ important fac-

tor in your adjustment to your new city.

---

3. The definite article can be used with singular and plural nouns and with count and non-count nouns.

The woman is waiting in your office. (singular noun)

The women are waiting in your office. (plural noun)

We moved *the* new desk into your office. (count noun)

We moved *the* new furniture into your office. (non-count noun)

4. The definite article can also be used with a singular generic noun; that is, it can be used when you are making a generalization about a class of things.

The violin is a difficult instrument to play.

Usually, the indefinite article can also be used in a such a sentence. Both of the sentences below have the same meaning, and both are correct.

The grizzly bear is a dangerous animal.

A grizzly bear is a dangerous animal.

Do not use *the* with a plural count noun in the generic sense. Instead, use the plural form with no article: "Grizzly bears are dangerous." If you are referring to specific animals, though, you can use *the* with the plural count noun: "The grizzly bears in the park are dangerous."

Here is another example to illustrate the correct use of articles with generic and specific plural count nouns.

Problem: The teenagers are often moody and irritable with their parents.

This use of *the* is incorrect if you are referring to teenagers as a class of people; it is correct if it refers to a specific group of teenagers.

Correct: Teenagers are often moody and irritable with their parents.

Also correct: The teenagers in that family are often moody and irritable with their parents.

Exercise 30.4

Fill in each blank with *the* or leave it blank if *the* is not required. Do not use *a/an* in this exercise.

1. _____ elderly deserve _____ support of society.

2 _____ children are naturally curious, but _____ children in that class are very inquisitive.

3. Do we know who invented _____ wheel?

4. In _____ Far North, _____ sun never sets in _____ June.

5. _____ elephant and _____ whale are both huge animals that give birth to _____ live babies; in other words, they are _____ mammals.

6. I like to play games on _____ computers.

7. _____ medical care is usually paid for by _____ government through _____ taxes.

8. _____ college students need to spend _____ time studying if they want to be successful.

9. Is _____ money as important as _____ love to you?

10. Thank you for _____ bananas; I love to eat _____ fruit.

GO TO WEB

EXERCISES 30.3, 30.4

5. The definite article is used in many quantity expressions that contain *of*; for example, *some of the coffee, most of the children, each one of the judges, all of the exams, both of the rings*.

In many of these phrases it is also correct to omit the *of the* part of the phrase.

Many of the models in fashion shows are very young.

Many models in fashion shows are very young.

Both sentences are correct and mean the same thing.
    Note that you cannot omit the definite article from a quantity expression without omitting *of* as well.

Incorrect: Some of people in this building are very wealthy.

Correct: Some of the people in this building are very wealthy.

Also correct: Some people in this building are very wealthy.

6. Many idioms use the definite article.

Some common examples are

all the time   play the fool

clear the table   tell the truth

make the beds   wash the dishes

7. Other uses of the definite article are listed below.

- With superlative adjectives: He is *the* ugliest man I know.

- With number words (ordinals): *the* third child, *the* tenth chapter

- In phrases that specify time or space sequence: *the* next day, *the* end, *the* last desk in *the* row

- In phrases that rank things: *the* main reason, *the* only person

- With official titles: *the* prime minister, *the* president. (When the person's name is attached, however, the definite article is omitted: Prime Minister Blair, President Fox.)

- With names of governmental and military bodies, both with common nouns (*the* parliament, *the* police, *the* army) and with proper nouns (*the* Liberal Party, *the* United Nations, *the* Pentagon)

- With historical periods or events: *the* Renaissance, *the* Ming Dynasty, *the* 1960s

- With legislative bills and acts: *the* Canadian Charter of Rights and Freedoms, *the* Meech Lake Accord

Exercise 30.5

Fill in the blanks in the sentences below with *a, an*, or *the*. Do not leave the blank empty.

1. I want to take _____ trip to _____ West Coast.

2. _____ phase of _____ moon is one of _____ causes of ocean tides.

3. I bought _____ new CD online yesterday, and _____ CD should be here by tomorrow.

4. What is _____ name of _____ student you were talking to this morning? He is _____ first person I talked to in class, and I would like to know his name.

5. Although I had never seen her before, I spoke to _____ beautiful young woman in _____ supermarket this morning; she is one of _____ loveliest human beings I have ever seen.

6. _____ kind of vacation I enjoy most is _____ long train ride.

7. I don't need _____ special destination when I board _____ train; for me _____ most important thing is _____ journey.

8. Where did you park _____ car?

9. _____ job requires _____ person with _____ lot of energy, and Danielle is _____ energetic person.

10. In many parts of Canada, _____ college student who begins school in _____ last part of August finishes _____ school year in April.

GO TO WEB

EXERCISES 30.5, 30.6

No Article (Zero Article)

No article is used in general statements with non-count and plural nouns unless the noun is particularized or made specific in some way. Study the following guidelines and examples.

1. Do not use an article with non-count nouns: Water is necessary for life. Rice is good for you. Gold is valuable.

No article is required with *water*, *life*, *rice*, *food*, and *gold* in these sentences.

2. In general statements, no article is required with plural nouns: We like bananas. Bears are dangerous creatures. People need friends.

To decide whether or not you need an article with a plural noun, you must determine whether the word is being used in a general or a specific sense. The following exercise will give you practice in making the correct decision.

Exercise 30.6

Use either *the* or no article in the blanks below. Do not use *a/an*.

1. I like to study _____ history; I have learned that _____

history of Bosnia is tragic.

2. We like _____ food, but _____ most of _____ food

at _____ restaurant is awful.

3. Everyone has _____ problems in _____ life. _____

   problems may be big or small, but everyone must cope with them.

4. His group is playing _____ jazz in _____ park.

5. Some of _____ most important products that Canada buys from

   India are _____ tea, _____ cotton, and _____ rice.

6. _____ milk is my baby's favourite drink, but she often spills

   _____ milk that I put in her cup.

7. _____ kindness is an attractive quality in people, and _____

   kindness of that woman is known to all of us.

8. _____ jewellery is a popular gift; my boyfriend loved _____

   jewellery that I gave him.

9. Natasha studies _____ art in university, and her specialty is

   _____ art of _____ Renaissance.

10. _____ boots are a necessary item of winter clothing in Canada, but

   _____ boots I bought last year were not very warm.

Using *The* or No Article in Geographical Names

Place names in English are inconsistent in their requirement for the definite article or no article. For example, you use *the* with oceans (*the Pacific Ocean*, *the Indian Ocean*) but not with lakes (*Lake Ontario*, *Shuswap Lake*). Why? Is there a guiding principle here? Unfortunately, no. You must learn the conventions that govern the use of articles in geographical and other place names.

No Article	Examples
Continents	Asia, Australia, Europe, South America
Countries	Canada, China, Italy, Laos, Mexico
Cities	London, Paris, Penticton, Rio de Janeiro
Lakes, bays, falls	Lake Simcoe, Hudson Bay, Niagara Falls
Streets and parks	Princess Street, Portage Avenue, High Park
Colleges and universities with *College* or *University* after name	Humber College, Red Deer College, Oxford University, Trent University
Halls	Carnegie Hall, Convocation Hall

Definite Article (The)	Examples
Plural place names	the Americas, the Balkans, the Maritimes
Countries (or other bodies) that refer to a political union or association	the United Kingdom, the United States
Mountain ranges	the Himalayas, the Rocky Mountains
Groups of islands, *but* not individual islands	the Philippine Islands, the Thousand Islands, the West Indies, *but* Long Island, Manitoulin Island, Vancouver Island
Oceans	the Arctic Ocean, the Atlantic Ocean, the Indian Ocean
Groups of lakes	the Finger Lakes, the Great Lakes
Rivers, seas, straits	the St. Lawrence River, the Caribbean, the Straits of Magellan
Colleges and universities that have *of* in the name	the College of the Americas, the University of New Brunswick, the University of Saskatchewan
Buildings, towers, bridges, hotels, libraries, museums	the Empire State Building, the CN Tower, the Granville Street Bridge, the Banff Springs Hotel, the Library of Parliament, the Bata Shoe Museum
Deserts, forests, peninsulas	the Sahara Desert, the Black Forest, the Gaspé Peninsula
Points of the globe or compass	the Equator, the Tropic of Capricorn, the Middle East, the North Pole, the Southern Hemisphere

Use either *the* or no article in the blanks below.

1. _____ earthquakes sometimes happen in _____ British

   Columbia, but they almost never occur in _____ Prairie provinces,

   _____ central Canada, _____ Quebec, or _____

   Maritimes.

2. Many of _____ geographical names in Canada are derived from

   _____ languages of Aboriginal peoples who lived here for thou-

   sands of _____ years before _____ first European settlers

   arrived.

3. For example, _____ Manitoulin Island, in _____ Lake

   Huron, got its name from the Algonkian word *Manitou*, which means

   "spirit."

4. _____ Queen Charlotte Islands (also known as Haida Gwaii) off

   _____ British Columbia coast consist of about 150 islands, the

   largest of which are _____ Graham Island and _____

   Moresby Island.

5. _____ Saskatchewan, _____ province of Ontario,

   _____ Magnetawan River, _____ Lake Okanagan, and even

   _____ name "Canada" itself are all examples of _____ influ-

   ence of native people's languages on Canada's place names.

6. Pat began his studies at _____ Langara College and then trans-

ferred to _____ University of British Columbia.

7. _____ Niagara Falls is on _____ Niagara River, which flows

from _____ Lake Erie to _____ Lake Ontario.

8. _____ People's Republic of _____ China is also known as

_____ China.

9. _____ St. Lawrence River forms _____ boundary between

_____ Ontario in _____ Canada and _____ New York

in _____ United States.

10. _____ Bering Strait is between _____ state of Alaska and

_____ former U.S.S.R, now known as _____ Russia.

GO TO WEB

EXERCISES 30.7, 30.8

Exercise 30.8

Fill in each space with the correct article or leave it blank if no article is required.

You can tell all you need to know about _____ person from

_____ shoes he or she wears. Our economics teacher, for example,

wears _____ worn-out, old, brown leather loafers. These shoes tell us

that he doesn't care about _____ appearances, that he likes to save

_____ money, and that he enjoys _____ comfort more than

_____ style. On the other hand, our computer teacher is _____

fashionably dressed woman who wears _____ different pair of shoes

almost every day. My favourites are her black patent leather pumps with

gold buckles on _____ toes. Such _____ stylish selection of

_____ shoes tells me that she is _____ fashion-conscious person

who cares what _____ people think of her appearance. She appreci-

ates quality and is willing to spend money to get it. If my theory about

_____ relationship between _____ character and footwear is

valid, I would be interested in _____ analysis of my English professor,

who wears _____ black army boots for two days, _____ white

running shoes _____ next day, then _____ pair of cowboy boots,

and ends the week with _____ pair of platform disco shoes.

Exercise 30.9

Correct any misused or missing articles in the paragraph below. There are 10
errors.

An hurricane is the severe tropical storm with winds between 120 and

240 km per hour. Hurricanes are most likely to form in Atlantic Ocean, and

they usually blow west across Caribbean and the Gulf of Mexico from the

Africa. Hurricanes gain their energy as they pass over warm ocean waters,

so warmest parts of year are known as "hurricane season," from the June

through month of October. Hurricanes rotate in a counterclockwise direction around a "eye." When a hurricane comes onshore, heavy rain, wind, and waves can do a tremendous amount of damage to the trees, buildings, and people in its path.

Exercise 30.10

Correct any misused or missing articles in the paragraph below. There are 10 errors.

Highest place on Earth is an mountain called Mount Everest, which is 8,850 metres high. It is located in Asia, at border of Tibet and Nepal, in a mountain range known as Himalayas. First people to climb Everest were the Tenzing Norgay and Edmund Hillary, who reached peak in 1953. According to a CBC Web site,* 2,249 people had climbed the Mount Everest by the end of 2004, but 186 people died trying. Now there is a small industry of guides who make a good living taking adventurous climbers to the top of Everest. Ascending the mountain is expensive proposition, though. The average cost of a guided climb is about US$65,000. Save your money if you want to make it to top!

CBC News Indepth: www.cbc.ca/news/background/mount_everest.

Exercise 30.11

Edit these paragraphs for errors in the use of articles. There are 25 errors.

I love the travelling and have been to many interesting places around world. My favourite places are the China and the Morocco because they are very different from Canada in culture, language, architecture, and cuisine. When I go to United States or the Great Britain or Australia, I find an experiences much like those here in Canada. In China and Morocco, I am always conscious that I am far away from a home.

In Morocco, I sampled couscous, which is very popular dish in the North Africa. In the markets, people dress in long, flowing robes and a tasselled red hats called fez. The buildings are all made of the clay, and many of cities are surrounded by large walls.

The China, too, is fascinating to me as the Canadian because it is so different. The Beijing is the very interesting city to visit, and I also enjoyed a trip to a Great Wall. In a countryside, an oxen are used to plow fields, and bicycles are more common than automobiles. The food is very spicy in some areas of country, and visitors will be surprised by variety of foods in different regions.

Morocco and China are not the countries like Canada where food, dress, and architecture are same wherever you go. Travel is wonderful way to learn about the world.

31

Practising with Prepositions

Prepositions are small words that often cause big problems for second-language learners. People who speak English as a first language are never confused by the distinction between *in* and *on* or *from* and *for*. But these little words often puzzle and frustrate second-language learners.

Prepositions have no special endings or inflections that make them easy to identify. (For instance, *-ous* endings usually indicate adjectives; e.g., *prosperous*; and *-ity* endings suggest nouns; e.g., *prosperity*.) The only characteristic that prepositions have in common is that most of them are short words.

Sometimes two short prepositions are joined to make a one-word compound (e.g., *into, without, upon*). People who learn English as a second language must memorize these words and their sometimes multiple meanings. There is no other way to learn how to use prepositions correctly.

A preposition is a word that begins a group of words known as a **prepositional phrase** (preposition + object).

after lunch	*to* school
during the week	*under* the car
in the closet	*with* my brother

In each of these phrases, the first word is a **preposition**. You can see from these examples that prepositions often clarify such relationships as time, place, or direction. Every prepositional phrase requires an **object** (a noun or pronoun); *lunch, week, closet, school, car, brother* are the objects in the prepositional phrases above.

Below is a list of common prepositions used in English.

above	beneath	into	throughout
about	beside	like	till
across	between	near	to
after	beyond	of	toward
against	by	off	under
along	despite	on	underneath
among	down	out	until
around	during	outside	up
at	for	over	upon
before	from	past	with
behind	in	since	within
below	inside	through	without

We'll break up this long list into four categories to make it easier for you to learn the various uses of prepositions. Each of the four charts on the following pages is organized according to the relationship that the preposition points to. The charts also provide brief definitions and examples of prepositions used correctly.

One of the reasons that prepositions are confusing is that the same word can be used with more than one meaning; hence, some occur in more than one chart. See *at*, *by*, and *from*, for example. Please note that the following charts include only the most common prepositions and their meanings. Your dictionary provides more extensive definitions and examples.

Check your understanding of prepositions by doing the exercises that follow each chart. Occasionally, there is more than one preposition that could be used correctly in a blank. Answers for exercises in this chapter begin on page 533. If you make any mistakes, study the chart again, and do the Web exercises that we have provided.

PREPOSITIONS THAT INDICATE TIME RELATIONSHIPS

Preposition	Uses/Meaning	Examples
after	one event follows another event	We will have dinner *after* the concert.
at	used with a specific time of the day	The bell rang *at* midnight. He has dinner *at* 7:00 p.m.
before	one event comes before (precedes) another	Mail your tax return *before* April 30.
by	no later than	Finish your assignment *by* Friday.
during	indicates a period of time, usually undivided	I usually sleep *during* a long flight.
for	indicates a quantity of time	The photographer needs you *for* an hour.
from	indicates the time in the future when something starts	The concert is three days *from* now.
in	used with a part of the day/month/year/season	I'll see you *in* the morning. My birthday is *in* March. Jessamyn was born *in* 1976. Birds fly south *in* the fall.

Preposition	Uses/Meaning	Examples
in	identifies a period of time by which something will happen; also means *during*	I'll see you *in* an hour. Traffic congestion has gotten much worse *in* recent years.
of	used with a date and month	People light fireworks on the first *of* July.
on	used with a day of the week or a specific date	I work *on* Saturday. Passover begins *on* April 7 this year.
since	from one time until now	I have not eaten *since* breakfast.
until, till	as far as the time when another event will occur	I won't have anything to eat *until* dinner.
within	not more than the specified period of time	Call me if you don't receive a cheque *within* a week.

Exercise 31.1

1. They were married _____ 1990, so they've been married _____ many years.

2. The blood tests are supposed to be taken _____ the morning on an empty stomach, so don't eat anything _____ your arrival at the lab.

3. Borat has owned a small store _____ his arrival in Canada.

4. You will finish your degree a year _____ now, and I would like to have a party for you when you graduate _____ June.

5. Francisco arrived _____ the summer; he was born _____ noon _____ July 11, 1962.

GO TO WEB

EXERCISE 31.1

PREPOSITIONS THAT INDICATE PLACE OR POSITION

Preposition	Uses/Meaning	Examples
above	directly higher	His apartment is *above* ours.
across	on the other side	She lives *across* the street.
among	included in a group (more than two)	She sat *among* her 12 grandchildren.
at	indicating a specific location; also with specific addresses	Xhonghong is *at* school. We live *at* 1507 Marine Drive.
behind	in back of	The grizzly bear is *behind* you!
below	directly lower	Her apartment is *below* ours.
beneath	under	Your coat is *beneath* mine in the pile.
beside	next to	Please sit *beside* me.
between	in the middle of two	She sat *between* her two grandchildren.
by	very near to, beside	He has a house *by* the river.
in	within an area or space	Wawa is located *in* Ontario.
near	close to; within a short distance	I live *near* the subway.

Preposition	Uses/Meaning	Examples
on	covering or forming part of a surface	Please write *on* the blackboard.
over	higher than something else	The helicopter flew *over* the highway.
under	lower than something else	The subway runs *under* this theatre.
underneath	beneath, close under	Her purse was *underneath* the bed.
within	not farther than the distance from	The school is *within* a kilometre of her apartment.

Exercise 31.2

1. Either put the dishes _____ the table or put them away _____ the cupboard.

2. What time does my plane land _____ Vancouver, and who will take me to my hotel, which is _____ Main and Hastings?

3. Saskatchewan is _____ Manitoba and Alberta.

4. I was _____ the people whose elevator got stuck _____ two floors for an hour.

5. Skunks live _____ holes called burrows, and that awful smell suggests you have a skunk burrow _____ a few metres of your back door.

GO TO WEB

EXERCISE 31.2

PREPOSITIONS THAT INDICATE DIRECTION OR MOVEMENT

Preposition	Uses/Meaning	Examples
across	from one side to the other	She walked *across* the room.
around	indicating movement within a larger area; moving past something in a circle	The sprinters ran *around* the track. Assad sailed *around* the world.
by	moving past someone or something	Michel walked *by* his ex-wife without speaking. The car drove *by* the restaurant.
down	from a higher to a lower level	I walked quickly *down* the stairs to the basement.
from	indicating place where movement away began	Our flight to Vancouver left *from* Hong Kong.
into	moving to a point inside	Nguyen dived *into* the cold water.
out of	moving away from	She jumped *out of* bed happily.
past	moving by someone or something	Michel walked *past* his ex-wife without speaking. The car drove *past* the restaurant.
through	passing from one side to another	The Assiniboine River flows *through* Winnipeg.
to	movement in the direction of a specific place	She walks *to* school every day.
toward	in the general direction of something	Walk *toward* the ocean and enjoy the beautiful sunset.
up	from a lower to a higher point	I walked quickly *up* the stairs to the attic.

Exercise 31.3

1. We drove _____ your house last night, but we didn't stop because no one seemed to be home.

2. After Javier reached the top of the hill, he walked back _____ the slope heading _____ the cabin.

3. The man ran _____ the middle _____ the crowd and jumped _____ the lake.

4. They'll return _____ their vacation next week.

5. The thief climbed _____ the ladder and crawled _____ the house _____ an open upstairs window.

GO TO WEB

EXERCISE 31.3

OTHER PREPOSITIONAL RELATIONSHIPS: RELATION, SOURCE, MANNER, POSSESSION, QUANTITY

Preposition	Uses/Meaning	Examples
about	on the subject of someone or something	This book is *about* love. We know *about* your family.
about	concerning something	We can do something *about* the problem.
for	indicating the person receiving something	The message is *for* you. What can I do *for* you?
for	with regard to purpose or function	Tharshini received roses *for* her birthday. He works *for* a car dealership.

Preposition	Uses/Meaning	Examples
from	indicating the source of someone or something; indicating the product or material from which something is made	Réné comes *from* the Gaspé. Wine is made *from* grapes. Penicillin is an antibiotic that was originally made *from* mould.
from	indicating the reason for something	The baby cried *from* hunger.
from	used to make a distinction between two things	English is very different *from* French.
of	belonging to somebody or something	He is a friend *of* mine. Please close the lid *of* the box.
of	concerning, relating to, or showing something	This is a photograph *of* my boyfriend. Do you have a map *of* Mexico?
of	indicating what is measured, counted, or contained	We drank a litre *of* wine.
of	used with *some, many, a few*, etc.	Some *of* the students failed the exam. A few *of* us are coming.
with	in the company of someone or something	I took a vacation *with* my husband. Please leave the keys *with* the parking attendant.
with	having or carrying something	The child *with* the red hair is her son. Take the coffee *with* you.
with	indicating the manner or condition	She did her homework *with* care. He was trembling *with* rage.
with	indicating the tool or instrument used	You can see the stars *with* a telescope.

Preposition	Uses/Meaning	Examples
without	not having, not using	No one can live *without* water. Can you see *without* your glasses?

Exercise 31.4

1. Farida took only one picture _____ me together _____ you.

2. After spending a day _____ the twins, we recognized that they are very different _____ one another.

3. We must do something _____ the problem _____ poverty _____ the world.

4. There were lots _____ adults because many _____ the children came _____ their parents.

5. Immigrants _____ South America often find that working in Canada is difficult _____ a good knowledge of English or French.

GO TO WEB

EXERCISE 31.4

The exercises that follow will give you practice in using prepositions correctly. Fill in the blanks with appropriate prepositions. When you have completed the exercise, compare your answers with our suggestions on pages 533–34.

Exercise 31.5

1. We wake up _____ 7:00 and finish our breakfast sometime _____ 7:30.

2. The old lady _____ the attic is a secret _____ you and me.

3. No one is permitted to leave _____ the conclusion _____ the performance.

4. I'll meet you _____ front of the restaurant that is located _____ the corner _____ Princess and Division Streets _____ Kingston.

Exercise 31.6

1. You should drink this milk _____ tomorrow.

2. There was a pool _____ oil _____ the car, so we knew that we would have to take it _____ a mechanic _____ repairs.

3. He came _____ the house quickly, jumped _____ his car, and sped _____ the street right _____ a police car.

Exercise 31.7

1. _____ tonight's play, drinks will be sold _____ intermission.

2. If you look _____ the painting _____ the wall, you will find a safe _____ a lot _____ money _____ it.

3. We couldn't find the cottage _____ the woods; it was hidden in the trees.

4. I work _____ 8:00 _____ the morning _____ 8:00 _____ night, and I am usually exhausted _____ the end _____ that time.

Exercise 31.8

My friend Jamil goes _____ school _____ the King Edward

campus _____ Vancouver Community College. _____ the same

time, he works full-time _____ his family's grocery business. The store is _____ the street _____ the college, so Jamil doesn't have to travel very far _____ school and work. He has to leave school _____ 4:00 p.m. every day so that he can work _____ the counter of the store selling goods _____ customers. _____ September, Jamil has been studying computer and business courses at the college, and he puts a lot _____ effort _____ his schoolwork. Because he works every night _____ midnight, he sometimes does his homework _____ quiet moments _____ the store. _____ his hard work, Jamil's family couldn't keep the store going. Jamil is working _____ two important goals: he is determined to succeed _____ his studies, and he is equally determined to help his family prosper.

GO TO WEB

EXERCISE 31.5

Exercise 31.9

Fill in the blanks with appropriate prepositions chosen from the list on page 395.

1. We fixed the hole _____ the ceiling _____ duct tape.

2. Pete is looking _____ a job _____ sales.

3. The child was standing _____ his father and mother.

4. The police arrived _____ minutes and broke _____ the house.

5. Michelle has a very large nose _____ a pair of small, close-set eyes. She wears a lot _____ heavy make-up _____ her face.

6. They told us all _____ their trip _____ Australia _____ their return _____ Canada.

7. _____ the opposition _____ the neighbours, they are going to go ahead and build a fence _____ the two properties.

8. Even if you have been speaking English _____ a long time, it is easy to make occasional mistakes _____ prepositions.

Test your mastery of grammar in this unit by identifying the 15 errors in the following passage. Check your answers on page 534.

[1]Let's say that you been learning English for a number of years now. [2]Perhaps you've been living and studying in English for much of your life. [3]Yet you still not feel entirely confident about your ability to make yourself understood when you're speaking, particularly when you are speak to a group of people at school or at work. [4]And you're also not always sure exactly what English speakers mean when they speak within you. [5]Are there any practical ways to improve your fluency in spoken English? [6]Yes, there are. [7]Here are a few tips to help you feel more confident when you are speaking and when you are listening.

[8]One good suggestion for everyone who is speaking English as a second language is to s-l-o-w down. [9]Especially if you are presenting in academic or professional situation, it's important to remember to speak slower and louder than you normally do. [10]Often what makes your speech difficult to

understand isn't the pronunciation of specific sounds ("t" vs. "th," for instance), but rather the intonation or rhythm that is rooted in your first language and doesn't sound natural to native English speakers. [11]Slowing down often helps. [12]Make sure that you pause frequently at appropriate places in your speech or presentation, and use transition words such as "next," "then," and "in conclusion" to help your listener or reader stay with you.

[13]If you are preparing short presentation, keep in mind that spoken language is simpler than written language. [14]Your sentences and vocabulary should be relatively simple. [15]Repeat key points, and use the board or cards to present important vocabulary that you think people might not understand. [16]Try to relax as much as possible, smile occasionally, and look from the people you're speaking to. [17]Eye contact is important and actually helps to communicate your meaning. [18]If you looking at people, you can usually tell when someone doesn't understand you, and you can repeat or clarify the point you're making.

[19]There are also a number of ways that you shall improve your comprehension of spoken English. [20]Listening to English radio and TV is helpful; listen to interested programs that you already know something about, whether that is sports, horoscopes, celebrity gossip, or the new. [21](Repeat key phrases to practise the rhythm of spoken English.) [22]Listen to recorded

phone messages; you might even get native-speaker friends to leave complicated messages for you so that you can practise understanding what they are saying. [23]Try to navigate through the phone loops of banks, airlines, or utility companies: "Press 6 if you would like to hear about our payment options."

[24]There are lots of Internet sites designed to help people learn the English. [25]A site such as the BBC World Service has much resources, including audio and video clips that help people improve their listening comprehension. [26]Of course, you may find that voices on the BBC have what Canadians call a "British accent." [27]But learning to understand the many varieties of spoken English is important to your overall mastery by the language.

[28]Above all, practise. [29]Try to keep yourself immersed in the English-speaking world around you. [30]Engage people in conversation, listen to what they have to say, and ask questions when you need to. [31]Mastering another language is a long and arduous task. [32]Nevertheless, time and lot of practice will give you the confidence in your speaking and listening skills that you want to achieve.

UNIT 7

Readings

Brian Green, "Career Consciousness"
Sun-Kyung Yi, "An Immigrant's Split Personality"
Eva Tihanyi, "Resolving Conflict in the Workplace"
Shandi Mitchell, "Baba and Me"
Germaine Greer, "Ottawa vs. New York"
Sarah Norton, "Metamorphosis"
Jeffrey Moussaieff Masson, "Dear Dad"
Deenu Parmar, "Labouring the Wal-Mart Way"
Nell Waldman, "The Second-Language Struggle"
    (MLA Documentation Style)
Aliki Tryphonopoulos, "A City for Students"
    (APA Documentation Style)

CAREER CONSCIOUSNESS
Brian Green

1   A career can be defined as the employment you prepare for during the first quarter of your life, engage in during the best years of your life, and reap the rewards from when you are least able to enjoy them. Behind the cynicism of this observation lies an important truth: choosing a life's vocation is not a decision to be taken lightly. To justify the time and effort you will invest in your career, it should be stimulating, rewarding, and productive. The better you know yourself, the more likely you are to choose a career you can live with happily.

2   What would a stimulating career be like? Picture yourself getting up in the morning and looking forward to your day with eager anticipation. This may not be the popular image of most jobs, but it is one that can be achieved. Most people participate in leisure activities that they find interesting, even energizing. There's no rule that says you can't be as enthusiastic about your work as you are about your play. Many successful people have turned their interests into careers, thus getting paid for what they like to do. Many career professionals in the arts, for example, make their living by doing what they feel they were born to do: write, act, paint, dance, play or compose music, sing, design, or sculpt. Clive Beddoe loved to fly, and from that passion grew his career as a bush pilot, and, later, his founding of one of Canada's most successful airlines, WestJet. Of course it is not always possible to turn a passion into a career, but to deny what excites you, to relegate it to after-hours activities without trying to incorporate it into your working life, means you will spend most of your life wishing you were doing something else.

3   If your career is stimulating, then chances are good that it can also be rewarding. A good career offers two kinds of rewards: financial and emotional. Rewarding work doesn't just happen; it's something you need to plan for. The first and most important step is to know yourself. Only if you know who you are and what you need to be happy can you consciously seek out career experiences that will bring you satisfaction and steer clear of those that will annoy or stress you. Are you genuinely ambitious, or is power something you seek because you think it is expected of you? The pursuit of status and a high salary brings some people pure pleasure. Many people, however, find leadership positions excruciatingly stressful. Career enjoyment depends to some extent on whether or not you are successful, and success is a state of mind. Consider two graduates from the same college program. One is a technician in a small-town television station who loves his work, takes pride in keeping the station on the air, and delights in raising his family in a community where he is involved in volunteer activities ranging from sports to fire-fighting. The other is a news director at one of Canada's major television networks. Her work is highly stressful, full

of risks, and continually scrutinized by viewers, competitors, and her supervisors. She thrives on the adrenaline rush of nightly production, and loves the big-city life, the financial rewards of her position, and the national recognition she receives. Which graduate is "successful"? Certainly, both feel their careers are rewarding, according to their individual definitions of the term.

4   A job at which you do not feel useful cannot be either rewarding or stimulating for very long. It is human nature to want to contribute, to feel that your efforts make a difference. Camaraderie with fellow workers, a pleasant daily routine, even a good salary cannot compensate in the long run for a sense that your work is meaningless or unappreciated. Sadly, some people spend their entire working lives at jobs in which their contribution is so insignificant that their absence would scarcely be noticed. Everyone knows people who boast about reading paperback novels on the job, and others who sleep through their night shift so they can spend their days fishing or golfing. Is this the way you want to spend 45 years of your life? All the paperbacks and the rounds of golf don't add up to much without a sense that you are doing something worthwhile. It may take a few years, but when it comes, the realization that your work lacks meaning is soul-destroying.

5   It is not easy to find a career that provides stimulating, enjoyable, and meaningful work. Understanding yourself—your interests, needs, values, and goals—is an essential first step. Making long-term decisions consistent with your values and goals is the difficult second step. Too many people spend their lives in careers that make them miserable because they allow themselves to be governed by parents, friends, or simple inertia. Finally, once you have launched your career, never rest. Actively seek challenges and opportunities that stimulate you. Relish the rewards of meeting those challenges, being productive, and doing your job well. Continually strive to improve, not for the sake of your employer, but for your own sake. Your career will occupy three-quarters of your life, so make the most of it!

QUESTIONS FOR DISCUSSION

1. What kind of attention-getter does the writer use to open his essay?
2. In paragraph 5, identify the two main parts of the author's conclusion: the summary of the essay's main points and the memorable statement. What kind of memorable statement has he used? Is it appropriate for this essay? Why?
3. In what order has Green arranged his points: chronological, logically linked, climactic, or random? Can you rearrange the points without diminishing the effectiveness of the piece?
4. How do the topic sentences of paragraphs 2, 3, and 4 contribute to the coherence of this essay? Identify three or four transitional words or phrases the author has used within his paragraphs to make them read smoothly.

SUGGESTIONS FOR WRITING

1. How would you define a satisfying career?
2. Who is the most satisfied (dissatisfied) worker you know? What makes him/her happy (unhappy) with the job?
3. If you had enough money invested so that you could live comfortably without paid employment, would you be happy? Why or why not?

AN IMMIGRANT'S SPLIT PERSONALITY
Sun-Kyung Yi

1   I am Korean-Canadian. But the hyphen often snaps in two, obliging me to choose to act as either a Korean or a Canadian, depending on where I am and who I'm with.

2   When I was younger, toying with the idea of entertaining two separate identities was a real treat, like a secret game for which no one knew the rules but me. I was known as Angela to the outside world, and as Sun-Kyung at home. I ate bologna sandwiches in the school lunch room and rice and kimchee for dinner. I chatted about teen idols and giggled with my girlfriends during my classes, and ambitiously practiced piano and studied in the evenings, planning to become a doctor when I grew up. I waved hellos and goodbyes to my teachers, but bowed to my parents' friends visiting our home. I could also look straight in the eyes of my teachers and friends and talk frankly with them instead of staring at my feet with my mouth shut when Koreans talked to me. Going outside the home meant I was able to relax from the constraints of my cultural conditioning, until I walked back in the door and had to return to being an obedient and submissive daughter.

3   The game soon ended when I realized that it had become a way of life, that I couldn't change the rules without disappointing my parents and questioning all the cultural implications and consequences that came with being a hyphenated Canadian.

4   Many have tried to convince me that I am a Canadian, like all other immigrants in the country, but those same people also ask me which country I came from with great curiosity, following with questions about the type of food I ate and the language I spoke. It's difficult to feel a sense of belonging and acceptance when you are regarded as "one of them." "Those Koreans, they work hard. . . . You must be fantastic at math and science." (No.) "Do your parents own a corner store?" (No.)

5   Koreans and Canadians just can't seem to merge into "us" and "we."

6   Some people advised me that I should just take the best of both worlds and disregard the rest. That's ideal, but unrealistic when my old culture demands a complete conformity with very little room to manoeuvre for new and different ideas.

7   After a lifetime of practice, I thought I could change faces and become Korean on demand with grace and perfection. But working with a small Korean company in Toronto proved me wrong. I quickly became estranged from my own people. My parents were ecstatic at the thought of their daughter finally finding her roots and having a working opportunity to speak my native tongue and absorb the culture. For me, it was the most painful and frustrating two and one-half months of my life.

8   When the president of the company boasted that he "operated little Korea," he meant it literally. A Canadianized Korean was not tolerated. I looked like a Korean; therefore, I had to talk, act, and think like one, too. Being accepted meant a total surrender to ancient codes of behaviour rooted in Confucian thought, while leaving the "Canadian" part of me out in the parking lot with my '86 Buick. In the first few days at work, I was bombarded with inquiries about my marital status. When I told them I was single, they spent the following days trying to match me up with available bachelors in the company and the community. I was expected to accept my inferior position as a woman and had to behave accordingly. It was not a place to practice my feminist views, or be an individual without being condemned. Little Korea is a place for men (who filled all the senior positions) and women don't dare speak up or disagree with their male counterparts. The president (all employees bow to him and call him Mr. President) asked me to act more like a lady and smile. I was openly scorned by a senior employee because I spoke more fluent English than Korean. The cook in the kitchen shook her head in disbelief upon discovering that my cooking skills were limited to boiling a package of instant noodles. "You want a good husband, learn to cook," she advised me.

9   In less than a week I became an outsider because I refused to conform and blindly nod my head in agreement to what my elders (which happened to be everybody else in the company) said. A month later, I was demoted because "members of the workplace and the Korean community" had complained that I just wasn't "Korean enough," and I had "too much power for a single woman." My father suggested that "when in Rome do as the Romans." But that's exactly what I was doing. I am in Canada so I was freely acting like a Canadian, and it cost me my job.

10   My father also said, "It doesn't matter how Canadian you think you are, just look in the mirror and it'll tell you who you *really* are." But what he didn't realize is that an immigrant has to embrace the new culture to enjoy and benefit from what it has to offer. Of course, I will always be Korean by virtue of my

appearance and early conditioning, but I am also happily Canadian and want to take full advantage of all that such citizenship confers. But for now I remain slightly distant from both cultures, accepted fully by neither. The hyphenated Canadian personifies the ideal of multiculturalism, but unless the host culture and the immigrant cultures can find ways to merge their distinct identities, sharing the best of both, this cultural schizophrenia will continue.

Source: Yi, Sun-Kyung. "An Immigrant's Split Personality." *Globe and Mail*. 12 April 1992. Reprinted by permission of Sun-Kyung Yi.

QUESTIONS FOR DISCUSSION

1. In point form, summarize the main characteristics of the Korean and the Canadian halves of the author's personality.
2. What method of paragraph development does the author use in paragraph 8?
3. Identify five examples of parallel structure in paragraph 2. How does the author's use of parallelism serve to reinforce her thesis?
4. Identify the summary of main points and the memorable statement in paragraph 10.

SUGGESTIONS FOR WRITING

1. Do you sometimes feel that you are two people trapped inside a single body? Write an essay in which you contrast the two sides of your personality.
2. Contrast three or four significant values of your generation with those of your parents' (or grandparents') generation.

RESOLVING CONFLICT IN THE WORKPLACE
Eva Tihanyi

1   Imagine you are the supervisor of a call centre that employs a full-time staff of 40 telephone sales representatives. During the past few months, there has been an increase in employee requests for schedule changes in order to accommodate personal needs. These employees, of course, would prefer not to lose pay, so they want to make sure they work their regular number of weekly hours. Unfortunately, the growing number of schedule changes is having an adverse effect, creating confusion and inconvenience for you, the

payroll department, and the employees in general. You, as the person in charge, recognize that you must deal with this situation quickly and fairly—before it escalates. There are four methods of conflict resolution to consider: deference, competition, compromise, and co-operation.

2   If the scheduling issue is not a major one, you might opt to defer; in other words, "let the other side win." Employees could continue to ask for schedule changes as they saw fit, and you would do your best to accommodate them and ignore the inconvenience. Maintaining employee morale would be more important than enforcing a smooth scheduling process.

3   If, on the other hand, you view the scheduling issue as so important that it must be resolved to the company's advantage, you will want to exercise your authority and insist on a no-change policy. Employees would be assigned to particular shifts, and if they wanted time off, they would have to take it without pay. There would be no re-scheduling. This is a competitive approach, one which ensures that you "win" while the other side "loses"—and one which also ensures that your relationship with the "losers" will be tarnished.

4   A more empathetic way of managing the situation would be to compromise. You could circulate a memo in which you laid out parameters, specific guidelines for how and when schedule changes could occur. This would allow some flexibility, but would at the same time limit the frequency and nature of schedule change requests. In this way, both you (i.e., the company) and the employees would "win"—partially. Both sides would get a part of what they wanted, but both would also lose a part. And so long as both sides were satisfied, this could be an effective solution.

5   Finally, if you're a supervisor who believes in the concept of mutual benefit, in the notion that it's possible for both sides to "win," you will choose the method of co-operation. You and the employees might brainstorm the scheduling issue together and in the process discover new ways in which it might be settled to the satisfaction of both sides—not compromise, but resolution. Because co-operation produces no "loser," it fosters an atmosphere of trust and respect; and, although certainly more time-consuming than the other three methods, it is generally the best way to encourage goodwill in the workplace.

6   Deference, competition, compromise, and co-operation are all viable ways of handling conflict. The one you choose will most likely depend on how significant the issue is, how much time you have to deal with it, to what extent you value employee morale, and what the word "winning" means to you.

Source: Tihanyi, Eva. Originally entitled "Methods of Conflict Resolution."

QUESTIONS FOR DISCUSSION

1. What introductory strategy does the author use to set up her thesis? (See pages 298–99 for a review of five different ways to introduce an essay.) A good introduction intrigues readers, involves them in the subject, and makes them want to read on. Does Tihanyi's introductory paragraph accomplish these goals?

2. One of the reasons this essay is so easy to read is the author has structured it very carefully. She outlines the problem in paragraph 1, then offers four different solutions to the problem, using a single pattern of development, in paragraphs 2 to 5. For each possible solution, she offers a definition, remarks on the practical effects of its implementation, and comments on how the implementation would affect company morale. Identify these three components in paragraphs 2, 3, 4, and 5.

3. Another reason this essay is easy to read is that the author has made skilful use of transitions. Turn to page 300 to review four kinds of transitional expressions that an author can employ. Which ones does Tihanyi use in this essay?

4. In Chapter 25, you learned that a good conclusion should (a) summarize or reinforce the main points of the paper and (b) end with a memorable statement. Does Tihanyi's conclusion satisfy these criteria?

SUGGESTIONS FOR WRITING

1. Describe a workplace conflict in which you were involved. What led up to it? How was it resolved? How did you feel about the resolution?

2. If you were the manager responsible for assigning workers to one of three eight-hour shifts, how would you go about it? Assume that no one wants the graveyard shift (midnight to 8:00 a.m.), workers with child-care responsibilities want the day shift (8:00 a.m. to 4:00 p.m.), and those without children hate the late shift (4:00 p.m. to midnight). You can't satisfy everybody, but can you schedule the work so that no one feels unfairly treated?

BABA AND ME

Shandi Mitchell

1   In 1922, my father, at the age of two, came to Canada with his parents and five brothers and sisters from the Ukraine. They landed at Pier 21 in Halifax and headed west to homestead in northern Alberta. They lived in a sod-and-log

house and suffered the prejudice of the times and the poverty of a barren existence. Forty years later, I was born into a lower-middle-class Canadian existence.

2   In that short span, the Ukrainian culture had been lost to me. My Baba (grandmother) never learned to speak English and I knew no Ukrainian. She was as much a stranger to me as were her customs, foods, thoughts, and life. As a child, I was frightened of her.

3   I knew nothing of her past and none of her secrets. No one spoke of my grandfather. I remember the family visiting a weed-infested lot set aside from the main cemetery. It wasn't until many years later that I was told he had killed himself.

4   It was then 1938: the prairies were choking on dust and Baba was newly widowed, with six children to support. In the next town over, Old Man Kurik's wife had died in childbirth. And so began Baba's next marriage. The old man used the kids as field hands and boxing bags, excepting his own son, whom he schooled to become a "gentleman." Then World War II exploded. One by one all of Baba's children left for the cities. They ran from the wheat fields and their rich, decaying earth.

5   They ran to the plastic, shiny chrome worlds filled with starched sailors and armed forces personnel. They ran to heroes' deaths and cowards' retreats. They fell in love and became "Canadians" or "Americans." They changed their names and became Marshalls, Smiths, and Longs. They travelled the world and sent postcards back home to Baba. She saved the exotic images in a cookie tin under her bed. Eventually, even Baba and Old Man Kurik moved to town. Baba became a grandmother and was asked not to speak Ukrainian around her grandchildren.

6   Baba wrote letters in Ukrainian to the old country, but they remained unanswered. Undaunted by political barriers, she continued to save her pennies, quarters, and nickels for her visit home. She didn't believe that she wouldn't be let in. Her children shushed her when she spoke of her Communist brother. It was as if the world grew up around Baba. Then one day, she found herself a widow again. That morning, she opened every window and door in the house and breathed deeply. It was January.

7   My Baba got old in the seventies. Sometimes, she babysat my brother and me. My parents would drop us off for the weekend. I hated going there. She didn't speak any English, and I blocked out her Ukrainian. She dressed funny, she cooked funny, and she smelled of garlic. She tried to teach me about Ukrainian things. I didn't want to know. My friends were outside playing, the first McDonald's in town was opening down the street, and the Bay City Rollers had a new record. . . . I had better things to do than hang around with Baba. Back then, I didn't know the word "ashamed."

8   Baba didn't need English in the town where she lived. There were Ukrainian newspapers, TV and radio stations, stores, neighbours, churches and all the

essentials in this weed of a town poking up out of nowhere in northern Alberta. The town of 1600 was divided neatly into French in the north, Ukrainians in the south, Cree in the east, English in the centre, and everyone else crammed into the west. It was in Baba's town that I first learned about poverty, alcoholism, domestic abuse, and racism.

9   When the old man next door died, his house was boarded up, and it became a popular place to sniff glue and drink aftershave. The neighbours pretended not to see. In the safety of daylight, we kids would venture in and gather up the few bottles amongst the cans and then cash them in at the confectionery for nickel candy. Once, we thought we'd found a dead body, but he had only passed out. Baba tended her garden, seemingly oblivious to the world next door, and kept on planning her trip home to the old country.

10   When the neighbourhood began to gentrify with condos and supermarkets and it was decided that Baba's best friend, Mrs. Westavich, couldn't keep her chickens anymore, Baba rallied to help her and used her precious savings in the process. When the two old women lost their battle, they took the chickens out to the front yard. Baba swung the axe while Mrs. Westavich held the birds down. They chopped their heads off one by one and let the birds' bodies flail and flop over the manicured lawns.

11   When the family decided it was best for Baba to go into a Home, there was no one left to fight for her. The first place was called Sunnyvale. The kids pulled her out from there when they found that she hadn't been bathed in a month and was covered in bed sores; also, her bank account was unaccountably low. Baba liked the new place better. She had a window box there, and grew tomatoes. I went to visit her, once. I called out, "Hi Baba!" and twenty wizened babas turned expectantly to me.

12   I hear Baba's house rents cheap now. The garden is filled with three cars up on blocks. I don't know what happened to her belongings. Her body is buried in Edmonton. I think the family felt it was a greater tribute to be buried in a city lot.

13   So here I sit in front of my computer with cellphone in hand and a coffeemaker brewing, and wonder about my grandmother. I have only one black and white photograph of her. She is squat and round, with huge breasts. She wears a cotton shift dress. Her nylon stockings are bunched at her ankles. A babushka covers her head. She stands shyly beside a shiny late-model 1950s car. Next to her is my mother, with dark glasses, over-sized sun hat, and wasp waist, posed very much like Greta Garbo. I stand at the edge of the frame, a skinny kid looking as if I'm about to run.

Source: Mitchell, Shandi. "Baba and Me." *Confluence*. Edmonton: Grant MacEwan College, 2001. 53–55.

QUESTIONS FOR DISCUSSION

1. State in one sentence what you think the purpose or "lesson" of the story is. How did this story affect you?
2. Identify the separate events in this story. In what order are they arranged? Write a point-form outline for this narrative.
3. What is the function of paragraph 1? Why does the author begin with this information?
4. Baba married twice. What do you think these marriages were like? Use details from the essay to support your opinion.
5. Why do you think Baba and Mrs. Westavich killed the chickens in the front yard (paragraph 10)?
6. The concluding paragraph is a description of a photograph. What do the specific details tell you about the people in the photograph: the grandmother, the mother, and the author as a child? What does this description imply about the relationships among these people?

SUGGESTIONS FOR WRITING

1. Write an essay describing an older relative or other person you know (or knew) well. Include physical details, but focus primarily on the kind of life the person had, as well as your own feelings about him or her.
2. Write an essay explaining the difficulties of being a new immigrant. How does it feel (or how do you think it would feel) to leave one's familiar world and move to a different country to establish a new life?

OTTAWA VS. NEW YORK

Germaine Greer

1   Waking up in Ottawa is not something I expect to do more than two or three times in this lifetime, and two of those times have already happened. This is not solely because Ottawa coffee is perhaps the worst in Canada and Canadian coffee on the whole the bitterest and weakest you will ever encounter, though these truths have some bearing. The badness of the coffee could be directly related to the . . . weakness of the currency; there was certainly an air of poverty-strickenness about the once great hotel I woke up in. My room was huge; as long as it was lit only by the forty-watt bulbs in the four lamps that cowered by the walls I could not see the dispiriting dun colour of the quarter-acre or so of carpet, but I could smell its depressing cocktail of sixty years of food, drink, smoking, cosmetics and sex, overlaid by a choking amalgam of air-freshener, carpet-deodoriser, -dry cleaner and -shampoo. I slept with the window open as

the first line of defence, and then leapt out of bed and into a shower that could not be regulated heatwise or pressurewise, and scooted off to an equally dun, dispiriting and malodorous dining room for breakfast, to wit, one bran muffin and juice made from concentrate. It is sybaritism, rather than self-discipline, that has reduced me to the semi-sylph-like proportions that I at present display. Mind you, giving interviews and making speeches "over lunch" effectively prevents ingestion of anything solid. The Women of Influence lunches I spoke at in Canada featured cold noodle salad and polystyrene chicken thighs, suggesting more plainly than words could that Canadian businesswomen have at their command small influence and less money.

2   To escape from Ottawa . . . to New York and the Pierpont Morgan Library, I took a plane to LaGuardia. Air Canada, as desperate to penny-pinch as all other Canadian operations, was sneakily folding the Newark flight into mine, which made me forty-five minutes late, and all the good people who needed to travel to New Jersey a great deal later. In that forty-five minutes the best-run hotel on the planet, or on Fifth Avenue, which comes to the same thing, let some interloper have my room.

3   The yingling at reception was so very, very sorry. Would I endure a night in a suite at the room rate instead of the statutory $3,000 a night, and let them move me to my own room tomorrow? I hummed and hawed and sighed for as long as I thought decent, then leapt at the chance. The yingling took me up himself, and threw open the door. I strode past him into a forty-foot mirrored salon hung with yellow silk damask; through the French windows a terrace hedged with clipped yew offered a spectacular view of aerial New York, as well as serried ranks of terracotta planters in which green and rose parrot tulips exhibited themselves. The east end of my salon was crowded with sofas and armchairs, all paying homage to a state-of-the-art music centre which, if I'd come equipped, I could have programmed for the whole evening. The west end featured a baronial fireplace and a ten-seater dining table. The yingling showed me my kitchen, my two bathrooms, and my seven-foot-square bed in my twenty-foot bedroom, and swept out before I could decide whether he should be tipped or not.

4   The only way to bring such magnificence into perspective was to take off all my clothes and skip about as naked as a jaybird, opening and shutting my closets, cupboards and drawers, turning all my appliances off and on, my phones, my faxes, my safe. If I had been anything more substantial than a nude scholar, I could have invited forty friends for cocktails, nine friends for dinner and a hundred for after-dinner drinks, and scribbled my signature on a room service check somewhere in the high six figures.

5   The salon soon felt less welcoming than vast, so I took a Roederer from the fridge and a salad into the bedroom, where, perched amid piles of pillows and bolsters stuffed with goosedown, I watched the fag-end of the Florida Marlins'

batting order knock the Atlanta Braves' relief pitcher all over the park. The bed was meant for better things; under the television there was a VCR player. I could have ordered a selection of video-porn from room service, and had a cute somebody sent up to watch them with me.

6   Which is the great thing about New York. Anything, but anything, can be had for money, from huge diamonds of the finest water, furs of lynx and sable, wines of vintages long said to have been exhausted, important works of art and rock cocaine, to toy-boys of the most spontaneous, entertaining and beautifully made, of any sexual orientation and all colours. Every day, planes land at JFK freighted with orchids from Malaysia, roses from Istanbul, mangos gathered that morning from trees in Karnataka, passion-fruit from Townsville, limes from Barbados, truffles from Perigord, lobsters brought live from the coldest seas on the planet. Within twenty-four hours all will have been put on sale and consumed. The huge prices are no deterrent. The New York elite likes to be seen to pay them with nonchalance, on the J. P. Morgan principle that if you need to know how much something costs you can't afford it. Nobody looks at the tab; the platinum credit card is thrown down for the obsequious salesperson to do his worst with.

7   That is what I don't like about New York. Below the thin upper crust of high rollers there is a dense layer of struggling aspirants to elite status, and below them dead-end poverty, which no longer aspires, if it ever did. The vast mass of urban New Yorkers are struggling to get by, in conditions that are truly unbearable, from the helots who open the hair salons at six in the morning and lock them up at eight at night to the dry-cleaners who have worked twelve hours a day in the steam and fumes ever since they stepped off a boat from Europe sixty or even seventy years ago. It's great that I can get my hair washed at any hour of day or night and my clothes altered or invisibly mended within four hours of dropping them off, but it is also terrible. If I ask these people about their working lives they display no rancour; they tell me that they cannot afford to retire and are amused at my consternation. They would rather keep on working, they say. What else would they do? The pain in the hairdresser's feet and back, the listlessness and pallor of the dry-cleaner, can't be complained of. Everybody has to be up.

8   The power of positive thinking is to persuade people that the narrative of their grim existence is a success story. Though New Yorkers have been telling themselves that story for so long that they have stopped believing it, they cannot permit themselves to stop telling it. Everywhere in New York, wizened ancients are drudging. The lift-driver who takes me up to my hotel room looks ninety if a day. Her bird-body balances on grossly distorted feet; the hands in her white gloves are knobby with arthritis; her skeletal face is gaily painted and her few remaining hairs coloured bright auburn and brushed up into a transparent crest. She opens and shuts the doors of her lift as if her only ambition

had ever been to do just that. I want to howl with rage on her behalf. The covers of the bolsters I frolic on have all been laundered, lightly starched and pressed by hand; as I play at being a nabob, I imagine the terribleness of the hotel laundry-room, all day, every day.

9   Though I love New York, I disapprove of it. Dreary as Ottawa was, it was in the end a better place than New York. Canadians believe that happiness is living in a just society; they will not sing the Yankee song that capitalism is happiness, capitalism is freedom. Canadians have a lively sense of decency and human dignity. Though no Canadian can afford freshly squeezed orange juice, every Canadian can have juice made from concentrate. The lack of luxury is meant to coincide with the absence of misery. It doesn't work altogether, but the idea is worth defending.

———————————

Source: Greer, Germaine. "Ottawa vs. New York." *Times Literary Supplement* 27 August 1999: 17.

QUESTIONS FOR DISCUSSION

1. Greer is in Ottawa as the essay begins. How does she feel about Canada's capital city?
2. The topic of paragraph 6 is developed by examples. Identify the topic sentence. Which of the examples do you recognize? Which are unfamiliar to you? Do these examples effectively support Greer's main idea?
3. According to the author, what is "the great thing about New York"?
4. What doesn't Greer like about New York? What contrast is the basis of her dislike? (See paragraph 7.)
5. The thesis of this essay is most clearly stated in the concluding paragraph. Summarize it in your own words.

SUGGESTIONS FOR WRITING

1. Write an essay comparing or contrasting two cities with which you are familiar. Without telling the reader directly, make it clear which city you would prefer to live in.
2. Write an essay contrasting life in a wealthy family, city, or country with life in a poor family, city, or country.

METAMORPHOSIS
Sarah Norton

1   Meet newborn Jeanie. Weak and helpless as a caterpillar, Jeanie's only defence against hunger and pain is the one sound she can make at will: crying. Eighteen months later, Jeanie will be a busy toddler who asks questions, expresses opinions, and even makes jokes. From helplessness to assertiveness: how does this wondrous transformation take place? To discover how we learn to speak, let's follow Jeanie as she develops from infant to toddler, from caterpillar to butterfly.

2   Infancy, the first stage of language development, literally means "unable to speak." For the first six months of her life, Jeanie isn't able to talk, but she can respond to speech. Shortly after birth, she'll turn her head toward the sound of a voice. By two weeks of age, she will prefer the sound of a human voice to non-human sounds. Between two and four months, she will learn to distinguish the voices of her caregivers from those of strangers, and she knows whether those voices are speaking soothingly or angrily. By the time she is two months old, Jeanie will have learned to coo as well as cry, and she coos happily when people smile and talk to her. Now she can express contentment as well as discomfort. At around four months of age, Jeanie's happy sounds become more varied and sophisticated: she registers delight on a scale ranging from throaty chuckles to belly laughs. All this vocal activity is actually a rehearsal for speech. As Jeanie cries and coos and laughs, her vocal cords, tongue, lips, and brain are developing the co-ordination required for her to speak her first words.

3   At six or seven months of age, Jeanie is no longer an infant; she's moved on to the baby stage of language development. Like a pupa in its cocoon, Jeanie is undergoing a dramatic but (to all but her closest observers) invisible change. She looks at her mother when someone says "Mama." She responds to simple directions: she'll clap her hands or wave "bye-bye" on request. By the time she is a year old, Jeanie will recognize at least twenty words. The sounds Jeanie produces at this stage are called babbling, a word that technically describes a series of reduplicated single consonant and vowel sounds and probably derives its name from a common example: "ba-ba-ba-ba." About halfway through this stage of her development, Jeanie progresses to variegated babbling, in which sounds change between syllables. "Da-dee, da-dee, da-dee," she burbles, to the delight of her father (who doesn't know that Jeanie cannot yet connect the sounds she makes to the meaning they represent to others). But by the time Jeanie celebrates her first birthday, the variety, rhythm, and tone of her babbling have become more varied, and her family begins to sense consistent meaning in the sounds she makes. "Go bye-bye!" is as clearly meant as it is spoken—Jeanie wants to get going!

4   Jeanie's recognition of the link between sounds and meanings signals her entry into the toddler stage—twelve to eighteen months. At eighteen months, Jeanie will understand approximately 250 words—more than ten times the number she understood at twelve months. Most of what she says are single-word utterances: "kitty" for a cat in her picture book, "nana" for the bananas she loves to squish and eat. But even single words now function as complex communications depending on the intonation Jeanie gives them. "Kitty?" she inquires, looking at a picture of a tiger. She demands a "nana!" for lunch. About halfway through the toddler stage, Jeanie begins to link words together to make sentences. "Mama gone," she cries when her mother leaves for work. "Me no go bed," she tells her father. Though it marks the beginning of trouble for her parents, this development marks a triumph for Jeanie. She has broken out of the cocoon of passive comprehension into the world of active participation.

5   In less than two years, Jeanie has metamorphosed from wailing newborn to babbling baby to talking toddler. Through language, she is becoming her own woman in the world. Now she can fly.

Source: Norton, Sarah. "Metamorphosis." *Canadian Content*. 5th ed. Ed. Sarah Norton and Nell Waldman. Toronto: Thomson Nelson, 2003. 67–68. (Revised).

QUESTIONS FOR DISCUSSION

1. What is the subject of this essay? State the author's thesis in your own words.
2. This essay is based on an extended comparison. What is it? Do you think the comparison is effective?
3. Identify the stages of development that are described in paragraphs 2, 3, and 4.
4. What two aspects of speech development are discussed in paragraphs 2, 3, and 4?
5. The concluding paragraph is very short. Do you think it is effective? Why?

SUGGESTIONS FOR WRITING

1. Describe the process of learning to talk of a child you know. How and when did this child begin to talk? Did you contribute to the process? How did observing the child's progress affect you?
2. Do some research and then summarize several of the later stages of speech development. For example, how different are a three-year-old child's speech patterns from those of 18-month-old Jeanie in this essay?

DEAR DAD

Jeffrey Moussaieff Masson

1   One reason that so many of us are fascinated by penguins is that they resemble us. They walk upright, the way we do, and, like us, they are notoriously curious creatures. No doubt this accounts for our fondness for cartoon images of penguins dressed up at crowded parties, but as fathers, penguins are our superiors.

2   Unlike mammals, male birds can experience pregnancy as an intimate matter, with the father in many species helping to sit (brood) the egg. After all, a male can brood an egg as well as a female can. But in no other species does it reach this extreme.

3   The emperors usually wait for good weather to copulate, any time between April 10 and June 6. They separate themselves somewhat from the rest of the colony and face each other, remaining still for a time. Then the male bends his head, contracts his abdomen, and shows the female the spot on his belly where he has a flap of skin that serves as a kind of pouch for the egg and baby chick. This stimulates the female to do the same. Their heads touch, and the male bends his head down to touch the female's pouch. Both begin to tremble visibly. Then the female lies face down on the ice, partially spreads her wings and opens her legs. The male climbs onto her back and they mate for 10 to 30 seconds.

4   They stay together afterward constantly, leaning against one another when they are standing up, or if they lie down, the female will glide her head under that of her mate. About a month later, between May 1 and June 12, the female lays a single greenish-white egg. French researchers noted that the annual dates on which the colony's first egg was laid varied by only eight days in 16 years of observation. Weighing almost a pound [.45 kilograms], and measuring up to 131 millimetres long and 86 millimetres wide, this is one of the largest eggs of any bird. The male stays by the female's side, his eyes fixed on her pouch. As soon as he sees the egg, he sings a variation of what has been called the "ecstatic" display by early observers, and she too takes up the melody.

5   She catches the egg with her wings before it touches the ice and places it on her feet. Both penguins then sing in unison, staring at the egg for up to an hour. The female then slowly walks around the male, who gently touches the egg on her feet with his beak, making soft groans, his whole body trembling. He shows the female his pouch. Gently she puts the egg down on the ice and just as gently he rolls it with his beak between his large, black, powerfully clawed feathered feet, and then, with great difficulty, hoists the egg onto the surface of his feet. He rests back on his heels so that his feet make the least contact with the ice. The transfer of the egg is a delicate operation. If it falls on the ice and rolls away, it can freeze in minutes or it might even be stolen. If it is snatched

away by a female penguin who failed to find a mate, its chances of survival are slight because the intruder will eventually abandon the egg, since she has no mate to relieve her.

6   With the egg transfer successfully completed, the happy couple both sing. The male parades about in front of the female, showing her his pouch with the egg inside. This thick fold, densely feathered on the outside and bare inside, now completely covers the egg and keeps it at about 95 degrees Fahrenheit, even when the temperature falls to 95 degrees below zero.

7   The female begins to back away, each time a little farther. He tries to follow her, but it is hard, since he is balancing the egg. Suddenly she is gone, moving purposefully toward the open sea. She is joined by the other females in the colony, who, by the end of May or June, have all left for the ocean almost 100 kilometres away. The females have fasted for nearly a month and a half, and have lost anywhere between 17 to 30 per cent of their total weight. They are in urgent need of food.

8   The female must renew her strength and vitality so that she can return with food for her chick. Going to the sea, she takes the shortest route to reach a polynya (open water surrounded by ice). Penguins appear to be able to navigate by the reflection of the clouds on the water, using what has been called a "water sky."

9   The male penguin, who has also been fasting, is now left with the egg balanced on his feet. The first egg was laid on the first of May; a chick will emerge in August. Since the seasons are reversed south of the equator, full winter has arrived, with many violent blizzards and the lowest temperatures of the year. Emperor penguins are well adapted to the almost unimaginable cold of these 24-hour Antarctic nights: Their plumage is waterproof, windproof, flexible and renewed annually. They may not need tents, but as soon as the bad weather starts, generally in June, the males need some protection from the bitter cold, and nearly all of them find it by forming a *tortue*, which is a throng of very densely packed penguins. When the storms come they move in close to one another, shoulder to shoulder, and form a circle. The middle of the tortue is unusually warm and one would think that every penguin fights to be at the epi-centre of warmth. But in fact what looks like an immobile mass is really a very slowly revolving spiral. The constantly shifting formation is such that every penguin, all the while balancing that single precious egg on his feet, eventually winds up in the middle of the tortue, only to find himself later at the periphery.

10   What early French explorers noticed during the two- to three-month incubation period is an almost preternatural calm among the males. This is no doubt necessitated by the long fast that is ahead of them. Many of them have already fasted, like the females, for two months or more, and must now face another two months of fasting. And moving about with an egg balanced on one's feet is difficult at the best of times.

11   The only time a father will abandon an egg is if he has reached the maximum limit of his physiological ability to fast, and would die if he did not seek food. Not a small number of eggs are left for this reason, and it would seem that in each case the female is late in returning.

12   In July or August, after being gone for almost three months, the female emperor returns from the sea, singing as she penetrates various groups of birds, searching for her mate and her chick or egg. The males do not move, but make small peeping noises. When she finds her partner, she sings, she makes little dance steps, then she goes quiet and both birds can remain immobile for up to 10 minutes. Then they begin to move around one another. The female fixes her eyes on the incubatory pouch of her partner, while her excitement grows visibly. Finally, if it is the right bird, the male allows the egg to fall gently to the ice, whereupon the female takes it and then turns her back to the male, to whom, after a final duet, she becomes completely indifferent. The male becomes increasingly irritated, stares at his empty pouch, pecks at it with his beak, lifts up his head, groans, and then pecks the female. She shows no further interest in him and eventually he leaves for the open sea, to break his long fast. The whole affair has lasted about 80 minutes. . . .

13   The miracle is that the mothers usually return on the day their chicks hatch. How is it, one wonders, that the female emperor penguin is able to return just in time for the birth of her chick? As Alexander Skutch notes in his wonderful book, *The Minds of Birds*, it is improbable that she has consciously counted the 63 days or whatever the exact number is between the laying of her egg and the hatching of her chick. "Some subconscious process, physiological or mental, was evidently summing the days to prompt the birds to start homeward when the proper number had elapsed."

14   If the egg has hatched before her arrival and the male already has a chick between his legs, the female is even more excited to hear it peep, and quickly removes it from the male. She immediately regurgitates food to the chick. If she is late in coming, the male, in spite of his near starvation, has a final resource: He regurgitates into the beak of his peeping newborn a substance known as penguin milk, similar to pigeon's milk, or crop milk, which is secreted from the lining of his esophagus. The secretion is remarkably rich, containing essential amino acids, much like the milk of marine mammals such as seals and whales. These feedings allow the young birds to survive for up to two weeks after hatching. Many of these males have now fasted for four and a half months, and have lost up to half of their body weight. It is a sight to see the well-nourished, sleek, brilliantly feathered, healthy-looking females arrive, and the emaciated, dirty, tired males leave.

15   How difficult it is for us to understand the emotions involved in these events. Yet it is hard to resist the anthropomorphic urge. Obviously the male emperor is aware of the loss of what has, after all, been almost a part of his body for two

to three months. Is he disappointed, bewildered, relieved, or are his feelings so remote from our own (not inferior, mind you, just different) that we cannot imagine them? We would groan, too, under such circumstances, but the meaning of a penguin's groan is still opaque to us. Yet we, too, are fathers and mothers with babies to protect and comfort, negotiating meals and absences and other obligations, just like our Antarctic cousins. Sometimes, when we are overwhelmed by an emotion, we are hard-pressed to express ourselves. If penguin fathers could speak about this moment in their lives, perhaps they would be at a similar loss for words. Perhaps the songs and groans of the male penguin are all the expression they need.

Source: Masson, Jeffrey Moussaieff. *The Emperor's Embrace.* New York: Atria, 1999. Chapter 1 excerpt.

QUESTIONS FOR DISCUSSION

1. What kind of attention-getter does the author use in the introduction (paragraphs 1 and 2)? (See pages 298–99.)
2. Masson's thesis is implied but not stated in this essay. In your own words, write a thesis statement for this piece.
3. Which paragraphs are developed primarily by means of numerical facts and statistics? Why is this an effective way of supporting the main ideas of these paragraphs?
4. The language of this essay combines scientific terms with words and phrases associated with human emotions, such as "happy couple" in paragraph 6 and "increasingly irritated" in paragraph 12. That is, Masson carefully chooses his words to imply similarities between penguins and humans. What do you think is his purpose in comparing the two very different species?
5. What is the author's attitude toward the emperor penguins? Identify three or four examples to support your opinion.

SUGGESTIONS FOR WRITING

1. Write an essay about a father's role in his child's life. What are the essential responsibilities of a father?
2. Write an essay about being a caregiver. Describe a situation in which you have cared for someone on an ongoing basis. How did you feel about the responsibilities you assumed?

LABOURING THE WAL-MART WAY

Deenu Parmar

1   *Always low prices. Always.* This is the slogan of the world's largest corporation, a U.S.-based retailer whose big-box stores offer a one-stop shop, from groceries to garments to garden hoses. The secret of Wal-Mart's success is to give consumers the lowest prices—14 percent lower than its competitors—by increasing the efficiency of the supply chain, the productivity of the labour force, and the use of labour-saving technology. Competitors must adopt a similar business plan, offer something Wal-Mart does not, or go out of business—as Woolco, Eaton's, Simpsons, and Woodwards have in Canada. The influence of the Wal-Mart model is not likely to wane in the near future. With over 235 stores in Canada and plans for rapid expansion, Wal-Mart and its effects on labour are worth considering. Are its offers of jobs, its attitude toward unionization, and its influence on industry labour practices worth the low price on the shelf?

2   One of the most frequent complaints about Wal-Mart, which employs 1.4 million people worldwide, is its failure to pay workers a living wage. Store employees are paid 20–30 percent less than the industry average, making many of them eligible for social assistance. It is estimated that American taxpayers fork out $2.5 billion a year in welfare payments to Wal-Mart employees. Because the retailer hires hard-to-place workers, like recent immigrants, seniors, and single mothers, its employees are often afraid they will not find work elsewhere. The kind of work Wal-Mart does offer is gruelling: stores are intentionally understaffed—the strategy behind the company's legendary productivity gains—so that existing employees will work harder. It is alleged that systemic discrimination against women within the corporation has denied the majority of Wal-Mart workers the chance at promotion, a charge that is now the subject of the largest civil-rights suit in U.S. history.

3   The corporation's staunch anti-unionism is its main defence in keeping workers' wages down and profits up. Without a union to give them collective clout, the store's employees suffer not only lower wages and benefits but abuses like being forced to work overtime without pay. The hiring process is designed to weed out union sympathizers; however, if organizing activity is reported in the store, an anti-union team is flown out from the headquarters in Bentonville, Arkansas, to break it up. The recent unionizing of the first Wal-Mart store in Canada (Jonquière, Quebec) exposed the company's strategy in the event that its anti-union efforts fail: condemn the store as unprofitable and announce a closing date. Although Wal-Mart's methods of keeping its workforce union-free have been ruled illegal in the United States, the company often finds it cheaper to pay labour violations than abide by labour rules. As a result,

litigation is a common but costly form of redress for Wal-Mart workers whose rights have been violated.

4   One of the main reasons retail workers at other stores want to see Wal-Mart unionized is to preserve the gains their own unions have made. The necessity of competing with Wal-Mart has already been used as an excuse for supermarkets all over the United States to lower the wages and benefits of their employees. In early 2004, unionized grocery workers in southern California were forced to accept cuts to their benefits so their employers could compete with a soon-to-open Wal-Mart Supercenter. Wal-Mart's reputation for putting local stores out of business also means that employees of the competition may find themselves working at Wal-Mart for less.

5   Although Wal-Mart's record of paying low wages, crushing unionizing efforts, and lowering industry employment standards bodes ill for Canadian labour, it is unlikely that Canadians will refrain from shopping there. The lure of good prices is hard to resist, and the company's widely admired business model would continue to thrive, even if Wal-Mart were to vanish tomorrow. In the interest of justice and fairness—and in avoiding pitting the customer's savings against the worker's ability to make a living—it falls on the government to pass laws that balance the interests of big business with the protection of labour, environmental, and community rights. This kind of legislation will require pressure from organized citizens acting not as consumers but as workers and concerned members of a community. The price on the shelf might rise as a result, causing Wal-Mart supporters to point out that the poor can no longer afford to shop there. However, the ability to buy at rock-bottom prices does not address the systemic causes of poverty—though it may contribute to them.

QUESTIONS FOR DISCUSSION

1. In this essay, is the author addressing Wal-Mart, Wal-Mart's customers, or Wal-Mart itself? What effect does she hope the essay will have on her target audience?

2. Consider the essay's attention-getter and memorable statement. Given the author's purpose and target audience, are they effective? Why?

3. What are the main kinds of evidence the author uses to support her thesis?

4. The author says that even if Canadians are aware of the effects of Wal-Mart's policies and practices, they will continue to shop there. Do you agree?

SUGGESTIONS FOR WRITING

1. If you live in a community with a Wal-Mart outlet, explain how that outlet has affected your community. Consider its effects on local merchants, local consumers' shopping habits, your community's tourist

trade, and even traffic patterns—whatever changes you have noticed as a result of Wal-Mart's presence.

2. Have you shopped at a Wal-Mart store? If so, write a narrative essay outlining the details of your experience. Describe your experience step by step, from the time you entered the store to the point of checking out and leaving the store.

3. Whether or not you have ever shopped at a Wal-Mart outlet, you must have seen the Wal-Mart television commercials. What do you think of them? Explain your opinion.

THE SECOND-LANGUAGE STRUGGLE

Nell Waldman
(MLA Documentation Style)

The essay below is an example of a short research paper formatted in MLA style. The annotations point out some features of MLA format and documentation. If your instructor requires a separate title page, ask for guidelines.

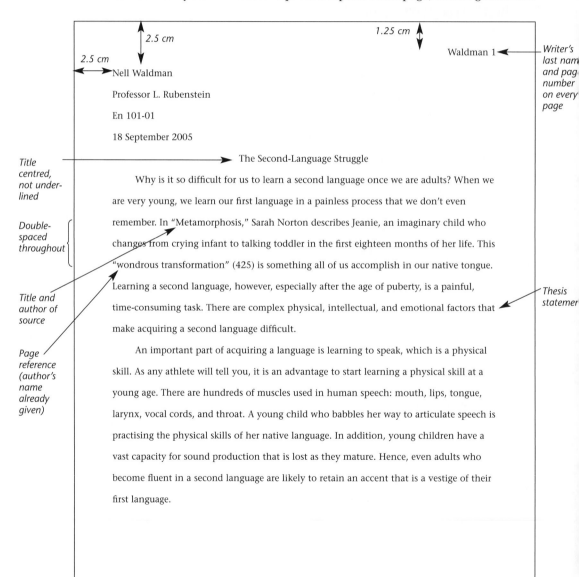

2.5 cm

2.5 cm

1.25 cm

Waldman 1

Writer's last name and page number on every page

Nell Waldman

Professor L. Rubenstein

En 101-01

18 September 2005

Title centred, not underlined

The Second-Language Struggle

Double-spaced throughout

Title and author of source

Page reference (author's name already given)

Why is it so difficult for us to learn a second language once we are adults? When we are very young, we learn our first language in a painless process that we don't even remember. In "Metamorphosis," Sarah Norton describes Jeanie, an imaginary child who changes from crying infant to talking toddler in the first eighteen months of her life. This "wondrous transformation" (425) is something all of us accomplish in our native tongue. Learning a second language, however, especially after the age of puberty, is a painful, time-consuming task. There are complex physical, intellectual, and emotional factors that make acquiring a second language difficult.

Thesis statement

An important part of acquiring a language is learning to speak, which is a physical skill. As any athlete will tell you, it is an advantage to start learning a physical skill at a young age. There are hundreds of muscles used in human speech: mouth, lips, tongue, larynx, vocal cords, and throat. A young child who babbles her way to articulate speech is practising the physical skills of her native language. In addition, young children have a vast capacity for sound production that is lost as they mature. Hence, even adults who become fluent in a second language are likely to retain an accent that is a vestige of their first language.

Waldman 2

An adult has intellectual and cognitive skills that a child lacks. An adult can think abstractly and is able to memorize and use dictionaries (Crystal 373). These skills might seem to make it easier to learn a new language. However, an adult already has a firmly established first language in his intellectual repertoire, and the native language actually interferes with mastering the second language. H. Douglas Brown describes the process whereby remnants of the native language collide with the new language: "The relatively permanent incorporation of incorrect linguistic forms into a person's second language competence . . . [is] referred to as *fossilization*" (217). The fossils of our native language tend to keep turning up as errors in the new language we are struggling to learn.

Emotional factors also complicate the process of learning a second language. Young children are naturally open and lack the self-consciousness that leads to inhibition. Adults, on the other hand, have a highly developed language ego; their control of language is bound up with self-esteem. As one language-learning Web site observes, "The biggest problem most people face in learning a new language is their own fear. They worry that they won't say things correctly or that they will look stupid, so they don't talk at all" ("How to Learn English"). Making mistakes, as any language learner must do, makes an adult anxious, shy, and reluctant to communicate in the new language. These emotions make the process of mastering it even more difficult.

Many linguists argue that humans are born with an innate capacity for learning language, that we have what is known as a "language acquisition device (LAD) hard-wired into our genetic make-up" (Crystal 234). This LAD is what makes it possible for us to learn our native language with such ease. Knowing more than one language is, of course, an extremely valuable ability. Yet acquiring a second language is a complex and demanding process for most people, especially if they undertake it as adults. Eva Hoffman writes movingly about language and identity and the troubling feelings that accompanied her struggle to master English and transfer her identity, so to speak, from her native Polish language:

> What has happened to me in this new world? I don't know. I don't see what I've seen, don't comprehend what's in front of me. I'm not filled with language anymore, and I have only a memory of fullness to anguish me with the knowledge that, in this dark and empty state, I don't really exist. (110)

Paraphrase (with author and page reference of source)

Quotation introduced by complete sentence + colon

Web site title only (no author identified and no page number)

Quotation integrated into writer's sentence

Long quotation set off 10 spaces (2.5 cm) from left margin

Ellipses indicate word(s) omitted; square brackets indicate word(s) changed or added

Quotation introduced by phrase + comma

Author and page reference of source

Waldman 3

Heading is centred, not underlined

Works Cited

Brown, H. Douglas. *Principles of Language Learning and Teaching*. 3rd ed. Englewood Cliffs,

Indent five spaces or 1.25 cm

NJ: Prentice Hall, 1994.

Crystal, David. *The Cambridge Encyclopedia of Language*. Cambridge: Cambridge UP, 1992.

Hoffman, Eva. "Lost in Translation." *Canadian Content*. 5th ed. Ed. Sarah Norton and Nell

Waldman. Toronto: Thomson Nelson, 2003. 309–313.

Entries are alphabet-ized

"How to Learn English." *world-english*. 2004. 18 Aug. 2005 <http://

www.world-english.org> (1 July 2005).

Norton, Sarah. "Metamorphosis." *Canadian Content*. 5th ed. Ed. Sarah Norton and Nell

Double-spaced throughout

Waldman. Toronto: Thomson Nelson, 2003. 67–68.

QUESTIONS FOR DISCUSSION

1. In your own words, identify the subject and main points of this essay.
2. How many different kinds of research sources does the essay rely on? How many are used in each paragraph? Are they all quotations?
3. What contrast is the second paragraph based on? Is this contrast developed in any other paragraphs?
4. What kind of concluding strategy does this essay use? Is it effective?

SUGGESTIONS FOR WRITING

1. Have you ever learned (or tried to learn) a new language? Were you successful? Why?
2. What is the value of learning another language as an adult? Why do people choose to make the effort to do so?

A City for Students

Aliki Tryphonopoulos
(APA Documentation Style)

The essay below is an example of a short research paper written in APA style. The annotations point out some features of APA format and documentation.

First two or three words of title on every page

Title, author's name, course name and section number, instructor's name, and date centred on page

All lines centred and double-spaced

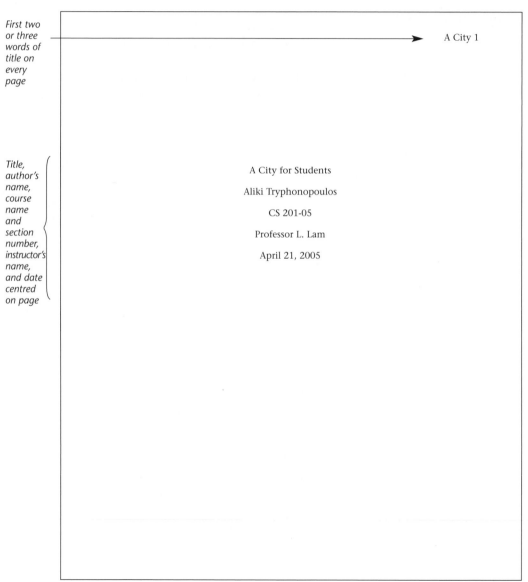

A City 1

A City for Students

Aliki Tryphonopoulos

CS 201-05

Professor L. Lam

April 21, 2005

A City 2

A City for Students

It is hard to think of a city more exhilarating for a student to live in than Montreal. Where else can you hear a conversation shift between two or even three languages with ease and playfulness at the local coffee shop? Cosmopolitan and cultured, *la belle ville* is unique in North America for its intersection of two historically established language groups with a large and growing immigrant population. Montrealers have translated this rich cultural diversity into a vibrant civic life with world-renowned festivals, a well-established art scene, lively café culture, and acclaimed international cuisine and fashion. Few cities in the world offer the affordable living, student amenities, and cultural dynamism that Montreal does.

Long-standing socioeconomic factors make Montreal an affordable city for students—no small consideration given that Canadian undergraduate tuition has risen by 111 percent since 1990 ("Bottom line," 2004, p. 72). Naysayers point out that although Quebec has the lowest tuition rates in Canada (frozen since 1994), out-of-province students must pay roughly twice as much as Quebec residents, placing them in the higher bracket of national tuition payers. Some students get around this disadvantage by working and taking part-time classes for a year in order to qualify for the in-province tuition rates. For those who are required to pay the higher rates, however, the financial burden is more than offset by the relatively low cost of rental housing in Montreal (Canada Mortgage, 2004, Table 2). One of the best ways for students to economize is by living close to the university. Montreal is a walking city, so it is possible for students to conduct all of their business within a five-block radius.

Pedestrian-friendly urban planning plays a large part in Montreal's reputation as a festival city that hosts over 40 events annually. In the sultry summer months, streets shut down for the Jazz Festival, the Montreal Grand Prix, and Just for Laughs, while the Fête des Neiges and the Montreal High Lights Festival provide outdoor activities and culinary delights in the winter. Students find plenty of ways to keep active—cycling, jogging, skating, skiing, dancing and drumming at Montreal's sexy Tam-Tams in Mount Royal Park—and gain an appreciation of the city's vibrant arts scene, from the numerous galleries in Old Montreal to fine art cinemas such as Cinema du Parc and Ex-Centris. Students

A City 3

can argue the merits of the latest Denys Arcand film in one of the many cafés along St.
Denis frequented by their compatriots from Concordia, McGill, Université de Montréal,
and Université du Québec à Montréal. As for ambience, the eclectic mix of old European
limestone mansions and North American glass towers lends this oldest of Canadian cities a
unique architectural allure.

Montreal's cultural dynamism, whose historic roots draw comparisons to such international cities as Barcelona and Brussels, is not only the city's most attractive attribute, but
sadly, what scares many students away. Bill 101, meant to protect the French language in
Quebec, contributed to the exodus of nonfrancophones from Montreal during the 1980s
and 1990s. That trend is slowly reversing (DeWolf, 2003). A recent study reveals what
Montrealers already know: the unique interaction of francophone, anglophone, and allo-
phone (languages other than French or English) cultures in Montreal is characterized by
mutual respect, accommodation, and even a sense of fun (Lamarre, 2002). Students can
absorb and appreciate the international flavour of the various boroughs and contribute to
the daily cultural exchange. With the city's high rates of bilingualism and trilingualism,
anglophone students do not need to know French in order to function, but their social
and cultural life will be far richer if they do. And what better place to learn *la langue
française* than in the second-largest French-speaking city in the world!

Education is as much about what goes on outside the classroom as in it. Those students who are willing to embrace Montreal's vibrant cultural milieu will find their world-
views challenged and broadened. In a global environment fraught with the dangers of
intercultural miscommunication and ignorance, that kind of education is vital.

Paraphrase

*Author
and year
of source*

*Source
citation of
the study
referred to*

A City 4

References

The bottom line. (2004, November 15). *Maclean's*, 72.

Canada Mortgage and Housing Corporation. (2004, December 1). Average rents in privately initiated apartment structures of three units and over in metropolitan areas (Table 2). Retrieved December 22, 2004, from http://www.cmhc.ca/en/News/nere/ 2004/2004-12-21-0715.cfm

DeWolf, C. (2003, May 25). The road to Montreal. *The Gazette* [Montreal]. Retrieved December 20, 2004, from http://maisonneuve.org/about_media .php?press_media_id=21

Lamarre, P. (2002). Multilingual Montreal: Listening in on the language practices of young Montrealers. *Canadian Ethnic Studies, 34*(3), 47–75.

*ntries are
lphabet-
ed*

*ndent
ive
paces
r 1.25
m*

*Heading
is centred,
not
under-
lined*

*Double-
spaced
throughout*

QUESTIONS FOR DISCUSSION

1. In addition to establishing the author's thesis and previewing her main points, what purpose is served by the introduction to this essay?
2. What is the primary method of paragraph development used in paragraph 2? In paragraph 3?
3. This essay is primarily an opinion piece rather than an academic research paper. Why do you think the author chose to cite reference sources to support her argument?
4. Consider the concluding paragraph. Is it effective? Why?

SUGGESTIONS FOR WRITING

Write a short essay in which you try to persuade a friend to attend your college or university. Focus on the positive features of the city or town in which your institution is located, not on the academic programs of the institution itself.

Appendixes

Appendix A   **Spelling Matters**
Three Basic Rules
Rule 1: Dropping the Final *e*
Rule 2: Doubling the Final Consonant
Rule 3: Words Containing *ie* or *ei*
Spelling Spoilers

Appendix B   **A Review of the Basics**
Sentences: Kinds and Parts
    Function: Four Kinds of Sentences
    Structure: Basic Sentence Patterns
    The Parts of a Sentence
Parts of Speech
    1. Nouns
    2. Verbs
    3. Pronouns
    4. Adjectives
    5. Adverbs
    6. Prepositions
    7. Conjunctions
    8. Articles
    9. Expletives

Appendix C   **List of Grammatical Terms**
Appendix D   **Answers to Exercises**

APPENDIX A

Spelling Matters

Obviously, misspellings can mislead or confuse readers. Certainly, they ruin your image as an intelligent and careful writer. If you *never* write except with a word processor, and if you *always* use its spell-check function, you can skip this section. But if, like most of us, you have to fill out forms and occasionally write memos or messages in longhand, you'd be wise to learn three basic rules and rid your writing of spelling spoilers.

Three Basic Rules

Ninety percent of English words are spelled the way they sound. Unfortunately, many of the words we use most frequently have irregular spellings. No rule holds true in all cases, but the three that follow do hold for most words.

Before learning the three rules, you need to know the difference between **vowels** and **consonants**. The vowels are *a*, *e*, *i*, *o*, and *u* (and sometimes *y*). All the other letters are consonants.

Rule 1
Dropping the Final *e*

The first rule tells you when to drop the final, silent *e* when adding an ending to a word.

Drop the final, silent *e* when adding an ending that begins with a vowel.
Keep the final, silent *e* when adding an ending that begins with a consonant.

Keeping the rule in mind, look at these examples:

Endings Beginning with a Vowel

-ing: amuse + ing = amusing
-ed: live + ed = lived
-able: like + able = likable
-ible: force + ible = forcible
-er: use + er = user

Endings Beginning with a Consonant

-ment: amuse + ment = amusement
-ly: live + ly = lively
-ness: like + ness = likeness
-ful: force + ful = forceful
-less: use + less = useless

GO TO WEB

EXERCISES A.1, A.2

EXCEPTIONS TO RULE 1

Three common words do not follow the rule.

argue + ment = argument
nine + th = ninth
true + ly = truly

There is one more exception to rule 1: after soft *c* (as in *notice*) and soft *g* (as in *courage*), keep the final, silent *e* when adding an ending beginning with *a* or *o*. Here are two examples:

notice + able = noticeable
courage + ous = courageous

Rule 2
Doubling the Final Consonant

The second rule tells you when you need to double the final consonant before adding an ending to a word.

When adding an ending that begins with a vowel (e.g., *-able*, *-ing*, *-ed*, or *-er*), double the final consonant of the root word if the word
1. ends with a single consonant preceded by a single vowel
and
2. is stressed on the last syllable.

Notice that a word must have *both* characteristics for the rule to apply. Let's look at a few examples. The accent on each word indicates the syllable that is stressed when you pronounce the word.

begin + er	ends with a single consonant *(n)* preceded by a single vowel *(i)* and is stressed on the last syllable *(begín)*, so the rule applies, and we double the final consonant:	**beginner**
control + ed	ends with a single consonant *(l)* preceded by a single vowel *(o)* and is stressed on the last syllable *(contról)*, so the rule applies:	**controlled**
drop + ing	ends with a single consonant *(p)* preceded by a single vowel *(o)* and is stressed on the last syllable (there is only one: *dróp*), so the rule applies:	**dropping**
appear + ing	ends with a single consonant *(r)* preceded by two vowels *(ea)*, so the rule does not apply, and we do not double the final consonant:	**appearing**
turn + ed	ends with two consonants *(rn)*, so the rule does not apply:	**turned**
open + er	ends with a single consonant *(n)* preceded by a single vowel *(e)* but is not stressed on the last syllable *(ópen)*, so the rule does not apply:	**opener**

In words such as *equip*, *quit*, and *quiz*, the *u* should be considered part of the *q* and not a vowel. These words then follow the rule: *equipping*, *quitter*, and *quizzed*.

Note 1: There are a few common words ending in *l, s,* or *t* that, according to the rule, do not need a double consonant before the ending. Some examples are *cancel, counsel, format, level,* and *travel.* In Canadian spelling, however, the final consonant is usually doubled: for example, *cancelled, counsellor,* and *travelling.*

GO TO WEB

EXERCISES A.3, A.4

Note 2: When it comes to adding *-ence,* three words cause problems. *Prefer, refer,* and *confer* all appear to require a doubled final consonant. But they don't because, when you add *-ence,* the stress shifts to the first syllable of the word:

prefér	preférring	*but*	préference
refér	reférring	*but*	réference
confér	conférring	*but*	cónference

Rule 3
Words Containing *ie* or *ei*

There are almost a thousand common English words containing *ie* or *ei,* so remembering the rule that governs them is worthwhile. It helps to keep in mind that *ie* occurs approximately twice as often as *ei.*

The old rhyme tells you most of what you need to know to spell these words.

> Write *i* before *e,* except after *c,*
> or when sounded like *a,* as in *neighbour* and *weigh.*

If you remember this rhyme, you'll have no difficulty in spelling words such as *belief, piece, ceiling, receive,* and *freight.*

Unfortunately, the rhyme covers only two of the cases in which we write *e* before *i*: after *c,* and when the syllable is pronounced with a long *ā* sound. So we need an addition to the rule.

If short ĕ or long ī is the sound that is right,
write *e* before *i*, as in *their* or in *height*.

This rule covers words such as *Fahrenheit, seismic, heir,* and *leisure* (pronounce it to rhyme with *pleasure*). *Either* and *neither* can be pronounced "eye-ther" and "nye-ther," so they too require *ei*.

There are, of course, exceptions. This silly sentence contains the most common ones:

A *weird species* of *sheik seized caffeine, codeine,* and *protein.*

GO TO WEB

EXERCISE A.5

There are three or four more spelling rules we could explain here, but we won't—for two reasons. First, there are many exceptions to the remaining rules for English spelling. And second, you don't need to memorize more rules if you use your dictionary and a spelling checker.

Spelling Spoilers

After homonyms (see Chapter 2), "spelling spoilers"—the most frequently misspelled words in English—are a writer's worst enemy. These demons can trip up even the most careful writer. Not all the words on our list will cause you trouble; in fact, not even most of them will. To discover which ones are your personal spelling demons, ask someone to dictate the list to you slowly while you write the words. Then compare your handwritten list to the print list that follows and highlight any words you misspelled. Post the list above your desk and memorize the ones you got wrong, a few at a time. Review your list once a week or so, until you have mastered every word. Making up memory aids will help you to conquer your personal "spoilers." Here are a few examples to get you started:

accommodate	It means "make room for," and the word itself makes room for two *c*'s and two *m*'s.
business	*Busi**ness* is no **sin**.

environment	The word *environment*, has **iron** in it, like the Earth.	
friend	He is a *fri**end*** to the **end**.	
grammar	Poor *gram**mar*** will **mar** your writing.	

absence	familiar	planned
accommodate	February	possess
achievement	finally	prejudice
acknowledge	forty	privilege
acquire	friend	procedure
across	gauge	proceed
address	government	professor
adolescence	grammar	psychology
among	guarantee	recommend
answer	guidance	relevant
apparent	height	repetition
argument	hoping	restaurant
beginning	hypocrisy	rhythm
business	immediately	ridiculous
careful	independent	safety
category	indispensable	schedule
clothes	laboratory	secretary
committee	library	separate
conscious	licence (noun) *or*	shining
convenience	license (verb)	similar
criticism	likely	somewhat
definitely	loneliness	speech
dependent	lonely	studying
desperate	maintenance	succeed
development	marriage	surprise
disappear	mentally	technique
disappoint	necessary	thorough
discipline	ninety	tragedy
dissatisfied	ninth	truly
doesn't	occasion	unnecessary
eighth	occasionally	until
embarrassed	omission	unusual
environment	opinion	usually
exercise	opportunity	vacuum
existence	paid	Wednesday
explanation	parallel	writing
extremely	perform	written

Exercise

Make up sentences containing the words you misspelled when the list of spelling spoilers was dictated. Underline the spelling spoiler(s) in each sentence, exchange papers with another student, and mark each other's work.

One final suggestion. Despite all your efforts, you may find that there are a few words you just cannot spell correctly. The solution? Either write them on the inside cover of your dictionary or, even simpler, don't use them. Look in your dictionary or in a thesaurus to find synonyms (different words with the same or similar meanings) and use those instead.

A Review of the Basics

This appendix contains a brief overview of the basic building blocks of the English language. At the very least, you should know the kinds and parts of a sentence and the parts of speech before you tackle the complex tasks involved in correcting and refining your writing.

Sentences: Kinds and Parts

A sentence is a group of words expressing a complete thought. Sentences can be classified in two different ways: by function and by structure.

FUNCTION: FOUR KINDS OF SENTENCES

1. The **declarative** sentence makes a statement or conveys information.

George Clooney starred in *O Brother, Where Art Thou?,* a Coen brothers' film.

He played a character named Ulysses Everett McGill.

2. The **interrogative** sentence asks a question.

Did George Clooney do his own singing in *O Brother, Where Art Thou?*

Was Pete really turned into a frog, or was he turned in to the police?

3. The **imperative** (command) sentence gives an order or a directive.

Stop talking! I'm trying to listen!

The **request** is a modified form of imperative sentence. Its tone is softer:

Let's rent a DVD of *O Brother* and watch it tonight.

4. The **exclamatory** sentence is a strong statement of opinion or warning.

The scene in which Clooney insists on wearing a hair net to bed is hilarious!

Don't answer the phone! This is my favourite part of the movie!

STRUCTURE: BASIC SENTENCE PATTERNS

Every sentence can be classified into one of four patterns, depending on the number and kind of clauses the sentence contains. (In the examples below, subjects are underlined with one line, verbs with two.)

1. A **simple** sentence consists of one independent clause. It has one subject and one verb, either or both of which may be compound (multiple).

a. <u>Matt</u> <u>plays</u> hockey for McGill. (single subject, single verb)

b. <u>Matt</u> and <u>Caro</u> <u>play</u> hockey with their friends on weekends. (compound subject, one plural verb)

c. <u>Matt</u> and <u>Caro</u> <u>play</u> hockey and <u>drink</u> beer with their friends on week-
    ends. (compound subject, compound verb)

2. A **compound** sentence is made up of two or more independent
   clauses. The clauses may be joined by a *coordinating conjunction* or
   by a semicolon. (See Chapters 7 and 18.)

<u>Geoff</u> <u>paid</u> for the flight to Cuba, *and* <u>Kendra</u> <u>paid</u> for their accommoda-
tion.

Either or both clauses in a compound sentence may contain a compound
subject and/or a compound verb:

<u>Geoff</u> and <u>Kendra</u> <u>flew</u> to Cuba, *but* <u>Matt</u> and <u>Caro</u> <u>stayed</u> home and
<u>sulked</u>.

3. A **complex** sentence has one independent clause and one or more
   dependent clauses introduced by *subordinate conjunctions*
   (dependent clause cues). (See page 462.)

<u>We</u> <u>flew</u> to Cuba for our vacation *while* my <u>brother</u> <u>stayed</u> home to take
care of our dogs.

<u>Geoff</u> and <u>Kendra</u> <u>flew</u> to Cuba, *but* <u>Matt</u> and <u>Caro</u> <u>stayed</u> home *because*
<u>they</u> <u>couldn</u>'t <u>afford</u> the trip.

4. The **compound-complex** sentence combines the features of sentence patterns 2 and 3 above. That is, it contains two (or more)
   independent clauses, together with one or more dependent clauses.

<u>Geoff</u> and <u>Kendra</u> <u>flew</u> to Cuba, *but* <u>Matt</u> and <u>Caro</u> <u>stayed</u> home *because*
<u>they</u> <u>couldn</u>'t <u>afford</u> the trip and *because* <u>someone</u> <u>needed</u> to care for the
dogs.

THE PARTS OF A SENTENCE

Every sentence or independent clause can be divided into two parts: subject and predicate. The subject half contains the **subject** (simple or compound), together with its modifiers. The predicate half contains the **verb** (simple or compound), with its modifiers and any other words or phrases that complete the sentence's meaning. These predicate completers may be **direct objects**, **indirect objects**, or **complements**.

1. The **subject** of a sentence is a noun/pronoun (or phrase or clause used as a noun).

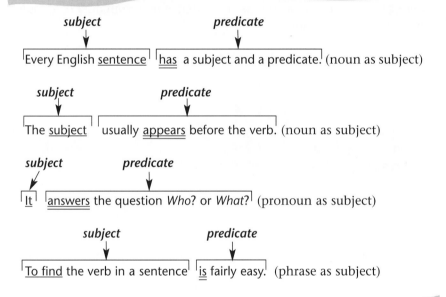

2. The **verb** is the word or phrase that tells the reader what the subject is or does.

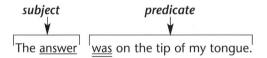

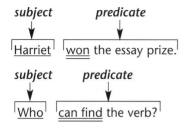

subject *predicate*

Harriet won the essay prize.

subject *predicate*

Who can find the verb?

In the examples below, <u>direct objects</u> are indicated by a triple underline; indirect objects by a dotted underline; and <u>complements</u> by a broken underline.)

3. The **direct object** is the noun or pronoun that names the receiver of the action of the verb.

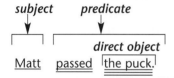

subject *predicate*

direct object

Matt passed the puck.

4. The **indirect object** is a noun or pronoun that tells to whom something is (was/will be) done. The indirect object comes before the direct object.

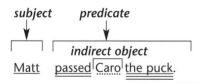

subject *predicate*

indirect object

Matt passed Caro the puck.

5. An **object of a preposition** is a noun or pronoun that follows the preposition in a prepositional phrase.

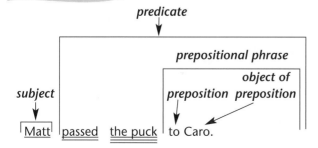

predicate

prepositional phrase

object of preposition *preposition*

subject

Matt passed the puck to Caro.

6. A **complement** is a noun, pronoun, or modifier that explains, renames, or describes the subject of a linking verb (e.g., *is, seems, appears, smells, tastes,* etc.).

Caro is the captain of the team. (noun complement)

The goal and the game are ours! (pronoun complement)

The crowd went wild. (adjective complement)

Parts of Speech

The words that make up sentences can be classified into nine grammatical categories or word classes. The function of a word in a sentence determines what part of speech it is. The word *rock*, for example, can belong to any one of three categories, depending on its context.

We stopped to rest in the shadow of an enormous *rock*. (noun)

The baby will usually stop fussing if you *rock* her. (verb)

I used to listen only to *rock* music, but now I prefer rap. (adjective)

Here's another example, illustrating three functions of the word *since*.

We have not seen Lucy *since* Saturday. (preposition)

We haven't seen Lucy *since* she left. (subordinate conjunction)

We haven't seen Lucy *since*. (adverb)

1. NOUNS

A noun is a word that names a person, place, object, quality, or concept.

A. **Common nouns** are general names for persons, places, and objects: e.g., *artist, politician; city, suburb; train, computer.*

- **Concrete** nouns name things that can be seen and touched: *telephone, sister, puppy.*
- **Abstract** nouns name thoughts, emotions, qualities, or values—things that cannot be seen or touched: e.g., *ambition, success, honesty.*

B. **Proper nouns** name specific persons, places, and things and are capitalized: *Queen Elizabeth, Homer Simpson, Bugs Bunny, CN Tower, Calgary, General Motors.*

C. **Collective nouns** name groups of people or things that act as a single unit: *jury, class, committee, herd.*

2. VERBS

A. A verb is a word or phrase that tells what the subject of the clause is or does.

- **Action verbs** tell what the subject does: The <u>driver</u> <u>braked</u> suddenly.
- **Linking** (or **copula**) **verbs** connect the subject to a word or phrase identifying or describing the subject of a sentence: The <u>driver</u> <u>was</u> my older brother. <u>He</u> <u>felt</u> sleepy.

B. All verbs have different forms (called tenses) to indicate past, present, or future time.

Our team <u>played</u> badly last night. (action verb in past tense)

Mario <u>thinks</u> that we <u>will win</u> tonight. (present tense, future tense)

I <u>am</u> not so confident. (linking verb in present tense)

C. **Auxiliary** (or **helping**) **verbs** are used with a main verb to show tense or voice.

The auxiliary verbs are *be, have, do, may, can, ought, must, shall, will,* and their various forms.

By November, <u>we will have been</u> in Canada for six months. (future perfect tense)

D. The way verbs interact with their subjects is shown through a quality called **voice**. Active voice and passive voice verbs give different messages to the reader.

- **Active voice** verbs show the subject doing or acting:

  A <u>woman</u> in a BMW <u>took</u> my parking place.

  The <u>tornado</u> <u>destroyed</u> everything in its path.

- **Passive voice** verbs show the subject being acted upon:

  My parking <u>place</u> <u>was taken</u> by a woman in a BMW.

  Our <u>home</u> <u>was destroyed</u> by the tornado.

  (See Chapter 11, pages 148–49, for instructions on when to use passive voice verbs.)

3. PRONOUNS

Pronouns are words that substitute for nouns. They can act as subjects or objects.

There are seven classes of pronouns:

1. Personal Pronouns

	Singular (Subject/Object)	*Plural (Subject/Object)*
1st person	I/me	we/us
2nd person	you/you	you/you
3rd person	he, she, it/him, her, it	they/them

We would like *you* to come with *us*, but *they* can fit only four people in the car.

2. Possessive Pronouns

	Singular	*Plural*
1st person	mine	ours
2nd person	yours	yours
3rd person	his, hers, its	theirs

The wonton soup is *yours*; the chicken wings are *hers*; the spareribs are *mine*; and the spring rolls are *ours* to share.

3. Indefinite Pronouns

Singular	*Plural*
any, anyone, anybody, anything	some, all, many
everyone, everybody, everything	some, all, many
someone, somebody, something	some people, some things
no one, nobody, nothing, none (*sing.*)	none (*pl.*)
one	several
each	both
either, neither	few, several, many

Is *no one* curious about *anything someone* is doing for the good of us *all*?

4. Demonstrative Pronouns

Singular	*Plural*
this	these
that	those

This paper is mine; *these* papers are yours.

That is my magazine; I've read *those,* so you can have them if you wish.

5. Relative Pronouns

Singular and Plural (Subject/Object)

who/whom; whoever/whomever; which/whichever; what/whatever; that; whose

The Order of Canada, *which* was created in 1967, is awarded each year to Canadians *who* have distinguished themselves in the arts and sciences, politics, or community service, and *whose* contributions in *whatever* field are deemed worthy of national honour.

6. Interrogative Pronouns

Singular and Plural (Subject/Object)

who?/whom?
which? what?/which? what?

Jan is the leader on *whom* the team depended. *Who* could take her place? *What* can the team do now?

7. Reflexive/Emphatic Pronouns

	Singular	*Plural*
1st person	myself	ourselves
2nd person	yourself	yourselves
3rd person	himself, herself, itself	themselves

We had planned to go by *ourselves*, but since Sharon invited *herself* along, Leo and Jon should have included *themselves* on the outing, too.

4. ADJECTIVES

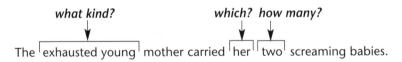

An adjective is a word that modifies or describes a noun or pronoun.

- Adjectives usually answer one of these questions: "What kind?" "Which?" "How many?"

    what kind?   *which? how many?*

The ⌈exhausted young⌉ mother carried ⌈her⌉ ⌈two⌉ screaming babies.

- Pay special attention to the possessive pronoun adjectives: *my, our; your; his, her, their*. These words follow the same rules for agreement that govern the possessive pronouns listed above. See Chapter 15, pages 181–82.
- Most adjectives have three forms:

Positive (Base) Form: short, brief, concise

Comparative Form:

- Add *-er* to one-syllable words: shorter, briefer
- Use *more* + base form for adjectives of two or more syllables: more concise

Superlative Form:

- Add *-est* to one-syllable words: shortest, briefest
- Use *most* + base form for adjectives of two or more syllables: most concise

A few adjectives such as *bad* have irregular comparatives (*worse*) and superlatives (*worst*). Your dictionary will list these irregular forms.

5. ADVERBS

An adverb is a word that modifies or describes a verb, an adjective, or another adverb.

- Adverbs commonly answer the questions "When?" "Where?" "How?"
- Adverbs often—but not always—end in *-ly*.

Rocco *foolishly* challenged the police officer. (adverb modifies verb)

The baby is an *extremely* fussy eater. (adverb modifies adjective)

My elderly father drives ⌐*very slowly.*⌐ (adverb modifies another adverb; adverb phrase modifies verb)

6. PREPOSITIONS

A preposition is a word (or words) such as *in, on, among, to, for, according to, instead of* that introduces a prepositional phrase. A **prepositional phrase** = preposition + object of the preposition (a noun or pronoun).

Prepositional phrases can function as adjectives, adverbs, or nouns.

Celeste is an old friend *of mine* *from Paris.* (prepositional phrases as adjectives modifying noun *friend*)

I'll wait *until seven o'clock.* (prepositional phrase as adverb modifying verb *wait*)

We all hope *for a better world.* (prepositional phrase as noun object of verb *hope*)

7. CONJUNCTIONS

Conjunctions are connecting words used to join two words, two phrases, or two clauses.

- **Coordinating conjunctions** (*and, but, or, for, so, nor, yet*) join grammatically equal elements in a sentence (e.g., the two parts of a compound subject; two independent clauses).

  Moreen *and* Gina are coming, *but* Tessa is not.

- **Subordinating conjunctions** are dependent clause cues: *because, although, when, since,* etc. They link dependent (or subordinate) clauses to independent clauses.

  Tom must go home early *because* he promised to cook dinner.

- **Conjunctive adverbs** are transitional expressions (e.g., *however, therefore, nevertheless, in fact*) usually used after a semicolon to join two independent clauses.

  I would like to go to the club tonight; *however,* I have no money.

- **Correlative conjunctions** are conjunctions used in pairs: e.g., *both . . . and, not only . . . but (also), either . . . or, neither . . . nor.* These constructions are intensifiers. They make the meaning of a statement more emphatic by focussing the reader's attention on each element separately.

Eva is beautiful *and* intelligent. (coordinating conjunction = statement)

Eva is *both* beautiful *and* intelligent. (correlative conjunctions = emphatic statement)

Luca invited all his friends to the party *and* gave everyone a gift. (coordinating conjunction = statement)

Not only did Luca invite all his friends to the party, *but* (*also*) he gave everyone a gift. (correlative conjunctions = emphatic statement)

8. ARTICLES

An article precedes the noun it modifies. The **definite article**, *the*, may be used with a singular or a plural noun; it denotes a particular person or thing. The **indefinite article** *a/an* is generally used with a singular, countable noun, and signals an unspecified one of others. (Use *an* before vowel *sounds,* not just vowels; e.g., *an apple, an honest* person.)

The student sitting next to you is asleep. (a particular student)

A student in the back row is snoring. (one of a number of students)

A number of factors determine the use or non-use of articles. For a summary of rules governing articles, go to "ESL Tips" under More Information on the Student Resources page of our Web site at www.essentialsplus3e.nelson.com.

9. EXPLETIVES

Here and *There* are expletives, which are words used at the beginning of a sentence to postpone the subject until after the verb and thus emphasize it.

Here is your mail. (= Your mail is here.)

There are hundreds of copies still available. (= Hundreds of copies are still available.)

See Chapter 5, page 66.

List of Grammatical Terms

abstract and **concrete**	See **noun**.
adjective	A word that modifies (describes, restricts, relates to, makes more precise) a noun or pronoun. Adjectives answer the questions **What kind? How many? Which?**—e.g., the *competent* student; *five* home runs; my *last* class. When two or more adjectives modify a noun, they may require commas between them. See Chapter 17 for the differences between **coordinate** and **cumulative adjectives**.
adverb	A word that modifies a verb, adjective, or other adverb. Adverbs answer the questions **When? How? Where? Why? How much?**—e.g., Nino talks *fast* (*fast* modifies the verb *talks*); he is a *very* fast talker (*very* modifies the adjective *fast*); he talks *really* fast (*really* modifies the adverb *fast*). Adverbs often—but not always—end in *-ly*.
anecdote	A short account of an event or incident, often humorous, that is used to catch the reader's interest and illustrate a point.
antecedent	The word that a pronoun refers to or stands for. Literally, it means "coming before, preceding." The antecedent usually comes before the pronoun that refers to it—e.g., *Karen* believes *she* is possessed. (*Karen* is the antecedent to which the pronoun *she* refers.)
article	A determiner that precedes a noun. *A/an* is the **indefinite article** that signals an unspecified one of others—e.g., *a* stockbroker, *an* accountant, *a* village, *an* animal, *an* opportunity. Use *a/an* with a singular count noun when making a generalization: *A* stockbroker's job is stressful.

The is the **definite article** that signals a particular person, place, or thing that has been singled out from others—e.g., *the* stockbroker who lives next door; *the* accountant who audits our books; *the* village where I was born. *The* is used when the speaker or writer and the audience are thinking about the same specific person(s) or thing(s). *The* is also used when an unspecified noun is mentioned a second time: I bought a box of chocolates, and my roommate ate half *the* box.

No article (zero article) is used in general statements with non-count and plural nouns unless the noun is particularized or made specific in some way—e.g., *Tea* contains less caffeine than *coffee. Diamonds* are a girl's best friend. (Contrast: *The diamond in my ring* weighs 1.25 carats.)

audience The writer's intended reader or readers. Knowledge of your audience's level of understanding, interests, attitude toward the subject, and expectations of you as a writer are critically important to successful communication. Your level of vocabulary, sentence structure, organization of material, the amount of specific detail you include, and tone will all be influenced by the needs of your audience.

chronological order Events or ideas that are organized chronologically are discussed in order of time sequence.

clause A group of words that contains a subject and a verb. If the group of words can stand by itself and makes complete sense, it is called an **independent clause** (or **principal clause** or **main clause**). If the group of words does not make complete sense on its own but is linked to another clause (depends on the other clause for its meaning), it is called a **dependent** or **subordinate clause**. Here's an example: The porch collapsed. This group of words can stand by itself, so it is called an independent clause. Now consider this clause: When Kalim removed the railing with his tractor. This group of words has a subject, *Kalim*, and a verb, *removed*, but it does not make complete sense on its own. It depends for its meaning on *the porch collapsed*; therefore, it is a dependent clause.

climactic order The arrangement of key ideas in order of importance. The most important or strongest idea comes last. Thus, the paper builds to a climax.

colloquialism   A word or phrase that we use in casual conversation or in informal writing.

> Steve *flunked* his accounting exam.
> *Did* you *get* what the teacher said about job placement?
> I can't believe that *guy* is serious about learning.

comma splice   The error that results when the writer joins two independent clauses with a comma—e.g., The comma splice is an error, it is a kind of run-on sentence. See Chapter 7.

compound   A compound construction is made up of two or more equal parts. For example:

> <u>Matt</u> and <u>Caro</u> are late. (**compound subject**)
>
> Matt <u>came</u> late and <u>left</u> early. (**compound verb**)
>
> Caro is <u>sick</u> and <u>tired</u>. (**compound complement**)
>
> The <u>team</u> <u>had</u> no time to warm up, but <u>they</u> <u>won</u> the game anyway. (**compound sentence**)

count noun   A common noun that has a plural form and can be preceded by an indefinite article *(a/an)* or a quantity expression such as *one, many, several, a few of, hundreds of.* Examples: car, letter, dollar.

dependent clause cue   A word or phrase that introduces a dependent clause—e.g., when, because, in order that, as soon as. Also called a **subordinate conjunction**. See page 84.

homonyms   Two or more words that are identical in sound (e.g., bear, bare) or spelling (e.g., bank—a place for money; bank—a slope) but different in meaning. See Chapter 2.

logically linked order   A pattern of organization that depends on a causal connection among the main points. One point must be explained before the next can be understood.

modifier   A word or group of words that adds information about another word (or phrase or clause) in a sentence. See **adjective, adverb, dependent clause**, and Chapter 8.

non-count noun   A common noun that cannot be preceded by an indefinite article *(a/an)* or by a quantity expression (e.g., *one, several, many, a couple of*) and that has no plural form. Examples: traffic, mail, money.

noun   A word that names a person, place, thing, or concept and that has the grammatical capability of being possessive. Nouns are most often used as subjects and objects. There are two classes of nouns: concrete and abstract.

Concrete nouns name things we perceive through our senses; we can see, hear, touch, taste, or smell what they stand for. Some concrete nouns are **proper**: they name people, places, or things and are capitalized—e.g., Michaëlle Jean, Beijing, Canada's Wonderland. Other concrete nouns are **common** (woman, city, car, coffee); still others are **collective** (group, audience, swarm, committee).

Abstract nouns name concepts, ideas, characteristics—things we know or experience through our intellect rather than through our senses—e.g., truth, pride, feminism, self-esteem.

object The "receiving" part of a sentence. The **direct object** is a noun or noun substitute (pronoun, phrase, or clause) that is the target or receiver of the action expressed by the verb. It answers the question **What?** or **Whom?**—e.g., John threw the *ball*. (John threw *what?*)

> He wondered where the money went. (He wondered *what?*)
> Munira loves Abdul. (Munira loves *whom?*)

The **indirect object** is a noun or pronoun that is the indirect target or receiver of the action expressed by the verb in a sentence. It is *always* placed in front of the direct object. It answers the question **To whom?** or **To what?**

> Doug threw *me* the ball. (Doug threw *to whom?*)
> Lisa forgot to give her *essay* a title. (Give *to what?*)

The **object of a preposition** is a noun or noun substitute (pronoun, phrase, or clause) that follows a preposition—e.g., after the *storm* (*storm* is a noun, object of the preposition *after*); before *signing the lease* (*signing the lease* is a phrase, object of the preposition *before*); he thought about *what he wanted to do* (*what he wanted to do* is a clause, object of the preposition *about*). Notice that what follows a preposition is always its object; that is why the subject of a sentence or clause can never be found in a prepositional phrase.

parallelism Consistent grammatical structure. In a sentence, for example, all items in a series would be written in the same grammatical form: words, phrases, or clauses. Julius Caesar's famous pronouncement, "I came, I saw, I conquered," is a classic example of parallel structure. The symmetry of parallelism appeals to readers and makes a sentence read smoothly and rhythmically. Lack of parallelism, on the other hand, is jarring: "My favourite sports are water-skiing, swimming, and I particularly love to sail."

paraphrase   To paraphrase is to rephrase another writer's idea in your own words. A good paraphrase reflects both the meaning and the tone of the original; it is usually about the same length or shorter than the original. Whenever you borrow another writer's ideas, you must acknowledge your source; otherwise you are guilty of plagiarism.

participle   The form of a verb that can be used as an adjective (the *completed* work, the *weeping* willows) or as part of a verb phrase (am *succeeding*, have *rented*).

> The **present participle** of a verb ends in *-ing*.
> The **past participle** of a **regular verb** ends in *-d* or in *-ed*. For a list of **irregular verbs**, see pages 140–42.

person   A category of pronouns and verbs. **First person** refers to the person who is speaking (I, we). **Second person** refers to the person being spoken to (you). **Third person** is the person or thing being spoken about (he, she, it, they). Verb forms remain constant except in the present tense third-person singular, which ends in *-s*.

phrase   A group of meaning-related words that acts as a noun, a verb, an adjective, or an adverb within a sentence. Phrases do not make complete sense on their own because they do not contain both a subject and a verb.

> Please order *legal-size manila file folders.* (phrase acting as noun)
> I *must have been sleeping* when you called. (verb phrase)
> *Sightseeing in Ottawa,* we photographed the monuments *on Parliament Hill.* (phrases acting as adjectives)
> Portaging a canoe *in this weather* is no fun. (phrase acting as adverb)

prefix   A meaningful letter or group of letters added to the beginning of a word to change either (1) its meaning or (2) its word class.

> 1. *a* + moral = amoral
>   *bi* + sexual = bisexual
>   *contra* + diction = contradiction
>   *dys* + functional = dysfunctional

2. *a* + board (noun) = aboard (adverb, preposition)
   con + temporary (adjective) = contemporary (noun, adjective)
   de + nude = denude (verb)
   in + put (verb) = input (noun)

Some prefixes require a hyphen, as here:
   all-Canadian
   de-emphasize
   mid-morning

preposition   A word that connects a noun, pronoun, or phrase to some other word(s) in a sentence. The noun, pronoun, or phrase is the **object** of the preposition.

> I prepared the minutes *of the meeting*. (*of* relates *meeting* to *minutes*)
> One *of the parents* checks the children every half hour. (*of* relates *parents* to *One*)

prepositional phrase   A group of grammatically related words beginning with a preposition and having the function of a noun, adjective, or adverb. See the list on page 71.

pretentious language   Sometimes called *gobbledygook*, pretentious language is characterized by vague, abstract, multi-syllable words and long, complicated sentences. Intended to impress the reader, pretentious language is sound without meaning; readers find it irritating, even exasperating.

pronoun   A word that functions like a noun in a sentence (e.g., as a subject, or as an object of a verb or a preposition). Pronouns usually substitute for nouns, but sometimes they substitute for other pronouns.

> *He* will promote *anything that* brings in money.
> *Everyone* must earn *her* badges.

There are several kinds of pronouns:

> **personal:** *I, we; you; he, she, it, they; me, us; him, her, them*
> **possessive:** *mine, ours; yours; his, her, its, theirs*
> **demonstrative:** *this, these; that, those*
> **relative:** *who, whom, whose; which, that*
> **interrogative:** *who? whose? whom? which? what?*
> **indefinite:** all *-one, -thing, -body* pronouns, such as *everyone, something,* and *anybody;* and *each; neither; either; few; none; several*

Note: Possessive pronouns also have adjective forms: *my, our; your; his, her, their.* Possessive adjectives follow the same rules for agreement that govern pronouns. They must agree with their antecedents in person, number, and gender—e.g.,

> Every young *boy* wants to be the goalie on *his* team. (not *their* team)

random order　A shopping-list kind of arrangement of main points in a paper. The points could be explained in any order. Random order is appropriate only when all points are equal in significance and are not chronologically or causally connected to one another.

subject　In a sentence, the person, thing, or concept that the sentence is about (see Chapter 5). In an essay, the person, thing, or concept that the paper is about (see Chapter 22).

suffix　A letter or group of letters that is added to the end of a word to change (1) its meaning, (2) its grammatical function, or (3) its word class.

1. king + *dom* = kingdom
   few + *er* = fewer
   tooth + *less* = toothless
2. buy (infinitive) + *s* = buys (third-person singular, present tense)
   eat (infinitive) + *en* = eaten (past participle)
   instructor + *s* = instructors (plural)
   instructor + *'s* = instructor's (possessive singular)
3. your (adjective) + *s* = yours (pronoun)
   act (verb) + *ive* = active (adjective)
   active (adjective) + *ly* = actively (adverb)
   ventilate (verb) + *tion* = ventilation (noun)

Some words add two or more prefixes and/or suffixes to the base form. Look at antidisestablishmentarianism, for example. How many prefixes and suffixes can you identify?

tense　The different forms of the verb used to indicate past, present, or future time are called **tenses.** The verb ending (e.g., play*s,* play*ed*) and any helping verbs associated with the main verb (*is* playing, *will* play, *has* played, *had* played, *will have* played) indicate the tense of the verb.

There are simple tenses:　**present:** ask, asks
　　　　　　　　　　　　　past: *asked*
　　　　　　　　　　　　　future: *will ask*

and perfect tenses:

present: *has (have) asked*
past: *had asked*
future: *will (shall) have asked*

The simple and perfect tenses can also be **progressive:** am asking, have been asking, etc.

thesis   A thesis is the idea or point about a subject that the writer wants to communicate to the reader. A summary of the writer's thesis is often expressed in a **thesis statement**. See Chapters 22 and 23.

tone   Reflects the writer's attitude toward his or her topic. For instance, a writer who is looking back with longing to the past might use a nostalgic tone. An angry writer might use an indignant tone or an understated, ironic tone—depending on the subject and purpose of the paper.

topic sentence   A sentence that identifies the main point or key idea developed in a paragraph. The topic sentence is usually found at or near the beginning of the paragraph.

transition   A word or phrase that helps readers to follow the writer's thinking from one sentence to the next or from one paragraph to another. See Chapter 25.

verb   A word or phrase that says something about a person, place, or thing and whose form may be changed to indicate tense. Verbs may make a statement (declarative), ask a question (interrogative), give a command (imperative), or express strong emotions or feelings (exclamatory). They may express action (physical or mental), occurrence, or condition (state of being). See Chapter 5.

> Wesley *hit* an inside curve for a home run. (physical action)
> Laurence *believed* the Blue Jays would win. (mental action)
> Father's Day *falls* on the third Sunday of June. (occurrence)
> Reva eventually *became* interested in English. (condition)

Some verbs are called **linking verbs:** they help to make a statement by linking the subject to a word or phrase that describes it.

> William Hubbard *was* Toronto's first Black mayor. (*was* links *William Hubbard* to *mayor*)
> Mohammed *looks* tired. (*looks* links *Mohammed* and *tired*)

In addition to *am*, *is*, *are*, *was*, *were*, and *been*, some common linking verbs are *appear, become, feel, grow, look, taste, remain, seem, smell, sound.*

Another class of verbs is called **auxiliary** or **helping verbs**. They show the time of a verb as future or past (*will* go, *has* gone) or as a continuing action (*is* reading). They also show the passive voice (*is* completed, *have been* submitted).

voice

Verbs may be **active** or **passive**, depending on whether the subject of the verb is *acting* (active voice) or *being acted upon* (passive voice).

In 2006, the government *introduced* a new set of tax reforms. (active)

A new set of tax reforms *was introduced* in 2006. (passive)

APPENDIX D

Answers to Exercises

Answers for Unit 1 Quick Quiz

Note: Triple asterisks (***) indicate that a word or words have been deleted. Each set of triple asterisks counts as one error.

¹I decided to buy a new radio for my car, so I went to a local store **whose** reputation I trusted to see what new products were available. ²**There**, the clerk told me they were having a sale on **v**oice-**a**ctivated car **radios**. ³He demonstrated by saying, "**L**ouder," which had the **effect** of increasing the radio's volume. ⁴Then he said, "Hip Hop" and the radio changed to a **h**ip-**h**op station. ⁵**I liked the features of this radio**, so, despite the fact that it cost more **than** ordinary radios, I bought it. ⁶In *** fact, I felt that it was safer than radios that needed to be adjusted manually *** while I was driving the car. ⁷It was more attractive than the others, too. ⁸I **accepted** the store's offer to install it for a small additional cost. ⁹Soon I was driving along the road calling out, "Louder" to increase the volume and "**Oldies**" to get a station playing songs from the past. ¹⁰As I was turning a corner, however, another driver suddenly cut in front of me. ¹¹Surprised and annoyed, I yelled, "Stupid!" and the radio suddenly *** switched to a call-in show.

Answer Key

If you missed the error(s) in sentence . . .		See Chapter . . .	
1	who's	3	The Apostrophe
2	their	2	Hazardous Homonyms
	Voice-Activated	4	Capital Letters (two errors)
	radio's	3	The Apostrophe
3	"louder"	4	Capital Letters
	affect	2	Hazardous Homonyms
4	Hip Hop	4	Capital Letters (two errors)
5	I thought this radio was really cool	1	"Slang" section
	then	2	Hazardous Homonyms
6	in actual fact; manually, by hand	1	"Wordiness" section
8	excepted	2	Hazardous Homonyms
9	Oldie's	3	The Apostrophe
11	suddenly and abruptly	1	"Wordiness" section

Answers for Chapter 1: Choosing the Right Words

Exercise 1.2

1. ratios
2. criteria
3. analyses
4. personnel
5. crises
6. data (the singular is *datum*)
7. mothers-in-law
8. nuclei (or *nucleuses*)
9. appendixes
   (or *appendices*)
10. formulas
    (or *formulae*)

Exercise 1.3

1. delayed
2. journeys
3. player
4. destroying
5. repayment
6. loneliness
7. policies
8. easier
9. laziness
10. necessarily

The root words in 1 to 5 end in a **vowel** plus *y*; these words do not change spelling when you add an ending. The root words in 6 to 10 end in a **consonant** plus *y*; change *y* to *i* when you add an ending to such words.

Exercise 1.4

1. dis-cuss
2. man-age-ment
3. ac-com-mo-date
4. dis-trib-ute
5. through (Words of one syllable cannot be divided.)
6. cre-ate
7. so-lu-tion
8. tech-ni-cian
9. con-science
10. busi-ness

Exercise 1.7 (suggested answers)

1. Several close friends and I have decided to go to the gym.
2. We were amazed to learn that the painting hanging in our residence was the work of a famous artist.
3. Though small and light, she is the best forward on our team.
4. We can never be free of the violence that surrounds us.
5. The professor then destroyed my concentration by announcing that we had only five minutes left.

Exercise 1.9 (suggested answers)

Note: Triple asterisks (***) indicate that a word or words have been deleted. Each set of triple asterisks counts as one error.

1. **You** should **be careful** when **using** an axe.
2. We **live** at the **corner** of Maple Street and Rue Érable in *** Sherbrooke.
3. **After** we **looked closely at** the task ***, we knew **we would need help**.
4. When we **saw** storm clouds **ahead**, we knew that **it was soon going to rain**.
5. His gym teacher **knows** that Tom **doesn't like** physical **exercise**.

Exercise 1.10

Note: Triple asterisks (***) indicate that a word or words have been deleted. Each set of triple asterisks counts as one error.

1. Abdullah is **highly** talented, so he could **have** chosen **many** different careers.
2. **Regardless** of what you think, I believe the media **are** generally reliable.
3. We should **have** told Kevin there wasn't **anything** he could **have** done to help.
4. The reason **you** are failing is **that** you don't do **any** homework.
5. Between you and **me**, Karl didn't do **very** well at today's practice.
6. Sonji's father isn't **prejudiced**; he can't *** stand any of her boyfriends, **regardless** of their backgrounds.
7. For this party, you're **supposed** to dress the way you **used** to when you were in primary school.
8. She shouldn't be driving **anywhere**; we should **have** taken the car keys **from** her.
9. We were *** sure of ourselves going into the race, but once we fell off *** our bikes, we couldn't *** hope to win.
10. Our instructor doesn't have **any** patience with people who should **have** been coming to class and now can't write **very** well.

Answers for Chapter 2: Hazardous Homonyms

Exercise 2.1
1. This is a **course** that I should be able to pass easily.
2. My sister is a **woman** who **hears** everything and forgets nothing.
3. **Whose** radio is disturbing the **peace** and quiet?
4. **They're** still in bed because they stayed up **too** late.
5. This college values **its** students.
6. I'd like to **lose** four kilograms by Christmas, but I can't resist **desserts**.

Exercise 2.2
1. **It's** the perfect **site** for a small house.
2. I won't **accept** assignments submitted **later** than Thursday.
3. Our **morale** was given a lift by the **compliments** we received.
4. **Their** eating habits are having an **effect** on their health.
5. It was the **fourth** quarter of the game, and we **led** by 20 points.

Exercise 2.3
1. Is there anyone **whose advice** you will listen to?
2. **Your** confidence in statistics is an **illusion**.
3. Sometimes my **conscience** bothers me when I send **personal** e-mails on the office computer.
4. **Whose** turn is it to go to the storeroom for more **stationery**?
5. I believe in the **principle** of fairness more **than** the deterrent of punishment.

Exercise 2.4
1. After lunch, we **led** them to the **site** of the old mine.
2. She **cited** my essay in her paper on the **effects** of poor grammar.
3. If we **accept** your **counsel**, will you guarantee success?
4. He was still **conscious** after falling from his **stationary** bike.
5. My overindulgence at the **dining** table **led** to a night of discomfort.

Exercise 2.5
1. **Choose** carefully, because the candidate **who's** hired will **affect** all of us.
2. This company makes a better product **than** any of **its** competitors.
3. In a situation **where** a company has several owners, the **principal** owner is the one who has the most shares.
4. **It's** the law that, as a **minor**, she is not allowed to have ice wine with her **dessert**.

Exercise 2.6
1. **It's** clear that my ability to learn is **affected** by my **personal** well-being more **than** by my intellectual ability.
2. All employees, without **exception**, will be fined $10.00 a day until **morale** on the job **site** improves!
3. The **advice** given to us by the personnel firm we hired was to **choose** a **woman whose principal** qualifications were a huge ego and shoes that **complemented** her every outfit.
4. Emily is the supervisor **who's** responsible for monitoring the **effects** of automation on assembly-line personnel.

Exercise 2.7

I had a hard time **choosing** between two colleges, both of which offered the **courses** I wanted. Both had good placement records, and I just couldn't make up my mind. I asked my friends for **advice**, but they were no help. Several were surprised that any college would even

accept me! Their negative view of my academic ability did nothing to improve my **morale**; in fact, it **led** me to re-evaluate my selection of friends. My school counsellor, a **woman whose** opinion I respect, didn't think one college was better **than** the other, so she suggested that I choose the school that was located **where** I preferred to live. I followed her advice, and I haven't regretted it.

Exercise 2.8

Many people today are **choosing** a quieter way of life. They hope to live longer and more happily by following the "slower is better" **principle**. Some, on the **advice** of **their** doctors, have been forced to slow down. One heart surgeon, for example, directs his patients to drive only in the slow lane rather **than** use the passing lane. They may arrive a few minutes later, but their blood pressure will not be **affected**. Others don't need to be prompted by their doctors. They **accept** that living at a slower pace doesn't mean **losing** out in any way. In fact, the opposite is true: **choosing** a healthy lifestyle benefits everyone. **Peace** and **quiet** in one's **personal** life leads to increased productivity, higher **morale**, and greater job satisfaction. Sometimes the improvements are **minor**, but as anyone who has **consciously** tried to slow the pace of life can tell you, the slow lane is the fast lane to longevity.

Answers for Chapter 3: The Apostrophe

Exercise 3.1

1. can't	5. let's	8. won't
2. she'd	6. hasn't	9. she'll
3. he'll	7. you're	10. we'll
4. we'd		

Exercise 3.2

1. they're	5. everyone's	8. you're
2. I'll	6. couldn't	9. we'd
3. it's	7. who's	10. won't
4. can't		

Exercise 3.3

1. **We'd** be glad to help if **they'd** ask us.
2. There **won't** be a problem if **you're** on time.
3. **I'm** sure that contractions **shouldn't** be used in formal writing.
4. **They're** acceptable in conversation and for informal writing.
5. **Don't** worry about your heart; **it'll** last as long as you do.
6. Your **sister's** very nice, but your **brother's** weird.
7. **It's** certain that **he'll** be late.
8. **We'll** help you with your essay, but **you'll** have to get started right away.
9. In my culture, a **birthday's** the most important day of the year, and anyone **who's** celebrating is the centre of attention.
10. **It's** a shame that **they're** arriving for a three-week visit on the same day that **you're** leaving to go home.

Exercise 3.4

I am writing to apply for the position of Webmaster for BrilloVision.com that **you have** advertised in the *Daily News*. **I have** got the talent and background **you are** looking for. Currently, I work as a Web designer for an online publication, Vexed.com, where **they are** very pleased with my work. If you click on their Web site, I think **you will** like what you see. **There is** little in the way of Web design and application that I **have not** been involved in during the past two years. But **it is** time for me to move on to a new challenge, and BrilloVision.com promises the kind of opportunity **I am** looking for. I guarantee you **will not** be disappointed if I join your team!

Exercise 3.5

1. woman's beauty
2. heaven's gate
3. families' budgets
4. children's school
5. the soldiers' uniforms
6. the book's title
7. the Thousand Islands' climate
8. the Simpsons' daughters
9. the oldest child's responsibility
10. our country's flag

Exercise 3.6

1. **Juri's** greatest fear is his **mother's** disapproval.
2. **Students'** supplies can be expensive, so I buy mine at **Danny's** Dollar Store.
3. My parents would like to know **whose** yogurt was left in **their** fridge for three months.
4. After only a **month's** wear, my **son's** new jacket fell apart.
5. Unfortunately, the **book's** cover was much more interesting than **its** contents.
6. Our **team's** biggest win came at the same time as our **league's** other teams all lost.
7. **Texas'** (or **Texas's**) record of executing people is one of the **United States'** most notorious statistics.
8. This year, our **family's** Thanksgiving celebration will be a quiet one, as we think of other **families'** poverty.
9. This **week's** *Fashion* magazine devotes four pages to **men's** clothing and twelve pages to **women's**.
10. One way of overcoming writer's block is to disconnect **your** computer from **its** monitor, so you can't see **your** work as you type.

Exercise 3.7

1. **There's** a rumour that **you're** going to quit smoking.
2. **It's** true. My family **doctor's** concerns about my health finally convinced me to quit.
3. **Who's** perfect? I am, in my **mother's** opinion, at least.
4. **It's** a fact that most **mothers'** opinions about their children are unrealistically positive.
5. Most **fathers'** opinions are highly negative when they first meet their **daughters'** boyfriends.

Exercise 3.8

1. The **candidates'** debate was deadly boring until the fans started fighting in their seats.
2. **Today's** styles and **tomorrow's** trends will be featured in our display window.
3. **Hockey's** playoff schedule puts the **finals** into the middle of June.
4. My **in-laws'** home is about four **hours'** drive north of Red Lake.
5. **Today's** paper features a short article entitled "**It's** Clear the **Apostrophe's** Days Are Numbered."

Exercise 3.9

1. When you feel like a snack, you can choose between apples or **Timbits**.
2. **Anna's** career took off when she discovered **it's** easy to sell **children's** toys.
3. The Olympic **Games** are held every two years.
4. **Poker's** an easy game to play if you are dealt **aces** more often than your **opponents** are.
5. **Nobody's** perfect, but if you consistently make mistakes, you demonstrate that you don't understand **apostrophes**.

Exercise 3.10

1. **I've** posted a sign on my front lawn: "**Salespersons** welcome. Dog **food's** expensive."
2. The **leaders** of the European Union **countries** are meeting in Brussels.
3. Do you really think your **employees** will be disappointed when they hear that you've cancelled the **company's** annual picnic?
4. In Canada, when it's warm enough to expose **your** skin to the sun, the **insects'** feeding season is at **its** height.

Exercise 3.11
1. Candy is dandy, but **liquor's** quicker. (Ogden Nash)
2. The storm devastated the two small **towns** in **its** path.
3. Thank you for the **flowers** you sent us on the occasion of the **twins'** graduation.
4. **Somebody's** going to be very disappointed when the panel releases its decision.
5. Four **months'** work was wasted by a few **minutes'** carelessness.
6. Don't forget your three o'clock appointment at the **Fingers** and **Toes** salon.

Answers for Chapter 4: Capital Letters

Exercise 4.1
1. **T**he pen is mightier than the sword.
2. Pietro hurried back inside and said, "**I**t's too cold to go to school today."
3. **M**y parents have a bumper sticker that reads, "**M**oney isn't everything, but it sure keeps the kids in touch."
4. **T**aped to the door, there was a sign that read "**N**ot to be used as an exit or entrance."
5. **I**n conclusion, I want you to think about the words of Wendell Johnson: "*A*lways and *never* are two words you should always remember never to use."

Exercise 4.2
1. After a brief stay in the **M**aritimes, **C**aptain Tallman and his crew sailed west up the **S**t. **L**awrence.
2. The **B**roadcast Department of **N**iagara College has ordered six **S**ony cameras for its studios in **W**elland, Ontario.
3. Do you find that **V**isa is more popular than American **E**xpress when you travel to faraway places such as Mexico, France, or Jupiter?
4. Our stay at the Seaview Hotel overlooking the **P**acific **O**cean certainly beat our last vacation at the **B**ates **M**otel, where we faced west, overlooking the city dump.
5. As a member of the **A**lumni **A**ssociation I am trying to raise funds from companies like Disney, **T**oyota, **M**icrosoft, and the **CBC**, where our graduates have positions.

Exercise 4.3
1. The **C**rusades, which were religious wars between **M**uslims and **C**hristians, raged through the **M**iddle **A**ges.
2. The **H**indu religion recognizes and honours many gods; **I**slam recognizes one god, **A**llah; **B**uddhism recognizes none.
3. The **K**oran, the **B**ible, and the **T**orah agree on many principles.
4. The **J**ewish festival of **H**anukkah often occurs near the same time that **C**hristians are celebrating **C**hristmas.
5. After **W**orld **W**ar I, many **J**ews began to emigrate to Palestine, where they and the **M**uslim population soon came into conflict.

Exercise 4.4
1. My favourite months are **J**anuary and **F**ebruary because I love all **w**inter sports.
2. This **M**onday is **V**alentine's **D**ay, when messages of love are exchanged.
3. In the summer, big meals seem too much trouble; however, after **T**hanksgiving, we need lots of food to survive the winter cold.
4. A **n**ational **h**oliday named **F**lag **D**ay was once proposed, but it was never officially approved.
5. Thursday is **C**anada **D**ay and also the official beginning of my **s**ummer **v**acation.

Exercise 4.5

1. The review of my book, *The Life and Times of a Chocoholic*, published in *The Globe and Mail,* was not favourable.
2. Clint Eastwood fans will be delighted that the two early movies that made him internationally famous, *A Fistful of Dollars* and *For a Few Dollars More,* are now available on **DVD**.
3. Joseph Conrad's short novel *Heart of Darkness* became the blockbuster movie *Apocalypse Now.*
4. My poem, "**A B**right and **S**ilent **P**lace," was published in the **A**pril issue of *Landscapes* magazine.
5. Botticelli's famous painting, "**B**irth of **V**enus," inspired my poem "**W**oman on the **H**alf **S**hell."

Exercise 4.6

1. I want to take **I**ntroductory **F**rench this term, but it is not offered until **w**inter.
2. Although my favourite subject is **m**ath, I'm not doing very well in Professor Truman's course, **B**usiness **F**inance 101.
3. Correct
4. Laurie is studying to be a chef and is taking courses called **F**ood **P**reparation, **R**estaurant **M**anagement, and **E**nglish.
5. The prerequisite for Theology 210 is **I**ntroduction to **W**orld **R**eligions, taught by **P**rofessor Singh.

Exercise 4.7

1. Our youth group meets in the **O**ttawa mosque every second **T**hursday.
2. You must take some **s**cience courses, or you'll never get into the program you want at college in the **f**all.
3. Gore Vidal, author of *The Best Man*, once said, "**I**t is not enough to succeed; others must fail."
4. After the game, we went to the **B**urger **P**alace for a late snack and then went home to watch *This Hour Has 22 Minutes* on television.
5. In our **E**nglish course at **C**aribou **C**ollege, we studied *The Englishman's Boy,* a novel about life among the settlers of the **A**merican and **C**anadian west.

Exercise 4.8

1. I own a **F**ord and wear **L**evi's jeans but hope someday to drive a **P**orsche and wear **A**rmani.
2. Two of Vancouver's religious leaders, **R**abbi David Mivasair and **I**mam Fode Drome, held a joint service last month to bring their two **c**ommunities together.
3. In an award ceremony that **P**resident **G**eorge **W**. **B**ush did not attend, he was given the prize for stupidest political statement of 2005 for his remark, "**T**hey are always thinking of ways to harm **A**merica, and so are we."
4. I plan to travel on **A**ir **C**anada to **A**sia next summer to visit **S**ri **L**anka, **I**ndia, and **P**akistan, where I have many relatives.

Answers for Unit 1 Rapid Review

Note: Triple asterisks (*******) indicate that a word or words have been deleted. Each set of triple asterisks counts as one error. The Answer Key following the answers identifies the errors by sentence number and indicates the chapter you should review if you missed an error.

[1]Recently I read a book, published in 1908, in which the author, travelling in the Nova Scotia wilderness, reports being thrilled ******* when he **sighted** a beaver dam. [2]Beavers were

almost extinct at that time; he'd never seen one before, and he might never get a chance to see another. ³The author's excitement interested me because, far from being extinct, the beaver is now so common and so prolific that **it's** being hunted and trapped as a nuisance across Canada. ⁴Did you know that Canadian **trappers** are issued a quota for the number of beavers they are **allowed** to trap in their region, and they must reach that quota or **lose** their trapping licences?

⁵**We're** not alone in our struggle to control these *** pesky rodents, either. ⁶A *Canadian Geographic* film called *The* **S***uper* **B***eaver* documents the **creature's** introduction to Tierra del Fuego, at the tip of South America, which has led to *** devastation of the ecosystem there. ⁷The film tells us that only coral and humans have had a greater impact on Earth's environment than beavers. ⁸They have now migrated to the mainland of South America and, without radical government intervention, they threaten to destroy millions of hectares of **Argentina's** land as they expand their territory northward. ⁹It's difficult to **accept** the fact that only 100 years ago, travellers in **Canada's** wilderness longed for a glimpse of what was then a rare and exotic animal.

Answer Key

If you missed the error(s) in sentence . . .   See Chapter . . .

1	thrilled out of his mind	1	"Levels of Language" section
	cited	2	Hazardous Homonyms
3	its	2	Hazardous Homonyms/ 3 The Apostrophe
4	trapper's	3	The Apostrophe
	aloud; loose	2	Hazardous Homonyms
5	Were	2	Hazardous Homonyms/ 3 The Apostrophe
	humongous	1	"Slang" section
6	The super beaver	4	Capital Letters
	creatures	3	The Apostrophe
	complete and total devastation	1	"Wordiness" section
7	earth's	4	Capital Letters
8	Argentinas	3	The Apostrophe
9	except	2	Hazardous Homonyms
	Canadas	3	The Apostrophe

Answers for Unit 2 Quick Quiz

¹You know that the heart pumps blood through our bodies, but did you also know that the word "heart" appears in the English language in other interesting ways? ²Let's look at some of the idioms using the word "heart." ³An idiom **is** a phrase whose meaning is difficult to figure out from the meaning of its individual words**; for example,** "heart of gold" and "heart of stone." ⁴Some "heart" idioms have positive connotations, **some have** negative connotations, and some are neutral. ⁵Some have to do with love and loss**;** others have nothing at all to do with romance.

⁶After "losing your heart," **you begin** the romance. ⁷As the relationship develops, you have many "heart-to-heart" talks**.** ⁸**Y**ou love each other "from the bottom of your hearts." ⁹However, your "heart sinks" **when the relationship ends**. ¹⁰You might "cry your heart out" **because** you are "heartbroken" and your lover is "heartless."

¹¹Turning away from romance, **we find** many other heart idioms that apply to all aspects of life. ¹²**Examples include** learning something "by heart" (memorizing it) and having your "heart set" on something (wanting it very much). ¹³Scared nearly out of your wits, **you find** the "heart-stopping" movie you are watching is truly frightening. ¹⁴The "heartland" **is** the most important part of a country. ¹⁵Asking someone to "have a heart" **means** to ask for sympathy. ¹⁶To describe people as "young at heart" means they are youthful in spirit, though not in years.

[17]English idioms using the word "heart" have a bewildering number of meanings that we learn **only** through experience. [18]Experience teaches us not to say that spicy food gave us "heartache**,**" **or** that an ex-lover caused us to have "heartburn." [19]My "heart goes out" to the many language learners who are confused by the difference!

Answer Key

If you missed the error(s) in sentence . . .		See Chapter . . .	
3	sentence fragment	6	"'Missing Piece' Fragments" section
4	sentence fragment	6	"'Missing Piece' Fragments" section
5	*negative connotations cling*	9	The Parallelism Principle
6	run-on sentence	7	"Comma Splices" section
7	*After losing your heart, the*	8	"Dangling Modifiers" section
8	run-on sentence	7	Comma Splices" section
9	sentence fragment	6	"'Missing Piece' Fragments" section
11	sentence fragment	6	"Dependent Clause Fragments" section
12	*Turning away from romance, many*	8	"Dangling Modifiers" section
13	sentence fragment	6	"'Missing Piece' Fragments" section
14	*Scared nearly out of your wits, the*	8	"Dangling Modifiers" section
15	sentence fragment	6	"'Missing Piece' Fragments" section
16	sentence fragment	6	"'Missing Piece' Fragments" section
18	*we only learn*	8	"Misplaced Modifiers" section
20	sentence fragment	6	"Dependent Clause Fragments" section

Answers for Chapter 5: Cracking the Sentence Code

Exercise 5.1
1. <u>Canadians</u> <u>love</u> doughnuts.
2. <u>They</u> <u>eat</u> more doughnuts than any other nation.
3. Most <u>malls</u> <u>contain</u> a doughnut shop.
4. <u>Doughnuts</u> <u>taste</u> sweet.
5. Glazed <u>doughnuts</u> <u>are</u> my favourite.
6. Hot <u>chocolate</u> <u>is</u> good with doughnuts.
7. [<u>You</u>] <u>Try</u> a bran doughnut for breakfast.
8. <u>It</u> <u>is</u> good for your health.
9. Doughnut <u>jokes</u> <u>are</u> common on television.
10. <u>Dentists</u> <u>like</u> doughnuts too, but for different reasons.

Exercise 5.2
1. My <u>computer</u> <u>is</u> usually reliable.
2. Today, however, <u>it</u> <u>keeps</u> crashing.
3. [<u>You</u>] <u>Turn</u> it off.
4. Maybe the <u>processor</u> <u>is</u> tired.
5. Perhaps the <u>operator</u> <u>needs</u> a vacation.
6. <u>Computing</u> <u>is</u> a necessary part of my life.
7. My <u>work</u> <u>depends</u> on it.
8. Without a functioning computer, <u>I</u> <u>feel</u> frustrated and angry.
9. Eventually, <u>I</u> <u>decided</u> to hit it with my fist.
10. The <u>computer</u> <u>booted</u> right up!

Exercise 5.3
1. <u>Is</u> <u>Tomas</u> still on the team?
2. [<u>You</u>] <u>Consider</u> it done.

3. Here <u>are</u> the <u><u>answers</u></u> to yesterday's quiz.
4. <u>Is</u> <u><u>it</u></u> your birthday today?
5. Into the pool <u>leaped</u> the terrified <u><u>cat</u></u>.
6. Where <u>are</u> the <u><u>children</u></u>?
7. There <u>were</u> only two <u><u>students</u></u> in class today.
8. Which <u><u>elective</u></u> <u>is</u> easier?
9. <u>Are</u> <u><u>you</u></u> happy with your choice?
10. <u><u>Who</u></u> <u>let</u> the dogs out?

Exercise 5.4
1. Your sister <u>is calling</u> from Mexico.
2. Carina <u>will arrive</u> from Finland tomorrow.
3. <u>Have</u> you <u>arranged</u> accommodation for our guests?
4. The restaurant <u>could have prepared</u> a vegetarian meal.
5. They <u>might have moved</u> away from the city.
6. Xue <u>should have completed</u> her diploma by now.
7. <u>Do</u> you <u>know</u> anything about Linux?
8. They <u>have visited</u> Venezuela twice.
9. We <u>must have practised</u> enough by now.
10. I <u>will be looking</u> for verbs in my sleep.

Exercise 5.5
1. <u>I</u> <u>am making</u> a nutritious breakfast.
2. <u>It</u> <u>does</u> not <u>include</u> Coca-Cola.
3. <u>You</u> <u>can add</u> fresh fruit to the cereal.
4. The <u>toast</u> <u>should be</u> almost ready now.
5. My <u>doctor</u> <u>has</u> often <u>recommended</u> yogurt for breakfast.
6. <u>I</u> <u>could</u> never <u>eat</u> yogurt without fruit.
7. With breakfast, <u>I</u> <u>will drink</u> at least two cups of coffee.
8. <u>I</u> <u>don</u>'t <u>like</u> tea.
9. <u>I</u> simply <u>cannot</u> <u>begin</u> my day without coffee.
10. <u>I</u> <u>should</u> probably <u>switch</u> to decaf.

Exercise 5.6
1. <u>Winners</u> <u>are</u> always <u>watching</u> for opportunities.
2. <u>Losers</u> <u>are</u> usually <u>looking</u> for lucky breaks.
3. <u>I</u> <u>should be riding</u> my bicycle to work.
4. My <u>bike</u> <u>has been broken</u> for nearly two years.
5. <u>I</u> <u>cannot</u> <u>ride</u> a broken bike.
6. My broken <u>bike</u> <u>is</u> really just an excuse.
7. Given the opportunity, <u>I</u> <u>will</u> always <u>drive</u>.
8. Also, <u>I</u> <u>have been waiting</u> for the bicycle fairy to fix it.
9. <u>Wouldn</u>'t <u>that</u> <u>be</u> a lucky break?
10. Maybe <u>I</u> <u>should</u> simply <u>start</u> working on it myself.

Exercise 5.7
1. Many <u>people</u> ~~in the crowd~~ <u>were</u> confused.
2. <u>Fifty</u> ~~of her friends~~ <u>gave</u> her a surprise party.
3. The official <u>opening</u> ~~of the new city hall~~ <u>will be held</u> tomorrow.
4. ~~In the movies~~, the <u>collision</u> ~~of two cars~~ always <u>results</u> ~~in a fire~~.
5. A <u>couple</u> ~~of burgers~~ <u>should be</u> enough ~~for each of us~~.
6. [<u>You</u>] Please <u>decide</u> ~~on dessert before dinnertime~~.
7. Only a <u>few</u> ~~of us~~ <u>have finished</u> our homework.

8. ~~After class,~~ the <u>people</u> ~~in my carpool~~ <u>meet</u> ~~in the cafeteria.~~
9. There <u>is</u> a <u>show</u> ~~about laser surgery on television~~ tonight.
10. ~~In the land of the blind,~~ the one-eyed <u>man</u> <u>is</u> king. (Erasmus)

Exercise 5.8

1. A <u>party</u> ~~in our neighbours' apartment~~ <u>kept</u> us awake ~~until dawn.~~
2. The <u>meeting</u> ~~of all students in our class~~ <u>solved</u> nothing.
3. ~~From the hallway~~ <u>came</u> the <u>sound</u> ~~of a loud argument.~~
4. ~~According to the news,~~ the <u>temperature</u> ~~in Yellowknife~~ <u>fell</u> 20°C overnight.
5. My <u>naps</u> ~~in the afternoon~~ are necessary because ~~of my late night activities.~~
6. <u>Nothing</u> ~~in this world~~ <u>travels</u> faster than a bad cheque.
7. ~~For many students,~~ <u>lack</u> ~~of money~~ <u>is</u> probably their most serious problem.
8. The <u>plural</u> ~~of "choose"~~ <u>should be</u> "cheese."
9. ~~After my acceptance to this college,~~ <u>I</u> <u>became</u> interested ~~in learning~~ more ~~about the city.~~
10. My <u>guarantee</u> ~~of an A in this course~~ <u>is</u> valid only ~~under certain conditions.~~

Exercise 5.9

1. ~~In my opinion,~~ the <u>fear</u> ~~of flying~~ <u>is</u> entirely justifiable.
2. ~~In our basement~~ <u>are</u> <u>stacks</u> ~~of magazines~~ dating ~~from the 1950s.~~
3. The <u>rats</u> ~~in our building~~ <u>have written</u> letters ~~of complaint to the Board of Health.~~
4. Why <u>did</u> <u>Kai</u> insist ~~on purple for the bathroom?~~
5. ~~For reasons of privacy,~~ <u>I</u> <u>am listed</u> ~~in the telephone book under my dog's name.~~
6. ~~Into the classroom~~ and ~~up to the front~~ <u>marched</u> a tall <u>woman</u> ~~with a determined look in her eyes.~~
7. <u>Most</u> ~~of the students in the class~~ instantly <u>decided</u> not to argue ~~with her.~~
8. ~~In future,~~ [<u>you</u>] <u>be</u> sure to read ~~through your notes before the exam.~~
9. ~~In your brochure,~~ <u>you</u> <u>advertise</u> a "semi-annual after-Christmas sale" ~~of quality items.~~
10. ~~According to my dictionary,~~ the <u>word</u> "semi-annual" <u>means</u> twice a year.

Exercise 5.10

1. My <u>mother</u> and <u>father</u> <u>support</u> me ~~in college.~~
2. <u>I</u> <u>could study</u> tonight or <u>go</u> ~~to the movies.~~
3. My <u>parents</u> and the <u>rest</u> ~~of my family~~ <u>are expecting</u> me to do well ~~in school.~~
4. <u>Entertainment</u> and <u>clothing</u> <u>are</u> not <u>included</u> ~~in my budget.~~
5. <u>Tuition</u>, <u>books</u>, <u>lab fees</u>, and <u>rent</u> <u>take</u> all my money.
6. A student's <u>life</u> <u>can be</u> sad and lonely.
7. ~~In my letters home,~~ <u>I</u> <u>whine</u> and <u>moan</u> ~~at every opportunity about my lack of money.~~
8. Unfortunately ~~for me,~~ my <u>mother</u> and <u>father</u> <u>were</u> students too and <u>had</u> the same experience.
9. <u>They</u> <u>laugh</u> and <u>shake</u> their heads and <u>tell</u> me ~~about their college days.~~
10. ~~According to my parents,~~ <u>they</u> <u>ate</u> only Kraft Dinner, <u>lived</u> ~~in a shack,~~ <u>wore</u> hand-me-down clothes, and <u>walked</u> 10 kilometres ~~to school.~~

Exercise 5.11

1. <u>Verbs</u> and <u>subjects</u> <u>are</u> sometimes hard to find.
2. <u>Farmers</u>, <u>loggers</u>, and <u>fishers</u> <u>need</u> and <u>deserve</u> the support ~~of consumers.~~
3. [<u>You</u>] <u>Open</u> the bottle, <u>pour</u> carefully, <u>taste</u>, and <u>enjoy</u>.
4. Where <u>do</u> <u>you</u> and your <u>roommates</u> get the energy ~~for school, work, and fun?~~
5. <u>Werner</u>, <u>Italo</u>, and <u>Pierre</u> <u>discussed</u> and <u>debated</u> recipes all night.
6. ~~During the following week,~~ each <u>one</u> <u>chose</u> and <u>prepared</u> a meal ~~for the other two.~~
7. Werner's <u>sauerbraten</u> and Black Forest <u>cake</u> <u>amazed</u> and <u>delighted</u> his friends.
8. <u>Italo</u> <u>chopped</u>, <u>sliced</u>, <u>simmered</u>, and <u>baked</u> a magnificent Italian meal.

9. <u>Pierre</u> and his <u>sister</u> <u>worked</u> ~~in the kitchen for two days~~ and <u>prepared</u> a delicious cassoulet.
10. ~~By the end of the week~~, <u>Pierre</u>, <u>Italo</u>, and <u>Werner</u> <u>were</u> ready ~~for a diet~~.

Exercise 5.12

1. A <u>fool</u> and his <u>money</u> <u>are</u> soon <u>parted</u>.
2. I <u>dream</u> ~~of success~~ and <u>worry</u> ~~about failure~~.
3. <u>Nur</u> and <u>Aman</u> <u>paddled</u> and <u>portaged</u> ~~for 10 days~~.
4. ~~From the back seat of the tiny car~~ <u>emerged</u> a basketball <u>player</u> and a Newfoundland <u>dog</u>.
5. ~~In the mist of early morning~~, a <u>Brontosaurus</u> and a <u>Tyrannosaurus Rex</u> <u>sniffed</u> the moist air and <u>hunted</u> ~~for food~~.
6. [<u>You</u>] <u>Study</u> my methods, <u>use</u> my research, but <u>do</u> not <u>copy</u> my work.
7. Why <u>are</u> <u>goalies</u> ~~in hockey~~ and <u>kickers</u> ~~in football~~ so superstitious?
8. ~~In my dreams~~, the <u>maid</u>, <u>butler</u>, <u>housekeeper</u>, and <u>chef</u> <u>wash</u> the dishes, <u>vacuum</u> the floors, <u>do</u> the laundry, and <u>make</u> the meals.
9. ~~According to the official course outline~~, <u>students</u> ~~in this English course~~ <u>must take</u> notes ~~during every class~~ and <u>submit</u> their notes ~~to their instructor for evaluation~~.
10. ~~In the opinion of many Canadians~~, the <u>word</u> *politician* <u>is</u> a synonym ~~for "crook."~~

Answers for Chapter 6: Solving Sentence-Fragment Problems

Exercise 6.1

Many different sentences can be made out of the fragments in this exercise. Just be sure that each of your sentences has both a subject and a verb.

1. F   One <u>type</u> of sentence-fragment error <u>is called</u> a "missing piece" fragment.
2. F   <u>We</u> <u>were</u> glad to be able to help you.
3. F   Your <u>mother</u> <u>is hoping</u> to hear from you soon.
4. F   The <u>class</u> <u>was saved</u> by the bell from doing yet another exercise.
5. F   To prevent a similar tragedy from happening again, a policy and procedures <u>manual will be developed.</u>
6. F   <u>It</u> <u>was</u> not a good idea to leave the cat in the same room with the canary.
7. F   <u>Attaching</u> a DVD player to the television <u>was</u> a challenge for me.
8. S
9. F   A new <u>puppy</u>, <u>kitten</u>, or <u>baby</u> <u>gives</u> one no choice but to get up early.
10. S

Exercise 6.2

1. F	5. F	8. S
2. F	6. S	9. F
3. F	7. F	10. F
4. F		

Exercise 6.3 (suggested answers)

1. This apartment suits me in every way, **e**xcept for the price. I can't afford it.
2. In track and field, this college is very well respected. Our team won the championship last year, **s**etting three new provincial records.
3. Whenever I go fishing, the fish aren't biting, but the mosquitoes are. Maybe I should give up fishing **a**nd start collecting insects as a hobby instead.
4. My son is a genius. On his last birthday, he was given a toy that was guaranteed unbreakable. **He** <u>used</u> it to break all his other toys.
5. We weren't lost, but we were certainly confused. I realized this when we passed City Hall **f**or the third time.

6. S

7. My husband and I often go to the hockey arena, **n**ot to watch sports, but to hear the concerts of our favourite local bands. These concerts give new meaning to the word "cool."

8. S

9. I enjoy reading travel books **a**bout faraway, exotic places that I have never visited and will probably never get to see. The fun is in the dreaming, not the doing.

10. To spend the days skiing and the nights dining and dancing **is** how I picture my retirement. Unfortunately, by then I'll be too old to do it.

Exercise 6.4

1. S	4. S	7. S
2. F	5. F	8. F
3. F	6. F	9. S

Exercise 6.5 (suggested answers)

I decided to take swimming lessons for several reasons. First, I <u>know</u> that swimming is one of the best activities for physical fitness. Second, I <u>am concerned</u> about safety. You never know when the ability to swim might save your life **or** the life of someone you're with. Third, I <u>want</u> to be able to enjoy water sports such as diving and snorkelling instead of being stuck on shore watching others have fun. By summer, I hope to be a confident swimmer, **a**ble to enjoy myself in and on the water. I can hardly wait!

Exercise 6.6 (suggested answers)

1. F (After) class is over.

2. F (When) you wish upon a star.

3. S

4. F (Once) the batteries are charged.

5. F (Who) encouraged us to keep trying until we succeeded.

6. S

7. F (Even if) there is an earthquake.

Exercise 6.7 (suggested answers)

1. After class is over, I <u>am meeting</u> Manuel for coffee.

2. When you wish upon a star, your <u>dreams will come</u> true.

4. Once the batteries are charged, <u>you can use</u> the sweeper.

5. It <u>was</u> our coach who encouraged us to keep trying until we succeeded.

7. Even if there is an earthquake, <u>we should be</u> safe in our mountain retreat.

Exercise 6.8

1. Walking is probably the best form of exercise there is. *Unless you're in the water.* Then swimming is preferable.

2. Rain doesn't bother me. I like to stay inside and read. *When the weather is miserable.*

3. Please try this curry. *After you've tasted it.* I am sure you'll be able to tell me what's missing.

4. The report identifies a serious problem that we need to consider. *Whenever our Web site is revised or updated.* It is vulnerable to hackers.

5. Sanir and Jade asked us what we thought about their recent engagement. *Since they want to go to Canada's Wonderland for their honeymoon.* We think they are probably too young to get married.

Exercise 6.9

1. I keep the temperature in my apartment very low. *In order to save money.* My friends have to wear sweaters every time they visit.

2. Your idea that we should ask for directions was a good one. *If we had relied on the hand-drawn map we were given.* We would still be lost right now.

3. Home decoration isn't all that difficult. *When you don't have enough money for furniture, carpets, or curtains.* You have no choice but to be creative.
4. I believe that honesty is the best policy. *If I found a million dollars in the street and discovered it belonged to a poor, homeless person.* I'd give it right back.
5. The names of many Canadian landmarks have been changed over the years. The Oldman River, for example, which runs through Lethbridge, used to be called the Belly River. *Until local residents petitioned for a change to a more dignified name.*

Exercise 6.10
Corrections to the fragments in Exercise 6.8
1. Walking is probably the best form of exercise there is **u**nless you're in the water. Then swimming is preferable.
2. Rain doesn't bother me. I like to stay inside and read **w**hen the weather is miserable.
3. Please try this curry. After you've tasted it**,** I am sure you'll be able to tell me what's missing.
4. The report identifies a serious problem that we need to consider. Whenever our Web site is revised or updated**, it** is vulnerable to hackers.
5. Sanir and Jade asked us what we thought about their recent engagement. Since they want to go to Canada's Wonderland for their honeymoon**, w**e think they are probably too young to get married.

Corrections to the fragments in Exercise 6.9
1. I keep the temperature in my apartment very low **i**n order to save money. My friends have to wear sweaters every time they visit.
2. Your idea that we should ask for directions was a good one. If we had relied on the hand-drawn map we were given**, w**e would still be lost right now.
3. Home decoration isn't all that difficult. When you don't have enough money for furniture, carpets, or curtains**, y**ou have no choice but to be creative.
4. I believe that honesty is the best policy. If I found a million dollars in the street and discovered that it belonged to a poor, homeless person**,** I'd give it right back.
5. The names of many Canadian landmarks have been changed over the years. The Oldman River, for example, which runs through Lethbridge, used to be called the Belly River **u**ntil local residents petitioned for a change to a more dignified name.

Exercise 6.11 (suggested answers)
Because the chances of winning are so small, **l**otteries have been called a tax on people with poor math skills. Buying a lottery ticket will gain you about as much as betting that the next U.S. president will come from Moose Jaw, **o**r that the parrot in the pet store speaks Inuktitut. While winning a lottery is not impossible, **it** is so unlikely that you'd do better to use your money to light a nice warm fire. Though the winners are highly publicized, **n**o one hears about the huge numbers of losers **w**hose money has gone to pay the winners. In order for the lottery corporation to make its enormous profits, **m**illions of dollars must be lost whenever a lucky winner is declared.

Answers for Chapter 7: Solving Run-On Sentence Problems

Exercise 7.1
1. Press on the wound**;** that will stop the bleeding.
2. Get going**. T**he others are waiting.
3. I can't read it **because** the print is too small.
4. Here is my number**. G**ive me a call.
5. I'm busy right now**;** you'll have to wait.
6. I'm not afraid to die**.** I just don't want to be there when it happens. (Woody Allen)
7. Eat sensibly**;** exercise regularly**;** die anyway.
8. That was a great dive, **so** you get a perfect 10.

9. Listen to this man play. **H**e's a jazz–blues musician who calls himself Dr. John.
10. While you were out, you received one phone call; it was from a telemarketer.

Exercise 7.2

1. I hate computers; they're always making mistakes.
2. I'm trying to stop playing computer games, **for** they take up too much of my time.
3. My watch has stopped, **so** I don't know what time it is.
4. I'm innocent. **T**his is a case of mistaken identity.
5. This desk is made of pine with maple veneer, **and** the other is solid oak.
6. I'm going to stay up all night tonight **because** I don't want to miss my 8:30 class.
7. The microwave oven is the most important appliance in my home; without it, I'd starve.
8. Money may not be everything, **but** it is far ahead of whatever is in second place.
9. Correct
10. Teachers are finding more and more students who went from printing straight to a keyboard. **T**hey have never learned cursive script.

Exercise 7.3

1. His favourite music is the blues **because** it complements his personality and temperament.
2. This restaurant is terribly slow. **I**t will be dinnertime when we finally get our lunch.
3. I'm investing all my money in this week's lottery **because** the jackpot is over 10 million dollars.
4. **If you** smile when you speak, you can get away with saying almost anything.
5. Correct
6. If I never again see a fast-food breakfast, it will be too soon. **T**he last one I ate nearly put me in the hospital.
7. The fine art of whacking an electronic device to get it to work again is called "percussive maintenance." **N**ine times out of ten, it works.
8. The English language makes no sense. **W**hy do people recite at a play and play at a recital?
9. I write in my journal every day. **W**hen I'm 90, I want to read about all the important events in my life.
10. We have not inherited the Earth from our ancestors; we are borrowing it from our children.

Exercise 7.4 (suggested revision)

Last year, an exchange student from the south of France came to live with us. **H**er name was Simone, **and** she came to Canada to practise her English and learn something about our culture. Simone was amazed by ice hockey; she had never seen a game before and thought it was very exciting. In her first months here, Simone was surprised by what she perceived as Canadians' devotion to everything American, from television shows to sports events, to music, to fast food. **S**he confessed that she couldn't see much that was uniquely Canadian. **S**he was disappointed by our lack of a distinct culture, **but** after she made a week's trip to Chicago, she began to understand some of the differences between the two countries. **T**he relative cleanliness of Canada's cities, our support of multiculturalism, and our respect for law and order impressed her. **T**he vast size of our country, with its huge expanses of untouched wilderness, intimidated her a little. Although she was homesick, especially in the first few weeks, Simone enjoyed her year in Canada. **W**hen she was packing up to return to Provence, she was already planning her next visit. **S**he wants to go camping on Prince Edward Island.

Exercise 7.5

Once upon a time, three travellers came upon a raging river **that** prevented them from continuing their journey. **L**uckily, however, they got to the river just in time to rescue a magic elf from the rushing water. **S**he was so grateful to them for saving her life that she told them she would grant each of them one wish. **S**o, The first man wished for the strength to be able to cross the river, and instantly his arms and legs developed powerful muscles that enabled him to swim easily to the other side. **T**he second man wished for a boat that would carry him across. **H**is wish was granted in the form of a sturdy rowboat and strong oars, **which** allowed him to make his way safely to the other side. The third man, having observed the success of his two companions, wanted to show that he could outsmart them, **so** he asked for the intelligence that would enable him to cross the water with the least possible effort. **H**e was immediately transformed into a woman who realized there was a bridge a few metres downstream and walked across it to the other shore.

Exercise 7.6
1. The newspaper tells us that the weekend has set records, **b**oth for high temperatures and traffic accidents. **T**he two records are probably connected.
2. Computers are not intelligent; if they were, they wouldn't allow humans to touch their keyboards.
3. The snow continues to fall. **It** hasn't let up for three days.
4. **If** the pen is mightier than the sword, why is it that they confiscate swords but not pens at the airport check-in?
5. I have always driven a small car. I think gas-guzzling SUVs, vans, and pickup trucks are ridiculous for city driving. **They are** wastefulness on wheels.
6. A cup of coffee in the morning gets me started; another at midday helps keep me alert after lunch.
7. CRNC is the home of the million-dollar guarantee. **Y**ou give us a million dollars, **and** we guarantee to play any song you want.
8. We often hear people complain about the cost of gasoline for their cars, **but** the same people don't hesitate to spend $1.50 for a bottle of water, **which is t**he same water they get free from the tap.
9. Television is a mass medium. **T**here is an old saying that it is called a medium because it rarely does anything well. **This saying has n**ever **been** truer than in today's 300-channel world.
10. Winter is my favourite season **because** a blanket of white snow covers the ugliness of the city, **m**aking the world seem fresh, clean, and pure.

Answers for Chapter 8: Solving Modifier Problems

Exercise 8.1
1. They closed just before five.
2. We were splashed with mud by almost every car that passed.
3. The flag was raised just at sunrise.
4. She was exhausted after walking merely 300 metres.
5. After the fire, she took her clothes with the most smoke damage to the cleaners.
6. The French drink wine with nearly every meal, including lunch.
7. The suspect gave the police scarcely any information.
8. He was underwater for nearly two minutes before surfacing.
9. We camped during August in a national park with lots of wildlife.
10. A huge tree, even one more than 300 years old, can be cut by any idiot with a chainsaw.

Exercise 8.2
1. The president fired only those who had failed to meet their sales quotas.
2. I have nearly been fired every week that I have worked here.
3. I had answered scarcely 12 of the 25 questions when time was up.
4. Matti couldn't force the loudly braying donkey to take a single step.
5. We have computers with little memory and constant breakdowns for all office staff.
6. Canadians enjoy practically the highest standard of living in the world.

7. We bought gifts with batteries included for the children.
8. Although six of us went to the beach, Kevin took pictures only of his girlfriend.
9. This is a book with real weight and depth for avid readers.
10. With his binoculars, Vince crouched in the long grass and watched the lion. (*Or:* Vince crouched with his binoculars in the long grass and watched the lion.)

Exercise 8.3
1. When running competitively, you must have a thorough warm-up.
2. As a college teacher, I find dangling modifiers annoying.
3. After revising her résumé, filling out the application, and going through the interview, she lost the position to someone else.
4. Getting to the meeting room 20 minutes late, we found everyone had left.
5. After cooking all day long, we thought the gourmet meal was worth the effort.
6. Having arrived so late, our guests were served a cold meal.
7. Driving recklessly, André was stopped at a roadblock by the police.
8. Dressed in a new miniskirt, Jessa looked terrific to her boyfriend.
9. After waiting 20 minutes, we finally got the attention of the server.
10. Having been convicted of breaking and entering, Bambi was sentenced to two years in prison.

Exercise 8.4
1. Travelling in Quebec, you will find that knowing even a little French is useful.
2. Her saddle firmly cinched, the mare was led out of the barn.
3. After being seasick for two days, we were relieved when the ocean became calm.
4. Standing in the water for more than an hour, he was numbed to the bone by the cold.
5. Being very weak in math, I found the job was out of my reach.
6. Looking for a job, you'll find a good résumé is vital to success.
7. After spending two weeks quarrelling non-stop, they decided to end their relationship.
8. In less than a minute after applying the ointment, I found the pain began to ease.
9. Living kilometres from anything, I find a car is a necessity.
10. Having had the same roommate for three years, I was urged by my parents to look for another.

Exercise 8.5
1. When you are running competitively, a thorough warm-up is necessary.
2. Since I am a college teacher, I find dangling modifiers annoying.
3. After she had revised her résumé, filled out the application, and gone through the interview, the position was taken by someone else.
4. When we got to the meeting room 20 minutes late, everyone had left.
5. Although we had cooked all day long, the gourmet meal was worth the effort.
6. Since our guests arrived so late, the meal was cold.
7. Because André was driving recklessly, the police stopped him at a roadblock.
8. When Jessa was dressed in her new miniskirt, her boyfriend thought she looked terrific.
9. After we had waited 20 minutes, the server finally came to our table.
10. After Bambi had been convicted of breaking and entering, the judge sentenced her to two years in prison.

Exercise 8.6
1. When you are travelling in Quebec, knowing even a little French is useful.
2. As soon as the mare's saddle was firmly cinched, Marie led her out of the barn.
3. After we had been seasick for two days, the ocean became calm.
4. When he had stood in the water for more than an hour, the cold numbed him to the bone.

5. Since I am very weak in math, the job was out of my reach.
6. When you are looking for a job, a good résumé is vital to success.
7. After they had spent two weeks quarrelling non-stop, their relationship was over.
8. In less than a minute after I had applied the ointment, the pain began to ease.
9. Since I live kilometres away from anything, a car is a necessity.
10. Because I've had the same roommate for three years, my parents suggested that I look for another.

Exercise 8.7

1. The sign said that only students were admitted to the pub.
2. Swimming in these waters, you should know that the undertow can be dangerous.
3. The lion was recaptured by the trainer before anyone was mauled or bitten.
4. Swimming isn't a good idea if the water is polluted.
5. When the bus driver suddenly slammed on the brakes, several passengers were thrown to the floor.
6. Employees who are often late are dismissed without notice. (*Or:* Employees who are late are often dismissed without notice.)
7. After we waited for you for more than an hour, the evening was ruined.
8. Since we'd been munching on chicken wings during the game, our appetites for dinner were ruined.
9. Because of her experience, we hired the first designer who applied.
10. For 20 minutes, the president spoke glowingly of the retiring workers who had worked long and loyally.

Exercise 8.8

1. Everyone stared as she rode in a polka-dot bikini through town on a horse.
2. Though they drink city water daily, many residents distrust it.
3. Being a music lover, I always have an MP3 player in my pocket.
4. Although Jan lives more than 50 km away, he manages to come to nearly every class.
5. Before you begin to write the exam, prayer is a recommended strategy.
6. After her Dachshund had given birth to a litter of 12, my sister had the dog neutered.
7. I heard on a sports phone-in show about the team's star player being hurt.
8. If you listen to the rumours, the newlyweds are already on the road to separation.
9. The police recommend that you check the ownership records before buying a used car.
10. We were almost shot the first day we went into the forest during hunting season.

Answers for Chapter 9: The Parallelism Principle

Exercise 9.1

1. This is a book to read, enjoy, and remember.
2. The new brochure on career opportunities is attractive and informative.
3. Except that it was too long, too violent, and too expensive, it was a great movie.
4. He ate his supper, did the dishes, watched television, and went to bed.
5. Barking dogs and screaming children keep me from enjoying the park.
6. In this clinic, we care for the sick, the injured, and the disabled.
7. If she wasn't constantly eating chips, playing bingo, and smoking cigarettes, she'd have plenty of money for groceries.
8. Our team could win the Cup because it has speed, size, youth, and talent.

9. So far, the countries I have most enjoyed visiting are China for its people, France for its food, and Brazil for its beaches.
10. She was discouraged by the low pay, the long hours, and the office politics.

Exercise 9.2
1. Being unable to speak the language, I was confused, frustrated, and embarrassed.
2. Trying your best and succeeding are not always the same thing.
3. I hold a baseball bat right-handed but hold a hockey stick left-handed. (*Or:* I play baseball right-handed but hockey left-handed.)
4. A good student attends all classes and finishes all projects on time.
5. A good teacher motivates with enthusiasm, informs with sensitivity, and counsels with compassion.
6. A good college president has the judgment of Solomon, the wisdom of Plato, and the wit of Rick Mercer.
7. Licking one's fingers and picking one's teeth in a restaurant are one way to get attention.
8. To succeed in this economy, small businesses must be creative and flexible.
9. Canadians must register the cars they drive, the businesses they own, the contracts they make, the houses they buy, and the guns they possess.
10. The test required us to read a paragraph, answer some questions, and write a summary.

Exercise 9.3
1. taste the wine
2. understand
3. loosen
4. engineering
5. knowledge
6. well educated
7. entertainment
8. exploring fully

Exercise 9.5 (suggested answers)

The dictionary is a useful and educational resource. Everyone knows that its three chief functions are to check the spelling, **meanings, and pronunciation of words.** Few people, however, use the dictionary for discovery as well as learning. There are several ways to use the dictionary as an aid to discovery. One is randomly looking at words, another is **reading** a page or two thoroughly, and still another is **skimming** the text looking for unfamiliar words. By this last method I discovered the word *steatopygous*, a term I now try to use at least once a day. You can increase your vocabulary significantly by using the dictionary, and of course a large and varied vocabulary can be used to baffle your colleagues, **impress your employers**, and **surprise your English teacher**.

Exercise 9.6
1. A coach has four responsibilities:
   • To encourage and motivate
   • To teach skills and techniques
   • To develop teamwork and co-operation
   • To build physical and mental strength
2. The college will undertake the following steps to conserve energy:
   • Lowering building temperatures by two degrees in winter
   • Putting lights in all rooms on motion sensors
   • Raising building temperatures by two degrees in summer
   • Replacing all windows with high-efficiency glass
3. In selecting a location for the new college residence, we must be mindful of transportation factors:
   • Convenient access to mass transit
   • Ample parking for all residents with cars

- Easy connections to major highways
- Immediate access to the bicycle-path network
- On-site availability of pedestrian walkways

4. This summer, I have five goals that I want to accomplish:
   - Learn to kiteboard
   - Read the latest Harry Potter book
   - Participate in a 10-km Fun Run
   - Earn enough money to pay my tuition
   - Spend time with my friends at the beach

5. The duties of this position include
   - Greeting customers
   - Modelling the clothing we sell
   - Making sales
   - Stocking the shelves
   - Taking inventory
   - Opening and locking up the store

Answers for Chapter 10: Refining by Combining

Exercise 10.1

1. Although the test was difficult, I passed it. (*Or*: The test was difficult, but I passed it.)
2. After eating our lunch, we continued working. (*Or*: We ate our lunch, then we continued working.)
3. Correct
4. Since our essay is due tomorrow, we must stay up late tonight. (*Or*: Our essay is due tomorrow, so we must stay up late tonight.)
5. Even though the pictures are good, I hate seeing myself. (*Or*: The pictures are good, yet I hate seeing myself.)
6. Correct
7. Though having a car would be convenient, I need the money for other things. (*Or*: Having a car would be convenient, but I need the money for other things.)
8. If this book will help me, I will buy it. (*Or*: This book will help me, so I will buy it.)
9. Where a mistake has been found, it must be corrected. (*Or*: A mistake has been found, so it must be corrected.)
10. Correct

Exercise 10.2

1. I have a teacher who always wears a tie.
2. Here is the car that is always breaking down.
3. I am enrolled in an art class that meets Wednesday evenings.
4. That singer whose name I always forget just won a Grammy.
5. The pen that you gave me is broken.
6. My plant, which you never watered, is dead.
7. The cellphone that you always carry is ringing.
8. Lisa baby-sits for a man whose wife speaks only Japanese.
9. The taxi driver who took me to the airport drove 20 km over the speed limit all the way.
10. My roommate whose snoring keeps me awake is finally moving out.

Exercise 10.3

1. No one wants to answer when the teacher asks a question.
2. Our apartment is quite large and comfortable, yet it is very reasonably priced.
3. Some college students believe that high marks in college are a matter of luck.
4. Our company will sponsor a marathon runner, but one of the employees must enter the race.
5. Hybrid cars are becoming more popular, even though they cost more than comparable gas-powered models.
6. The VJ on Channel 12, who sounds like an experienced professional, is only 24 years old.
7. Just when they were down to their last loonie, they won the lottery.
8. I have a migraine headache that prevents me from working, reading, or even watching TV.
9. Your choice of outfit is not appropriate for the office, but it would look just right in an after-hours club.
10. Although I love the taste of very hot, strong coffee, it keeps me awake.

Exercise 10.4 (suggested answers)

1. The cursor is blinking, but there is no response.
2. The village that I grew up in is very small.
3. My car is in the repair shop because it needs a new alternator.
4. The textbook contains information that will be on tomorrow's exam.
5. I have read this book from cover to cover and completed all of the exercises, and now my writing skills are gradually improving.
6. Banging your head against a wall uses 150 calories an hour.
7. Although the movie was terrible and our car broke down, we had a good time anyway.
8. Many of my friends send me pictures with their e-mails, but my computer doesn't have enough memory to receive them.
9. This restaurant is very expensive, but I don't mind paying the price for good food and excellent service.
10. Some people enjoy hockey while others prefer soccer, the world's most popular spectator sport.

Exercise 10.5 (suggested answers)

1. A good manager must have many skills, but the most important is the ability to delegate.
2. The stapler that was clearly labelled with my name is missing.
3. Weyburn, Saskatchewan, is where I was born, but I have not lived there since I was a baby.
4. Although a sauna provides no proven health benefits, I find one very refreshing when the weather is cold.
5. English muffins were not invented in England nor were French fries invented in France.
6. My satellite TV reception, which is just fine in the winter, is very poor in the summer because the leaves on the trees block the dish.
7. Although Taylor is very good at reading a road map and can find her way anywhere, she cannot fold the map properly.
8. Our college has a Continuing Education Department that offers both credit and interest courses at night.
9. Tisa is a Canadian citizen who was born in Halifax, but she has American citizenship too because she has lived most of her life in Texas.
10. My roommate, who is not too bright, takes an hour and a half to watch *60 Minutes* on television.

Answers for Unit 2 Rapid Review

Note: Triple asterisks (***) indicate that a word or words have been deleted. Each set of triple asterisks counts as one error.

¹Imagination is the ability to visualize things that are not physically present. ²**It is o**ften thought to be important to artists, but not to anyone else. ³Of course, artists depend on imagination**;** their creativity consists of picturing things that do not exist in the real world and giving form to their visions in paintings, sculptures, music, or literature. ⁴Artists, however, are not the **only** ones who rely on imagination for a living. ⁵⁻⁷To be able to see a new way to accomplish a familiar task or a different approach to an old problem *** is a critical skill in many fields**, a**mong them, science, **medicine**, technology, construction, **manufacturing**, and lawmaking. ⁸Being vital to innovation and invention, **highly developed imaginations are found in** leaders in all fields. ⁹The critical importance of imagination applies not **just** to leaders, either. ¹⁰⁻¹¹All humans use imagination to find ways to improve their lives **a**nd entertain themselves with books, films, and games of all kinds.

¹²Lack of imagination leads to rigidity and stagnation, to doing the same old things in the same old way. ¹³It is true that some people are comfortable **only** in an environment in which there is little or no change. ¹⁴Such people become anxious, even helpless, when jobs *** requiring even a minimal amount of creativity are assigned them. ¹⁵There is a story about two men who were observed at work in a city park. ¹⁶One was digging holes**;** the other was filling in the holes. ¹⁷Being curious, **a bystander** asked them what they were doing. ¹⁸They replied that each of them had a job: Henry dug the holes, **Bill planted the trees**, and John filled the holes. ¹⁹**Since Bill was** sick today, Henry and John had to do their jobs without him.

Answer Key

If you missed the error(s) in sentence . . .		See Chapter . . .	
2	sentence fragment	5	"'Missing Piece' Fragments" section
3	run-on sentence	7	"Comma Splices" section
4	*are not only the ones*	8	"Misplaced Modifiers" section
5	sentence fragment	5	"'Missing Piece' Fragments" section
7	sentence fragment	5	"'Missing Piece' Fragments" section
	science, doctors . . . construction,		
	manufacturers	9	The Parallelism Principle
8	*Being vital to innovation . . . , you*	8	"Dangling Modifiers" section
9	*applies not to just leaders*	8	"Misplaced Modifiers" section
11	sentence fragment	5	"'Missing Piece' Fragments" section
13	*only are comfortable*	8	"Misplaced Modifiers" section
14	*when jobs are assigned them requiring*	8	"Misplaced Modifiers" section
16	run-on sentence	7	"Fused Sentences" section
17	*Being curious, they*	8	"Dangling Modifiers" section
18	*dug . . . were planted . . . filled*	9	The Parallelism Principle
19	*Being sick today, Henry and John*	8	"Dangling Modifiers" section

Answers for Unit 3 Quick Quiz

¹"What's in a name?" Shakespeare asked. ²The answer is, "a great deal." For instance, your name may indicate the decade in which you were born. ³Like skirt length, tie width, and hairstyles, names **go** in and out of fashion. ⁴If your grandparents were born in the 1940s or '50s, the chances are good that **he and she** (*or* **they**) **are called** Robert, Mark, or Richard; and Linda, Barbara, or Patricia. ⁵Interestingly, the name Michael first appeared on the top 10 list in the '50s and then **topped** the charts as the most popular male name for the next 40 years.

⁶In the 1960s, the most popular female name **was** Lisa. ⁷Other favourites **included** Kimberley, Donna, and Michelle. ⁸If you were born in the '70s, **your** parents may well have named you Jennifer, Amy, or Jessica; or Christopher, Matthew, or Justin. ⁹In the '80s, baby boys were likely to be named Joshua, Daniel, or Jason. ¹⁰Those little boys probably **went** to kindergarten with little girls called Amanda, Ashley, and Tiffany. ¹¹In the 1990s, the most popular names for boys were Jacob, Nicholas, and Tyler; for girls, Emily, Brittany, and Megan.

¹²What about the future? ¹³A Web site called Babyzone.com offers advice for couples who **are** expecting a child. ¹⁴The "power names" for the new century **include** one-syllable names such as Grace, Cole, and Claire. ¹⁵Place names also rank high on the list: Dakota, Dallas, and Brooklyn (for boys or girls); China and India (for girls). ¹⁶New parents **who** want to be on the leading edge of the naming culture often look to celebrities for guidance. ¹⁷Babyzone advises that Bob Geldof and his wife **named their** three daughters Peaches, Pixie, and Fifi Trixibelle. ¹⁸And, of course, everyone under 30 **knows** about Gwyneth's daughter, Apple.

¹⁹If you are interested in traditional English names, Babyzone posts a list of names found in Shakespeare's plays, which are full of beautiful names—at least for women: Miranda, Olivia, Ariel. ²⁰But if you're tempted to choose a Shakespearean name for your baby, **you should read the play first**. ²¹Burdening a helpless infant with a name such as Malvolio, Goneril, or Caliban is a form of child abuse!

Answer Key

If you missed the error(s) in sentence . . .		See Chapter . . .	
3	names will go	13	Keeping Your Tenses Consistent
4	him and her	14	Choosing the Correct Pronoun Form
	will be called	13	Keeping Your Tenses Consistent
5	tops the charts	13	Keeping Your Tenses Consistent
6	is Lisa	13	Keeping Your Tenses Consistent
7	include	13	Keeping Your Tenses Consistent
8	one's	16	Maintaining Person Agreement
10	go	13	Keeping Your Tenses Consistent
13	are expecting	11	Choosing the Correct Verb Form
14	includes	12	"Singular and Plural" section
16	parents that	15	"Relative Pronouns" section
17	names	11	Choosing the Correct Verb Form
	his three daughters	16	Maintaining Person Agreement
18	know	12	"Four Special Cases" section
20	the play should be read by you	11	"Active and Passive Voice" section

Answers for Chapter 11: Choosing the Correct Verb Form

Exercise 11.1

1. wear   You **wore** your good hiking boots only once, but after you have **worn** them several times, you won't want to take them off.
2. give   The tourists **gave** Terry a tip after she had **given** them directions to the hotel.
3. begin   After the project had **begun**, the members of the team soon **began** to disagree on how to proceed.
4. eat   I **ate** as though I had not **eaten** in a month.
5. cost   The vacation in Cuba **cost** less than last year's trip to Jamaica had **cost** and was much more fun.
6. bring   If you have **brought** your children with you, I hope you also **brought** enough toys and movies to keep them out of trouble during your stay.
7. grow   The noise from the party next door **grew** louder by the hour, but by midnight I had **grown** used to it, and went to sleep.

8. sit   Marc **sat** in front of the TV all morning; by evening he will have **sat** there for eight hours—a full working day!

9. write   After she had **written** the essay that was due last week, she **wrote** e-mails to all her friends.

10. pay   I **paid** off my credit cards, so I have not **paid** this month's rent.

Exercise 11.2

1. ride   I had never **ridden** in a stretch limo until I **rode** in one at Jerry's wedding.

2. sing   She **sang** a silly little song that her mother had **sung** when she was a baby.

3. teach   Harold had been **taught** to play poker by his father, and he **taught** his daughter the same way.

4. find   He **found** the solution that hundreds of mathematicians over three centuries had not **found**.

5. fly   Suzhu had once **flown** to Whitehorse, so when she **flew** north to Tuktoyaktuk, she knew what to expect.

6. feel   At first, they had **felt** silly in their new pink uniforms, but after winning three games in a row, they **felt** much better.

7. lie   The cat **lay** right where the dog had **lain** all morning.

8. go   We **went** to our new home to find that the movers had **gone** to the wrong address to deliver our furniture.

9. lose   The reason you **lost** those customers is that you have **lost** confidence in your sales technique.

10. steal   I **stole** two customers away from the sales representative who earlier had **stolen** my best account.

Exercise 11.3

1. think   I had **thought** that you were right, but when I **thought** more about your answer, I realized you were wrong.

2. buy   If we had **bought** this stock 20 years ago, the shares we **bought** would now be worth a fortune.

3. do   They **did** what was asked, but their competitors, who had **done** a better job, got the contract.

4. show   Today our agent **showed** us a house that was much better suited to our needs than anything she had **shown** us previously.

5. hurt   Budget cuts had **hurt** the project, but today's decision to lay off two of our workers **hurt** it even more.

6. throw   The rope had not been **thrown** far enough to reach those in the water, so Mia pulled it in and **threw** it again.

7. lay   Elzbieta **laid** her passport on the official's desk where the other tourists had **laid** theirs.

8. put   I have **put** your notebook in the mail, but your pen and glasses I will **put** away until I see you again.

9. fight   My parents **fought** again today, the way they have **fought** almost every day for the last 20 years.

10. break   She **broke** the Canadian record only six months after she had **broken** her arm in training.

Exercise 11.5

1. __A__   Our professor <u>checks</u> our homework every day.

2. __P__   The report <u>is being prepared</u> by the marketing department.

3. __P__   The car <u>was being driven</u> by a chauffeur.

4. __A__   Eva <u>will invite</u> Kiefer to the party.

5. __P__   The CN Tower <u>is visited</u> by hundreds of people every day.

6. __A__   Sula <u>designs</u> bracelets, necklaces, and earrings.

7. __P__ *The English Patient* <u>was written</u> by Canadian author Michael Ondaatje.
8. __A__ Hollywood <u>made</u> the book into a successful movie.
9. __P__ The song <u>was performed</u> by Eminem.
10. __P__ Two metres of snow <u>had to be shovelled</u> off the driveway.

Exercise 11.6
1. Our homework is checked by our professor every day.
2. The marketing department <u>is preparing</u> the report.
3. A chauffeur <u>was driving</u> the car.
4. Kiefer <u>will be invited</u> to the party by Eva.
5. Hundreds of visitors <u>visit</u> the CN Tower every day.
6. These bracelets, necklaces, and earrings <u>were designed</u> by Sula.
7. Canadian author Michael Ondaatje <u>wrote</u> *The English Patient.*
8. The book <u>was made</u> into a successful movie by Hollywood.
9. Eminem <u>performed</u> the song.
10. We <u>had to shovel</u> two metres of snow off the driveway.

Exercise 11.7
1. Lisa bought the gas for the trip.
2. Our houseguests washed the dishes.
3. The sales representative gave me his business card.
4. Our computer made an error in your bill.
5. My brother took the short route home.
6. On our first anniversary, we had our portrait taken by a professional photographer.
7. Canadians do not always understand American election practices.
8. Most Americans know very little about Canada.
9. In today's class, all of you will work on your research papers.
10. This book contains all the information you need to become a competent writer.

Exercise 11.8
1. Bambi told the professor that she was finding the course too difficult. (Active voice is more effective.)
2. A member of our staff did not type this document. (Passive voice is more effective; the person who did or did not type the document is unknown.)
3. Three firefighters carefully entered the burning building. (Active voice is more effective.)
4. My new bifocals helped me to read. (Active voice is more effective.)
5. Someone had left the lights on all the time we were away. (Passive voice is more effective because it places the emphasis on the lights—the object affected by the action—rather than on the unknown person who performed the action.)
6. At 4:00 each afternoon, the dining room servers lay the linens and set the tables. (Active voice is more effective.)
7. In the parade around the stadium, a biathlete carried the Olympic flag. (Passive voice is more effective because it puts the focus on the Olympic flag, an enduring symbol, rather than on the unknown athlete who happened to carry it in this particular parade.)
8. Poor communication between the members of the team delayed the project. (Active voice is more effective. Projects are often delayed, but we don't always know why they are delayed, so the emphasis on the "actors" gives useful information.)
9. My brother uses his bookcase to hold his bowling trophies and empty fast-food containers. (Active voice is more effective.)
10. The provincial government has declared a state of emergency and set up a special fund to aid the flood victims. (Active voice is more effective for two reasons: the doer of the action is known and so should occupy the subject position, and the passive construction is too wordy for easy reading.)

Answers for Chapter 12: Mastering Subject–Verb Agreement

Exercise 12.1
1. key
2. invoices
3. people

4. Professor Temkin
5. Jupiter, Saturn

Exercise 12.2
1. has
2. has
3. succeeds

4. shows
5. is

Exercise 12.3
1. My <u>paper</u> <u>is</u> due on Tuesday.
2. My passport <u>photo</u> <u>is</u> hideous!
3. The <u>technician</u> <u>is</u> away on a professional development course.
4. Under our back porch <u>lives</u> a huge <u>raccoon</u>.
5. <u>Has</u> the lucky <u>winner</u> <u>collected</u> the lottery money?
6. The <u>article</u> in this journal <u>gives</u> you the background information you need.
7. A <u>hotel</u> within walking distance of the arena <u>is</u> a necessity for our team.
8. Only recently <u>has</u> our track <u>coach</u> <u>become</u> interested in chemistry.
9. So far, only <u>one</u> of your answers <u>has been</u> incorrect.
10. The <u>pressure</u> of schoolwork and part-time work <u>has caused</u> many students to drop out.

Exercise 12.4
1. A good <u>example</u> <u>is</u> hockey players.
2. <u>Sardines</u> <u>are</u> a healthy type of oily fish.
3. A <u>necessity</u> in my job <u>is</u> palm-sized computers.
4. Noisy <u>speedboats</u> <u>are</u> what irritate us on our quiet lake.
5. An important <u>part</u> of a balanced diet <u>is</u> fresh fruits and vegetables.

Exercise 12.5
   A dog seems to understand the **mood** of **its owner**. **It is** tuned in to any **shift** in emotion or **change** in health of the **human it lives** with. **A doctor** will often suggest adding **a pet** to **a household** where there **is someone** (*or* **a person**) suffering from depression or **an** emotional **problem**. **A dog is a** sympathetic **companion**. The **mood** of **an elderly person** in **a** retirement **home** or even **a** hospital **ward** can be brightened by **a visit** from **a** pet **owner** and **a dog**. **A dog** never **tires** of hearing about the "good old days," and **it is** uncritical and unselfish in giving affection. **A doctor** will often encourage **an** epilepsy **sufferer** to adopt **a** specially trained **dog**. Such **a dog is** so attuned to the health of **its owner** that **it** can sense when **a seizure is** about to occur long before **its owner** can. The **dog** then **warns** the **owner** of the coming attack, so the **owner is** able to take safety precautions.

Exercise 12.6
1. live
2. reveals

3. have
4. fascinates

5. know

Exercise 12.7
1. wants
2. has

3. was
4. is

5. don't

Exercise 12.8

1. is
2. thinks
3. recommends
4. want
5. were

Exercise 12.9

1. is
2. is
3. goes
4. was
5. takes

Exercise 12.10

1. Not the weekly quizzes, but the final exam **is** what I'm worried about.
2. Unfortunately, not one of the women **agrees** to pose nude for a publicity photo.
3. Either the tires or the alignment **is** causing the steering vibration.
4. This province, along with six others, **has** voted in favour of the federal government's health care proposal.
5. Anything that could possibly go wrong, including wind, rain, hail, and snow, **has** gone wrong during this event.
6. When Kim emptied her pockets, she found that $2 **was** all she had left to buy lunch.
7. Neither the puppies nor their mother **was** enjoying the veterinarian's physical examination.
8. Get ready: 400 km of mountain roads **lies** ahead of us.
9. Everything you've told me about Katrina and her children **is** untrue and hurtful.
10. It seems that in every group project, there is one team member who **gets** stuck with most of the work.

Exercise 12.11

1. Each day that passes **brings** us closer to the end of term.
2. A Quetchua Indian living in the Andes Mountains **has** two or three more litres of blood than people living at lower elevations.
3. The swim team **have** been billeted with host families during their stay in Seattle.
4. Neither fame nor riches **are** my goal in life.
5. The original model for the king in a standard deck of playing cards **is** thought to be King Charles I of England.
6. A large planet together with two small stars **is** visible on the eastern horizon.
7. The lack of things to write about **is** my problem.
8. One faculty member in addition to a group of students **has** volunteered to help us clean out the lab.
9. Not only cat hairs but also ragweed **makes** me sneeze.
10. Everyone who successfully completed these exercises **deserves** high praise.

Exercise 12.12

The rewards of obtaining a good summer or part-time job **go** well beyond the money you earn from your labour. Contacts that may be valuable in the future and experience in the working world **are** an important part of your employment. Even if the jobs you get while attending school **have** nothing to do with your future **goals**, they offer many benefits. For example, when considering job applicants, an employer always **prefers** someone who can be counted on to arrive at the work site on time, get along with co-workers, and follow directions. Neither instinct nor instruction **takes** the place of experience in teaching the basic facts of working life. These long-term considerations, in addition to the money that is the immediate reward, **are** what **make** part-time work so valuable. Everyone who **has** worked part-time while going to school **is** able to confirm these observations.

Exercise 12.13

1. singular
2. singular
3. plural
4. singular
5. singular
6. singular
7. singular
8. plural
9. singular
10. singular

Answers to Chapter 13: Keeping Your Tenses Consistent

Exercise 13.1

1. As we walked through the park, we **saw** some people playing Ultimate Frisbee.
2. Alain went home and **told** Gulçan what happened.
3. Gil tried to laugh, but he **was** too upset even to speak.
4. After his fiancée broke up with him, she **refused** to return his ring.
5. Correct
6. The rebellion failed because the people **did** not support it.
7. I enjoy my work, but I **am** not going to let it take over my life.
8. Prejudice is learned and **is** hard to outgrow.
9. A Canadian is someone who thinks that an income tax refund **is** a gift from the government.
10. Although the sun is shining and the skies are clear, the temperature **is** bitterly cold.

Exercise 13.2

1. We need proof that the picture **is** genuine.
2. The couple living in the apartment next door had a boa constrictor that **kept** getting loose.
3. Correct
4. It was getting dark, but Stanley **was** not afraid.
5. My deadline is Friday, and I **have** to submit an outline and a rough draft by then.
6. Correct
7. I drank a half litre of milk, then I **ate** two curry wraps, and I **was** ready for anything.
8. It was great music for dancing, and it **was** being played by a super band.
9. I will download about 600 songs this year and **[will] pay** for all of them.
10. When the weekend paper arrives, we **fight** over who gets to read it first.

Exercise 13.3

My most embarrassing moment occurred just last month when I **met** an old friend whom I **hadn't** seen in years. We **greeted** each other and **began** to chat, and I **told** her that I **had** been reading her daughter's columns in the newspaper. I **congratulated** her on her daughter's talent. I **told** her that she must be very proud to see her offspring's name in print. My friend **looked** puzzled for a minute, then she **laughed** and **told** me that the writer I **was** praising so highly **wasn't** her daughter. My friend had divorced long ago; her former husband **had remarried**, and the columnist **was** her ex-husband's new wife.

Answers for Chapter 14: Choosing the Correct Pronoun Form

Exercise 14.1

1. The movie that Gina and **I** rented was a waste of time and money.
2. Dasha wants to come to the restaurant with Joshi and **me**.
3. Except for Vikram and **her**, there's no one else who knows how to enter the data manually.
4. **Sasha and I** are best friends.
5. The work will go much faster if **he** and Roland do it by themselves.

6. Sami and **he** wrote, shot, and edited the entire film.
7. I left my CD in the computer when my friends and **I** left the lab.
8. Surely your sister wasn't serious when she said that **they** and their children were coming to stay with us for three weeks.
9. I can't believe Chandra would break up with me after **she** and **I** got matching tattoos and navel rings.
10. **He and I** have completely different tastes in music.

Exercise 14.2

1. Have you and **she** ever tried skydiving?
2. My boyfriend and **I** have completely different tastes in music.
3. It is not up to you or **me** to discipline your sister's children.
4. She and Xan took the videos back before Tami or **I** had seen them.
5. Arranging the details and hiring the staff are up to **him** and his team, because **we** volunteers have done all the planning.
6. Was it **he** who served you? Or was it **she**?
7. **He** and Marie finished on time; except for **them** and their staff, no one else met the deadline.

Exercise 14.3

1. The prize is sure to go to Omar and [to] **her**.
2. No one likes our cooking class more than **I** [do].
3. In fact, nobody in the class eats as much as **I** [do].
4. It's not surprising that I am much bigger than **they** [are].
5. My mother would rather cook for my brother than [for] **me** because he never complains when dinner is burned or raw.
6. At last I have met someone who loves barbecued eel as much as **I** [do]!
7. More than **I** [do], Yuxiang uses the computer to draft and revise his papers.
8. He doesn't write as well as **I** [do], but he does write faster.
9. Only a few Mexican food fanatics eat as many jalapeño peppers as **he** [does].
10. I think you have as much trouble with English as **I** [do].

Answers for Chapter 15: Mastering Pronoun–Antecedent Agreement

Exercise 15.1

1. Each player on the team has **her** strengths.
2. It seemed that everybody in the mall was talking on **a** cellphone.
3. Would someone kindly lend **a** copy of the textbook to Mei Yu?
4. Anything found in the locker room will be returned to **its** owner, if possible.
5. A band leader is someone who is not afraid to face **the** music.
6. According to the reviews, not one of the movies at the mall is worth **the** admission price.
7. So far, no one on the wrestling team has been able to persuade **his** parents to host the team party.
8. Everyone is expected to pay **a** share of the expenses.
9. Is there anybody here who can bring **her** own car?
10. Anyone who wants a high mark for **this** essay should see me after class and write out **a** cheque.

Exercise 15.2 (deleted words are indicated by ***)

1. Everyone is a product of *** environment as well as heredity.
2. Nobody who is as smart as you needs to have help with **this** homework.
3. Each car in all categories will be judged on **its** bodywork, engine, and interior.

4. Every movie-, theatre-, and concert-goer knows how annoying it is to have **an** evening's enjoyment spoiled by a ringing cellphone.
5. Put the sign at the curb so anyone looking for our yard sale won't have to waste ******* time driving around the neighbourhood.
6. Everyone who pays **the** membership fee in advance will receive a free session with a personal trainer.
7. A true geek is somebody who has trouble deciding between buying flowers for **his** girlfriend and upgrading **his** RAM.
8. Ultimate is a game in which **all those who participate enjoy** themselves, whether their team finishes first or last.
9. No one on the football team has been able to get **his** parents to donate **their** house for the party.
10. The accident could not have been avoided, and fortunately no one was hurt, so no one should have to **apologize**.

Exercise 15.3 (suggested answers)
1. **Our college strictly enforces** the "no smoking" policy.
2. Kara didn't hear my question **because** she was listening to her iPod.
3. Every time David looked at the dog, **it** barked.
4. In a rage, Max hurled his cellphone at the computer and broke **the monitor**.
5. The big story on *Entertainment Tonight* was that Cher told Dolly that **Dolly** was losing her looks.
6. My wife was annoyed when I didn't notice she had fallen overboard; **I was distracted** because I was concentrating on landing my fish.
7. Kevin told Yu to leave his books on the table beside **Kevin's** computer.
8. When I learned that smoking was the cause of my asthma, I gave up **cigarettes** for good.
9. Nell didn't see her son score the winning goal ******* because she was talking on her cellphone at the time.
10. Being on time is a challenge for my girlfriend, so I'm getting her **a watch** for her birthday.

Exercise 15.4
1. Chi Keung is the technician **who** can fix your problem.
2. I would have won, except for one judge **who** placed me fourth.
3. A grouch is a person **who** knows himself and isn't happy about it.
4. The salesclerk **who** sold me my DVD player didn't know what he was talking about.
5. Everyone **who** was at the party had a good time, though a few had more punch than was good for them.
6. The open-office concept sounds good to anyone **who** has worked in a stuffy little cubicle all day.
7. I wish I could find someone in our class **who** could help me with my homework.
8. Thanks to the computer, I regularly order supplies from companies **that** are located in cities all across the country.
9. The tests **that** we wrote today were designed to discourage anyone **who** didn't have the knowledge, preparation, and stamina to endure them.
10. My roommate has just started on the term paper, **which** was assigned a month ago, for her political science course.

Exercise 15.5
　　North Americans seem obsessed with showing their grasp of useless information. Trivia games have been hugely popular for decades, and they continue to enjoy large audiences. **Trivia players are** expected to have at their fingertips all sorts of obscure information, from

sports statistics to popular music, from world geography to the film industry. Team trivia contests have become important fund-raising events for charity. Teams of eight to ten players answer trivia questions in competition with other teams. Each member of a team is expected to have **a** particular area of expertise and to help **the** team gain points by answering the questions in that area. At the end of the contest, the winning team will usually have answered correctly more than 80 percent of the questions called out by the quizmaster.

Another forum for trivia is the television shows in which **contestants** must demonstrate their knowledge individually in a high-pressure, game show format. Alone, each contestant faces the show's host, who may give *** assistance if **the contestant asks for it**. In other games, **contestants play** against each other and must demonstrate superior knowledge if they want to win. Playing trivia at home is also popular, and many households have **a game**.

Whether you play alone, with friends, on a team, or on television, **you** should keep the game in perspective. After all, the object of any trivia game is to reward the players **who demonstrate** that they know more about unimportant and irrelevant facts than anyone else in the game!

Answers for Chapter 16: Maintaining Person Agreement

Exercise 16.1
1. You shouldn't annoy the instructor if **you want** to get an A.
2. A person can succeed at almost anything if **he or she has** enough talent and determination.
3. When we laugh, the world laughs with **us**.
4. You can save a great deal of time if **you fill** out the forms before going to the passport office.
5. Clarify the question before beginning to write, or **you** may lose focus.
6. Our opinions will never be heard unless **we make** a serious effort to reach the public.
7. I wish that **we** had a few more options to choose from.
8. **You** should not question Professor Snapes in class because he loses his temper, and you don't want that to happen.
9. Anyone with a telephone can get **his or her** voice heard on the radio.
10. Call-in programs give everyone the opportunity to make sure the whole world knows **one's** ignorance of the issues.

Exercise 16.2 (suggested answers)
1. One is never too old to learn, but **one is** never too young to know everything. (**You are** never too old . . . ,)
2. One always removes **one's** shoes when entering a mosque.
3. The speed limit is the speed **you** go as soon as you see a police car.
4. You must improve your computer skills if **you are** to succeed at this job.
5. No one can blame you for trying to do your best, even if **you do** not always succeed.
6. Experience is that marvellous thing that enables us to recognize a mistake when **we** make it again. (F.P. Jones)
7. If you can't cope with the pressure, **you** must be expected to be replaced by someone who can.
8. We all believed his story because **we** couldn't believe he would lie.
9. I find that unconditional love is most reliably offered by **my** dog.
10. **My** colleagues and superiors can make **me** feel stupid and insignificant, but my dog's whole world revolves around me.

Exercise 16.3
Those of us who enjoy baseball find it difficult to explain **our** enthusiasm to non-fans. We baseball enthusiasts can watch a game of three hours or more as **we follow** each play with rapt

attention. We true fans get excited by a no-hitter—a game in which, by definition, nothing happens. **We** claim that the game is about much more than mere action, but non-fans must be forgiven if **they** don't get the point. To them, watching a baseball game is about as exciting as watching paint dry.

Exercise 16.4 (suggested answers)
(Words or phrases that have been omitted are indicated by ***.)

When **we are** at the beginning of our careers, it seems impossible that **we** may one day wish to work less. The drive to get ahead leads many of us to sacrifice **our** leisure, **our** community responsibilities, even **our** family life for the sake of **our** careers. Normally, as **we** age, **our** priorities begin to change, and career success becomes less important than quality of life. Not everyone, however, experiences this shift in priorities. Indeed, some people work themselves to death, while others are so committed to their work throughout their lives that they die within months of retirement—presumably from stress caused by lack of work. The poet Robert Frost once observed, "By working faithfully eight hours a day, you may eventually get to be a boss. Then you can work twelve hours a day." Those of **us** who are living and working in the early years of the 21st century would be wise to take Frost's words to heart.

Answers for Unit 3 Rapid Review

[1]Police officers in a small Manitoba town had **seen** too many people **who** were driving on the local roads while drunk, and they decided to make an example of one drunk driver to publicize the problem. [2]An officer, together with two reporters from the local newspaper, **was** stationed outside the town's most notorious bar in order to catch the worst drunk driver they **could** find. [3]As closing time neared, a man who clearly had **drunk** too much **came** out of the bar and tripped on the curb, staggered to the parking lot, and **began** trying to open car doors with his keys. [4]As the officer and the reporters **watched**, he tried 30 cars before his key worked. [5]Once he had succeeded in opening the car door, he **stumbled** to the front of the car and collapsed on the hood. [6]Meanwhile, the rest of the patrons **who** had been in the bar began to leave, but neither the reporters nor the officer **was** interested in anyone but the drunk on the hood of his car. [7]As the last car pulled out of the parking lot, the man rolled himself from the hood of his car, **got** in, and drove away. [8]The officer immediately pulled him over and, as the reporters watched, gave him a breathalyzer test. [9]"You should not be driving when **you are** inebriated," the policeman said. [10]"**The whole town** will read about you when they get their newspapers tomorrow morning."

[11]However, to the officer's surprise, the breathalyzer test showed a reading of 0.0. [12]When **he** and the reporters asked the man how it could be possible that the breathalyzer showed him to be sober, the man answered, "Tonight was my turn to be the decoy driver!"

Answer Key

If you missed the error(s) in sentence . . .		See Chapter . . .	
1	had saw	11	"The Principal Parts of Irregular Verbs" section
	people that	15	"Relative Pronouns" section
2	were stationed	12	"Four Special Cases" section (Rule 2)
	can find	13	Keeping Your Tenses Consistent
3	had drank	11	"The Principal Parts of Irregular Verbs" section
	come out	13	Keeping Your Tenses Consistent

If you missed the error(s) in sentence . . .		See Chapter . . .	
	begun trying	11	"The Principal Parts of Irregular Verbs" section
4	officer and reporters watch	13	Keeping Your Tenses Consistent
5	he stumbles	11	"The Principal Parts of Irregular Verbs" section
6	the rest of the patrons that	15	"Relative Pronouns" section
	the officer were interested	12	"Four Special Cases" section (Rule 1)
7	gets in	13	Keeping Your Tenses Consistent
9	one is inebriated	16	Maintaining Person Agreement
10	Everyone	15	"Pronoun–Antecedent Agreement" section
11	when him	14	"Subject and Object Pronouns" section

Answers for Unit 4 Quick Quiz

Note: Triple asterisks (***) indicate that a word or words have been deleted. Each set of triple asterisks counts as one error.

¹When we go to a movie**,** most of us like to sit back, munch away on a bucket of popcorn, and get lost in a good story. ²Some people**,** however**,** delight in examining each frame to see if the producers of the film have made mistakes called "bloopers." ³One kind of blooper is anachronisms. ⁴An anachronism is something that is inconsistent with the time period in which the movie is set. ⁵For example**,** in *Troy***,** when Brad Pitt is involved in a fight scene**,** a jumbo jet is clearly visible in the sky. ⁶In *Gladiator*, Russell Crowe walks past a field marked with tractor-tire tracks. ⁷Filter-tipped cigarettes in *Titanic***,** a Volkswagen Beetle in *The Godfather*, and white *** canvas sneakers in *The Ten Commandments* are other glaring examples of anachronisms. ⁸Whoops**!**

⁹Another kind of blooper is *** the "continuity" mistake. ¹⁰This kind of slip-up involves inconsistencies from one film sequence to the next. ¹¹For example, if a character drinks from a glass in one shot, the glass must contain less liquid, not more, in the next. ¹²Continuity problems abound**:** cigarettes get longer instead of shorter or appear and disappear from an actor's hand, hair changes style or length, and jewellery changes location. ¹³Did you notice any of these bloopers when you watched the following films**?** ¹⁴In *The Aviator*, the canopy on Leonardo DiCaprio's airplane pops on and off from sequence to sequence. ¹⁵In *Lord of the Rings: Return of the King*, Frodo's scar moves several times from the right side of his face to the left and back again. ¹⁶In *The Bourne Identity*, Matt Damon's watch changes from his right wrist to his left *** and back while he is cutting Franka Potente's hair.

¹⁷When we encounter a work of art, we want to experience what the poet Coleridge called **"**the willing suspension of disbelief.**"** ¹⁸We need to believe because getting lost in the story is the essence of a great movie. ¹⁹Bloopers can interfere with this belief**,** but so can looking too hard for mistakes!

Answer Key

If you missed the error(s) in sentence . . .		See Chapter . . .	
1	When we go to a movie most	17	The Comma (Rule 3)
2	people however delight	17	The Comma (Rule 4)
5	For example in	17	The Comma (Rule 3)
	in *Troy* when Brad Pitt is involved in a fight scene	17	The Comma (Rule 4)

If you missed the error(s) in sentence . . .		See Chapter . . .	
7	Filter-tipped cigarettes in *Titanic* a	17	The Comma (Rule 1)
	white, canvas sneakers	17	The Comma (Rule 5)
8	Whoops.	21	"The Exclamation Mark" section
9	is: the "continuity" mistake	19	The Colon
12	problems abound;	18	The Semicolon/19 The Colon
13	the following films.	21	"The Question Mark" section
16	to his left, and	17	The Comma (Rule 2)
17	the willing suspension of disbelief	20	Quotation Marks
19	belief but	17	The Comma (Rule 2)

Answers for Chapter 17: The Comma

Exercise 17.1

1. Hirako held two aces, a King, a Queen, and a Jack in her hand.
2. Cambodian food is spicy, colourful, nourishing, and delicious.
3. In Canada, the seasons are spring, summer, fall, winter, winter, and winter.
4. Correct
5. Fax machines are almost as outmoded as typewriters, black-and-white TV, and record players.
6. You need woollen underwear, snowshoes, and Arctic boots, but very little money to go winter camping.
7. Sleeping through my alarm, dozing during sociology, napping in the library after lunch, and snoozing in front of the TV all are symptoms of my overactive nightlife.
8. Once you have finished your homework, taken out the garbage, and done the dishes, you can feed the cat, clean your room, and do your laundry.
9. Of Paris, Moscow, Sydney, Madrid, and Beijing, which is not a national capital?
10. Both my doctor and my nutritionist agree that I should eat better, exercise more, and give up smoking.

Exercise 17.2

1. Pierre and I are good friends, yet we often disagree.
2. Correct
3. Please pay close attention, for the instructions are a little complicated.
4. Money can't buy happiness, but it makes misery easier to live with.
5. Correct
6. Correct
7. Flying may be the safest form of transportation, but why is the place where planes land called a "terminal"?
8. Pack an extra jacket or sweater, for evenings in September can be cold.
9. The phone hasn't worked for days, and the television has been broken for a month, but I haven't missed either of them.
10. Noah had the last two of every creature on his ark, so why didn't he swat those mosquitoes?

Exercise 17.3

1. First, we need to understand what an independent clause is.
2. In the end, we will be judged by how much happiness we have given others.
3. Driving 50 kph over the speed limit, Amin was soon pulled over.
4. According to company policy, you may not collect air mile points for business-related travel.
5. If you live by the calendar, your days are numbered.

6. According to my stomach, lunchtime came and went about an hour ago.
7. In most newspaper and magazine advertisements, the time shown on a watch is 10:10.
8. When you are right about something, it's considered polite not to gloat.
9. As her fortieth birthday approached, Eva met the challenge by trading in her minivan for a sports car and her husband for a boyfriend 20 years younger.
10. When the leaves turn colour, and the weather turns cold, I know it's time to put the snow tires on the car.

Exercise 17.4

1. Commas, like capitals, are clues to meaning.
2. Our hope, of course, is that the terrorists will be caught and punished.
3. Our family doctor, like our family dog, never comes when we call.
4. Our adventure began in Barcelona, which is the site of a famous unfinished cathedral designed by Gaudi.
5. Gaudi, who was killed by a bus in his 50s, began the cathedral as an atonement for the sins of mankind.
6. Correct
7. A compliment, like a good perfume, should be pleasing but not overpowering.
8. Our car made it all the way from Thunder Bay to Saskatoon, a piece of good luck that surprised us all.
9. Correct
10. The new office manager, now in her second month on the job, has made many changes to our procedures, not all of them welcome.

Exercise 17.5

1. Correct
2. Correct
3. Correct
4. Toronto in the summer is hot, smoggy, and humid.
5. Today's paper has an article about a new car made of lightweight, durable aluminum.
6. I think you'll like the new, improved model that has been assigned to all employees in your category.
7. This ergonomic, efficient, full-function keyboard comes in a variety of pastel shades.
8. We ordered a large, nutritious salad for lunch, then indulged ourselves with apple pie topped with vanilla ice cream.
9. When he retired, my father bought himself a large, comfortable, leather reclining chair.
10. We survived the long, high-velocity descent but almost didn't survive the sudden, unexpected crash landing.

Exercise 17.6

1. I call my salary "take-home pay," for home is the only place I can afford to go on what I make.
2. Madalena won my heart by laughing at my jokes, admiring my car, and tolerating my obsession with sports.
3. Though I try to remember my password, I forget it at least once a month.
4. Leo went to the bank to withdraw enough money to pay for his tuition, books, and the student activity fee.
5. In a moment of foolish optimism, I invested my life savings in a software development company.
6. The happiest years of my life, in my opinion, were the years I spent in college.
7. Sabina spends all day sleeping in bed, so she can spend all night dancing in the clubs.
8. Doing punctuation exercises is not very exciting, but it's cleaner than tuning your car.

9. This year, instead of the traditional gold watch, we will be giving retiring employees a framed photograph of our company's president.
10. Iqaluit, which was called Frobisher Bay until 1987, is a major centre on Baffin Island in Canada's eastern Arctic region.

Exercise 17.7

As long as you are prepared and confident, you'll find that an employment interview need not be a terrifying experience. Some people actually enjoy employment interviews and attend them with enthusiasm. Most of us, however, are intimidated by the prospect of being interrogated by an interviewer or (even worse) a team of interviewers.

To prepare for an interview, the first thing you should do is to find out as much as you can about the company. Among the things you need to know are the title of the job you are applying for, approximately how much it pays, the name of the person or persons who will conduct the interview, the address of the company, and the location of the washrooms. Employment consultants usually recommend that you make an advance visit to confirm how long it takes to get there and where the interview room is. While on your scouting mission, you can learn valuable information about the company's working conditions, employee attitudes, and even dress code.

On the day of the interview, be sure to show up 10 or 15 minutes in advance of your scheduled appointment. When the interviewer greets you, you should do three things: memorize his or her name, identify yourself, and extend your hand. Your handshake should be brief and firm, not limply passive or bone-crushingly aggressive. Practise! Now all you have to do is relax and enjoy the interview.

Answers for Chapter 18: The Semicolon

Exercise 18.1

2. Correct	7. Correct
3. Correct	10. Correct
4. Correct	

Exercise 18.2
Note: Triple asterisks (***) indicate that a word or words have been deleted. Each set of triple asterisks counts as one error.
1. We'll have to go soon; *** it's getting late. (*Or*: We'll have to go soon, for it's getting late.)
5. Make good notes on this topic; *** it could be on the exam. (*Or*: Make good notes on this topic, for it could be on the exam.)
6. If a tree falls in the woods where no one can hear it, does it make a noise?
8. Invented by a Canadian in the late 19th century, basketball is one of the world's most popular sports.
9. My neighbour works for a high-tech company, but he can't program his own VCR.

Exercise 18.3
1. We're late again; this is the third time this week.
2. Kiki is always late; however, she is worth waiting for.
3. Correct
4. I've found a delicious-sounding recipe for our dinner party, but you are allergic to two of the ingredients.
5. If you ever need a loan or a helping hand, just call Michel.
6. Travelling in Italy broadens the mind; eating Italian food broadens the behind.

7. North America's oldest continuously run horse race, the Queen's Plate, pre-dates the Kentucky Derby by 15 years.

8. We can't afford dinner at an expensive restaurant; instead, let's have spaghetti and meatballs at home.

9. I am a marvellous housekeeper; every time I leave a man, I keep his house. (Zsa Zsa Gabor)

10. A man has to do what a man has to do; a woman must do what he can't. (Feminist saying)

Exercise 18.4

1. An apple a day keeps the doctor away; however, an onion a day keeps everyone away.

2. Cash your paycheque right away; this company might be out of business by morning.

3. The telephone has been ringing all day, but there's no one home to take the call.

4. This note says that we are supposed to be at the interview by 9:00 a.m.; consequently, we'll have to leave home by 7:30.

5. Some people are skilled in many fields; Kumari, for example, is both a good plumber and a great cook.

6. After staring at a blank screen for half an hour, I decided to play solitaire.

7. The school counsellors maintain that to succeed at this level, you need excellent note-taking skills; organized study habits; and, most of all, good time-management strategies.

8. I know you need this report urgently, but until my computer is fixed, there's nothing I can do.

9. In 1813, Laura Secord trekked 25 km to warn the British and the Canadians of an American attack; her information resulted in victory at the Battle of Beaverdams.

10. Many years later, her name became famous, and a chocolate company was named after her.

Answers for Chapter 19: The Colon

Exercise 19.1

1. Correct	4. Correct
3. Correct	8. Correct

Exercise 19.2

(A deleted punctuation mark is indicated by ***.)

2. I stay fit by *** cycling and swimming.

5. My car is so badly built that, instead of a warranty, it came with *** an apology.

6. There are many species of fish in this lake, including *** pike, bass, and walleye.

7. Two common causes of failure are *** poor time management and inadequate preparation.

9. This apartment would be perfect if it had more storage: there aren't enough closets, bookshelves, or even drawers.

10. The difference between Canadians and Americans is that *** Canadians know there is a difference.

Exercise 19.3

(A deleted punctuation mark is indicated by ***.)

1. Our dog knows only one trick: pretending to be deaf.

2. Let me give you an example of a female role model: Adrienne Clarkson.

3. If at first you don't succeed, become a consultant and teach someone else.

4. There is a reason I have always felt my little brother was a mean, spiteful child: he always hit me back.

5. Leila spends too much time *** shopping at the malls, talking on the phone, and watching TV.

6. My roommate loved *Kill Bill: Vol. 1* and *Kill Bill: Vol. 2*, and I hated them both.
7. Your research paper lacks three important features: a title page, a Works Cited page, and some content in between.
8. The shortstop on our baseball team caught only one thing all season: a cold.
9. My mother always wanted a successful son, so I did my part: I urged her to have more children.
10. Every time I go to a club, I can hear my mother's warning: "Don't pick that up! You don't know where it's been."

Exercise 19.5

Imagine, if you can, Mario's surprise on being told that he had won a big prize in the lottery: one million dollars. At first, he didn't believe it; it was simply too good to be true. Once the reality had sunk in, however, he began to make plans for his fortune. As he thought about how to spend the money, he kept one goal in mind: "I want to help others as well as myself." He talked to the counsellors at the college, who advised him that setting up a scholarship would be a good use of his funds. Every year, five thousand dollars would go to three students who were doing well in school, but who couldn't afford to continue with their education without assistance. It was a perfect way for Mario to share his good fortune with others. Of course, he also bought himself the car of his dreams: a sleek, silver Porsche.

Answers for Chapter 20: Quotation Marks

Exercise 20.1
1. The most famous quotation in the history of Canadian sports is Foster Hewitt's "He shoots! He scores!"
2. The beaver, Canada's national animal, was once described by Michael Kesterton as "a distant relative of the sewer rat."
3. In the opinion of writer Barry Callaghan, "We Canadians have raised being boring to an art form."
4. "All we want," said Yvon Deschamps, "is an independent Quebec within a strong and united Canada."
5. Pierre Berton summed up the difference between Canadians and Americans as follows: "You ask an American how he's feeling, and he cries 'Great!' You ask a Canadian, and he answers 'Not bad,' or 'Pas mal.' "

Exercise 20.2
(The italicized titles are also correct if they are underlined.)
1. My favourite chapter in William Safire's book *How Not to Write* is Chapter 14, "Don't Use No Double Negatives."
2. Canada's national anthem is derived from a French song, "Chant national," which was first performed in Quebec City in 1880.
3. "O Canada," the English version of "Chant national," was written by R. Stanley Weir, a Montreal judge and poet, and was first performed in 1908.
4. In Shakespeare's play *The Winter's Tale*, there is a peculiar stage direction that has baffled scholars for 400 years: "Exit, pursued by a bear."
5. *Crouching Toad, Hidden Lizard*, a humorous documentary made by our college's television students, was shown on the CBC program *Short Shots*.
6. The video documentary *A War of Their Own* is the story of the Canadian troops in World War II who fought in the long, bloody Italian campaign.
7. The CD *Sparkjiver* features some great blues songs, such as "Harlem Nocturne" and "Try a Little Tenderness," performed by an unusual trio of electric organ, sax, and drums.

8. Go to **The Globe and Mail**'s Web page if you want to follow the links to Steve Galea's article "Thunder in the Snow," which describes the appeal and the dangers of snowmobiling.

9. The Diana Krall album **When I Look in Your Eyes** has three of my favourite jazz vocals: "Devil May Care," "I Can't Give You Anything But Love," and "Do It Again."

10. The Outdoors Channel is playing reruns of old **Survivor** episodes to show viewers, as **TV Guide** puts it, "how to live off the land while surrounded by cameras, microphones, TV technicians, and an obnoxious host."

Answers for Chapter 21: Question Marks, Exclamation Marks, and Punctuation Review

Exercise 21.1

1. Correct	5. Incorrect	9. Incorrect
2. Incorrect	6. Correct	10. Incorrect
3. Incorrect	7. Incorrect	
4. Correct	8. Incorrect	

Exercise 21.2

2. I want to know what's going on.
3. Why do they bother to report power outages on TV**?**
5. If corn oil comes from corn, I wonder where baby oil comes from.
7. I'm curious about where you plan to go for your vacation.
8. Theo wanted to know if Maria was going to the concert.
9. Do you know another word for *thesaurus***?**
10. As a Canadian, I often wonder if God ever considered having snow fall up.

Exercise 21.3

1. I quit**.** (*Or, if you want emphasis:* I quit!)
2. Stop**,** thief!
3. Don't you dare!
4. He's on the stairway**,** right behind you! (*Or, if you are describing a nonthreatening scene:* He's on the stairway, right behind you.)
5. We won! I can't believe it!
6. Brandishing her new credit card, Tessa marched through the mall shouting, "Charge it!"
7. Take the money and run**.**
8. I can't believe it's over! (*Or:* I can't believe it's over.)

Exercise 21.4

1. The question was whether it would be better to stay in bed or to go to the clinic.
2. Gregory asked Nell if she had ever been to Nanaimo.
3. Hurry, or we'll be late!
4. Did you ever notice that the early bird gets the worm, but the second mouse gets the cheese**?**
5. Just imagine! In only three hours, they are going to draw my ticket number in the lottery!
6. Is it true that those who live by the sword get shot by those who don't**?**
7. Stop! Do you want to be arrested for running a red light?
8. Shoot the puck! Why won't he shoot the puck**?**

Exercise 21.6

(Punctuation that has been omitted is indicated by ***.)

1. If you want to make your living as a comedian, you must *** remember the punch line.
2. Good health, according to my doctor, should be defined as *** "the slowest possible rate at which one can die."

3. The fast pace of life doesn't bother me; it's the sudden stop at the end that has me worried.
4. This new fad diet can be summed up in a single sentence: "If it tastes good, don't eat it."
5. Many years ago, Mark Twain warned us, (*or* :) "Be careful about reading health books; you may die of a misprint."
6. My brother doesn't think much of a healthy lifestyle; he often says, "Eat well, exercise regularly, and die anyway."
7. "Don't worry about avoiding temptation," advised Winston Churchill. "As you grow older, it will avoid you."
8. Did you know that Irish coffee is the perfect food? It provides in a single glass all four essential food groups: alcohol, caffeine, sugar, and fat.
9. The prescription for a healthy life is well known: eat a balanced diet; get regular exercise, even if it's just a five-minute walk each day; get regular checkups; and avoid stress.
10. Columbus first encountered turkeys, which were unknown in Europe at that time, on an island off the coast of Honduras; he was served roast turkey by the Native peoples. According to Margaret Visser, author of **The Rituals of Dinner**, "At ceremonial feasts, the Spaniards were served huge tamales containing a whole turkey each."

Answers for Unit Four Rapid Review

[1]A well-known Canadian politician was asked to make a major speech to the executives of Canada's major banks. [2]Since his staff included a professional speechwriter, he called her into his office and outlined for her the background of his audience, the policies and programs he wanted to talk about, and the tone and approach he thought were appropriate for the occasion. [3]The speechwriter asked only one question: she wanted to know how long the speech should be. [4]The politician told her that the speech should be exactly 20 minutes long. [5]Knowing how important this address would be for her boss, the writer went right to work; she stayed late to draft what she thought was a masterpiece.

[6]On the day after the big speech, the writer was at her desk early; she was curious to learn how her speech had been received. [7]When her boss called, she could tell from the tone of his voice that he was very angry. [8]"The speech was a disaster!" he bellowed. [9]"I asked for a 20-minute speech, not a 60-minute speech. [10]Before I was finished, half the audience had left the hall, and most of the others were asleep!" [11]The writer replied that she had given him exactly what he had asked for: notes for a 20-minute speech and two copies.

Answer Key

If you missed the error(s) in sentence . . .		See Chapter . . .	
2	speechwriter he	17	The Comma (Rule 3)
	audience the	17	The Comma (Rule 1)
	about and	17	The Comma (Rule 1)
3	question she	19	The Colon
5	boss the	17	The Comma (Rule 3)
	work she	18	The Semicolon
6	big speech the	17	The Comma (Rule 3)
	early she	18	The Semicolon
7	called she	17	The Comma (Rule 3)
8	The speech	20	Quotation Marks
	disaster he	21	"The Exclamation Mark" section
9	I asked	20	Quotation Marks
10	finished half	17	The Comma (Rule 3)
	asleep	21	"The Exclamation Mark" section
11	asked for notes	19	The Colon

Answers for Chapter 22: Finding Something to Write About

Exercise 22.1
 1. Not specific, and not supportable without a great deal of research
 2. Not significant. Every child knows what they are.
 3. Not significant
 4. Not single or specific
 5. Not significant
 6. Not single. Choose one.
 7. Not specific. Whole books have been written on this topic.
 8. Not supportable. How can we know?
 9. Not single
10. Not specific

Exercise 22.2
 1. Not significant; it's a commonplace fact.
 2. Possible, but too broad. You could make it specific and significant by applying one or more limiting factors to it. For example, "Canadian teenagers' notion of ideal female beauty" or "How the notion of physical attractiveness has changed since my parents' generation."
 3. Possible. Make it significant by broadening the topic a little: e.g., "How to increase the efficiency of your dishwasher." (If your dishwasher is a human being, the subject has humorous possibilities.)
 4. Not specific and not supportable for most of us without substantial research. To be a suitable subject, it would need limiting: e.g., "Some lessons to be learned from Russia's struggle to develop a market economy."
 5. Possible, but the subject needs to be limited if it is to be both significant and specific. You might, for example, discuss one influential Canadian woman or write a profile of one "unknown" Canadian woman—i.e., someone who is not a public figure.
 6. Unless you are Martha Stewart or can come up with some unusual and useful ideas, this is not significant.
 7. As it stands, this topic is unsupportable. It needs to be limited to be specific and supportable: e.g., "Basic palm-reading techniques" or "How computer miniaturization will change our lives."
 8. Possible. Make it specific by identifying two or three typical challenges.

Exercise 22.6
 1. Seattle Mariners (unrelated to the subject; it's an American team)
 2. Improved looks (overlaps with "improved appearance"); improved social life (not *directly* related to the subject)
 3. Travelling (unrelated; already accomplished by the immigrant to Canada); shovelling snow (overlaps with "adjusting to climate")
 4. Earthquakes (not a weather system)
 5. Alcohol (not a reason)
 6. Quiz shows (overlaps with "game shows"); Oprah (unrelated; not a "kind" of show)
 7. White shark; hammerhead shark (species, not characteristics, of sharks)
 8. Government has less money to spend on social services (not related to the subject; it contradicts the argument for lower taxes)

Exercise 22.8

Subject	Order	Main Points	
1. How to start a gas lawn mower	chronological	2	make sure there is enough gas in tank
		3	turn switch to start
		1	put lawn mower on flat ground
		5	when running, adjust to proper speed
		4	pull cord
		6	mow!
2. Differences between spoken and written language	climactic	3	speech is transitory; writing is permanent
		2	speech is direct and personal; writing isn't
		1	speech can't be revised; writing can
3. How to write a research paper	chronological	3	read and take notes on selected research sources
		4	draft the paper
		2	compile a working bibliography of research sources
		1	define the subject
		7	type and proofread paper
		6	prepare footnotes, if needed, and list of works cited
		5	revise the paper
4. How colleges benefit society	logical	2	they provide the individual with a higher level of general education
		3	society benefits from increased productivity and commitment of an educated populace
		1	they provide the individual with job skills
5. Effects of malnutrition	logical	3	malnutrition affects the productivity and prosperity of nations as a whole
		1	malnutrition impedes the mental and physical development of children
		2	undernourished children become sickly adults unable to participate fully in their society

Subject	Order	Main Points	
6. Why pornography should be banned	chronological	_1_	it degrades the people involved in making it
		_3_	it brutalizes society as a whole
		_2_	it desensitizes the people who view it

7. and 8. Decide on your own climactic arrangements for these questions. Be sure you can explain your choices.

Answers for Chapter 23: The Thesis Statement

Exercise 23.1

1. The essential features of a good novel (are) interesting characters, a stimulating plot, and exceptional writing.
2. My boss enjoys two hobbies (:) improving his golf game and tormenting his employees.
3. Well-known stars, stunning technical effects, and a hugely expensive advertising campaign (are) the requirements for a blockbuster movie.
4. If I were you, I would avoid eating in the cafeteria (because) the food is expensive, tasteless, and unhealthy.
5. The original Volkswagen Beetle, the Citröen CV, and the Morris Minor (are) three cars that will be remembered for their endearing oddness.
6. The responsibilities of a modern union (include) protecting the jobs of current employees, seeking to improve their working conditions and compensation, and protecting the pensions and benefits of pensioners.
7. Fad diets are not the quick and easy fixes to weight problems that they may seem to be; in fact, they are often costly, ineffective, and even dangerous.
8. (Because) they lack basic skills, study skills, or motivation, some students run the risk of failure in college.
9. *The Simpsons* amuses and provokes viewers (with its depiction of) a smart-aleck, underachieving son; a talented, overachieving daughter; and a hopeless, blundering father.
10. The Canadian political culture differs from the American political culture (in terms of) attitudes toward universal health care, gun control, and capital punishment.

Exercise 23.2

1. Parallel	3. Not parallel	5. Not parallel
2. Not parallel	4. Not parallel	

Exercise 23.3

1. Correct
2. Good writing involves applying the principles of organization, sentence structure, spelling, and punctuation.
3. Our company requires employees to be knowledgeable, honest, disciplined, and reliable.
4. Hobbies are important because they provide us with recreation, stimulation, and relaxation.
5. Some of the negative effects of caffeine are nervousness, sleeplessness, and heart palpitations.

Exercise 23.4

1. The four kinds of essay writing are description, narration, exposition, and argumentation. (parallelism)
2. Intramural sports offer students a way to get involved in their school, an opportunity to meet friends, and a way to keep fit. (parallelism and significance: "uniforms" is a trivial point)
3. Increasingly, scientists are finding links between the weather and diseases such as colds, cancer, and arthritis. (parallelism and relevance—aging isn't a disease)
4. The most prolific producers of pretentious language are politicians, educators, advertising copy writers, and sports writers. (overlap between *teachers and administrators* and *educators*; parallelism)
5. There are three categories of students whom teachers find difficult: those who skip class, those who sleep through class, and those who disrupt class. (parallelism—and wordiness! *Better* ... skippers, sleepers, and disrupters)

Exercise 23.5 (suggested answers)

1. Qualities needed to succeed in college
   Living in a college residence rather than one's own home is not a quality needed for success. It is a choice based on personal circumstances and preferences.
   B. Three important qualities required for students to succeed in college (are) good academic skills, organizational skills, and motivation.
2. Living in Canada has some advantages over living in the United States.
   - Universal medical care: Yes, good point.
   - Pleasant climate: No, not true. Canada's climate is cold and snowy for much of the year.
   - Less crime: Yes.
   - Tundra: No, the tundra is an Arctic region where no trees grow.
   - More affordable post-secondary education: Yes, generally true.
   - Multicultural environment: No, both countries are immigrant societies made up of people from many cultures.
   A. Three advantages that living in Canada has over living in the United States (are) universal medical care, more affordable post-secondary education, and less crime.
   B. Canada is a better place to live than the United States (because) Canada has universal medical care, more affordable post-secondary education, and less crime.
3. Some forms of electronic communication can improve a person's social life.
   - Instant messaging: Yes, this service helps people to stay in touch.
   - iPods: No; if anything, once you're plugged into an iPod, you are isolated from the social life around you.
   - Blogging: Yes, you can communicate with people who have similar interests.
   - Expensive gadgets: No. Many are available, but by themselves, they have nothing to do with the subject. How you use them is what may or may not have an impact on your social life.
   - Internet dating: Yes, people date people they meet online.
   A. Some forms of electronic communication can improve a person's social life; (for example,) Internet dating, instant messaging, and blogging.
   B. Some forms of electronic communication that can improve a person's social life (are) Internet dating, instant messaging, and blogging.
4. What most immigrant parents encourage their Canadian-born children to learn
   - Their native language: Yes, this is important for many parents.
   - Their native footwear: No, not really significant.
   - Their cultural history: Yes.
   - Their ethical/religious beliefs: Yes.

- Canadian tax law: No, not related to the subject.
- Nothing about their homeland: No, most immigrant parents want their children to know about their original culture.
- A Most immigrant parents encourage their Canadian-born children to learn (about) their native language, cultural history, and ethical/religious beliefs.
- B. The things that most immigrant parents encourage their Canadian-born children to learn (include) their native language, cultural history, and ethical/religious beliefs.
5. Maintaining a healthy lifestyle
  - Balanced diet
  - Adequate exercise
  - (Your choice)
  - A. (Main points first) A balanced diet, adequate exercise, and (your main point) (are) essential to maintaining a healthy lifestyle.
B. Answers will vary.

Answers for Chapter 25: Paragraphs

Exercise 25.1

Paragraph 3:

Topic sentence — If, on the other hand, you view the scheduling issue as so important that it must be resolved to the company's advantage, you will want to exercise your authority and insist on a no-charge policy.

Supporting sentences — Employees would be assigned to particular shifts, and if they wanted time off, they would have to take it without pay. There would be no re-scheduling.

Conclusion — This is a competitive approach, one which ensures that you "win" while the other side "loses"—and one which also ensures that your relationship with the "losers" will be tarnished.

Paragraph 4:

Topic sentence — A more empathetic way of managing the situation would be compromise.

Supporting sentences — You could circulate a memo in which you laid out parameters, specific guidelines for how and when schedule changes could occur. This would allow some flexibility, but would at the same time limit the frequency and nature of schedule change requests. In this way, both you (i.e., the company) and the employees would "win"— partially. Both sides would get a part of what they wanted, but both would also lose a part.

Conclusion — And so long as both sides were satisfied, this could be an effective solution.

Paragraph 5:

Topic sentence — Finally, if you're a supervisor who believes in the concept of mutual benefit, in the notion that it's possible for both sides to "win," you will choose the method of co-operation.

Supporting sentences — You and the employees might brainstorm the scheduling issue together and in the process discover new ways in which it might be settled to the satisfaction of both sides—not compromise, but resolution. Because co-operation produces no "loser," it fosters an atmosphere of trust and respect; and, although certainly more time-consuming than the other three methods,

Conclusion — it is generally the best way to encourage goodwill in the workplace.

Exercise 25.7

1. Series of steps/stages
2. Quotation
3. Specific details
4. Series of steps/stages
5. Definition + contrast
6. Specific numerical details
7. Comparison/contrast
8. Descriptive details
9. Quotations
10. Quotation and contrast

Exercise 25.10

(We have italicized the words and phrases that need to be revised to change the tone of this paragraph from tactless to tactful and provided some suggestions in square brackets following the offensive phrases.)

I'm from the city, so I may not know much about the subject, but it seems to me that we urban dwellers have lost touch with the food we eat. By this I mean, *obviously,* [delete] that we no longer appreciate the farmers and farm workers who supply the food that we enjoy every day. *Anyone with half a brain should realize that* [delete] Most of the food we buy is prepackaged in Styrofoam, wrapped in plastic, or precooked and frozen by huge corporations *whose goal is to make humongous profits by selling us the packaging, not the contents.* [who put at least as much effort into designing attractive packaging as they do into preparing food.] *Do any urban consumers understand that* [How many urban consumers think about the fact that] their ketchup is made from farm-grown tomatoes? Do *any advertising-driven* [delete] supermarket shoppers *really think about the fact* [stop to consider] that those *overpackaged* [delete] frozen pork chops, so irresistible with their sprig of parsley, were once a pig, raised by a farmer? *Not only are we ignorant, but also we could care less* [Let's face the facts: Do many of us know or even care] about the journey our food makes from farm to fridge[?] My guess is that if you asked most *city kids* [urban children] where their food comes from, they'd say, "the store."

Here is how a final draft of this revision might read. (Note that we've added a conclusion to the paragraph.)

It seems to me that we urban dwellers have lost touch with the food we eat. By this I mean that we no longer appreciate the farmers and farm workers who supply the food that we enjoy every day. Most of the food we buy is prepackaged in Styrofoam, wrapped in plastic, or precooked and frozen by huge corporations who put at least as much effort into designing attractive packaging as they do into preparing food. How many urban consumers think about the fact that ketchup is made from farm-grown tomatoes? Do supermarket shoppers stop to consider that those frozen pork chops, so irresistible with their sprig of parsley, were once a pig, raised by a farmer? Let's face facts: how many of us know or even care about the journey our food makes from farm to fridge? My guess is that if you asked most urban children where their food comes from, they'd say, "the store." But the correct answer is, "Canadian farmers." They deserve our attention and support.

Answers for Chapter 26: Revising Your Paper

Exercise 26.1

Attention-getter: As the recipient of approximately 1,000 business-related e-mail messages every month, I am something of an expert on what is effective and what is not in e-mail correspondence.

Thesis statement: The three areas that need attention in most e-mail messages are the subject line, the content and format of the message, and the use of attachments.

Main points:

 I. Subject line
   A. Never leave the subject line blank (*or* Always include a subject line)
   B. Make sure the subject line states clearly what the message is about

 II. Message
   A. Content
     1. Be concise and to the point
     2. Tell the reader what action is needed, by whom, and when
     3. Use plain English, not "cyberspeak"

    4. Use an appropriate level of language in your message as well as in your salutation and signature
- B. Format
    1. Use bullets to identify points you want to emphasize
    2. Leave white space between points
    3. Avoid sending your message in upper-case letters (shouting)
    4. Avoid smilies and other "cute" computer shorthand symbols
III. Attachments
- A. Use only if necessary
    1. may carry viruses
    2. take time to transfer and to open
- B. Attach text-only files unless a graphic is absolutely necessary

Summary: If you follow my recommendations on these three points whenever you write an e-mail, you will make the recipient of your message very happy.
Memorable statement: Especially if you're writing to me.

Exercise 26.2 (suggested answer)
In the following answer, we have corrected only the errors in paragraph structure, sentence structure, and grammar. The passage still contains errors in spelling, punctuation, and usage. We will correct those errors at Step 3.

1   As the recipient of almost 1,000 business-related e-mail messages every month, I am something of an expert on what is effective and what is not in e-mail correspondence. The three areas that need attention in most e-mail messages are the subject line, the **content and format** of the message**,** and the use of attachments.

2   Some people leave the subject line blank**. T**his is a mistake. I want to know what the message is about before I open it**,** so I can decide if it needs my immediate attention **or** can wait until later. A message with no subject line**,** or with a line that **doesn't** tell me **anything** about the content of the e-mail**, gets** sent to the bottom of my "to-do" list. There are lots of readers like me: busy people who receive tons of e-mail, much of it unsolicited advertising that **clutters** up **our** in-boxes. For this reason the subject line should always clearly state the subject of the message and should never be vague or cute**,** like "hello**,**" or "message**,**" or "are you there?"

3   As for the message itself, it's function should be to tell the reader what action **you want. Y**ou need to be clear about this and be as brief as possible. What is it that you want the recipient to do. Who else needs to be involved. By when does the action need to take place. Communicate your message in plain English, not in "cyberspeak**.**" Not everyone knows Net lingo, and even some who are famliar with it find it irritating**,** not charming. Use an appropriate level of language (general-level Standard English **is** always appropriate) to convey you're message. Use the same level of language in you're salutation and closing or "signature." **Never** sign off a message to you're client or you're boss with "love and kisses."

4   Format you're message so that the recipient **can read it quickly and understand** it easily. Use bullets to identify points you want to emphasize **and** separate the bullets with white space so **that your points** can be read at a glance and reviewed individually if neccessary.

5   There are some important points of e-mail etiquette that you should observe. Don't type you're message in upper-case letters**. This is** considered "shouting." Do avoid "smilies" and other "cute" computer shorthand symbols. Some of you're readers won't understand them**. O**thers will have seen them so often they will be turned off.

6   Attachments should be included only if they are really necessary**. One reason is that** they may carry virruses and some people won't open them. Another disadvantage is that **attachments** take time to send download and open. Unless I am sure that an attachment is both

urgent and vitally important—the agenda of tomorrow's meeting, for example—I don't bother to open it. **F**or all I know, it might contain not only a virus but also footage of the sender's toddler doing her latest photogenic trick. As a general rule **you should** attach only what you must and attach text-only files. Try to include everything you need to say in the message itself**;** use attachments only as a last resort. Think of them as equivalent to footnotes**:** supplementary to the message**,** not an essential part of it.

7   If you follow my recommendations on these three points whenever you write an e-mail, you will make the recipient of your message very happy, especially if you're writing to me.

Exercise 26.3 (suggested answer)
(Words that have been omitted are indicated by ***.)

1   As the recipient of approximately 1,000 business-related e-mail messages every month, I am something of an expert on what is effective and what is not in e-mail correspondence. The three areas that need attention in most e-mail messages are the subject line, the content *** and format of the message**,** and the use of attachments.

2   Some people leave the subject line blank. This is a mistake. I want to know what the message is about before I open it, so I can decide if it needs my immediate attention or can wait until later. A message with no subject line, or with a line that doesn't tell me anything about the content of the e-mail, gets sent to the bottom of my "to-do" list. There are lots of readers like me: busy people who receive tons of e-mail, much of which is unsolicited advertising that clutters up our inboxes. For this reason**,** the subject line should always clearly state the subject of the message and should never be vague or cute. **Some examples of inappropriate subject lines include** "Hello," *** "Message," **and** "Are you there?"

3   As for the message itself, **its** function should be to tell the reader what action you want **taken**. *** Be clear about this**,** and be as brief as possible. What is it that you want the recipient to do**?** Who else needs to be involved**?** By when does the action need to **be completed?** Communicate your message in plain English, not in "cyberspeak." Not everyone knows Net lingo, and even some who are **familiar** with it find it irritating, not charming. Use an appropriate level of language (general-level standard English is always appropriate) to convey **your** message. Use the same level of language in **your** salutation and closing or "signature." Never sign off a message to **your** client or **your** boss with "love and kisses."

4   Format **your** message so that the recipient can read it quickly and understand it easily. Use bullets to identify points you want to emphasize, and separate the bullets with white space so that your points can be read at a glance and reviewed individually**,** if **necessary**.

5   There are some important points of e-mail etiquette that you should observe. Don't type **your** message in upper-case letters. This is considered "shouting." Do avoid "smilies" and other "cute" computer shorthand symbols. Some of **your** readers won't understand them. Others will have seen them so often **that** they will be turned off.

6   Attachments should be included only if they are really necessary. One reason is that they may carry **viruses,** and some people won't open them. Another disadvantage is that attachments take time to send**,** download**,** and open. Unless I am sure that an attachment is both urgent and vitally important—the agenda of tomorrow's meeting, for example—I don't bother to open it. For all I know, it might contain not only a virus but also footage of the sender's toddler doing her latest photogenic trick. As a general rule**,** you should attach only what you must**,** and attach text-only files. Try to include everything you need to say in the message itself; use attachments only as a last resort. Think of them as equivalent to footnotes: supplementary to the message, not an essential part of it.

7   If you follow my recommendations on these three points whenever you write an e-mail, you will make the recipient of your message very happy, especially if you're writing to me.

Answers for Unit 6 Quick Quiz

¹People learn their first language very early and very easily. ²Most of us understand spoken words and respond to them **by** the time we are two or three years old. ³It takes another few years for us to learn how to read and write, but we acquire our first language fairly easily. ⁴**For** most of us, however, learning a second language is a slow and exasperating process. ⁵Most people who study English as a second language are especially **frustrated** by three of its peculiarities: its unsystematic pronunciation, its inconsistent spelling, and its enormous vocabulary.

⁶English **has** sounds that are difficult for speakers of other languages. ⁷The *th* sound is one of them. ⁸Why is it pronounced differently in words such as *this* and *think*? ⁹The consonant sounds *l, r,* and *w* also present problems. ¹⁰Many new English speakers don't hear the differences between *light, right,* and *white,* and so they don't pronounce them. ¹¹There are also more vowel sounds in English than in most other **languages**. ¹²The *a* sound in the words *bat* and *mat* is peculiar to English, so second-language learners often pronounce *bet, bat,* and *but* identically. ¹³To native speakers of English, these words **have** quite distinct sounds that many second-language learners do not hear and so cannot pronounce. ¹⁴Many ESL **speakers** find it difficult to pronounce the unusual vowel sounds that occur in words *bird, word,* and *nurse.* ¹⁵The fact that the same sound occurs in words with three different vowels—*i, o,* and *u*—is **an** example of **the** second major difficulty with English: its inconsistent spelling system.

¹⁶Most native speakers would agree that English spelling is challenging. ¹⁷Why do *tough* and *stuff* rhyme when their spelling is so different? ¹⁸Shouldn't *tough* rhyme with *cough?* ¹⁹But *cough* rhymes with *off.* ²⁰Why does *clamour* rhyme with *hammer* while *worm* and *storm*—which should rhyme—don't? ²¹There **is no** single answer, but part of the reason is that English is a language that has absorbed many words and sounds from other languages, along with their spellings. ²²Almost 75% of English words have regular spellings, but, unfortunately, the most frequently used words in English are the irregular **ones**. ²³All of us, second-language learners and native speakers alike, simply have to learn to cope.

²⁴English also has a huge vocabulary, in part because it borrows freely from other languages. ²⁵The roots of English are Germanic, but the Celts, Romans, French, and many others have contributed heavily to the language. ²⁶The gigantic *Oxford English Dictionary* lists about 500,000 words and does not include about another half million technical and scientific **words**.

²⁷English is **a** difficult language for all of these **reasons**, but it's a rich and **satisfying** one that is well worth the effort to learn.

Answer Key

If you missed the error(s) in sentence . . .		See Chapter . . .	
2	since the time	31	Practising with Prepositions
4	By most of us	31	Practising with Prepositions
5	especially frustrating	28	"Participial Adjectives" section
6	English is having sounds	27	Choosing the Correct Verb Tense
11	most other language	29	"Quantity Expressions" section
13	these words are having	27	Choosing the Correct Verb Tense
14	Many ESL speaker	29	"Quantity Expressions" section
15	is example	30	"The Indefinite Article: *A/An*" section
	of second major difficulty	30	"The Definite Article: *The*" section
21	isn't no single answer	28	"Forming Negatives" section
22	the irregular one	29	Solving Plural Problems
26	scientific word	29	"Quantity Expressions" section
27	is difficult language	30	"The Indefinite Article: *A/An*" section
	these reason	29	Solving Plural Problems
	satisifed one	28	"Participial Adjectives" section

Answers for Chapter 27: Choosing the Correct Verb Tense

Exercise 27.1

1.	(present perfect progressive)	He **has** been **going**.	He **has** been **seeing**.
2.	(past progressive)	I was **going**.	I was **seeing**.
3.	(simple present)	He **goes**. They **go**.	He **sees**. They **see**.
4.	(present progressive)	You **are going**.	You **are seeing**.
5.	(simple past)	We **went**.	We **saw**.
6.	(future progressive)	She **will** be **going**.	She **will** be **seeing**.
7.	(present perfect progressive)	He **has** been **going**.	He **has** been **seeing**.
8.	(past perfect)	We had **gone**.	We had **seen**.
9.	(simple future)	You **will go**.	You **will see.**
10.	(past perfect progressive)	Someone had **been going**.	Someone had **been seeing**.

Exercise 27.2

1. He will **be going** with us. (future progressive)
2. The new year **starts/begins** on January 1. (simple present)
3. My parents **have** always **been** good to me. (present perfect)
4. Linda and Joy **are leaving** for China a week from now. (present progressive expressing future)
5. My friend **had** lived in Canada for two years, but he returned to Poland last week.
6. You **have been working** very hard, so why not take a break? (present perfect progressive)
7. The movie **had been playing** for 30 minutes by the time we got there. (past perfect progressive)
8. I **read** all the stories last night to prepare for the quiz. (simple past)
9. I **am taking** off my running shoes right now because they **are killing** my feet. (present progressive)
10. He **was watching** TV when I **called** him last night. (past progressive; simple past).

Exercise 27.3

1. It **is snowing** again today. In my country, it often **rains**, but it never **snows**.
2. My father usually **comes** to see my games, but tonight he **is working** a late shift.
3. I **study** almost every night, but tonight I **am going** to visit some friends.
4. A ticket home **costs** so much that I **doubt** that I can afford the trip.
5. We still **believe** we have a good team, and now we **are trying** to develop a winning strategy.
6. My mother usually **phones** me every day at 6:00, but it is now 6:30 and I am **still waiting** for her call. I wonder what she **is doing.**
7. The baby **is crying** again. He always **cries** when his mother **leaves**.
8. What **are you doing** right now? I **am learning** English verb tenses.
9. The little girl **looks** tired, but right now she **is looking** at her favourite storybook.
10. Wanda **wants** to get a good job, but she **has** to finish her college education first.

Exercise 27.4

1. Does Rahim like to travel?
   Yes, he does. He **has gone** to many different places during his life. He **has visited** both Asia and Africa **since** 2002.

2. Are you taking an ESL course this semester?

No, I **have already taken** it. I **have studied** English **for** 11 years.

3. Do you love me?

Yes, I **have always loved** you. I **have known** you **since** I was a little girl, and I **have never loved** anyone but you.

4. Does Mira like to shop?

Yes, she loves to shop. She **bought** four pairs of shoes last week. She already **has** dozens of pairs of shoes in her closet.

5. When did you move here?

I moved here in _____. I **have been** here **for** _____ years.

Exercise 27.5

1. It **has been snowing** all day.
2. They **have been studying** physics for three days straight.
3. We **have been working** hard on our grammar.
4. She **has been answering** all of the e-mail messages.
5. The phone **has been ringing** all morning.

Exercise 27.6

1. It **has been raining** all night, and the basement is flooded.
2. There **have been** four big rainstorms already this week.
3. I always **have done** my homework carefully, and I also **am working** with a tutor right now.
4. Marty **has known** the man for many years.
5. How long **have you lived** (*or* **have you been living**) in Canada?

Exercise 27.7

1. Three of us **were smoking** in the upstairs washroom when the boss **walked** in.
2. The cat **was hiding** behind the fish tank when I **saw** his tail twitch and **caught** him.
3. While their sister **was preparing** their lunch, the children **ran** into the house and **turned** on the television.
4. When we **were working** outside in the yard last night, we **felt** the jolt of a small earthquake.
5. Marco **was trying** to park his new SUV in the narrow driveway when he **hit** the neighbour's hedge. The branches **made** deep scratches in the paint.
6. As Julio **was telling** (**or told**) his friends about his new job, one of them **asked** him how he **had found** the position.
7. The professor **was teaching** an important lesson when two men **came** in late and **disturbed** the class.
8. I **did not hear** you arrive last night because I **was sleeping**.
9. **Were** you **eating** breakfast this morning when I **phoned**?
10. I **was studying** in the library when I **became** ferociously hungry and **knew** that I **had** to eat.

Exercise 27.8

1. Dick was late for class. The professor **had just given** a quiz when he **got** there.
2. Yesterday my friend Ronit **saw** an old friend whom she **had not seen** in years.
3. I almost missed my flight. Everyone **had already boarded** the plane by the time I **rushed** in.
4. We **had** scarcely **begun** the test when the fire alarm **rang**.
5. The movie **had** hardly **started** when the audience **walked** out.

Exercise 27.9

1. It is 6:00 p.m. I **have been working** for 10 hours straight, so it is time to go home.
2. It was 6:00 p.m. I **had been working** for 10 hours straight, so it was time to go home.
3. I woke up feeling strange this morning because I **had been dreaming** about dinosaurs all night.
4. Sam is tired because he **has been working** all morning.
5. They **had been dating** for a year when they got engaged.

Exercise 27.10

1. By the time I **realized** that I needed an elective to graduate, I **had already dropped** my history course.
2. He **lived** in Beijing until he **was** 20.
3. Karin's sister **arrived** about 10 minutes after Karin **had left** (*or* **left**).
4. I **wasn't listening** when they **made** the announcement.
5. By the time Kim **had been working** (*or* **had worked**) the night shift for three months, she **thought** that she would never have a social life again.
6. We **had been looking** forward to our vacation for months when my wife **got** a promotion, and we **had** to cancel our plans.
7. If I **had known** how difficult this course **was**, I would have signed up for something easier.
8. When he **retired**, Professor Green **had been teaching** creative writing for 30 years.
9. We **had decided** (*or* **decided**) to sell our condominium, but we **changed** our minds when the real estate agent **told** us the low price we would get.
10. Kim **never thought** about her friend's feelings; she **was** (*or* **was being**) very selfish when she made the decision.

Exercise 27.11

1. When I **got** home last night, everyone **had already eaten** dinner.
2. I **had never seen** any of Monet's paintings until I **went** to the Museum of Modern Art in New York last year.
3. We **have been planning** to renovate our house for a long time, but we **decided** on a contractor only last week.
4. Hockey **has always been** Canadians' favourite sport; we **have been playing** the game for more than 150 years.
5. Although Ali **has lived** (*or* **has been living**) in Toronto since he was 10, he **has never visited** the CN Tower.
6. While Igor **was talking** on the phone, the bathtub **overflowed**.
7. For six weeks, I **have been waiting** for my transcript to come in the mail. I wonder if the Registrar's Office **has gone** on strike.
8. **Have** you **finished** your homework yet?
9. Yesterday my father **made** me go to the barber who **has been cutting** (*or* **has cut**) his hair for the past 20 years.
10. While I **was waiting** (*or* **waited**) for my turn, I **noticed** that I **was** the only person in the shop under 50.

Exercise 27.12

1. He **is going to arrive** tonight, but I **won't be** here.
2. Tomorrow is his birthday, so he **is going to have** dinner with friends.
3. Since you **are going to take** an elective course next semester, I suggest you sign up for sociology. You **will enjoy** Professor Singh's sense of humour.
4. Our neighbours **are going to build** an addition onto their home next summer. I hope we **will be** on vacation when the construction begins.

5. I **am going to buy** a daytimer schedule because my counsellor says that it **will help** me put some order into my life.

Exercise 27.13

1. I have no idea where I **will be working** next week, but I **will let** you know as soon as I find out.
2. My fiancée insists that I buy her a diamond ring before she **will marry** me, so I **will be buying** a lot of lottery tickets.
3. I **won't have** (*or* **will not have**) time to talk on the phone this afternoon because I **will be cooking** a traditional dinner for 14 people.
4. Ravi says that he **is going to teach** in Tokyo next year.
5. We **won't stay** at this hotel again.

Exercise 27.14

1. I **am going to go** (*or* **will go**) to Florida with Josef next spring because by then he **will have earned** (*or* **will earn**) enough money to pay for his share of the trip.
2. We are going to be late because of the terrible traffic. By the time we **reach** the airport, Miryam's plane **will already have arrived.** She **will be worrying** (*or* **will worry**) that something has happened to us.
3. At this pace, we **will have walked** 30 km by tonight.
4. You were born in _____. By the year 2050, you **will have lived** (*or* **will have been living**) for _____ years. You **will have seen** (*or* **will see**) many changes!
5. I **will have already cleaned** the house by the time you get here.

Exercise 27.15

1. As soon as Val **graduates**, he **will leave** (*or* **is leaving** *or* **will be leaving**) for Africa.
2. If the wind **blows** hard, that house **will collapse**.
3. They **are returning** (*or* **are going to return**) to China next year.
4. If it **rains** on the weekend, we **will cancel** (*or* **are going to cancel**) our plans for a beach party.
5. Pierre **will be** here in Canada for at least another year before he **returns** home to Haiti and **gets** a job.

Exercise 27.16

Many of us are studying computers as part of our college programs. In fact, computer skills have become essential for success in almost all of the jobs we **will be doing** in the next decade. Most Canadians take the presence of a computer in the home, at work, and at school for granted. It is astonishing, therefore, to reflect that not so long ago, many people **were treating** computers as a mere fad. During the 1940s, for example, engineers **were predicting** that computers in the future would weigh over a tonne. In the same decade, the chairman of IBM told his company, "We **are not losing** (*or* **aren't going to lose**) sleep over these machines." He thought there would be a world market for "maybe five computers." A decade later, book publishers **were assuring** their employees that data processing was a fad that wouldn't last a year. In 1977, the president of Digital Equipment Corporation **was telling** the company's shareholders that there was no reason for anyone to want a computer in the home.

Today, all of us who **are using** computers know about Bill Gates, the president of Microsoft. In the years to come, his company **will be producing** many of the programs and applications that will become the standard of the future. These programs will use gigabytes of memory. It is hard to believe that in 1981 Bill Gates **was telling** anyone who would listen, "640K ought to be enough for anybody."

Exercise 27.17

Many of us **study** computers as part of our college programs. In fact, computer skills have become essential for success in almost all of the jobs we **will do** (*or* **are going to do**) in the next decade. Most Canadians take the presence of a computer in the home, at work, and at school for granted. It is astonishing, therefore, to reflect that not so long ago, many people **treated** computers as a mere fad. During the 1940s, for example, engineers **predicted** that computers in the future would weigh over a tonne. In the same decade, the chairman of IBM told his company, "We **won't lose** (*or* **will not lose** *or* **are not going to lose**) sleep over these machines." He thought there would be a world market for "maybe five computers." A decade later, book publishers **assured** their employees that data processing was a fad that wouldn't last a year. In 1977, the president of Digital Equipment Corporation **told** the company's shareholders that there was no reason for anyone to want a computer in the home.

Today, all of us who **use** computers know about Bill Gates, the president of Microsoft. In the years to come, his company **will produce** (*or* **is going to produce**) many of the programs and applications that will become the standard of the future. These programs will use gigabytes of memory. It is hard to believe that in 1981 Bill Gates **told** anyone who would listen, "640K ought to be enough for anybody."

The second set of paragraphs, using simple tenses, is a better description of the events described in this passage. Most of the events occurred once, not over a period of time. Simple tenses depict an action; progressive tenses emphasize the duration of an action.

Answers for Chapter 28: More about Verbs

Exercise 28.1

2. I **do not** (**don't**) trust the bank.
3. No one **trusts** the bank.
4. The passengers **do not** (**don't**) have their passports in order.
5. You **should not** (**shouldn't**) have given the students a quiz on negatives.
6. The man **does not look** (**doesn't look**) suspicious to me.
7. Ling **did not** (**didn't**) **forget** to pick us up yesterday.
8. We **never** watch our diet.
9. José and Marta **did not** (**didn't**) **want** to eat before the movie.
10. The class **does not** (**doesn't**) **need** more exercises on verb forms. *Or*: The class needs **no** more exercises on verb forms.

Exercise 28.2

1. Mohammed and Hassan **have not** enjoyed the winters in Canada.
2. I certainly **do not** want to see you.
3. I certainly **did not want** to see you.
4. We **were not** (**weren't**) sleeping when you called.
5. Most of the class **did not attend** the reception for international students.
6. The Montreal Canadiens **did not succeed** in winning many new fans last season.
7. Susana **never** wants to come to the movies with us, even when we **want** her to join us.
8. The computer **is not** (**isn't**) working very well.
9. The computer **was not** (**wasn't**) working very well.
10. She **didn't come** to the meeting alone.

Exercise 28.3

1. Bob *loves* Mary. He is a **loving** man.
2. Bob *loves* Mary. She is a **loved** woman.
3. The movie *interests* the children. They are **interested** children. They are watching an **interesting** movie.

4. The news *surprised* my brother. He is a **surprised** person. The news was quite **surprising**.
5. The cartoons *amused* me. The cartoons were **amusing**. I was **amused**.
6. The lecture *stimulated* the students. The lecture was **stimulating**. The students were **stimulated**.
7. The task *exhausted* me. I was **exhausted** by this **exhausting** task.
8. The possibility *excites* everyone. The possibility is **exciting**. Everyone is **excited**.
9. The child's tantrum *embarrassed* his father. The father was **embarrassed**. The child's tantrum was **embarrassing**.
10. The test results *shocked* the whole town. The **shocked** people could hardly believe the **shocking** test results.

Exercise 28.4

2. an annoying neighbour; I'm annoyed
3. a horrifying accident; I'm horrified
4. I am disgusted; disgusting garbage
5. a satisfying meal; I am satisfied
6. disappointing; He was disappointed.
7. Jan isn't bored; Jan's job isn't boring.
8. I'm pleased; pleasing music
9. an amazing answer; I'm amazed
10. I am inspired; inspiring

Exercise 28.5

2. **Would** you please **hand** me the phone?
3. You **must not tell** Rani about the party because we want it to be a surprise for her.
4. The baby is just learning to talk but he **can say** five or six words. A few weeks ago he **couldn't talk** at all.
5. Pat **may live** at her parents' home, but I'm not sure.
6. **Shall** we **eat** at the new restaurant?
7. I didn't get much sleep last night. I **should go** to bed early tonight, but I want to wait up for you.
8. I promise I **will clean** my room tomorrow.

Exercise 28.6

1. It **is going to** rain later, so you **ought to** take your umbrella.
2. I **used to** go to the United States with just a passport, but now I **have to** get a visa.
3. We **were supposed to** go to the beach yesterday, but it was too cold. We hope that we **are able to** go tomorrow.

Exercise 28.7

1. (see) The doctor **may be able to see** you later this afternoon.
2. (finish) If he works very hard, Paulo **may** (*or* **might** *or* **will**) **finish** the project before the deadline.
3. (complete) He **must** (*or* **has to**) **complete** it on time if he wants to get paid.
4. (visit) You **should** (*or* **ought to**) **visit** your grandmother because she misses you.
5. (run) When Oswaldo was younger, he **could run** very fast.
6. (love) Felix bought his girlfriend a beautiful engagement ring; he **must love** her very much.
7. (drink) Her parents **used to drink** heavily, but they have stopped entirely since joining Alcoholics Anonymous.
8. (suppose) I **was supposed** to study for the quiz yesterday, but I forgot.
9. (rain) The sky is getting darker; it **may** (*or* **might**) **rain.**
10. (smoke, not) You **can't smoke** in public buildings in Canada.

Exercise 28.8

1. I wonder when the boat will arrive. It **was supposed to** be here an hour ago.
2. You **shouldn't** (*or* **mustn't**) answer your cellphone in class.
3. If you have a food processor, you **can** prepare this salad in a few minutes.
4. What did you say? **Will/would** you please repeat it?
5. You **can't** be in two places at once.
6. The mayor is not in her office; she **may/might/must** be at a meeting.
7. Their whole house is decorated in red; they **must** really love the colour!
8. Jon **should** know better than to call me at midnight.
9. Our instructor **used to** give us quizzes every day, but now he gives only three a semester.
10. **Will** you **be able to** come to our party? *Or:* **Are** you **able to** come to our party?

Exercise 28.9

People choose to immigrate to Canada for many reasons. They **may** (*or* **might**) want to have more economic opportunity. Or they **might** (*or* **may**) be looking for a better education for their children. Or they **may** (*or* **might**) want to **be able** to practise their beliefs openly. Perhaps the country where they **used to** live denied them certain rights that they **can** (*or* **are able to**) take for granted in Canada. Whatever their reasons for coming, immigrants to Canada **must** (*or* **have to**) work very hard to adjust to their new country. They **must** (*or* **have to**) find new homes and jobs, and most of them **have to** (*or* **must**) learn a new language. Immigrating is not an easy process, but new immigrants hope that they **will** build a better life in their new home.

Answers for Chapter 29: Solving Plural Problems

Exercise 29.1

2. Your little **girls love their** new **toys**.
3. **Students learn** to take **tests**.
4. Good **doctors listen** to **their patients**.
5. The **sharks are** swimming around the **boats**.
6. The **boys visit their girlfriends** every night.
7. These **rooms are** very large.
8. Angry **dogs are** dangerous **animals**.
9. Should **our brothers** find **their** own **apartments**?
10. **Our houses have** swimming **pools**.

See Chapter 12, Mastering Subject–Verb Agreement, if you missed any of the verb shifts (e.g., is/are, has/have). See Chapter 13, Keeping Your Tenses Consistent, if you missed any of the pronoun shifts (e.g., her/their, this/these).

Exercise 29.2

2. yourselves
3. categories
4. woman
5. moose
6. feet
7. eyelash
8. criterion
9. themselves
10. photos
11. zoos
12. tomato
13. stimulus
14. monarchs
15. theses
16. thieves
17. husbands
18. tooth
19. heroes
20. chiefs

Exercise 29.3

1. children, classes
2. mushrooms, berries
3. trees, leaves
4. courses, quizzes
5. scissors, knives
6. cities, communities
7. inquiries, replies
8. potatoes, yourselves
9. nineties, attorneys
10. activities, studies

Exercise 29.4

	NC	NC	NC
1.	milk	sugar	coffee

	NC	C
2.	advice	problems

	NC	NC
3.	knowledge	math

	NC	C
4.	beef	dinner

	C	NC
5.	suitcases	baggage

	NC	C
6.	water	chemicals

	C	NC
7.	vitamins	health

Exercise 29.5

1. money, luck
2. luggage, backpacks
3. pianos, furniture
4. advice, homework
5. cattle, beef
6. light, lights
7. times, time
8. garbage, work
9. history, music
10. jeans, wardrobe

Exercise 29.6

1. Robert is going bald and wants to know where he can get **information** on **hair** replacement.
2. Correct
3. You can have **fun** in sports, but the **enjoyment disappears** if you play too much **hockey** or **football**.
4. We want to give you some new **clothes** to wear as an expression of our **thanks**.
5. The **rich** get richer, and the **poor** get poorer.
6. Having two **businesses** go bankrupt was a learning **experience**.
7. All of my relatives had **advice** for me when I came to Canada.
8. Did you get any new **information** about the computer **data** we lost?
9. We didn't hear much **laughter** coming from the back of the van as we drove through the rush-hour **traffic**.
10. Correct

Exercise 29.7

Note: Triple asterisks (***) indicate that a word or words have been deleted. Each set of triple asterisks counts as one error.

 *** **Sharks are** *** scary **animals** to most people. **They are** considered to be *** **fish** that **attack** and **eat** humans from the depths of the ocean. **Sharks are**, in fact, an ancient species.

Their ancestors date back about 350 million years, as **fossil records** show. In size, ***
sharks range from **tiny angel sharks** that **are** less than a metre in length to *** huge 15-metre whale **sharks** that can weigh 700 kilograms.

*** **Sharks are** *** very effective **predators** in the ocean. **They have** very good eyesight, and even in total darkness, *** **sharks** can sense the movement of **their** prey by means of special pores in **their** skin that sense **other animals'** electrical vibrations. In addition, ***
sharks actually **smell their** prey from a long way off. These characteristics make *** **sharks** *** good killing **machines** as **they hunt** for food.

Although *** **sharks are** high on the food chain, **they** usually **eat** smaller fish, crabs, seals, and other sea creatures. *** **Sharks do** not seek out humans to eat. We may fear ***
sharks, but there are only about 100 shark attacks on humans in the world in a year, and perhaps 25 to 30 of these are fatal. Given our increasing appetite for shark meat, the truth is that we eat many more of them than they eat of us.

Exercise 29.8
1. I will read _____ reports. (four, several, ~~much~~, ~~a great deal of~~, some, few, a lot of, too many, ~~every~~, most, ~~a little~~)
2. I will study _____ information. (~~three~~, ~~each~~, much, a lot of, ~~several~~, a great deal of, plenty of, ~~a few~~, a little, hardly any)
3. My friend has _____ comfortable chairs on the patio. (~~too much~~, hardly any, four, a few, ~~a great deal of~~, no, plenty of, some, ~~every~~)
4. My friend has _____ comfortable furniture on the patio. (~~a few~~, ~~three~~, ~~one~~, some, ~~several~~, hardly any, much, a lot of, lots of, ~~a couple of~~)

Exercise 29.9
1. **A little** extra money is good to have.
2. Several **businesses** lost money.
3. Roberto has **few** friends here in Canada, so he feels very homesick.
4. **Most** of the **students** found the course very boring. Only two or three people found it interesting.
5. Very **few** tourists visit the country because of the war.
6. My best friend has **several** good-looking brothers, so I like to spend as **much** time at her house as I can.
7. **Every** one of her **brothers** is tall, dark, handsome, and smart.
8. **Many** of my friends will be at my party, so we must have **lots** of **food**.
9. It takes **plenty of** practice to learn how to ice skate.
10. **Both** of us got home from the game quickly because there was **hardly any** traffic.

Answers for Chapter 30: Using Articles Accurately

Exercise 30.1
1. an ugly dog, a strange-looking old man
2. a zoologist, a scientist
3. a dentist
4. a hasty retreat
5. a bad fall, an X-ray
6. a half-hour lesson
7. an extremely difficult test
8. A European man
9. a college, a university
10. a VIP pass

Exercise 30.2
1. a veterinarian, a doctor, (no article) animals
2. A child, (no article) parents
3. a last drink, a half-bottle
4. A man, a big nose, (no article) huge feet
5. As a rule, a rich person
6. an hour and a half, a counsellor
7. Twice a year, an adventure, a friend
8. A baby, (no article) milk
9. a cup, of (no article) coffee
10. a break

Exercise 30.3

When you move to **a** new city, you have to think about your housing needs. If you are going to be there for only **a** short time, you can rent **a** furnished apartment. **The** apartment should be in **a** convenient location. Perhaps you should locate yourself in **the** downtown area near public transportation. **The** furnished apartment you rent needs to have **a** decent kitchen. **The** kitchen should have **a** working stove and refrigerator. **The** place where you live is **an** important factor in your adjustment to your new city.

Exercise 30.4
1. **The** elderly deserve **the** support of society.
2. **(No article)** Children are naturally curious, but **the** children in that class are very inquisitive.
3. Do we know who invented **the** wheel?
4. In **the** Far North, **the** sun never sets in **(no article)** June.
5. **The** elephant and **the** whale are both huge animals that give birth to **(no article)** live babies; in other words, they are **(no article)** mammals.
6. I like to play games on **(no article)** computers.
7. **(No article)** Medical care is usually paid for by **the** government through **(no article)** taxes.
8. **(No article)** College students need to spend **(no article)** time studying if they want to be successful.
9. Is **(no article)** money as important as **(no article)** love to you?
10. Thank you for **the** bananas; I love to eat **(no article)** fruit.

Exercise 30.5
1.   I want to take **a** trip to **the** West Coast.
2. **The** phase of **the** moon is one of **the** causes of ocean tides.
3. I bought **a** new CD online yesterday, and **the** CD should be here by tomorrow.
4. What is **the** name of **the** student you were talking to this morning? He is **the** first person I talked to in class, and I would like to know his name.
5. Although I had never seen her before, I spoke to **a** beautiful young woman in **the** supermarket this morning; she is one of **the** loveliest human beings I have ever seen.
6. **The** kind of vacation I enjoy most is **a** long train ride.
7. I don't need **a** special destination when I board **the/a** train; for me **the** important thing is **the** journey.
8. Where did you park **the** car?
9. **The** job requires **a** person with **a** lot of energy, and Danielle is **an** energetic person.
10. In many parts of Canada, **a** college student who begins school in **the** last part of August finishes **the** school year in April.

Exercise 30.6
1. I like to study **(no article)** history; I have learned that **the** history of Bosnia is tragic.
2. We like **(no article)** food, but **(no article)** most of **the** food at **the** restaurant is awful.

3. Everyone has **(no article)** problems in **(no article)** life. **The** problems may be big or small, but everyone must cope with them.
4. His group is playing **(no article)** jazz in **the** park.
5. Some of **the** most important products that Canada buys from India are **(no article)** tea, **(no article)** cotton, and **(no article)** rice.
6. **(No article)** Milk is my baby's favourite drink, but she often spills **the** milk that I put in her cup.
7. **(No article)** Kindness is an attractive quality in people, and **the** kindness of that woman is known to all of us.
8. **(No article)** Jewellery is a popular gift; my boyfriend loved **the** jewellery that I gave him.
9. Natasha studies **(no article)** art in university, and her specialty is **the** art of **the** Renaissance.
10. **(No article)** Boots are a necessary item of winter clothing in Canada, but **the** boots I bought last year were not very warm.

Exercise 30.7
1. **(No article)** Earthquakes sometimes happen in **(no article)** British Columbia, but they almost never occur in **the** Prairie provinces, **(no article)** central Canada, **(no article)** Quebec, or **the** Maritimes.
2. Many of **the** geographical names in Canada are derived from **the/no article** languages of Aboriginal peoples who lived here for thousands of **(no article)** years before **the** first European settlers arrived.
3. For example, **(no article)** Manitoulin Island, in **(no article)** Lake Huron, got its name from the Algonkian word *Manitou*, which means "spirit."
4. **The** Queen Charlotte Islands (also known as Haida Gwaii) off **the** British Columbia coast consist of about 150 islands, the largest of which are **(no article)** Graham Island and **(no article)** Moresby Island.
5. **(No article)** Saskatchewan, **the** province of Ontario, **the** Magnetawan River, **(no article)** Lake Okanagan, and even **the** name "Canada" itself are all examples of **the** influence of native people's languages on Canada's place names.
6. Pat began his studies at **(no article)** Langara College and then transferred to **the** University of British Columbia.
7. **(no article)** Niagara Falls is on **the** Niagara River, which flows from **(no article)** Lake Erie to **(no article)** Lake Ontario.
8. **The** People's Republic of **(no article)** China is also known as **(no article)** China.
9. **The** St. Lawrence River forms **the** boundary between **(no article)** Ontario in **(no article)** Canada and **(no article)** New York in **the** United States.
10. **The** Bering Strait is between **the** state of Alaska and **the** former U.S.S.R., now known as **(no article)** Russia.

Exercise 30.8
You can tell all you need to know about **a** person from **the** shoes he or she wears. Our economics teacher, for example, wears **(no article)** worn-out, old, brown leather loafers. These shoes tell us that he doesn't care about **(no article)** appearances, that he likes to save **(no article)** money, and that he enjoys **(no article)** comfort more than **(no article)** style. On the other hand, our computer teacher is **a** fashionably dressed woman who wears **a** different pair of shoes almost every day. My favourites are her black patent leather pumps with gold buckles on **the** toes. Such **a** stylish selection of **(no article)** shoes tells me that she is **a** fashion-conscious person who cares what **(no article)** people think of her appearance. She appreciates quality and is willing to spend money to get it. If my theory about **the** relationship between **(no article)** character and footwear is valid, I would be interested in **an** analysis of

my English professor, who wears **(no article)** black army boots for two days, **(no article)** white running shoes **the** next day, then **a** pair of cowboy boots, and ends the week with **a** pair of platform disco shoes.

Exercise 30.9

A hurricane is **a** severe tropical storm with winds between 120 and 240 km per hour. Hurricanes are most likely to form in **the** Atlantic Ocean, and they usually blow west across **the** Caribbean and the Gulf of Mexico from ~~the~~ Africa. Hurricanes gain their energy as they pass over warm ocean waters, so **the** warmest parts of **the** year are known as "hurricane season," from ~~the~~ June through **the** month of October. Hurricanes rotate in a counterclockwise direction around **an** "eye." When a hurricane comes onshore, heavy rain, wind, and waves can do a tremendous amount of damage to the trees, buildings, and people in its path.

Exercise 30.10

The highest place on Earth is **a** mountain called Mount Everest, which is 8,850 metres high. It is located in Asia, at **the** border of Tibet and Nepal, in a mountain range known as **the** Himalayas. **The** first people to climb Everest were ~~the~~ Tenzing Norgay and Edmund Hillary who reached **the** peak in 1953. According to a CBC Web site, 2,249 people had climbed ~~the~~ Mount Everest by the end of 2004, but 186 people died trying. Now there is a small industry of guides who make a good living taking adventurous climbers to the top of Everest. Ascending the mountain is **an** expensive proposition, though. The average cost of a guided climb is about US$65,000. Save your money if you want to make it to **the** top!

CBC News Indepth: www.cbc.ca/news/background/mount_everest.

Answers for Chapter 31: Practising with Prepositions

Sometimes more than one preposition can be used in the context of a sentence. The answers we have provided are those that most native speakers would supply in the context; the alternatives given in parentheses are also common and correct responses. Other answers may also be correct; if your answers differ from ours, check with your instructor.

Exercise 31.1
1. in, for
2. in, before
3. since
4. from, in
5. in, at, on

Exercise 31.2
1. on, in
2. in, at
3. between
4. among (with), between
5. in, within

Exercise 31.3
1. by (past)
2. down, toward (to)
3. through (out of), of, into
4. from
5. up, into, through

Exercise 31.4
1. of, with
2. with, from
3. about, of, in
4. of, of, with
5. from, without

Exercise 31.5
1. at, around
2. in, between
3. until (before), of
4. in, at, of, in

Exercise 31.6

1. before (by)
2. of, under (underneath, beneath), to, for
3. out of, into, up (down), by (past)

Exercise 31.7

1. At, during
2. behind (under), on, with, of, in
3. in, among (in)
4. from, in, to (until), at, at (by), of

Exercise 31.8

My friend Jamil goes **to** school **at** the King Edward campus **of** Vancouver Community College. **At** the same time, he works full-time **in** (*or* **at**) his family's grocery business. The store is **across** the street **from** the college, so Jamil doesn't have to travel very far **between** school and work. He has to leave school **at** (*or* **by**) 4:00 p.m. every day so that he can work **behind** (*or* **at**) the counter of the store selling goods **to** customers. **Since** September, Jamil has been studying computer and business courses at the college, and he puts a lot **of** effort **into** his schoolwork. Because he works every night **until** midnight, he sometimes does his homework **during** (*or* **in**) quiet moments **in** (*or* **at**) the store. **Without** his hard work, Jamil's family couldn't keep the store going. Jamil is working **toward** two important goals: he is determined to succeed **at** (*or* **in**) his studies, and he is equally determined to help his family prosper.

Answers for Unit 6 Rapid Review

[1]Let's say that **you've** (*or* **you have**) been learning English for a number of years now. [2]Perhaps you've been living and studying in English for much of your life. [3]Yet you still **don't** (*or* **do not**) feel entirely confident about your ability to make yourself understood when you're speaking, particularly when you **are speaking** to a group of people at school or at work. [4]And you're also not always sure exactly what English speakers mean when they speak **to** you. [5]Are there any practical ways to improve your fluency in spoken English? [6]Yes, there are. [7]Here are a few tips to help you feel more confident when you are speaking and when you are listening.

[8]One good suggestion for everyone who is speaking English as a second language is to s-l-o-w down. [9]Especially if you are presenting in **an** academic or professional situation, it's important to remember to speak slower and louder than you normally do. [10]Often what makes your speech difficult to understand isn't the pronunciation of specific sounds ("t" vs. "th," for instance), but rather the intonation or rhythm that is rooted in your first language and doesn't sound natural to native English speakers. [11]Slowing down often helps. [12]Make sure that you pause frequently at appropriate places in your speech or presentation, and use transition words such as "next," "then," and "in conclusion" to help your listener or reader stay with you.

[13]If you are preparing **a** short presentation, keep in mind that spoken language is simpler than written language. [14]Your sentences and vocabulary should be relatively simple. [15]Repeat key points, and use the board or cards to present important vocabulary that you think people might not understand. [16]Try to relax as much as possible, smile occasionally, and look **at** the people you're speaking to. [17]Eye contact is important and actually helps to communicate your meaning. [18]If you**'re** (*or* **you are**) looking at people, you can usually tell when someone doesn't understand you, and you can repeat or clarify the point you're making.

[19]There are also a number of ways that you **can** improve your comprehension of spoken English. [20]Listening to English radio and TV is helpful; listen to **interesting** programs that you already know something about, whether that is sports, horoscopes, celebrity gossip, or the **news**. [21](Repeat key phrases to practise the rhythm of spoken English.) [22]Listen to recorded phone messages; you might even get native-speaker friends to leave complicated messages for you so that you can practise understanding what they are saying. [23]Try to navigate through the phone loops of banks, airlines, or utility companies: "Press 6 if you would like to hear about our payment options."

[24]There are lots of Internet sites designed to help people learn ~~the~~ English. [25]A site such as the BBC World Service has **many** resources, including audio and video clips that help people improve their listening comprehension. [26]Of course, you may find that voices on the BBC have what Canadians call a "British accent." [27]But learning to understand the many varieties of spoken English is important to your overall mastery **of** the language.

[28]Above all, practise. [29]Try to keep yourself immersed in the English-speaking world around you. [30]Engage people in conversation, listen to what they have to say, and ask questions when you need to. [31]Mastering another language is a long and arduous task. [32]Nevertheless, time and **lots** (*or* **a lot of**) of practice will give you the confidence in your speaking and listening skills that you want to achieve.

Answer Key

If you missed the error(s) in sentence . . .		See Chapter . . .	
1	you been	27	"The Present Perfect Tense" section
3	you still feel	28	"Forming Negatives" section
	you are speak	27	"The Present Progressive Tense" section
4	they speak within you	31	"Prepositions that Indicate Direction or Movement" section
9	in academic or professional situation	30	"The Indefinite Article: *A/An*" section
13	preparing short presentation	30	"The Indefinite Article: *A/An*" section
16	look from the people	31	"Prepositions That Indicate Place or Position" section
18	you looking	27	"The Present Progressive Tense" section
19	that you shall improve	28	"Modal Auxiliaries" section
20	listen to interested programs	28	"Participial Adjectives" section
	the new	29	"Count vs. Non-Count Nouns" section
24	help people learn the English	30	"No Article (Zero Article)" section
25	has much resources	29	"Quantity Expressions" section
27	mastery by the language	31	"Other Prepositional Relationships" section
32	time and lot of practice	29	"Quantity Expressions" section

Index

a, an, 376–80
about, 401
above, 398
Abstract noun, 359, 457, 467
accept, except, 23
across, 398, 400
Action verb, 64, 457
Active voice, 146–49, 458, 472
"Add -*s* for plural" rule, 359
Adjective, 460–61, 464
Adverb, 461, 464
advice, advise, 23
a few, few, 373
affect, effect, 23
after, 396
Agreement
   person, 194–200
   pronoun–antecedent, 181–93
   subject–verb, 153–67
a little, little, 373
allusion, illusion, 23
alot, 17
a lot, allot, 23
among, 398
Anecdote, 464
Answers to exercises, 473–535
Antecedent, 181, 464
anyways, 17
anywheres, 17
APA documentation style, 235, 441
Apostrophe, 38–49
   contraction, 39
   plurals, 47
   possession, 42–45
   possessive pronoun, 44
are, our, 24
around, 400
Arrangement of ideas (order), 263–65
Article, 376–93, 463, 464–65
   definite *(the),* 380–86
   geographical names, 387–88
   indefinite *(a/an),* 376–80
   no article (zero article), 386–87
at, 396, 398
Attention-getter, 298–99
Audience, 465

Auxiliary verb, 346, 457. *See also* Helping
   verb

"Baba and Me" (Mitchell), 418–21
Basic sentence patterns, 452–53
be able to, 355
before, 396
be going to, 355
behind, 398
below, 398
beneath, 398
beside, 398
beside, besides, 24
be supposed to, 355
between, 398
Bibliography, 236–37. *See also*
   Documentation style
Bilingual students. *See* ESL students
Blasphemy, 17
Block indentation, 234
Brainstorming, 256
by, 396, 398, 400

can, 352
can't hardly, 18
Capitalitis, 50
Capitalization, 50–56
   days of week, 53
   first word of sentence, etc., 50
   holidays, 53
   months of year, 53
   names of historical events, 52
   names of religions, holy texts, 52
   names of school courses, 54
   names of specific people, places, etc.,
     51
   titles of published works, 53
"Career Consciousness" (Green), 412–14
Checklist
   content and organization, 307–08
   editing, 315
   paragraph and sentence, 310–11
choose, chose, 24
Chronological order, 264
cite, sight, site, 24
Citing sources, 234–37, 296–97

"City for Students, A" (Tryphonopoulos), 438–42
Clause, 84, 465
Climactic order, 264–65
Closing paragraph, 299
Clustering, 256
coarse, course, 24
Collective noun, 457
Colloquialism, 466
Colon, 226–31
Combining sentences, 117–30
Comma, 207–18
Comma splice, 90, 91, 466
Command (sentence), 452
Common noun, 456
Comparative form (adjective), 460
Comparison, 294
Comparison and contrast, 294–95
Complement, 456
complement, compliment, 25
Complex sentence, 453
Compound, 466
Compound complement, 466
Compound-complex sentence, 453
Compound sentence, 453, 466
Compound subject, 74–77, 466
Compound verb, 74–77, 466
Conclusion, 299
Concrete noun, 359, 457, 467
Conjunction, 119–20, 462–63
Conjunctive adverb, 462
conscience, conscious, 25
consul, council, counsel, 25
Content and organization checklist, 307–08
Contraction, 39
Contrast, 294
Coordinating conjunction, 462
Copula verb, 457
Correlative conjunction, 462
could, 352
couldn't hardly, 18
could of, 18
Count noun, 365–70, 466

Dangling modifier, 103–04
"Dear Dad" (Masson), 427–30
Declarative sentence, 451
Definite article *(the),* 380–86, 465
Definition, 289–90
Demonstrative pronoun, 459
Dependent clause, 84, 465
Dependent clause cue, 84, 462, 466

Dependent clause fragment, 84–86
desert, dessert, 25
Developing paragraphs, 289–98
    comparison and contrast, 294–95
    definition, 289–90
    examples, 290–92
    paraphrase, 295–96
    process/series of steps, 292–93
    quotation, 296
    specific details, 293–94
Dictionary, 4–6
didn't do nothing, 18
dining, dinning, 25
Direct object, 455
Documentation style, 234–37, 296–97
does, dose, 26
down, 400
during, 396

Editing, 313–15
Editing checklist, 315
effect, affect, 23
either ... or, 159
Electronic translating dictionaries, 8–9
E-mail, 17
Emphatic pronoun, 460
Endnote, 234
English as a second language. *See* ESL students
ESL students, 317–409
    article, 376–93 (*see also* Article)
    count *vs.* non-count nouns, 365–70
    modal auxiliaries, 351–55
    negatives, 346–47
    participial adjectives, 348–49
    preposition, 394–406 (*see also* Preposition)
    quantity expressions, 371–73
    quick quiz, 320–21
    rapid review, 407–09
    singular *vs.* plural nouns, 359–64
    verb tense, 322–45 (*see also* Verb tense)
Essay writing. *See* Paragraphs and essays
Examples, 290–92
except, accept, 23
Exclamation mark, 241–42
Exclamatory sentence, 452
Exercises, answers to, 473–535
Expletive, 463

"fanboys," 209
few, a few, 373
Finding something to write about, 252–68

First person, 153, 468
Footnote, 234
for, 396, 401
Foreign students. *See* ESL students
Formal outline, 283–84
forth, fourth, 26
4-S guidelines, 252–54
Fragments, 79–89
Freewriting, 256
from, 396, 400, 402
Fused sentence, 90–91
Future perfect progressive tense, 341
Future perfect tense, 340
Future progressive tense, 339
Future tense, 338–41
    future perfect progressive tense, 341
    future perfect tense, 340
    future progressive tense, 339
    simple future tense, 338

Gage Canadian Dictionary, 5
General level of English, 10
Geographical names, 387–88
Glossary of grammatical terms, 464–72
Gobbledygook, 469–70
good, 18
Grammar, 133–202
    person agreement, 194–200
    pronoun form, 173–80 (*see also*
      Pronoun)
    quick quiz, 134–36
    rapid review, 201–02
    verb form, 137–52 (*see also* Verb)
    See also Pronoun–antecedent agree-
      ment; Subject–verb agreement; Verb
      tense
Grammar checker, 9, 313–14
Green, Brian, 291, 412–14
Greer, Germaine, 295, 421–24

Hand-held spell checker, 8
have/has/had to, 355
he, she, 195
hear, here, 26
Helping verb, 67–70, 457, 472
Homonym, 22–37, 466

Idea generation, 252–68
"Immigrant's Split Personality, An" (Sun-
    Kyung Yi), 414–16
Imperative sentence, 452
in, 396, 397, 398
Indefinite article *(a/an),* 376–80

Indefinite pronoun, 182, 459
Independent clause, 84, 465
Indirect object, 455, 467
Infinitive, 137–42
Informal level of English, 10
Informal outline, 282–83
Interrogative pronoun, 460
Interrogative sentence, 452
into, 400
Introduction, 298–99
irregardless, 18
Irregular verbs, 138–42
its, it's, 26–27, 44

knew, new, 26–27
know, no, 26–27

"Labouring the Wal-Mart Way," 431–33
later, latter, 26–27
lead, led, 26–27
Levels of language, 10
Linking verb, 64, 457, 471
Listing, 256
List of grammatical terms, 464–72
little, a little, 373
Logically linked order, 265, 466
loose, lose, 27–28

Main clause, 465
Main points, 255–63, 270–71
Masson, Jeffrey Moussaieff, 289, 427–30
may, 352
media, 18
Memorable statement, 299
"Metamorphosis" (Norton), 425–26
might, 353
miner, minor, 28
Misplaced modifier, 99–102
"Missing piece" fragment, 79–84
Mitchell, Shandi, 418–21
MLA documentation style, 235, 436
*MLA Handbook for Writers of Research
    Papers,* 235
Modal auxiliaries, 351–55
Modifier, 99, 466
Modifier problems, 99–109
moral, morale, 28
Multiple subjects and verbs, 74–77
must, 353

near, 398
Negatives, 346–47
neither … nor, 159

Nelson Canadian Dictionary of the English Language, 5
new, knew, 26–27
Nikiforuk, Andrew, 290
no, know, 26–27
No article (zero article), 386–87, 465
Non-count noun, 365–70, 466
Non-progressive tenses, 326–27
Norton, Sarah, 292, 425–26
not ... but, 159
Noun, 456–57, 466–67
    abstract, 457
    collective, 457
    common, 456
    concrete, 457
    count, 365–70
    defined, 456
    non-count, 365–70
    proper, 457

Object, 394, 467
Object of a preposition, 455, 467
Object pronoun, 174–76
Obscene words, 17
of, 397, 402
Offensive language, 16–17
off of, 18
on, 397, 399
one, 195
Order (arrangement of ideas), 263–65
Organizing main points, 263–65
"Ottawa vs. New York" (Greer), 421–24
ought to, 355
our, are, 24
Outline, 281–87
    formal, 283–84
    informal, 282–83
    scratch, 282
out of, 400
over, 399
Owner words (possession), 42–45
Oxford Advanced Learner's Dictionary, 5
Oxford Thesaurus of English, 9

Paragraph and sentence checklist, 310–11
Paragraphs and essays, 251–316
    attention-getter, 298–99
    conclusion, 299
    finding something to write about, 252–68
    4-S guidelines, 252–54
    introduction, 298–99
    main points, 255–63, 270–71

    organizing main points, 263–65
    outline, 281–87
    subject to write about, 252–68
    thesis, 255–56
    thesis statement, 269–80
    tone, 301–02
    topic determination, 252–68
    topic sentence, 288
    transitions, 300–301
    See also Developing paragraphs; Revision
Parallelism, 110–16, 467–68
Paraphrase, 295–96, 468
Parenthetical citations, 234
Parmar, Deenu, 431–33
Participial adjectives, 348–49
Participle, 468
Parts of speech, 456–63
    adjective, 460–61
    adverb, 461
    article, 463 (*see also* Article)
    conjunction, 462–63
    expletive, 463
    noun, 456–57 (*see also* Noun)
    preposition, 461–62 (*see also* Preposition)
    pronoun, 458–60 (*see also* Pronoun)
    verb, 457–58 (*see also* Verb)
passed, past, 28
Passive voice, 146–49, 458, 472
past, 400
Past participle, 137–42, 468
Past perfect progressive tense, 335
Past perfect tense, 333–34
Past progressive tense, 332–33
Past tense, 332–35
    past perfect progressive tense, 335
    past perfect tense, 333–34
    past progressive tense, 332–33
    simple past tense, 332
peace, piece, 28
Person, 153, 468
Person agreement, 194–200
personal, personnel, 28
Personal pronoun, 458
Phrasal modal auxiliaries, 354–55
Phrase, 468
Plurals, 47, 359–64
Possession, 42–45
Possessive pronoun, 44, 458–59
Prefix, 468–69
prejudice, 18
prejudism, 18

Preposition, 394–406, 461–62, 469
  direction/movement, 399
  other prepositional relationships,
    401–03
  place/position, 398–99
  relationship, 396–97
Prepositional phrase, 70, 394, 461–62, 469
Present participle, 137–42, 468
Present perfect progressive tense, 330–31
Present perfect tense, 329–30
Present progressive tense, 326–27
Present tense, 326–31
  present perfect progressive tense,
    330–31
  present perfect tense, 329–30
  present progressive tense, 326–27
  simple present tense, 326
  using, to indicate future tense, 342
Pretentious language, 15–16, 469
principal, principle, 29
Principal clause, 465
Principal parts of verbs, 137–46
Process/series of steps, 292–93
Progressive tenses, 326–27
Pronominal adjective, 181n
Pronoun, 458–60, 469–70
  antecedents, and, 181–93
  contrast constructions, 177–78
  defined, 458
  demonstrative, 459
  indefinite, 459
  interrogative, 460
  object, 174–76
  personal, 458
  reflexive, 460
  relative, 189–90, 459
  subject, 174–76
Pronoun–antecedent agreement, 181–93
  pronoun ending in *-one, -body, -thing,*
    182–84
  relative pronouns, 189–90
  vague reference, 186–87
Proofreading, 316
Proper noun, 457
*Publication Manual of the American
  Psychological Association,* 235
Punctuation, 203–49
  colon, 226–31
  comma, 207–18
  exclamation mark, 241–42
  question mark, 240–41
  quick quiz, 204–06
  quotation mark, 232–39

  rapid review, 248–49
  semicolon, 219–25

Quantity expressions, 371–73
Question mark, 240–41
quiet, quite, 29
Quotation, 296
Quotation mark, 232–39
Quotation within quotation, 234

Racist language, 17
Random order, 265
real, 18
Redundant phrase, 11–12
References list, 296–97, 441
Reflexive pronoun, 460
Relative pronoun, 189–90, 459
"Resolving Conflict in the Workplace"
  (Tihanyi), 416–18
Revision, 305–16
  content and organization, 306–10
  editing, 313–15
  paragraphs/sentences, 310–13
  proofreading, 316
  steps in process, 306
Roget's Thesaurus, 9
Run-on sentence, 90–98

Scratch outline, 282
Second-language learners. *See* ESL students
"Second-Language Struggle, The"
  (Waldman), 434–37
Second person, 153, 468
Semicolon, 219–25
Sentence, 59–132
  combining, 117–30
  complex, 453
  compound, 453
  compound-complex, 453
  declarative, 451
  exclamatory, 452
  fragments, 79–89
  fused, 90–91
  imperative, 452
  interrogative, 452
  key principle, 62
  modifier problems, 99–109
  parallelism, 110–16
  parts of, 454–56
  quick quiz, 60–61
  rapid review, 131–32
  run-on, 90–98
  simple, 452–53

topic, 288
See also Subject; Verb
Sentence combining, 117–30
Sentence fragment, 79–89
shall, 353
she, he, 195
Shifting tenses, 168–72
should, 353
should of, 18
sight, site, cite, 24
Simple future tense, 338
Simple past tense, 137–42, 332
Simple present tense, 326
Simple sentence, 452–53
since, 397
Single-word modal auxiliaries, 352–53
Singular, 153
Singular *vs.* plural nouns, 359–64
Slang, 13–14
sort of speak, 19
Source identification, 234–37, 296–97
Specific details, 293–94
Spell checker, 8, 313–14
Spelling, 444–50
    difficult words, 448–49
    rule 2 (doubling final consonant),
        446–47
    rule 1 (drop final *e*), 444–45
    rule 3 (words containing *ie* or *ei*),
        447–48
Spelling spoilers, 448–49
"States of being" verbs, 327
stationary, stationery, 29
Student exercises, answers to, 473–535
Subject, 470
    compound, 74
    defined, 63, 454
    finding, 63–67
    See also Subject–verb agreement
Subject pronoun, 174–76
Subject to write about, 252–68
Subject–verb agreement, 153–67
    collective noun, 161
    compound subject joined by "either …
        or," etc., 158–59
    singular and plural, 153–58
    units of money, time, distance, etc.,
        161
Subordinate clause, 84, 465
Subordinate/subordinating conjunction,
    84, 462, 466
Suffix, 470
Summary, 299

Sun-Kyung Yi, 291, 294, 414–16
Superlative form (adjective), 461
suppose to, 19
Swear words, 17
Synonym, 9

Tact, 301
Tense. *See* Verb tense
that, which, 190
the, 380–86, 465
their, there, they're, 29, 44
themselfs, 19
then, than, 29
the reason is because, 18
Thesaurus, 9
Thesis, 255–56, 471
Thesis statement, 269–80, 471
Third person, 153, 468
threw, through, 30
through, 400
Tihanyi, Eva, 416–18
till, 397
Title
    capitalization, 53
    italicize/underline, 236–37
to, 400
Tone, 301–02, 471
too, two, to, 30
Topic determination, 252–68
Topic sentence, 288, 471
toward, 400
Transitions, 300–301, 471
Tryphonopoulos, Aliki, 438–42

Uncountable noun, 365–70
under, 399
underneath, 399
until, till, 397
up, 400
used to, 355

Vague reference, 186–87
Verb, 457–58, 471–72
    action, 457
    active voice, 146–49
    compound, 74
    defined, 63, 454, 457
    finding, 63–67
    helping, 67–70, 457
    irregular, 138–42
    linking, 457
    passive voice, 146–49
    principal parts, 137–46

"states of being," 327
    voice, 458
    See also Subject–verb agreement; Verb
       tense
Verb tense, 322–45, 470–71
    formation, rules, 333–34
    future tense, 338–41
    past tense, 332–35
    present tense, 326–31
    shifting tenses, 168–72
Verb tense formation, 333–34
Voice, 458, 472

Waldman, Nell, 296, 434–37
wear, were, where, we're, 30
weather, whether, 30
which, that, 190
who, whom, 189
who's, whose, 30–31, 44
will, 353
with, 402
within, 397, 399
without, 403
woman, women, 31
Wordiness, 11–13
Words, 1–58
    abusages, 17–19

dictionary, 4–6
grammar checker, 9
homonyms, 22–37
levels of language, 10
offensive language, 16–17
pretentious language, 15–16
quick quiz, 2–3
rapid review, 57–58
slang, 13–14
spell checker, 8
thesaurus, 9
wordiness, 11–13
writer's toolkit, 4–9
See also Apostrophe; Capitalization
Works Cited list, 236–37, 296–97, 436
would, 353
would of, 18
Writer's toolkit, 4–9

Yi, Sun-Kyung, 291, 294, 414–16
you're, your, 31, 44
youse, 19

Zero article (no article), 386–87, 465

Credits

CORRECTION ABBREVIATIONS AND SYMBOLS

When marking essays, instructors often use editing/proofreading marks as a kind of shorthand to show students what errors they've made. You need to know the meaning of these abbreviations and symbols so you can look up and correct your errors. Many teachers create their own shorthand, so we've left space in the right-hand column for you to record your teacher's correction code.

Correction Mark	Meaning and Chapter/Page Reference	Instructor's Code
agr	Agreement error: Subject–verb (Ch. 12) or pronoun–antecedent (Ch. 15)	
apos	Insert ($\lor$) or delete ($\mathscr{G}$) apostrophe (Ch. 3)	
awk	Awkward sentence	
cap/ ≡	use capital letter (Ch. 4)	
colloq	Colloquial language (pp. 13–14)	
⌃	Insert comma (Ch. 17)	
cs	Comma splice (pp. 90–91)	
DM	Dangling modifier (pp. 103–04)	
frag	Sentence fragment (Ch. 6)	
FS	Fused sentence (pp. 90–91)	
Ital/no ital	Use _italics_ (do not use italics) (p. 236)	
lc or /	Use lower-case (small) letters, not capitals (Ch. 4)	
MM	Misplaced modifier (Ch. 8)	
¶	Start a new paragraph (Ch. 25)	
no ¶	Do not start new paragraph here	
para	Use parallel structure (Ch. 9)	
pass	Incorrect use of passive voice (pp. 148–49)	
pro	Pronoun error (Ch. 14)	
⟨⟨ ⟩⟩	Insert quotation marks (Ch. 20)	
ref	Vague pronoun reference (pp. 186–87)	
R-O	Run-on sentence (Ch. 7)	
sl	Slang (pp. 13–14)	
sp	Spelling error (Ch. 2, Appendix A)	
trans	Transition needed (pp. 300–301)	
tr	Transpose lettre words or	
vb	Verb form error (Ch. 11, 13)	
wordy	Omit unnecessary words (pp. 11–13)	
W (or WW)	Wrong word (check your dictionary)	
?	Word/phrase is illegible or makes no sense	
$\mathscr{G}$	Delete the marked letter, word word, or punctuation mark	
⋀	Add missing letter or word	
(⁏)/(∶) ⊙/ =	Insert missing punctuation: semicolon⁏colon ∶ period⊙or hyphen ≖	
✓	Good idea, detail, phrasing	